943.08 / ELE   940115

FROM UNIFICATION
TO NAZISM

FROM UNIFICATION TO NAZISM

Reinterpreting the German Past

GEOFF ELEY

London and New York

First published in 1986 by Unwin Hyman Ltd
Second impression 1990

Reprinted 1992 by
Routledge
11 New Fetter Lane, London EC4P 4EE

Simultaneously published in the USA and Canada
by Routledge
a division of Routledge, Chapman and Hall, Inc.
29 West 35th Street, New York, NY 10001

Printed and bound in Great Britain by
Mackays of Chatham PLC, Chatham, Kent

British Library Cataloguing in Publication Data
Eley, Geoff
   From unification to Nazism: reinterpreting the German past.
   1. Germany – History – 1866–1871 2. Germany – History – 1871–
   I. Title
   943.08   DD210

Library of Congress Cataloging in Publication Data
Eley, Geoff, 1949–
   From unification to Nazism.
   Includes index
   1. German – History – 1848–1870. 2. German – History – 1871– .
   I. Title
   DD210.E48 1985   943.08   85–11183

ISBN 0–415–08488–1

Contents

Acknowledgements

Of the contents of this collection, the Introduction has been specially written, and Chapters 1 and 4 are previously unpublished. Of the rest, the original places of publication were as follows:

Chapter 2: *Historical Journal*, vol. 21, no. 3 (1978), pp. 737–50.

Chapter 3: Raphael Samuel and Gareth Stedman Jones (eds), *Culture, Ideology and Politics. Essays for Eric Hobsbawm* (London: Routledge & Kegan Paul, 1983), pp. 277–301.

Chapter 5: *Militärgeschichtliche Mitteilungen*, vol. 15 (1974), pp. 29–63.

Chapter 6: Joachim Radkau and Imanuel Geiss (eds), *Imperialismus im 20. Jahrhundert. Gedenkschrift für Georg W. F. Hallgarten* (Munich: Verlag C. H. Beck, 1976), pp. 71–86.

Chapter 7: *Radical History Review*, no. 28–30 (1984), pp. 13–44.

Chapter 8: *East European Quarterly*, vol. 18, no. 3 (1984), pp. 335–64.

Chapter 9: Richard J. Evans (ed.), *Society and Politics in Wilhelmine Germany* (London: Croom Helm, 1978), pp. 112–35.

Chapter 10: *Politics and Society*, vol. 12, no. 1 (1983), pp. 53–82.

Introduction

Taken as a whole, these essays try to develop a particular way of approaching the German past between Bismarck and Hitler, which is at some variance with how German history has mainly been written since the Second World War. They were written at various times over the last ten years, the oldest as long ago as 1973, some as recently as 1983. Most have been published before, with varying degrees of accessibility. My purpose in bringing them together is to revive some of their arguments and to set them before a larger public than is sometimes the case with articles published in specialized journals. Because they represent instalments of a larger plan, reflecting aspects of a general vision of the German past, I also believe that they make a relatively coherent collection. Quite aside from the merits of the individual essays, therefore, this is the basis on which I would like the volume to be judged.

In this sense, the essays follow several different lines of inquiry. One concerns the best way of conceptualizing the continuity in German history if we are to do justice both to the origins of Nazism and to the autonomies of the imperial period that came before. Another concerns what has become the abiding problem of historical analysis in the last third of the twentieth century, namely the best way of relating the economic and social-structural levels of a society's existence to the political, cultural and ideological ones, or to put it another way, the best way of integrating different kinds of history together in a comprehensive view of the whole. Yet a third is focused more closely on some particular areas of German historical writing, including the impact of the Great Depression of 1873–96, the weaknesses of German liberalism, the pivotal importance of 1878–9 and 1897–1902 to the empire's political history, the extent of the SPD's radicalism as opposed to its degree of integration in imperial German society, and so on.

It will not escape the reader's attention that these arguments are explored via the medium of critique. My work in German history has been conducted through a kind of running dialogue with existing approaches in the field. This began with the first of my published articles (Chapter 5 in this volume), and continued with a series of further essays considering the usefulness of some of the concepts and interpretations that have come to dominate modern German history since the late-1960s.[1] The summation of this critical writing, which sought to combine the various particular discussions into a general argument about the course of German history, was a book which I jointly published with David

1

Blackbourn in West Germany in 1980, and which subsequently appeared in English in a much revised form as *The Peculiarities of German History. Bourgeois Society and Politics in Nineteenth-Century Germany* (Oxford, 1984).[2] The same cumulative critique also set the scene for my own first book on the changing bases of right-wing politics between the fall of Bismarck and the early 1920s.[3]

Amongst German historians, it is fair to say, this critique has not enjoyed unqualified assent. Some of its aspects have been extremely contentious, provoking widespread disagreement (particularly in the Federal Republic of Germany) and considerable unease, even in circles inclined to be sympathetic. This is partly a matter of generations. Since the war, Anglo-American writing about Germany has been dominated by people who directly experienced the horrors of Nazism in their own lives, intellectual development and moral-political formation, often as a result of growing up in Germany itself and the ensuing traumas of personal loss and forced emigration, and invariably through some form of participation in the anti-fascist war effort.[4] They were a generation, as Leonard Krieger put it, who were 'politically educated by the totalitarian process that ended a united Germany'.[5] Their approach is best described as forthrightly liberal. They proceeded from the essential authoritarianism and associated backwardness of German political culture before 1945, stressing the historic weaknesses of German liberalism by comparison with the West. Despite the imposing strengths of the German capitalist economy by the start of the twentieth century, they argued, there was no corresponding 'modernization' of the political system, which continued to reflect the reactionary predilections of traditional elites amongst the landowners, army and civil service. Thus the failure to extirpate the power of 'pre-industrial traditions' at the centre of the state vitiated any progress towards liberal democracy before 1914 and undermined the foundations of the Weimar Republic. The two senior representatives of this approach in the USA and West Germany have probably been Hajo Holborn and Karl Dietrich Bracher, while Gordon Craig's *Germany 1866–1945* (Oxford, 1978) may stand as its literary monument.[6]

This way of thinking received decisive further impetus from developments in West Germany in the 1960s. Apart from the early advocates of contemporary history (amongst whom Bracher was a leading voice), few historians in the Federal Republic had joined the Anglo-American liberal critique until the way was opened by the celebrated Fischer Controversy surrounding the work of the Hamburg historian Fritz Fischer on Germany's aims in the First World War. This is not the place for another detailed commentary on the ramifications of this affair. We need only to note that it dramatically exposed the problem of continuity in modern German history for intensive discussion. By showing similarities between German expansionism in both world wars, Fischer both located Nazism in the deeper German past and directed attention to the social factors that may have produced it. Interest quickly focused on the social and political system of the *Kaiserreich* between 1871 and 1918. In effect, Fischer and his followers took the Anglo-American notion of pre-industrial continuity ('authoritarian and anti-democratic structures in state and society', in Bracher's phrase), and grounded it in a new kind of socio-economic analysis. In this case, German political culture's peculiar 'backwardness' became attributed to the political dominance of a particular cluster of interests – the 'alliance of iron and rye' or the political bloc of heavy industry and big agriculture – which were thought to have continuously blocked the development of liberal democratic institutions.[7]

This became the starting-point for what amounted to a remarkable renaissance of historical studies in the Federal Republic. The impact of the Fischer Controversy extended far beyond the character of Fischer's own interpretations and type of history, because it cleared the way for a wide-ranging discussion of German history as a whole. Partly such discussion focused on the nature of the policies and coalitions of interest that sustained Germany's drive for foreign expansion before and during the First World War. The domestic counterpart to such aggressive expansion-ism, it seemed, was the entrenched social defensiveness of the traditional élites, who tried to preserve the bastions of their power against the consequences of industrialization. After successfully surmounting the frontal assault of the bourgeoisie in 1848 and the renewal of a liberal challenge in the 1860s, the pre-industrial élite managed to co-opt the leaderships of the industrial, commercial and professional bourgeoisie under the empire, and held the line against further demands for political reform by a variety of manipulative and diversionary techniques. This sort of analysis made the history of the empire increasingly basic to the discussion of German fascism. The successful 'defence of inherited ruling positions by pre-industrial élites against the onslaught of new forces', it is argued, stacked the situation against the chances of democracy. Not only was this true under the empire, but it also undercut the republican experiment of Weimar.[8]

In other words, the continuity of German imperialist ambition across the two world wars was seen to reflect a more basic continuity of dominant socio-economic interests at home. This view has spawned a rich variety of conceptual innovation and monographic research. One result has been a definite view of the political process – as being primarily constituted from the interaction of organized economic interests and, at the same time, heavily overdetermined by pre-industrial traditions at the centre of the state – that is probably the enduring legacy of the Fischer Controversy and the changes it helped begin, with a powerful imprint on current approaches to political history under both the *Kaiserreich* and the Weimar Republic. This is accompanied by polemical advocacy of 'the primacy of domestic policy' (a phrase taken from the influence of Eckart Kehr), which was originally a means of grounding the continuity thesis in the kind of socio-economic analysis of politics just mentioned. Finally, the concept of 'social imperialism' should also be mentioned, for it was this that mediated the connection between the postulated continuity of foreign-policy ambitions and the domestic power structure by stressing the manipulative interventions of successive German governments. In Hans-Ulrich Wehler's classic definition, social imperialism was 'the diversion outwards of internal tensions and forces of change in order to preserve the social and political status quo', and a 'defensive ideology' against the 'disruptive effects of industrialization on the social and economic structure of Germany'. It was also a principal means by which the dominant agrarian-industrial bloc secured its popular support, because popular nationalism was consciously manipulated as a 'long-term integrative factor' for stabilizing the 'anachronistic social and power structure'. Indeed, 'If there is a continuity in German imperialism', it consists in 'the primacy of social imperialism from Bismarck to Hitler'.[9]

This systematic revisiting of pre-1914 history under the sign of continuity had many other aspects. For instance, it involved the careful reappropriation of radical or other dissenting scholarship from the interwar years, which had been either marginalized or suppressed by the Nazis and the prevailing conservatism of the German historical profession (the *Zunft* or guild, as it is frequently known).[10] It also gave much impetus to the growth of social history by fixing attention on the interrelations of economy, politics and social structure. In addition, there developed a much greater theoretical and methodological self-consciousness, as the exponents of the post-Fischer viewpoints were called upon to justify their history against the established canon of the West German profession. In each of these respects work on the *Kaiserreich* converged with other tendencies towards intellectual renewal. Some of these came from cognate historical debates, including the discussion of the workers' councils in 1918–19 (which reopened the question of missed democratic opportunities in the foundation years of the Weimar Republic) and the various interpretations of National Socialism, which increasingly shifted discussion away from concepts of totalitarianism and Hitler's personal dictatorship towards a theory of polycracy and the regime's broader social and economic context.[11]

The 1960s were also a very special conjuncture. The renovation of historical studies could not have happened if the time had not been ripe in other ways. In this respect West Germany shared in an international synchrony of affluence, ideological loosening and expanding higher education, which was compounded by some German particularities, from the dissolution of the so-called CDU state and its suffocating conformities to the beginnings of a dialogue with the German Democratic Republic and the Brandt government's *Ostpolitik*. In the universities the demands for relevance and democratization were briefly linked to the maturing discontents of historians. Amongst the latter there was talk of 'emancipation' and the discipline of intellectual relevance, a wide-ranging eclecticism of theoretical reference, an opening up of new subjects (especially in social history), and a general atmosphere of experiment. Above all, there was an unbending commitment to critically interrogating the German past – *Bewältigung der Vergangenheit*, coming to terms with the past – so that Nazism's deeper origins in German history could be laid bare. The new 'critical history' was perhaps characterized most of all by this strong sense of pedagogic political purpose, a principled determination that uncomfortable realities of the German past should finally be faced.

This was the moment in which the German historiography of the 1970s – including the essays in this book – was formed. Not its least notable feature was the fleeting convergence of very different intellectual tendencies on the common ground of the continuity question – not just the advocates of social-scientific history around Hans-Ulrich Wehler, but many who later moved into other kinds of social history oriented more towards 'Anglo-Marxism' and historical anthropology, and various currents of the German New Left, who in the late-1960s unfolded an intensive theoretical discussion on the subject of fascism.[12] But ultimately it was the notion of a 'historical social science' that made the deepest inroads into the structure of the West German profession, and this 'Western' orientation facilitated a close relationship with British and American Germanists of a similar age and background. As Wehler says, speaking of his own generation, namely, 'the advanced students and doctoral candidates, assistants and lecturers who were active in history departments around 1960': 'An interested and approving opening to the West European and American world was for them as self-evident as was a liberal-democratic point of view.'[13] From our present perspective, the point worth stressing here is the pervasive popularity of an idea with a long pedigree in Western social and political thought, namely the idea of a German *Sonderweg* – a special path of historical development, which was distinct from those in Britain, France and the USA, and which basically explains German society's vulnerability to fascism – or the 'social origins of dictatorship', as Barrington Moore put it in the title of his famous book.[14]

By now it should be clear that the views under discussion are inextricably bound up with deeply held political opinions. This is true in their different ways of both the older Anglo-American and the newer West German versions of the *Sonderweg* thesis. But the latter, in particular, has been argued through, these last twenty years, against the accumulated complacency of a society which actively suppressed the questions of deeper-rooted historical responsibility for fascism, and against the obdurate resistance of conservatives in the profession who commanded enormous reserves of institutional power and bitterly contested not only the validity of the interpretations but the very legitimacy of their expression. Furthermore, the West German advocates of critical history have been equally conscious of an adversary further to the east. Their struggle for a progressive science of history has been conducted as a two-front war – not only with the hulking dinosaurs of the *Zunft*, but also with the Marxist–Leninist beast. Since the early 1970s, 'critical historians' have carefully negotiated a middle path, exposing the limitations of traditional history of whatever stripe, but strictly demarcating themselves from the German Democratic Republic.[15] This is a matter of no small importance. In practice, this proscription of Marxism has extended not just to the works of orthodox communist historiography, but to all forms of a Marxist approach, whatever their distance from the latter.[16]

This political dimension of German historical writing helps explain some of what one observer has called the 'negative, defensive, allergic response' to my interventions.[17] It is perhaps understandable if the exponents of such hard-won positions should be less than enthusiastic about the appearance of a fresh critique. Having established themselves so painfully against the right, they are hardly likely to be very patient with critical arguments from the left which appear to undercut them. But sometimes their reactions have taken a rather extreme form. On occasion the seriousness of my intentions has been impugned as a 'cynical' effort at 'stirring' on the part of an unknown outsider anxious to make a reputation.[18] At other times my work has been dismissed as the misguided ignorance of an Englishman who cannot possibly understand the mainsprings of German history. It has been suggested that I have not done enough reading or research, that I do not know what I am writing about, that ultimately my arguments are based on 'bluff'.[19] More reasonably, it has been said that I am better at knocking down other people's arguments than at building my own, while my occasional polemical style has sometimes given offence.

All of this has been strong stuff. Arguing against the primacy of pre-industrial traditions and the simplifications of the post-Fischer continuity thesis from a flexible Marxist perspective – one of the main connecting threads of my German essays – has been no easy business. Sometimes I have been accused of playing into the hands of the conservatives by suggesting that the *Kaiserreich* was perhaps more stable and less crisis-ridden than we had thought; at others (often by the same people) I have been charged with promulgating a reductionist and economistic Marxism–Leninism, despite all my protestations to the contrary.[20] Such attacks are all the harder to deal with because I have always upheld the progressive importance of the late 1960s' departures, and have tried to state this clearly in the course of my writing. There has never been any doubt in my mind that they liberated West German historiography from its stultifying political and methodological conservatism and opened up the serious scholarly investigation of the imperial era. To clarify the nature of my stance, therefore, it may be worth saying something about the evolution of my own thinking during the last fifteen years. This may also help position my individual essays against the broader historiographical developments I have been describing.

I began graduate work in September 1970 dimly aware of the Fischer Controversy and its implications. Fischer had lectured in Oxford that previous year, but being up to my neck in student politics (that is, more important things, as they seemed at the time), I had missed him. I had spent a good part of my final undergraduate year digesting John Röhl's *Germany without Bismarck* (London, 1967) which was then virtually the only work in English on its period based on the archives, and in the same year Röhl also gave a paper to my college history society on Germany's responsibility for the First World War.[21] My closest undergraduate teacher, Hartmut Pogge von Strandmann, had also pointed me at some of the contemporary debates, but without as yet much coherent effect. Otherwise, I carried the usual set of German history interests for the time, when the new research had still to make much of an impact on the sort of materials generally available to a British student: the origins of the Second World War, the role of the German army in politics, the character of the SPD (Sozialdemokratische Partei Deutschlands – Social Democratic Party), and so on. Looking back over my undergraduate essays, they are strikingly innocent of the German revisionism already in train. To the extent that I was already aware of the changing approaches, it was more in connection with the German Revolution of 1918 (whose existence I had just then discovered), than with the social and political history of the *Kaiserreich*.

The first book I read in German as a graduate student was Hans-Ulrich Wehler's *magnum opus* entitled *Bismarck und der Imperialismus* (Cologne, 1969). This came as a revelation – in the extraordinary weight of its erudition, in the enormous density of its empirical research (and the vastness of its footnotes), in the imposing plenitude of its bibliography (24 separate archives, 65 collections of private papers, some 2,300 individual titles), and in the openness and ambition of its theoretical framework. The combination of economic theory, concrete analytical detail, political narrative and overarching historical interpretation was particularly impressive. It not only contained a challenging and finely articulated theoretical framework (with Lukács quoted in the final sentence of the foreword and Marx in the motto to the introduction, followed in the next few pages by Horkheimer and Habermas, Hans Rosenberg and Eckart Kehr), but a comprehensive analysis of Germany's commercial and colonial expansion in all parts of the world in the 1870s and 1880s, and a detailed discussion of Bismarckian policy-making. Historians in Britain, I remember thinking at the time, simply did not write this kind of book.

7

Having jumped into the deep end of the post-Fischer revisionism, I proceeded to swim with the current. As my reading continued, the basic works of the 1960s followed in rapid succession: Helmut Böhme's *Deutschlands Weg zur Grossmacht* (Cologne, 1966); Hans Rosenberg's *Grosse Depression und Bismarckzeit* (Berlin, 1967); Hans-Jürgen Puhle's *Agrarische Interessenpolitik und preussischer Konservatismus im Wilhelminischen Reich 1893–1914* (Bonn and Bad Godesberg, 1975; originally published 1966); Fritz Fischer's second book *Krieg der Illusionen. Die deutsche Politik 1911–1914* (Düsseldorf, 1969; later translated as *War of Illusions* [London, 1974]); and a number of others. Three volumes of essays, edited by Böhme, Wehler and Michael Stürmer, had a particularly strategic place in this reading, as of course did the writings of Eckhart Kehr.[22] Finally, I worked with a fine-tooth comb through the newly appeared monographs of two Fischer students, Peter-Christian Witt's *Die Finanzpolitik des Deutschen Reiches von 1903–1913* (Lübeck, 1970) and Dirk Stegmann's *Die Erben Bismarcks* (Cologne, 1970), to which at this stage my grasp of Wilhelmine politics probably owed more than any other single work. I mention this reading not to imply that it was anything other than usual for someone entering Wilhelmine history at the time, but simply to suggest the general sense of freshness and excitement at the time I was trained. By the time I went out to the archives in October 1971, I was steeped in the latest research. With the appearance of Volker Berghahn's study of the big navy policy, *Der Tirpitz-Plan* (Düsseldorf, 1971), the first generation of post-Fischer monographs on Wilhelmine Germany was basically complete. In February 1972, just before returning to Germany, I attended a panel in St Antony's on the domestic origins of Germany's expansionism in the First World War, which seemed to confirm the strength of the consensus behind the new perspectives.[23]

As I took the ferry from Ehrenbreitstein to Coblenz in mid-October 1971 and crossed the threshold of the Bundesarchiv, I was very clear about the kind of contribution my dissertation would make: it would add one more building block to the emerging revisionist edifice.[24] During the previous year I had adopted one of several topics suggested by my supervisor and had chosen to write my thesis on the Navy League, which was the largest of the various nationalist pressure groups that played such a prominent part in Wilhelmine politics. It was an axiom of the new writing that the naval issue was crucial in reviving the agrarian-industrial alliance during 1897–1902 by offering the positive incentives for industrial participation and by providing access to the necessary popular support, amongst both the propertied classes and the people at large.[25] From this point of view, the Navy League seemed to provide an excellent opportunity for showing the dominant politics at work. As a mass agitational organization of the right eventually mobilizing over a million people, with intimate links to government and the spokesmen of the agrarian-industrial alliance, it seemed the perfect exemplar of the 'manipulative social imperialism' as Wehler had defined it, and as every other writer on the subject seemed to accept. Moreover, its foundation in 1898 coincided with the first stage of the government's *Sammlungspolitik* ('the politics of concentration or rallying-together'), as the effort to unite industry and agriculture became known. Its moving spirits were drawn from the *Sammlung's* leading circles in collusion with the government, and it was usually thought to have played a key role in the 1898 elections which followed a few weeks after the foundation. Here, I thought, was a golden chance to illustrate the value of the new ideas.[26]

At first, I found little to shake my confidence in these certainties. But then in February 1972 I began a period of intensive work on the daily press, partly to reconstruct the detailed activity of the Navy League, partly to see how it fitted into the national political picture. This included a comprehensive search through several national and regional newspapers for the period between the major government reconstruction of summer 1897 and the climax of the Reichstag elections twelve months later.[27] Rather to my surprise, I seemed to be finding little evidence of the naval issue's positive involvement in the protracted negotiations surrounding *Sammlungspolitik* and hardly any evidence at all of its part in the elections. Still more surprising, the foundation of the Navy League seemed to have passed without significant comment. The press carried a brief notice of its appearance, but thereafter the silence was deafening. This was a major setback: if the press did not reflect the naval issue's central importance to *Sammlungspolitik*, let alone the Navy League's key part in the government's right-wing election tactic, then what would I do for evidence?

Once I began working through the unpublished sources, unease turned to active doubt. For one thing, the naval records (that is, the Imperial Navy Office documents and the private papers of Alfred von Tirpitz and some others), including departmental memoranda, minutes of ministerial discussions affecting the navy, records of key meetings between Tirpitz's assistants and the Finance Minister and main architect of *Sammlungspolitik* Johannes von Miquel, and general correspondence, showed the naval question to have been quite separate from the main concerns of the *Sammlung*. These were to do with protectionist economic policies, the government's need for a solid parliamentary majority of the right, and the paramount urgency of anti-socialist unity for the forthcoming elections. Tirpitz doggedly and successfully pursued his own goal of a legislative basis for naval construction (realized in the two Navy Laws of 1898 and 1900). But at the same time Miquel had his way, too, by keeping the navy out of the negotiations between industry and agriculture and successfully excluding it from the planned election campaign.

For me, this was a disconcerting revelation. Berghahn, who had just used these materials, had insisted rather forcefully that the navy was 'the catalyst which was supposed to facilitate a *Sammlung*' between industry and agriculture and supplied the creative key to government thinking in these years.[28] Yet here were the key policy-makers bending over backwards to stress that the navy should be kept out of the picture. The reason was Conservative and agrarian anxieties about untrammelled industrialism, for the naval issue was too redolent of triumphal commercialism, expanding industry, bourgeois ideologies of technological and economic progress, and the kind of low-tariff trading policies that the agrarian lobby was currently seeking to overturn.[29]

It seemed increasingly to me that the naval issue had been a disruptive factor in the preferred strategy of the government and the party-political right. Historians had been seduced by Eckart Kehr's fetching formula ('for industry the fleet, *Weltpolitik* and expansion, for the agrarians the tariffs and the upholding of the social supremacy of the Conservatives') into assuming a tight and constructive relationship between the big navy policy and *Sammlungspolitik* which the primary sources could not sustain.[30] Instead, the two questions had simply coincided in time, to be discretely handled in the political process. At first somewhat hesitantly, and then with the full vigour of conversion, I pursued this insight as systematically as possible through the available sources, most of which had not been properly exploited by previous historians. These included the daily press (to which I returned for another thorough going-over); several collections of private papers, some of which I was the first to use (including those of the chairman of the Central Association of German Industrialists Theodor von Hassler, the first chairman of the Navy League Fürst Wilhelm zu Wied, the leading Pan-German and industry-oriented newspaper editor Theodor Reismann-Grone, and a number of others); the holdings of the Gutehoffnungshütte firm archive (which gave me further access to inner-industry discussions); fragmentary records of the National Liberal Party (for the political articulation of industry's views on *Sammlungspolitik*); and the archive of the Pan-Germans (who had an independent stake of their own in a vigorous naval agitation).[31]

The result was my first published article, which is reprinted as the fifth chapter in this collection. More than anything else, I suppose, I had grown sceptical of the explanatory sufficiency of concepts like *Sammlungspolitik* and social imperialism. They were turning into unreflected habits of discourse, explanations in themselves rather than precisely what needed to be explained. They seemed to impute too much unity and coherence to the empire's 'ruling elites' and too much manipulative farsightedness to politicians like Bernhard von Bülow and Alfred von Tirpitz. It was to help specify the limits of such ideas that my original article was written, and from the same agenda came two further essays, only one of which is collected here, on different aspects of social imperialism.[32] Moreover, by now my desire to take stock of the post-Fischer revisionism was developing its own momentum. In the second half of the 1970s I produced a string of additional essays on other aspects of what, in 1976, James Sheehan felt able to call a 'new orthodoxy' and which by the start of the decade was heavily identified with the influence of Hans-Ulrich Wehler.[33] These included a discussion of Eckart Kehr's influence in a review of the 'second wave' of revisionist publication in the mid-1970s (reprinted as the second chapter in this collection); a general essay on the dynamics of radicalization on the right (the penultimate chapter in the collection); a discussion of 'pre-industrial traditions' in the army (later reworked as the fourth chapter below); and an unpublished paper on the influence of Hans Rosenberg (the first chapter below). The climax of this writing was a generalized polemic against Wehler's influential textbook *Das deutsche Kaiserreich 1871–1918* (Göttingen, 1973), which in retrospect contains a certain amount of youthful overstatement, and which on balance I decided not to republish in the current collection.[34]

What was the connecting theme of my cumulative critique? Basically, I had decided that the idea of authoritarian continuities – of 'pre-industrial traditions' whose dominance in a healthier course of development would have to have been swept away, but which in Germany survived to stymie the prospect of democracy – begged more questions than it resolved. In effect, I was arguing for a systematic shifting of perspective. Rather than seeing the empire as straightforwardly dominated by 'pre-industrial elites', for instance, perhaps it would be more useful to consider the consequences of German society's *embourgeoisement*. Rather than assuming that German history was distorted by an absence of bourgeois revolution and a failure of liberalism in the middle decades of the nineteenth century, perhaps it would be more useful to consider the forms of bourgeois predominance in a society increasingly dominated by capitalism. Rather than speaking of the German liberals' capitulation to Bismarck, one might continue, perhaps we should recognize areas of liberal achievement, from the creation of the nation-state to the mixed constitution, the rule of the law, and the triumph of distinctively bourgeois values. Rather than explaining all forms of authoritarianism by the baleful influence of the Junkers, perhaps they should also be referred to the structures and processes of Germany's extraordinarily dynamic capitalist development. Rather than seeing the imperial polity as gripped by a 'permanent structural crisis' resulting from the discrepancy between 'industrial growth and political backwardness', perhaps we should recognize tendencies towards political stabilization. Rather than viewing German history exclusively from Berlin, or from Prussia, or from the backward provinces east of the Elbe, perhaps we should see German society as a whole, in the full complexity of its regions. Rather than stressing the manipulative abilities of the governing elites, perhaps we should focus on the field of tensions between dominant and subordinate classes and the bases of the latter's independent mobilization. Rather than seeing just the linear continuities of Bismarckian, Wilhelmine and Nazi authoritarianism, perhaps we should explore the unevenness of the process from a less inevitabilist conception of Nazism's deeper origins. Perhaps we should stop seeing German history, in other words, as a site of pathology, where social and political development had from the beginning gone 'wrong'.

So from small beginnings – a rather specific argument about the basis of right-wing politics in 1897–8 – there grew a more general dissatisfaction with the approaches and interpretations that had come to dominate the study of imperial Germany since the late 1960s. From detailed disgreements over the politics of naval expansion at the turn of the century, I turned to a critique of central concepts like *Sammlungspolitik* and social imperialism; from there I began to rethink my ideas about continuity and the origins of Nazism; and from that point it was a short step to reconsider the underlying assumptions about the basis of authoritarianism and the primacy of pre-industrial traditions. Ultimately, this chain of thought brought me to the idea of the German *Sonderweg* itself, and by around 1977–8 I found myself questioning the whole notion of German exceptionalism when compared with the 'West'. I wanted both to loosen the deterministic grip of the 'road to 1933' on our perceptions of the period before 1914 and to render the imperial German experience more constructively comparable to that of its peer societies west of the Rhine. At the same time, this was no exercise in mere apostacy. I had no desire to repudiate the post-Fischer perspectives as a whole. As a matter of principle I continued to affirm their importance. But I did start to think about how else the questions of continuity and authoritarianism could be understood.

There was also another dimension to my intellectual development in the 1970s. I began graduate work fresh from the radical excitements of the student movement, but with a grasp of theory that was still pretty unformed and only hesistantly Marxist.[35] Indeed, my 'Marxism' was hardly more than a belief in the causal efficacy of 'social and economic factors', and it was precisely one of the attractions of the West German revisionist history that it seemed to take 'economic explanations' seriously. By the end of 1970–1 I had already put a large amount of fresh reading behind me, including the start of a long and continuing engagement with the ideas of Antonio Gramsci. But it was only later, from around 1974, with the new freedom of a completed dissertation, that I began seriously training myself in theory, working my way through Marx and Engels, Gramsci, Nicos Poulantzas and the emerging corpus of British post-Althusserian or structural Marxist theory, together with Max Weber and various British 'left-Weberians'. As it happened, this was also a time of far-reaching revisionism within the Marxist tradition, which greatly helped my own graduation from the rudimentary 'economism' and 'class-deter-minism' (as they came to be known) of my student initiation. Such revisionism was especially important for discussions of the state, politics and ideology, which by the later 1970s were also becoming heavily influenced by developments in feminist theory, whose exponents came at similar questions from another direction.

By the present time of writing (October 1984), these developments have brought me a long way from the political and intellectual optimism of 1970, when Marxism seemed to provide the answers rather than just a better set of questions. In that sense my historiographical critique also reflects a critical discussion within the Marxist tradition. At the risk of simplifying some extremely complex and ramified debates, the latter has been centrally concerned with the limitations of the classical 'base-superstructure' metaphor. Since the late 1960s Marxists have increasingly sought ways of freeing analysis of the state, politics, ideology and culture (the 'super-structure' of the classical metaphor) from their instrumentalist, functional-ist and expressive dependence on the causal sovereignty of the economy and the class structure (the 'base'). Now, I would not claim much originality for my own writing in this particular respect. But I have tried to explore some of the implications of these theoretical developments for my German work, by applying some of their insights and by revisiting some accustomed or fashionable interpretations. As well as their immediate historical and historiographical purposes, therefore, the essays in this volume also reflect a continuing effort to assimilate the lessons of recent theoretical debates and by an intensive examination of one historical experience to concretize their value.

The essay with the lowest theoretical profile in this respect is the earliest (the fifth chapter in the volume), where the argument could stand fairly easily without the underlying Marxist perspective, even allowing for the grand implication of its concluding sentence. But the essay on social imperialism, which was conceived immediately after, already reflects a stronger theoretical engagement and anticipates in a practical form many of the arguments made more confidently later in the 1970s. At this time I was trying hard to grasp the consequences of the emerging Marxist discussions referred to above, and some of this intellectual process is also reflected in the second essay in this collection, which was written and rewritten many times during 1977. Otherwise, I was dealing in my own research with questions that had been either neglected by previous Marxist writing or else treated very unsympathetically, like the predicament and political mobilization of the petty bourgeoisie; this was the immediate subject of my dissertation and first book and is also addressed in the penultimate essay of the collection, which was originally drafted in 1975–6. By 1977–8, when I completed most of the writing for *Reshaping the German Right*, I felt very much in control of the particular version of structural Marxism I had come to find most congenial, and the essay on the Great Depression which opens this collection originated in 1979 as an explicit attempt to implement its relentlessly anti-reductionist prescriptions. The subsequent essays (especially the third, seventh and last in the collection), for better or worse, reflect the maturity of this theoretical perspective.[36]

This aspect of my writing is worth drawing attention to, because it is one that is frequently singled out for criticism in West Germany. More generally during the 1970s there was a discouraging diminution of tolerance for Marxist ideas in the West German universities, a situation which contrasted unfavourably with the attractive and invigorating intellectual pluralism of the later 1960s. This intellectual closure was paralleled and partially encouraged by the attack on the position of radicals in the public service through the infamous *Berufsverbot*, which for most of the 1970s rendered the expression of Marxist or other 'extremist' opinions reasonable grounds for dismissal or exclusion from public employment.[37] Regrettably, the West German historical profession has not been immune to these developments, and by contrast with their earlier public engagement for progressive political causes, few of the 'critical historians' seemed willing to raise their voices in defence of this particular cause of academic freedom. Indeed, such historians have routinely neglected the possibility of a Marxism distinct from the dogmatic Marxism–Leninism usually attributed to the historians of the German Democratic Republic, so that any appropriation of current Marxist theory for historical analysis tends to be rendered suspect. But for whatever reason, and by contrast with Britain, North America, Scandinavia and the Mediterranean, there is very little of a contemporary Marxist presence in the West German historical profession.

One purpose of my essays has been to help establish the legitimacy of Marxist analysis in the plural discourse of German historians. The various positions these essays seek to explore are obviously not the last word, but they are an attempt to think through some difficult problems, and as such deserve to enter the discussion. West German writing sometimes leaves the uneasy feeling that an explicitly Marxist approach is equated too readily with 'dogmatism' as such without considering the ideas on their merits, so that the very possibility of a constructive Marxist intervention is ruled out from the beginning, forever tainted by the palpable sterility of one particular 'orthodox Marxist' tradition. It is my firm conviction that this is a harmful and unnecessary narrowing of any genuinely 'critical' or liberal discussion. Recent Marxist debates have much to offer, and the discourse will be much the poorer for their exclusion.

All of this may help to make more sense of the critical writing contained in these assembled essays. This introduction has been more heavily autobiographical than is usual, but as I believe with E. H. Carr that one must know one's historian, it may be of more than passing interest to know how my own modest contribution was produced. More so than many such collections, perhaps, the essays represent an unfinished intellectual agenda, part of a continuing effort to clarify my views of the German past and an example, in that sense, of thinking-in-progress. I was encouraged, on returning to the older essays in the collection, by how little I wanted to change. But at the same time, I also hope that the more recent ones reflect greater maturity of analysis and conceptual sophistication, in addition to carrying the argument into new empirical terrain.

The individual essays have been selected to give a fairly rounded sense both of my own interests and of the main areas of current concern in the literature on the *Kaiserreich*. The two essays in Part One are meant to identify some strategic influences and patterns of interpretation in the post-Fischer revisionist writing. The four in Part Two are meant to explore those interpretive figures more concretely by looking at various aspects of the Second Empire's social and political system. Here the discussion is fairly open and (especially in the third and sixth essays) is meant to deliver an agenda for the future. Part Three connects with two of my larger interests, in the social history of socialism and the left and in the general problem of nationalism, as well as directing attention to the underside of the empire's social and political system. The last two essays in Part Four are meant to bring the argument back to what remains the overriding focus of interest for German historians, namely, the best way of explaining the origins of Nazism. Here again, the thinking should be viewed as provisional, in the sense of wanting more than anything else to provoke discussion.

I have made few substantive alterations for the purposes of republication. Mainly the changes consist of minor corrections and elaborations, a few adjustments of conceptual terminology for the purposes of consistency and clarity, and an occasional stripping away of excess verbiage. The essays on Hans Rosenberg and the problem of militarism have not previously been published, while one or two of the others originally appeared in places not very easily accessible to an English-speaking audience. On reflection, I decided not to include a separate bibliography, on the grounds that the notes to the introduction and the prefaces to each essay should provide an adequate guide to further reading. Taken as a whole, the collection is intended to communicate a coherent view of the German past, in the context of the debates outlined in this introduction.

Most of my debts are acknowledged in the notes to the individual essays of the volume. But this introduction would barely be complete without mentioning the people whose influence and advice have been especially important in shaping the direction and content of my thinking. Hartmut Pogge deserves first place in this respect, as without him I would never have become a German historian to begin with. In retrospect his influence was even greater than I appreciated at the time, and a number of these essays originated in suggestions he subtly introduced into our many discussions in the early-1970s when I was writing my dissertation. Our contact has necessarily been less regular since, but I know that the essays' strengths still bear the traces of his influence.

At a later stage, Jane Caplan and David Crew also had an enormous influence on my thinking, as we worked through a number of these questions together. One of the settings in which we did so was the Cambridge Social History Seminar in King's College, whose weekly meetings between 1975 and 1979 (when I left Cambridge) provided the essential comparative stimulus for my German interests. I could not have wished for a more supportive and challenging intellectual environment.

It is impossible to mention all the individuals and groups whose criticisms and advice have contributed to whatever strengths my writing may possess. Collectively I should thank the various meetings and seminars to whom versions of the texts were presented and the editors in whose journals and collections they originally appeared. In their different ways Richard Evans, Dieter Groh, Jonathan Steinberg and Wolfgang Mommsen were all extremely supportive at a time in the later 1970s when my ideas were exciting a certain amount of adverse controversy. In the meantime I have also benefited greatly from friendly critiques of my work published by Roger Fletcher, Robert Moeller and James Retallack. My good friend and colleague Ron Suny cast an outsider's eye across the introduction and gave me good advice on the shape of the volume, while a last-minute reading of the introduction by Fred Cooper also gave me much reassurance.

I would like to thank Rebecca Reed for retyping most of the essays and the Faculty Assistance Fund of the College of Literature, Science and Arts of the University of Michigan for defraying most of the costs. I am grateful to Bryan Skib for help in preparing the index, and to Richard Bodek for reading the proofs. I should also thank the editors and publishers of the original essays for permission to reprint, and a full listing appears at the beginning of this introduction. Not least, I would like to thank Jane Harris-Matthews and Allen & Unwin for giving me the chance to keep these essays alive.

Finally, I would like to acknowledge two debts of particular importance. One is to the broader community of German historians – especially in Britain – for providing the indispensable intellectual stimulus for this writing during the last ten years and for making it such a good time to be a German historian. The other is to David Blackbourn. Our collaboration began in a library canteen in Stuttgart one spring afternoon in 1972 and has continued in various forms ever since. During 1975–8, when the argumentation for most of these essays was first laid down and we were writing our various books, this was especially close, so much so that it is hard to know where one of us begins and the other stops. In its virtues, this book is to a great extent also his.

INTRODUCTION: NOTES

1 As well as the essays in this volume, the following should also be mentioned: 'Defining social imperialism: use and abuse of an idea', *Social History*, vol. 1 (1976), pp. 265–90; 'Memories of under-development: social history in Germany', *Social History*, vol. 2 (1977), pp. 785–92; 'Die "Kehrites" und das Kaiserreich: Bemerkungen zu einer aktuellen Kontroverse', *Geschichte und Gesellschaft*, vol. 4 (1978), pp. 91–107; 'Reshaping the right: radical nationalism and the German Navy League, 1898–1908', *Historical Journal*, vol. 21 (1978), pp. 327–54; 'Recent work in modern German history', *Historical Journal*, vol. 23 (1980), pp. 463–79; 'Zum Problem der Verbände im Kaiserreich', *SOWI (Sozialwissenschaftliche Informationen für Unterricht und Studium)*, vol. 11 (January 1982), pp. 22–8. One other text should be mentioned which was originally written in 1977 and revised for publication in 1982, but which at the time of writing had still not appeared: 'The populist moment of the 1890s: agrarian mobilisation and the decomposition of the Bismarckian system', J. C. Fout (ed.), *Politics, Parties and the Authoritarian State: Imperial Germany 1871–1918* (New York, 1985).

2 This was an expanded and revised version of *Mythen deutscher Geschichtsschreibung: die gescheiterte bürgerliche Revolution von 1848* (Frankfurt-on-Main, 1980), which originated as two separately written essays in the mid-1970s.

3 *Reshaping the German Right. Radical Nationalism and Political Change after Bismarck* (New Haven, Conn. and London, 1980).

4 The most useful works on the Central European emigration are: J. Radkau, *Die deutsche Emigration in den USA, ihr Einfluss auf den amerikanische Europapolitik 1933–1945* (Düsseldorf, 1971); H. S. Hughes, *The Sea Change. The Migration of Social Thought 1930–1965* (New York, 1975); M. Jay, *The Dialectical Imagination: A History of the Frankfurt School and the Institute of Social Research 1923–1950* (Boston, Mass. and London, 1973).

5 L. Krieger, 'German history in the grand manner', *American Historical Review*, vol. 84 (1979), pp. 1011 f.

6 Although his comments are not always a very accurate guide to the detailed literature under discussion, there is a useful critique of this prevailing liberal approach in three articles by Geoffrey Barraclough in the *New York Review of Books*: 'Mandarins and Nazis' (19 October 1972); 'The liberals and German history' (2 November 1972); 'A new view of German history' (16 November 1972).

7 Fischer's book was originally published in Germany in 1961 and was translated as *Germany's Aims in the First World War* (London, 1967). There are now numerous introductions to the Fischer Controversy. The most useful for English readers is J. A. Moses, *The Politics of Illusion. The Fischer Controversy in German Historiography* (London, 1975).

8 The quotation is taken from H.-U. Wehler, *Das deutsche Kaiserreich 1871–1918* (Göttingen, 1973), p. 14 which contains one of the best summaries of the general interpretation these developments produced.

9 The quotations are taken from the following: H.-U. Wehler, *Bismarck und der Imperialismus* (Cologne, 1969), p. 115; Wehler, 'Industrial growth and early German imperialism', in R. Owen and B. Sutcliffe (eds), *Studies in the Theory of Imperialism* (London, 1972), pp. 89, 87, 88; Wehler, 'Probleme des Imperialismus', *Krisenherde des Kaiserreichs 1871–1918* (Göttingen, 1970), p. 131. I have discussed Wehler's concept of social imperialism at length in several essays, two of which are republished in this volume (Chapters 5 and 6 below). See also Eley 'Defining social imperialism', cit. at n. 1 above.

10 I am referring here to a disconnected minority of talented outsiders who won little academic recognition in their own country during the 1920s, and most of whom left after 1933, thereby enriching the historical profession in their country of adoption, usually the USA. The key individuals here were Eckart Kehr, G. W. F. Hallgarten, Alfred Vagts and, of course, Hans Rosenberg, who did compose something of a loose intellectual network. To them we might add a few others like Gustav Mayer, Arthur Rosenberg and Veit Valentin. On the whole they continued to receive little recognition in West Germany after 1945 until the new generation of the 1960s rediscovered them. The person who can take much of the credit for this is Hans-Ulrich Wehler, who during the last two decades has produced many valuable editions of their works. His writings in this area are now

conveniently collected in Wehler, *Historische Sozialwissenschaft und Geschichts-schreibung* (Göttingen, 1980).

11 There is a helpful summary of this larger historiographical context in H.-U. Wehler, 'Historiography in German today', in J. Habermas (ed.), *Observations on the Spiritual Situation of the Age* (Cambridge, Mass., 1984), pp. 221–59.

12 The openness of Wehler in particular to Marxism and other forms of New Left radicalism in the 1960s can be easily obscured by his writings of the mid-1970s, which have increasingly marked his polemical distance from Marxist approaches, which are usually identified implicitly with orthodox Marxist–Leninist perspectives. For some valuable insights into the intellectual convergence of the late 1960s, see H. Grebing, *Aktuelle Theorien über Faschismus und Konservatismus* (Stuttgart, 1974), and for a stimulating review of the subsequent field of fire, see R. Fletcher, 'Recent developments in German historiography: the Bielefeld School and its critics', *German Studies Review*, vol. 7, no. 3 (October 1984), pp. 451–80.

13 Wehler, 'Historiography in Germany today', cit. at n. 11 above, pp. 230f.

14 B. Moore Jr, *The Social Origins of Dictatorship and Democracy* (Boston, Mass., 1966).

15 See esp. H. A. Winkler (ed.), *Organisierter Kapitalismus* (Göttingen, 1974); Winkler, *Revolution, Staat, Faschismus. Zur Revision des Historischen Materialismus* (Göttingen, 1978); J. Kocka, 'Ursachen des Nationalsozialismus', *Aus Politik und Zeitgeschichte*, 21 June 1980, pp. 9–13.

16 I speak from chastened experience. My own attempt to offer what I thought was a careful Marxist approach explicitly distanced from orthodox Marxist–Leninist ones was brusquely dismissed as just another rendition of the old vulgar Marxist line. See my contribution to D. Blackbourn and G. Eley, *The Peculiarities of German History. Bourgeois Society and Politics in Nineteenth-Century Germany* (Oxford, 1984), esp. pp. 95, 115, 131 ff. For two of the offending reviews of the earlier German edition of the book, see H.-U. Wehler, ' "Deutscher Sonderweg" oder allgemeine Probleme des westlichen Kapitalismus? Zur Kritik einiger "Mythen deutscher Geschichts-schreibung" ', *Merkur*, vol. 35 (1981), pp. 478–82; H. -J. Puhle, 'Deutscher Sonderweg. Kontroverse um eine vermeintliche Legende', *Journal für Geschichte*, vol. 4 (1981), pp. 44–5.

17 R. G. Moeller, 'Die Besonderheiten der Deutschen? Neue Beiträge zur Sonderwegs-diskussion', *Internationale Schulbuchforschung*, vol. 4 (1982), p. 72.

18 See J. A. Moses, 'Restructuring the paradigm: West German historians between historicism and social history', *Australian Journal of Politics and History*, vol. 29 (1983), p. 377. In explaining the tone of his published response to one of my articles, Hans-Jürgen Puhle once told me that he had assumed I was some young scholar out to make a name for himself.

19 For a good example of such a measured and judicious response, see Heinrich August Winkler's review of my *Reshaping the German Right* in *Journal of Modern History*, vol. 54 (1982), pp. 170–6.

20 Friends and colleagues have often cautioned me against pressing my criticisms of Wehler and his co-thinkers too far, essentially on the grounds that they need to be defended against the right in the West German profession. This is a difficult argument to deal with, not least because I would myself uphold the political and intellectual value of the late 1960s departures. But, on the whole, such arguments usually function to suppress difficulties and debate.

21 This was published as J. C. G. Röhl, 'Admiral von Müller and the approach of war, 1911–1914', *Historical Journal*, vol. 12 (1969), pp. 651–73.

22 See H. Böhme (ed.), *Probleme der Reichsgründungszeit 1848–1879* (Cologne and West Berlin, 1968); H.-U. Wehler (ed.), *Moderne deutsche Sozialgeschichte* (Cologne, 1966); M. Stürmer (ed.), *Das kaiserliche Deutschland. Politik und Gesellschaft 1870–1918* (Düsseldorf, 1970); E. Kehr, *Schlachtflottenbau und Parteipolitik 1894–1901* (Berlin, 1930), and *Der Primat der Innenpolitik*, ed. H.-U. Wehler (West Berlin, 1965). In the meantime Kehr's works have been translated as *Battleship Building and Party Politics in Germany 1894–1901. A Cross-Section of the Political, Social and Ideological Pre-conditions of German Imperialism*, ed. and trans. P. R. and E. N. Anderson (Chicago and London, 1975), and *Economic Interest, Militarism and Foreign Policy*, ed. G. A. Craig (Berkeley, Calif., Los Angeles and London, 1977).

23 The panel consisted of Volker Berghahn, Wolfgang J. Mommsen, Hartmut Pogge von Strandmann and John Röhl, and despite some local disagreements and differences of emphasis, there seemed little interest in disputing the basic value of the post-Fischer perspectives.

24 Lest these references appear too arcane: the Bundesarchiv is the Federal Archive in Coblenz, and Ehrenbreitstein is the district across the Rhine where I lodged, beneath the shadow of the old fortress.

25 This view of the naval issue originated with Kehr and was taken up again by the post-Fischer revisionists, receiving its strongest statement in the detailed research of Volker Berghahn. Essentially, the expansion of the navy in the two laws of 1898 and 1900 is seen as part of a system of economic and political compensations designed to bolster up the existing system of power, terminate further progress towards social reform for the working class and keep popular democratic forces in subjection. The naval issue supposedly tempted heavy industry into joining this arrangement (just as higher tariffs tempted the agrarians), provided an object for the frustrated nationalism of the bourgeoisie, and offered a new means of whipping up broader popular support. The issues are discussed exhaustively in Chapter 5 below.

26 The historical literature dealing with the Navy League is dealt with at length in my book, *Reshaping the German Right*, and my unpublished dissertation, 'The German Navy League in German Politics, 1898–1914' (D.Phil., University of Sussex, 1974).

27 I focused on a number of issues: the circumstances surrounding the proclamation of *Sammlungspolitik* in July 1897 together with the associated government measures to facilitate agrarian-industrial understanding and the ensuing public reactions; the attempt in February–March 1898 to formulate a common economic policy through the so-called *Wirtschaftlicher Aufruf* (Economic Manifesto) as a basis for co-operation of the right-wing parties in the elections; and the election campaigning itself in May–June 1898.

28 V. R. Berghahn, *Germany and the Approach of War in 1914* (London 1973), p. 24. According to Berghahn, *Sammlungspolitik* began 'at the same time with and through the construction of the fleet'. 'The navy was to act as a focus for divergent social forces which the government hoped to bribe into a conservative *Sammlung* against the "Revolution". Promises of a great economic and political future were made with the aim of maintaining the big landowners, the military and the bureaucracy in their key positions within the power structure'. ibid., pp. 29 f.

29 The crucial documents in this respect are to be found mainly in the Bundesarchiv–Militärarchiv (Federal Military Archive) in Freiburg, mainly in the private papers of Tirpitz, and are discussed extensively in Chapter 5 below.

30 Kehr's much quoted statement may be found in *Battleship Building*, p. 217. There is a third element in his agrarian-industrial equation, namely, the key political position that rebounded to the advantage of the Catholic Centre Party as a result of the negotiations, which I have omitted from the quotation for the purposes of simplicity.

31 The Hassler papers were consulted in the town archive at Augsburg; the Wied papers at the Wied residence in Neuwied; the Reismann–Grone papers in the Essen town archive; National Liberal materials at the Federal Archive in Coblenz; and the Pan-German archive in the Central Archive of the German Democratic Republic in Potsdam. At the time I was denied access to the Krupp Archive, which would have added further illumination to the circumstances surrounding the foundation of the Navy League and possibly the inception of *Sammlungspolitik*.

32 See Chapter 6 below and 'Defining social imperialism', cit. at n. 1 above.

33 Sheehan's phrase was used in a review in the *Journal of Modern History*, vol. 48 (1976), p. 567.

34 See 'Die "Kehrites" und das Kaiserreich' (cit. at n. 1 above). While I would still uphold much of the argument in this article today, it contains too many unnuanced and exaggerated formulations to justify reviving in an unaltered form. In that sense it was more a personal reckoning with ideas and approaches I had originally found attractive than a lasting intellectual contribution. In the meantime Wehler's textbook has been published in an English translation, *The German Empire, 1871–1918* (Leamington Spa, Warwicks., 1985).

35 At that stage I had the haziest familiarity with the writings of Marx and Engels themselves. Most of my knowledge had been acquired at secondhand through the

burgeoning political literature of the late 1960s and through my own political activity. Much more important in this sense was my reading of certain Marxist historians, such as Edward Thompson, whose *Making of the English Working Class* (London, 1963) I spent most of the winter vaction in 1968–9 reading. Another explicitly theoretical essay that strongly influenced my approach to history was Eugene Genovese's 'Marxian interpretations of the slave South', in B. J. Bernstein (ed.), *Towards a New Past. Dissenting Essays in American History* (London, 1970), pp. 90–125, which contained a powerful critique of 'naive economic determinism'.

36 At the risk of becoming too self-indulgently autobiographical, I should also say that in the meantime I have also become more sceptical about the unrelieved structuralism of my preferred Marxism. Its insufficiency has emerged during two continuing discussions within the British left since around 1978–9, one centred on the writings of Marxist feminists, the other on the English-language reception of Antonio Gramsci. To a great extent this also mirrored a more general reckoning with so-called 'Althusserianism' within British Marxism, which was brought to a head by the reactions to E. P. Thompson's polemic on the subject, *The Poverty of Theory* (London, 1978). For a valuable discussion of this whole context, see T. Benton, *The Rise and Fall of Structural Marxism. Althusser and his Influence* (London, 1984).

37 The *Berufsverbot* was the generic name for a set of decrees and practices which, beginning in 1972, seriously compromised civil liberties in West Germany for anyone with a record of 'extremist' political involvement who held or applied for a civil service job. As this category of employment includes university and school teachers, railway and post office workers, doctors and nurses in state hospitals, as well as civil servants in the narrower sense, amounting to some 16 per cent of total employment in West Germany, the measure became a powerful device for tightening the public ideological climate and for delegitimizing certain kinds of Marxist and other radical ideas.

PART ONE

German Historical Writing

1

Hans Rosenberg and the Great Depression of 1873–96: Politics and Economics in Recent German Historiography, 1960–80

This essay originated as an attempt to take stock of Hans Rosenberg's seminal influence on recent historical writing about modern Germany. It came at the end of a period when I had been thinking critically about the various concepts that German historians were using to organize discussion of the *Kaiserreich*. '*Sammlungspolitik*' and 'social imperialism' were two of these and are considered in later essays in the collection below. I had also become quite critical of the view that 'pre-industrial élites' were dominant in the political system and of the manipulative model of political mobilization all these ideas seemed to imply. By the end of the 1970s these reconsiderations were also leading me back to the basic intellectual commitments of the post-Fischer revisionists – the belief in direct continuity between Bismarck and Hitler, the idea of a fundamental contradiction between economic modernity and political backwardness leading to the empire's structural instability, the view that German society lacked the progressive emancipating experience of a successful bourgeois revolution, and the belief that German history was the site of exceptional 'mis-development' by comparison with the healthier trajectories of the West – not in order to abandon them completely, but to work out how far their usefulness actually reached. From this point of view it made sense to include Rosenberg's argument about the Great Depression in my agenda, because most German historians seemed to accept that the latter was a vital 'founding period' in each of the other developments. Moreover, the middle and later 1970s were also a time of extensive discussion amongst Marxists of the need to avoid various kinds of economic and sociological reductionism, and I was becoming extremely sceptical of any views which seemed to explain major political phenomena too easily by reference to the changing character of the economy.

A first opportunity to evaluate Hans Rosenberg's general influence and achievements as a German historian came when I was asked to review his second Festschrift, *Sozialgeschichte Heute*, edited by Hans-Ulrich Wehler (Göttingen, 1974), for the special German issue of *Social History* (vol. 4, 1979, pp. 379–84). The appearance of a major monograph by one of Rosenberg's students, Shulamit Volkov's *The Rise of Popular Antimodernism in Germany. The Urban Master Artisans 1873–1896* (Princeton, NJ, 1978), which developed the 'Great Depression thesis' particularly strongly for a specific social group usually thought to be especially prominent in right-wing 'anti-modernist' political movements, also set me thinking in this direction. Then in December 1979 I was asked to contribute a paper on Rosenberg's influence for a session on 'Comparative perspectives on the political and social consequences of the Great Depression of 1873–96' for the Americal Historical Association annual convention. The following year I prepared the paper for publication in a volume of essays that failed to appear, and it has remained unpublished until the present occasion. It has been substantially rewritten for this volume and combines elements from the 1979 convention paper and the review of Rosenberg's Festschrift. So far as I am aware, there have been no significant discussions of the 'Great Depression thesis' in the meantime, although Margaret L. Anderson and Kenneth Barkin have published a highly revisionist essay whose argument is consonant with my own: 'The myth of the Puttkamer Purge and the reality of the *Kulturkampf*: some reflections on the historiography of Imperial Germany', *Journal of Modern History*, vol. 54 (1982), pp. 647–86.

I

Hans Rosenberg's *Grosse Depression und Bismarckzeit* (The Great Depression and the Time of Bismarck) was published in 1967, resuming and elaborating an argument he first mooted in 1940 and published in essay form three years later.[1] Its influence has been enormous and this was very much to do with the time of publication. The later 1960s were peculiarly propitious for that kind of intervention in the Federal Republic of Germany, given the renewal of interest in the *Kaiserreich* and the general turn to social and economic history, and in that sense the book's importance was symptomatic: it both condensed some emergent intellectual tendencies into a lucid interpretive argument and constructively specified the future direction of discussion. Together with his contemporary Eckart Kehr, whose writings were also discovered and avidly consumed in the 1960s, Rosenberg has profoundly influenced at least two generations of German historians, above all by the way in which certain 'German traditions' or 'peculiarities' have come to be perceived. This is especially clear when the book on the Great Depression is considered with his earlier work on Prussian bureaucracy and his essays on the Junkers.[2]

The nature of Rosenberg's influence has to be related to the 'interrupted' and 'displaced' development of German historical studies since the 1930s. The post-1960s upsurge of enthusiasm for social history has involved a deliberate act of recovery, to retrieve for the present the intellectual achievement of the past. This was made necessary – for good or ill it is hard to imagine British social historians returning quite as reverently to the Webbs, the Hammonds and G. D. H. Cole – by the notable backwardness imposed on West German historiography by the successive impact of Nazism and conservative restoration between the 1930s and early 1960s. As Arnold Sywottek has observed in an earlier assessment of Rosenberg's legacy, it was only by the end of the 1960s that the intellectual level of thirty years before was finally regained, so that the new activity around 1970 was 'in many respects hardly more than a reception of what was asked, thought and researched before the time of the Third Reich'.[3] Most left historians of that time (whose ranks were certainly not confined to the members of university history departments) had either died or stayed in emigration after 1945. It was therefore significant that when younger historians resumed certain kinds of theoretical and methodological discussion in the 1960s, they should choose to do so by consciously reconstituting the achievement of what they took to be a submerged dissenting historiography. In particular, Hans-Ulrich Wehler has conducted a series of forays into this terrain, appropriating first the work of Eckart Kehr, and then less prominently that of Gustav Mayer, Arthur Rosenberg and, more recently, Veit Valentin and Ludwig Quidde.[4] German historians are deeply in Wehler's debt for this intellectual archaeology, and it is entirely fitting that he should also have presided over a major tribute to Hans Rosenberg's work in the form of that extremely German phenomenon, a second Festschrift.[5]

Aside from this general ambience, which acquires much of its coherence only in the light of these recent historiographical events, Rosenberg can also be placed within a smaller circle of contemporary associates, who included Kehr, Alfred Vagts, Georg W. F. Hallgarten and the two Americans Eugene and Pauline Anderson.[6] Taken as a whole the work of these people amounts to an important body of non-Marxist but Marxist-influenced history, which made an early attempt to explore the impact of social forces on political decision-making and appears in retrospect as a potential dissident moment in the solidly conservative culture of the Weimar historical profession. In the event, this group was dispersed all too soon into emigration (where Kehr died at the tragically early age of 30 in May 1933), and lacking the collective institutional resources that sustained a larger grouping like the Frankfurt School, they failed to generate a distinctive intellectual tradition.[7] Considered individually, however, Rosenberg has proven the most manifestly influential of his peers, and by his capacity for intellectual development increasingly overshadowed the career of another distinguished *émigré*, Hajo Holborn, who came to occupy a more visible and prestigious position in the USA, but who remained far more beholden to the intellectual formation of his youth.[8] Though the enduring themes of his mature work were already present in the 1940s and in that way suggest an imposing continuity, Hans Rosenberg has consistently deepened his approach and extended his range. The great classic *Bureaucracy, Aristocracy and Autocracy: The Prussian Experience, 1660–1815* (Cambridge, Mass., 1958) was followed a decade later by *Grosse Depression und Bismarckzeit*, and the two were linked by a set of essays on German agriculture and the place of the Junkers, *Probleme der deutschen Sozialgeschichte* (Frankfurt-on-Main, 1969).[9] The sequential replacement of the English by the German language is significant and marked Rosenberg's adoption by a new generation of West German historians. This was confirmed in 1970 by the distinction of a German-language Festschrift, and then in 1972 his early essays from the 1930s on pre-unification liberalism were also reissued.[10]

What is the nature of Rosenberg's legacy? At one level his work reflects the general preoccupation of German historians since the 1930s with the origins of political authoritarianism, as I tried to outline in the introduction to this volume. But the hallmark of his contribution, which distinguished it from the studied urbanity of Holborn's intellectual history, was a solid commitment to grounding the analysis – at a general conceptual level – in a history of society rather than one of ideas. As he said in the Preface to *Bureaucracy, Aristocracy and Autocracy* (p. viii), his analysis 'approaches political, institutional and ideological changes in terms of social history, and it does not reduce social history to an appendix of economic history'. This became an organizing principle of Rosenberg's subsequent work, though again more as an axiom of general understanding than as an embodied practice of detailed social historical research. The specifically social history dimension in Rosenberg's work is achieved more by a sociological vocabulary of 'status', 'élites' and 'bureaucracy', than by a concrete exploration of social relations or social process (whether defined by a particular empirical terrain or a more 'Marxist' theory). In this way the departure from ordinary political or institutional history is registered mainly by an organizing framework of concepts, while the familiar focus on government, institutions and official values is left largely intact. When measured against the ideas of social history in the 1980s, Rosenberg's 'social history' seems more a matter of formal orientation than transformed actual practice.

But if Rosenberg's form of social history cannot be assimilated to the presently ascendant North American meanings or to the familiar British and French traditions, with their specific methodologies, objects of study and attention to place, it was none the less important for that. The recourse to social and political science had much to say for it in the 1950s and 1960s, given the resolute backwardness of the German historical establishment (not only in West Germany) and the failure of Marxism at that time to offer more than an unappealing economism. In this sense Rosenberg stands in a direct line with Kehr, whose writing was formed in a similar intellectual conjuncture. Indeed, Rosenberg's career has involved a systematic working-through of the discussions begun by Kehr before his death. This was true both of Kehr's general commitments to a notion of theorized history and to seeing politics in terms of large configurations of social forces, and of his particular topical interests. For example, Rosenberg's study of the Prussian bureaucracy may well be viewed as a resumption of Kehr's lost work on the Stein–Hardenberg era, the completed manuscript of which was apparently destroyed.[11] Like Kehr, he also acknowledged a specific debt to the theory of Max Weber and the more particularized work of Otto Hintze. Moreover, this included a *political* critique, which served simultaneously as a grand theory of German historical development: the belief that the specific authoritarianism of German political culture was contained in the 'contradiction between economic and political power', and in a political system dominated not by the 'legitimate representatives of the industrial-capitalist economic order, the bourgeoisie, but by the legitimate representatives of an economic system, feudalism, which has essentially been by-passed by history.[12]

The pursuit of this theme lends a unity to Rosenberg's whole career. Moreover, he deepened Kehr's legacy in two ways. First, he continued to examine the social historical rooting of Wilhelmine authoritarianism, which Kehr had begun to delineate in the famous 'cross-sectional' analysis of the battlefleet programme in 1897–1900. Thus, quite apart from the bureaucracy book, the long essay on the Junkers ('Die Pseudodemokrat-isierung der Rittergutsbesitzerklasse', in *Probleme der deutschen Sozial-geschichte*, pp. 7–50) belongs directly with Kehr's influential essays on the genesis of the Prussian bureaucracy and the reserve officer corps.[13] There are definite limits to this analysis. Bureaucracy is still understood primarily as a *political* phenomenon, a legal and administrative apparatus whose functioning is defined by the recorded statements of its own personnel; the stronger *social historical* aspects – how it affected social relations, how it was experienced by the ordinary population, or how it contributed to, inhibited, or helped transform the forms of appropriation of the economic surplus – are hardly discussed at all. Ultimately this reflects a deficit of theory – namely, a developed conception of the feudal mode of production and its complex articulation with other modes in the German social formation of the nineteenth century – leading to a disembodied 'statism' which cannot possibly comprehend the full particularity of Prussian absolutism. Given the strategic importance of the 'resurgent political influence of the landed aristocracy' in Rosenberg's view of the latter (*Bureaucracy, Aristocracy and Autocracy*, p. viii) and the supposed persistence of Junker domination under capitalism, this deficit becomes all the more vital. It is remarkable that we still lack an adequate social history of the 'Prussian road' of agricultural development. Yet it is only when embedded in such a deeper social analysis that the full value of Rosenberg's work on bureaucracy will finally become clear.[14]

Rosenberg's second major extension of Kehr's legacy was into specific conjunctural analysis. Already in 1934 Rosenberg had published *Die Weltwirtschaftskrisis von 1857–1859* (reissued Göttingen, 1974). But he is far better known for his work on the so-called 'Great Depression' of 1873–96, first sketched out in an essay of 1943. With the latter Rosenberg brought a dimension of hard economic analysis that Kehr's work had lacked, locating the foundations of the imperial political system in a particular period of social and economic crisis. In this way he conjoined his older conception of the authoritarian tradition of 'bureaucratic absolutism' and its legacy to a notion of cyclical economic development and its structural relation to politics. Accordingly, the Great Depression becomes a crucial founding period, generating a firm alliance of industrial and agrarian interests, badly weakening the forces of liberalism, spawning anti-semitism and other 'anti-modern' ideologies, and generally easing the way for 'pre-fascist' dispositions. There can be no doubt of this work's importance. More than any other, it helped dethrone Bismarck from his biographical domination of German historiography and opened the way for new approaches.

II

In general, therefore, Hans Rosenberg has provided a living bridge to the Weimar Republic, where the beginnings of a left liberal and democratically inclined intellectual culture were brutally shattered by the catastrophe of 1933. His exterior relationship to West German academic life (which in the 1950s was a matter of exclusion as well as personal choice), combined with the USA's cultural hegemony in the 1950s and 1960s, left him well placed for contributing to the eventual revival of a more creative historiography in the Federal Republic of Germany. In fact, one might say that his career anticipates the uneven trajectory of Germany's progressive non-Marxist historiography between the 1930s and the present – from the liberal history of ideas, through the discovery of deeper structural continuities in the German past, to a general interest in the role of socio-economic factors in political life. In these terms he is a very representative figure, upholding a certain left liberal critique of the 'Prussian tradition' which achieved remarkable popularity in the 1960s, straddling American and West German intellectual culture, and assisting in some vital historiographical departures.

In other words, Rosenberg's importance lies beyond dispute. In matters of substance and approach he has been a seminal influence on the best of recent German history. This is especially true of his support for social history and his use of economic theory. My aim in what follows is not to diminish his achievement, nor to produce a general and well-rounded assessment of his *œuvre*, but to consider a specific dimension of his work which is most powerfully represented in the book on the Great Depression, namely, the relationship of politics to economics. In so doing, I am intentionally raising an issue of broader importance for German historians of the later-nineteenth and twentieth centuries, and one which has received extensive exposure amongst Marxists and other social theorists during the past decade and a half.[15]

Now, there is a certain difficulty in broaching this question. On the one hand, Rosenberg's book on the Great Depression clearly contains a powerful notion of structural causality, in which movements of the economy are given a determining influence on developments in the political and ideological sphere. The crucial political changes hinging on the events of 1878–9 are causally related in Rosenberg's argument to the economic instability produced by the crash of 1873, and the Kondratiev downswing of 1873–96 is thought to be directly reproduced in a similar movement of social and political life. But, on the other hand, more recently Rosenberg has heavily qualified these causal implications. While denying reasonably enough any monocausal intentions for his stress on the economics of the Great Depression, with this disclaimer Rosenberg leaves us uncertain where exactly he stands on the question of structural causality (that is, the determination of the political by the economic, however subtle or mediated the relation). Instead, we are left with an unresolved tension at the centre of the argument – between the radical *in*determinacy of an analytical pluralism in which one factor has no more and no less weight than any other, and a practical logic in the construction of the book itself which belies this subsequent scepticism.[16]

Acknowledging the argument's 'heuristic' status only partially resolves this contradiction. Moreover, while it may be unfair to belabour Rosenberg himself with the misappropriation of his intentions by others, the book's reception has clearly stressed the causal primacy of the Kondratiev downswing in explaining the political history of those years. This is not to say that the argument is in itself crude or simplistic – in the two major texts of the later 1960s its application ranges from the mechanistic determinism of Helmut Böhme's *Deutschlands Weg zur Grossmacht* to the immense sophistication of Hans-Ulrich Wehler's *Bismarck und der Imperialismus*.[17] But as I shall try to show, it is not without its problems. The aim of the following pages is to revisit the central thesis bequeathed by the reception of Rosenberg's book, namely, that the so-called Great Depression is a crucial 'founding period' of modern German history. In so doing I wish to expose for discussion an abiding problem of theoretical and historical analysis, which has been too easily suppressed in the turn to social and economic history during the last two decades (in itself both necessary and overwhelmingly beneficial), namely, that of how the relationship between politics and economics is best to be conceived.

In raising this question certain things should be made absolutely clear. First, to emphasize the pitfalls in constructing social and economic explanations of political change is not to argue for the abandonment of the entire project, and to stress the difficulties in a type of analysis is not to question its fundamental desirability. This needs to be said, because criticisms of the turn to social and economic history are easily misunderstood, particularly in the Federal Republic of Germany, where its exponents have been so badly marginalized within the historical profession until very recently and even now are still vulnerable to the effects of a conservative counter-attack. More generally, the advocates of such a social history turn, with its potential for radically redefining the nature of political analysis, have fought such hard and protracted battles against the high priests of an older professional orthodoxy that *any* plea for the analytical separation of the political and the socio-economic is likely to be seen as a betrayal and a return to the former situation of a rigidly and narrowly compartmentalized type of history. But this is a dangerous situation, as it threatens to identify progressive or 'critical' history with a more or less sophisticated reductionism, in which political developments are explained by an implicitly behaviourist sociology and potential criticisms silenced by reference to a common enemy.

So lest there be any doubt on this score, I take my own stand uncompromisingly on the advances of the last two decades. My intention is not to belittle or dismiss the achievements of Rosenberg, Wehler, or anyone else, but to suggest how they might be built on. I remain committed in my own thinking to a notion of complex social totality, through which particular practices or events may be related to the history of whole societies in highly specified conjunctures. As already stated above, recognizing the difficulty of this project does not diminish its pressing desirability.[18] Finally, these comments should not be read as a hostile attack on either Rosenberg or his admirers, but are offered in a spirit of sympathetic provocation. Rosenberg's book contributed enormously to the contemporary West German vogue for social-scientific history, and stands with Wehler's *Bismarck und der Imperialismus* as an exciting and implicitly programmatic call for a desirable new practice. The legitimacy of investigating the structural connectedness between economic development, social structure and political system – after all still disputed in West Germany – owes much to Rosenberg's pioneering intervention. Yet at the same time, his substantive interpretations – which were offered at the time explicitly as hypotheses for future discussion with an avowedly heuristic intent – have been transformed by their very popularity into a barely questioned orthodoxy. The manner of the book's reception has rendered part of its achievement problematic.

III

Most obviously, perhaps, there has been astonishingly little attempt to explore the validity of Rosenberg's thesis in detailed economic analysis, so that the Great Depression's importance figures in most recent work largely as a deeply entrenched set of assumptions. This absence of serious discussion amongst Rosenberg's admirers (with the important exception of Wehler) leaves them rather vulnerable to such critical voices as may be raised, though so far these have been few and far between. Landes declared his scepticism at an early stage, as did Gerschenkron, and more recently both Robert Gellately and Dan S. White have cast doubts on the sharpness of Rosenberg's economic periodization.[19]

But the most substantial attack has come from one of the few general economic histories of the empire to be published since Rosenberg's study, Volker Hentschel's *Wirtschaft und Wirtschaftspolitik im wilhelminischen Deutschland* (Stuttgart, 1978). Here the objection is less to the theoretical validity of the Kondratiev long waves in which Rosenberg's periodization is ultimately founded, than to the empirical basis for the Great Depression's existence as a coherent and unitary period. Hentschel argues forcefully that by most criteria the German economy achieved rates of growth for 1880–94 which were already comparable with those achieved in 1895–1908, while the real period of stagnation was strictly confined to the years 1873–9. Economically speaking, this makes 1895–6 far less of a caesura than Rosenberg's argument suggests. In addition, Hentschel argues, particular explanations may be found for the shorter depression after 1873 that owe little to any 'long swing' in the business cycle. Industrial production had well recovered by 1880, and the continuing problems of agriculture had independent origins in the transformed conditions of the world market. All this leaves the status of the 'Great Depression' as a distinct period of German economic history somewhat indeterminate, to say the very least.[20]

But though important, in a sense this misses the main point. The special force of Rosenberg's argument always derived not directly from its economic validity, but from its bearing on a set of *political* problems. Once we consider the claim that the Great Depression was a founding period of German history, in fact, the focus shifts from the cyclical movements of the economy to a series of political developments, which are thought to explain the deeper origins of Nazism. Most of these have become familiar conventions of German historiography: the novel combination of industrial and agrarian interests into a stable anti-Socialist alliance simultaneously committed to a high-tariff economic policy; the decline of liberalism; the growth of anti-semitism and other 'anti-modern' ideologies; and the general implantation of 'pre-fascist' tendencies in the political culture. The origin of these processes is located confidently in the later 1870s and Bismarck's turn to the right in 1878–9.

But the nature of the causal relationship with the economic circumstances of the Great Depression is in urgent need of specification. How exactly the political and ideological appearances mentioned above are derived from the experience of economic crisis (assuming for the moment that this is a sensible description for the slowed rates of economic growth in the later 1870s) requires far more detailed elucidation than is actually provided in the accounts of Rosenberg and his admirers. The same goes for the precise nature of the theoretical relationship which is being constructed between the political and the economic. In other words, there is in Rosenberg's approach a kind of incipient reductionism, in which the legitimate stress on levels of structural determination threatens to relapse into a far less acceptable determin*ism* of social and economic circumstances.

This I take to be the most serious deficiency of the 'Great Depression thesis', as it is now conventionally accepted among German historians. There is a marked disposition to explain political ideas and political actions by direct reference to an immediate socio-economic situation or to the social origins and backgrounds of particular groups of human actors. To take an example of some prominence in both Rosenberg's own study and the work of his admirers, anti-semitism tends to be explained as a social-psychological response to the pressures of economic decline and as the 'natural' ideology of small producers threatened in their 'traditional' independence. Methodologically this sort of analysis proceeds from the identification of structural trends to the description of an ideological response in particular sections of the population, which is then invoked mechanically as a confirmation of the original trends. But the crucial step in this argument – that the political and ideological manifestations can be explained primarily by the structural pressures of economic modernization in a cyclical crisis rather than by, say, the operation of relatively autonomous social, cultural and political factors, or by more 'local' combinations of socio-economic and politico-ideological causality – is never properly laid out. First, a structural analysis is presented (for example, of the economy in general, or a particular type of industry, or a particular social group like master artisans), often very convincingly; then an argument is mounted concerning the ideological response, usually pieced together from a textual analysis of the pamphlet literature, the public proceedings of organizations, and the press; and finally a correspondence between the two is asserted, normally by ascribing the ideology in question to one of the social groups centrally affected by the structural changes originally described.

The most ambitious effort of this kind is still Wehler's *Bismarck und der Imperialismus*, with its stress on the political dynamics of an economic crisis and explicit linkage of social imperialism to the explanatory framework of the Great Depression. But the discrepancy between the magnitude of the causal claims and the paucity of the evidence to sustain them is also enormous. Thus Wehler tends to locate the effectiveness of social imperialist ideology in a sociological syndrome of status anxiety, popular disorientation and the break-up of traditional communities, and it is this contention that does the main work of linking the impact of the Great Depression to changes in popular consciousness, not only in Wehler but in the literature as a whole. More specifically, Wehler contends that 'broad social strata' responded to social imperialist strategies, including 'the petty bourgeoisie of craftsmen and small businessmen, parts of the industrial labour force, of the rural *Mittelstand* and of the larger landowners'.[21] Yet these important statements appear to be based on no empirical evidence and are little more than speculative assertions derived from widely disseminated sociological dogma.[22]

The thrust of these comments should not be misunderstood. My point here is *not* that the Great Depression had no impact on political consciousness or that public debate did not address the problems which the Depression posed. To argue this would be clearly ridiculous, because the economic problems of the years after 1873 left their imprint on public discussion in all kinds of ways. Instead, I am really saying two things. First, that there is a tendency in the Great Depression literature to assume that economic developments are *directly* and *causally* reflected in the dominant political and ideological trends of the day, in a way that reduces the latter to the mere epiphenomena of something that happens elsewhere, in the economy. Occasionally, this reductionism attains gigantic proportions, in which virtually everything is attributed to the originating influence of the Great Depression, from social darwinism to anti-semitism and even psychoanalysis.[23] This is not so far removed from a simple vulgar Marxist schema of base and superstructure, which in the writings of Marxists themselves would be roundly condemned. At its worst, it can completely deny the independence of ideology and its effects, especially at the popular level, where the subjective coherence of particular ideologies (like anti-semitism) is entirely collapsed into a kind of behaviourist psychology, in which people respond spontaneously to the stimulus of economic events.[24]

But secondly, there is a similar tendency, just as reductionist in its own way, to generalize the prevalence of a particular ideology to an entire social group and to explain its origins and appearance in terms of that group's objective situation. Anti-semitism is again a good example of this effect. First, the emergence of political anti-semitism in the 1870s is correctly interpreted as a commentary on the processes of capitalist transformation which the 1873 crash helped to dramatize. But then its concern with the problems of struggling small producers is taken to imply a functional and dependent relationship to the latter, while the presence of *some* artisans and other *Mittelständler* in the organized anti-semitic movement is taken to mean support from the artisanate and *Mittelstand* as a whole, so that political anti-semitism becomes categorizable in essentialist terms as a *class movement* of the traditional petty bourgeoisie. As a result, the autonomy of politics (relative or otherwise) is consistently compromised in this work, so that the forms and content of political life – the terrain on which politics could be found – become rather strictly delineated by the impact of the economy and its fluctuations on different categories of people.

IV

To illustrate some of the consequences of this syndrome for our practical understanding, it is worth looking at a particular example. In fact, the difficulties are exemplified very clearly in Shulamit Volkov's well-received study of urban master artisans, which is one of the few monographs actually done on the years 1873–96 and which takes its conceptual framework directly from Rosenberg's argumentation.[25] The book describes itself as a study of a particular social group – urban master artisans in traditional handicrafts – and purports to investigate its subject as a unified cultural formation – 'a total life experience', as she calls it.[26] But in practice it consists of two separate discussions, which together amount to considerably less than this stated intention: on the one hand, a valuable and well-researched economic analysis of the declining sectors of small-scale handicrafts production; but, on the other hand, a political analysis of a particular ideology and its representation in the public statements of certain artisanal organizations (namely, 'the rise of popular anti-modernism', from which the book also gets its title). The transition from one discussion to the other (which occurs somewhere near the middle of the book) blurs the basic question of how the one is to be related to the other – of how the political appearances are to be related to the economic change, in both theory and in the evidence. On the whole, the correspondence is simply assumed rather than positively demonstrated.

Moreover, an uncertainty in the definition of the book's original problematic is already present in the adoption of Rosenberg's periodization. For Volkov actually admits that the Great Depression has a very doubtful validity as 'a distinct economic period', arguing instead that the period also displayed 'a number of unique social, political and cultural features' and that this justifies the retention of the term 'Great Depression' to designate a reasonable unit for study.[27] This is rather extraordinary. The original basis for a concept is admitted to be inadequate. But then secondary criteria which only made sense in terms of the original definition are reintroduced as the primary justification for the concept's retention. The political and ideological phenomena then maintain an arbitrary existence, disembodied from the economic causes that supposedly spawned them.

In other words, the economic and political analyses are neither properly distinguished from one another nor coherently integrated together. In fact, by the explanatory primacy given to the 'Great Depression' (which surely must retain its essentially economic meaning), and by the causal progression of the argument from the economic to the political, reflected in the sequential organization of the book, the interpretation is implicitly reductionist. There is a gradual slippage in the terms of the discussion, for while the author begins by treating master artisans as an *economic* category, she ends by presenting a specific tendency in *politics*. The definitional criteria shift in the course of the book, from a 'traditional' organization of production (that is, excluding trades where technology, the division of labour, or the labour process were transformed) to the espousal in public life of a particular ideology (namely, 'anti-modernism'), while the author's original adoption of *cultural* criteria (for example, an artisan 'style of life', 'sense of community', 'consciousness of a shared past', 'uniformity of education and personal history', and so on) somehow gets lost in the main body of the book and is never adequate to bridge the gap.[28]

In this sense the author lacks consistency in how the object of study is to be constituted. *Either* the object is a particular form of petty commodity production, in which case we need more discussion of issues like proletarianization and the full diversity of master artisans' social and political reactions; *or else* it is a specific ideology, and we need a much fuller sense of its effectivity in politics (that is, the social breadth of its appeal, its forms of articulation into the life of the various parties, the bases of associational life, a stronger sense of locality, and so on). Without this theoretical consistency Volkov's reference to a 'total life experience' of master artisans and the 'integration of social with economic, political and cultural history' is purely rhetorical.[29] On the contrary, the political and the economic are elided reductively together, and there is no evidence in the book itself that master artisans in declining sectors and the spokesmen for anti-semitic organizations were actually the same people at all, let alone that the latter were representative of master artisans or the *Mittelstand* as a whole. As it is, Volkov's master artisans are transmogrified from an objectively specified economic category into a self-selecting and rather narrowly based *political* grouping, whose subjective perceptions of their changing situation are very doubtfully extended to characterize their social group in general.

In a way, it is unfair to single out this book in particular, as its component analyses are in themselves perfectly competent and in many of their conclusions very persuasive, although the economic discussion is far stronger than the other. But, on the other hand, the very strengths of the book make it particularly appropriate for exemplifying the general syndrome under discussion, as it marks not only the weakest of recent work but the best as well. It provides a very good example of how purely formal and, in the end, very arbitrary correspondences between structural economic analysis and the discussion of particular ideologies can masquerade as a properly founded argument. Of course, I would not pretend that the problem of thinking through the relations between the political and the economic is a simple or a straightforwardly answered process. That it is not is precisely the point of these comments, and in most of the work on the Great Depression this abiding theoretical conundrum goes by default. In particular, the conventional equation of anti-semitic ideology with economic decline, though in specific instances it may be empirically correct, should not be an a priori assumption.

Moreover, the social psychology that accompanies much of the ideological analysis (the disorientation resulting from the disintegration of traditional norms), and the ridiculous hyperbole of the acccompanying language (for example, 'a mood of lonely despair', 'political homelessness', and so on) can be badly misplaced. As David Crew has shown in his excellent study of Bochum, the *Mittelstand* kept an important place in municipal affairs, securely grounded in traditions of associational life, and this was especially true of prosperous masters in the traditional sector.[30] Moreover, as Crew points out, the distinctive problems of small businessmen resulted neither from the short-run consequences of the 1873 crash, nor from an ideological confrontation with 'modernity' which would eventually dissolve in the inevitable adjustment to realities of 'industrial society'. Instead, they came from some permanent features of the unevenly developing capitalist economy. These were partly economic, like the dependence of markets on the business cycles of bigger industry, or conflicts over the distribution of the local tax burden; they were partly social, like the organization and financing of poor relief, or the improvement of public amenities; and they were, above all, political, like the rise of Social Democracy and organized labour. Without exception, the full magnitude of these problems was faced *after* the real period of depression in the 1870s, certainly outlived the overall period 1873–96, and in many ways only fully appeared in the 1890s and after.

V

It will be clear from the general drift of my remarks that I think the political impact of the Great Depression has been greatly overstated, and given the space I would argue that the 1890s witnessed a far greater change in the character of the political system.[31] The status of the 'Great Depression' as a meaningful period is itself rather doubtful, and still awaits systematic discussion amongst German economic historians. Similarly, the longer view elaborated upon it, that between 1873 and 1896 developments were laid down that culminated several decades later in the triumph of fascism, also needs to be more adequately expressed. The suggestion that as a result of the Great Depression some old authoritarian structures became deeply entrenched and certain new ones created, partly by the clever manipulations of the 'old élites' and partly by the social psychological effects of popular disorientation in a period of accelerated and irregular industrialization, has become a well-worn convention of much German historiography. But the idea that 'prefascist' potentialities were thereby unleashed, to be strengthened by the manipulations and mobilizations of the Wilhelmine era, is ultimately too glib and question-begging an interpretation. As I argue in the concluding essay of this collection, this encourages the belief that fascism was *preordained* by malformations in the initial stages of capitalist industrialization. It resulted from the incompleteness of the original societal transformation, when too many features of the 'pre-industrial' society were left intact which should have been swept away, and not from the authentic contradictions of an advanced capitalist society itself.[32] But the causal implications of a term like 'pre-fascism' remain terribly obscure, and the overall argument seems depressingly teleological, as if the complex significance of late-nineteenth-century developments can be simply co-opted into the origins of Nazism, a narrative plot with a known resolution.

Moreover, the view that the Great Depression represents a meaningful period of *political* history, irrespective of its economic reality, rests on an economistic and behaviourist social psychology which has yet to receive adequate theoretical exposure, and has certainly never been specified through the concrete analysis of social experience, as opposed to the textual evaluation of governmental and organizational records. Since Rosenberg's book was published almost twenty years ago, there has been some fairly extensive analysis of one aspect of the Great Depression's political economy, the political and economic significance of the high tariffs first introduced in 1879 and raised several times during the 1880s, before being modified in the early 1890s and restored in 1902. But this is a very circumscribed discussion, which conceives its agenda almost completely in terms of interest-group politics and their penetration into the state, and has so far abstained from reviewing the larger socio-political interpretations set into motion by Rosenberg's book.[33] This leaves Rosenberg's Great Depression thesis hanging rather indeterminately in space. Correlations between political events and economic fluctuations are notoriously difficult to establish at anything other than a fairly high level of generalization, and until German historians begin extending our sketchy knowledge of the Bismarckian period's social history, we cannot possibly evaluate the final usefulness of Rosenberg's suggestions.

But beside this empirical deficit we must set the more serious lack of theoretical reflection. German historians increasingly conduct their political analysis on a shaky foundation of economic and sociological reductionism – that is, on the basis of assumptions concerning the mainsprings of political activity which are rarely exposed as such to critical discussion. Of course, it may be reasonably objected that my own exposition in this essay is based on an extremely small number of recent works and cannot stand in its present form as a critique of an entire historiography. I naturally make no such claims for my modest observations and have been concerned simply to provide food for thought. At the same time, I would insist that the reductionist syndrome is present in a much larger literature in a varying guise. A convincing case could be made,

for instance, that recent German historiography has reduced the character
of the political process to an institutional structure of corporate interest
representation within the economy, and has neglected the party political
and parliamentary arenas to the point now of distortion, with serious
consequences for our understanding of the imperial and Weimar states.[34]
But the discussion of these larger ramifications must await some future
occasion.[35] Here I have tried to identify what seems to me a rather
questionable economic interpretation of political change, to point to the
dangers of reductionism in social historical analysis (whether vulgar
sociological or vulgar Marxist), and to suggest that there is no easy
correspondence necessarily between change in the economy and change in
the political system or the dominant ideology.

CHAPTER 1: NOTES

1 Full title: *Grosse Depression und Bismarckzeit. Wirtschaftsablauf, Gesellschaft und Politik in Mitteleuropa* (West Berlin, 1967). The original essay was published as 'Political and social consequences of the Great Depression of 1873–1896 in Central Europe', *Economic History Review*, vol. 13 (1943), pp. 58–73.

2 *Bureaucracy, Aristocracy and Autocracy: The Prussian Experience, 1660–1815* (Cambridge, Mass., 1958); and *Probleme der deutschen Sozialgeschichte* (Frankfurt-on-Main, 1969).

3 A. Sywottek, 'Sozialgeschichte im Gefolge Hans Rosenbergs', *Archiv für Sozialgeschichte*, vol. 16 (1976), p. 603.

4 See in particular: E. Kehr, *Der Primat der Innenpolitik*, ed. H.-U. Wehler (West Berlin, 1965); G. Mayer, *Radikalismus, Sozialismus und bürgerliche Demokratie* (Frankfurt-on-Main, 1969); G. Mayer, *Arbeiterbewegung und Obrigkeitsstaat* (Bonn, 1972); A. Rosenberg, *Demokratie und Klassenkampf* (West Berlin, 1974); L. Quidde, *Caligula. Schriften über Militarismus und Pazifismus* (Frankfurt-on-Main, 1977) – all edited by H.-U. Wehler. See also Wehler, 'Staatsgeschichte oder Gesellschaftsgeschichte? Zwei Aussenseiter der deutschen Historikerzunft: Veit Valentin und Ludwig Quidde', in H. Berding et al. (eds), *Vom Staat des Ancien Régime zum Modernen Parteienstaat. Festschrift für Theodor Schieder* (Munich, 1978), pp. 349–68. Wehler has also edited a five-volume series of short biographical essays, *Deutsche Historiker* (Göttingen, 1971–2), which is meant to perform a similar function.

5 H.-U. Wehler (ed.), *Sozialgeschichte Heute. Festschrift für Hans Rosenberg zum 70. Geburtstag* (Göttingen, 1974).

6 See the following: E. Kehr, *Schlachtflottenbau und Parteipolitik 1894–1901* (Berlin, 1930), and *Primat der Innenpolitik*; A. Vagts, *Deutschland und die Vereinigten Staaten in der Weltpolitik*, 2 vols (New York, 1935); G. W. F. Hallgarten, *Imperialismus vor 1914*, 2 vols (Munich, 1951); E. N. Anderson, *The First Moroccan Crisis 1904–1906* (Chicago, 1930); P. R. Anderson, *The Background of Anti-English Feeling in Germany, 1890–1902* (Washington, DC, 1939). Both Kehr's book and his collected essays have now been translated as *Battleship Building and Party Politics in Germany 1894–1901. A Cross-Section of the Political, Social and Ideological Preconditions of German Imperialism*, ed. and trans. P. R. Anderson and E. N. Anderson (Chicago and London, 1973), and *Economic Interest, Militarism, and Foreign Policy*, ed. G. A. Craig (Berkeley, Calif., Los Angeles and London, 1977). It remains unclear just how closely associated a grouping this was in the 1930s, but some light can be shed from the editors' introductions to the English editions of Kehr's writings and from Wehler's various commentaries mentioned in note 4 above. See also Hallgarten's autobiography, *Als die Schatten fielen, 1900–1968* (West Berlin, 1969), and the interesting essay by Arthur Lloyd Skop, 'The primacy of

domestic politics: Eckart Kehr and the intellectual development of Charles A. Beard', *History and Theory*, vol. 13 (1974), pp. 119–31.

7   See M. Jay, *The Dialectical Imagination: A History of the Frankfurt School and the Institute of Social Research 1923–1950* (Boston, Mass. and London, 1973). There is now an extensive scholarly literature on the German emigration to Britain and the USA in the 1930s. For an introduction, see R. Boyers (ed.), *The Legacy of the German Refugee Intellectuals* (New York, 1972), and G. Hirschfeld (ed.), *Exile in Great Britain. Refugees from Hitler's Germany* (Leamington Spa, War., 1984).

8   Holborn was, amongst other things, the author of a three-volume *History of Modern Germany* (New York, 1959–69). Interestingly, Rosenberg was not among the contributors to Holborn's own Festschrift, who otherwise read like a roll call of significant postwar German history scholarship in North America at the time of publication. See L. Krieger and F. Stern (eds), *The Responsibility of Power. Historical Essays in Honor of Hajo Holborn* (London, 1968).

9   Each of these three projects was originally announced in a specific essay of the 1940s: 'The rise of the Junkers in Brandenburg-Prussia, 1410–1653', *American Historical Review*, vol. 49 (1943–4), pp. 1–22, 228–42; 'Political and social consequences of the Great Depression' (cit. in note 1 above); 'The economic impact of Imperial Germany: agricultural policy', *Journal of Economic History*, vol. 3 (1943), suppl., pp. 101–7.

10 G. A. Ritter (ed.), *Entstehung und Wandel der modernen Gesellschaft* (West Berlin, 1970); H. Rosenberg, *Politische Denkströmungen im deutschen Vormärz* (Göttingen, 1972). In his informative introduction to the later Festschrift, Wehler notes that during a visiting appointment at the Free University of Berlin in 1949–50, Rosenberg had established contact with a number of research students who became important in West German historical studies, including Gerhard A. Ritter, Karl Dietrich Bracher, Gilbert Ziebura, Gerhard Schulz, Otto Büsch, Wolfgang Sauer, Franz Ansprenger and Friedrich Zunkel. Sauer was subsequently to join Rosenberg in the history department at Berkeley, where the latter had moved from Brooklyn College in 1959. Rosenberg's early essays on German liberalism, which are mainly in an intellectual history mode, are not available in English. A further collection of his essays from various stages of his career has been published as *Machteliten und Wirtschaftskonjunkturen. Zur neueren deutschen Sozial- und Wirstschaftsgeschichte* (Göttingen, 1978).

11 This has now been published in a reconstituted form as E. Kehr, *Preussische Finanzpolitik 1806–1810. Quellen zur Verwaltung der Ministerien Stein und Altenstein*, ed. H. Schissler (Göttingen, 1984).

12 Kehr, *Battleship Building*, p. 277 (my amended trans.).

13 'The genesis of the Prussian bureaucracy and the *Rechsstaat*', and 'The genesis of the Royal Prussian Reserve Officer', in *Economic Interest, Militarism, and Foreign Policy*, pp. 141–63, 97–108.

14 The most important studies of Prussian agrarian politics, H.-J. Puhle's *Agrarische Interessenpolitik und preussischer Konservatismus im wilhelminischen Reich 1893–1914* (Hanover, 1966) and *Politische Agrarbewegungen in kapitalistischen Industriegesell-schaften* (Göttingen, 1975), together with many of the same author's essays, show no awareness of this need. More recently there have been signs of a more intelligent interest in the question: H. Schissler, *Preussische Agrargesellschaft im Wandel. Wirtschaftliche, gesellschaftliche und politische Transformationsprozesse von 1763 bis 1847* (Göttingen, 1978); J. A. Perkins, 'The agricultural revolution in Germany, 1850–1914', *Journal of European Economic History*, vol. 10 (1981), pp. 71–118; A. Winson, 'The "Prussian Road" of agrarian development: a reconsideration', *Economy and Society*, vol. 11 (1982), pp. 381–408; K. Tribe, 'Prussian agriculture – German politics: Max Weber 1892–7', *Economy and Society*, vol. 12 (1983), pp. 181–226.

15 I am referring here both to the prevalent approach to modern German political history in the period since the Fischer Controversy and to the manifold critiques of 'economism' and 'reductionism' in the fields of social and political theory.

16 See, for instance, this statement from Rosenberg's preface to the new (Frankfurt-on-Main, 1976) edition of his book: While long-term cyclical movements of the economy are cited as one element of explanation amongst many for 'non-economic accompanying manifestations' and 'structural changes' and are accordingly isolated for purely analytical purposes, 'this naturally does not mean that in principle the business cycle is being

attributed an overwhelming causative importance and a more or less originating, and even dominant role in modern historical life, however important this dimension may now have become' (p. xii).

17 Full references: H. Böhme, *Deutschlands Weg zur Grossmacht: Studien zum Verhältnis von Wirtschaft und Staat während der Reichsgründungszeit 1848–1881* (Cologne, 1966); H.-U. Wehler, *Bismarck und der Imperialismus* (Cologne, 1969).

18 This lengthy disclaimer is prompted by the ease with which in the past my arguments have apparently been misunderstood. So let me repeat: I have the highest respect for Hans Rosenberg, Hans-Ulrich Wehler and others; I have been much influenced by their work; and by critically reviewing their influence I cannot diminish their stature. Likewise, when I presented an earlier version of this paper on a panel at the American Historical Association in 1979, some listeners took it to be an atavistic plea for a return to old-fashioned political history removed from social and economic context, and the chairman of the session attacked me rather vociferously for traditional-minded 'tunnel vision'. Nothing could be further from the case. It is just that, by contrast with my younger days when I took the superiority of a 'social' approach and the sovereignty of social forces to be self-evident, I have become more impressed these last ten years with the complexities of arguing this relationship through. In that sense, this essay is really an exercise in constructive scepticism. But it does not mean that I have given up on the basic intellectual commitment. The principle of a materialist approach is still axiomatic; the task of thinking it through – and of showing its value concretely – is just more difficult. For a salutary statement of the problem, the reader might consult a couple of essays by Barry Hindess: 'Class and politics in Marxist theory', in G. Littlejohn *et al.* (eds), *Power and the State* (London, 1978), pp. 72–97, and 'Marxism and parliamentary democracy', in A. Hunt (ed.), *Marxism and Democracy* (London, 1980), pp. 21–54.

19 D. Landes, *The Unbound Prometheus* (Cambridge, 1969), pp. 232 ff.; A. Gerschenkron, 'The Great Depression in Germany', in *Continuity in History and Other Essays* (Cambridge, Mass., 1968), pp. 405–8; R. Gellately, *The Politics of Economic Despair: Shopkeepers and German Politics, 1890–1914* (London, 1974), pp. 20 ff.; D. S. White, *The Splintered Party. National Liberalism in Hessen and the Reich 1867–1914* (Cambridge, Mass. and London, 1976), pp. 52 ff. For a strong critique of the idea of the Great Depression in the British context, see S. B. Saul, *The Myth of the Great Depression 1873–1896* (London, 1972); also W. A. Lewis, *Growth and Fluctuations 1870–1913* (London, 1978), p. 68.

20 V. Hentschel, *Wirtschaft und Wirtschaftspolitik im wilhelminischen Deutschland* (Stuttgart, 1978), pp. 205–12. Gerschenkron made much the same case in his review of Rosenberg's book mentioned in the previous note, and Rosenberg himself has conceded much of its validity, shifting the emphasis from production to prices and profits in his definition of the Great Depression, and half substituting the new phrase 'Great Deflation'. See his preface to the new 1976 edition, p. xii. See also C. Trebilcock, *The Industrialization of the Continental Powers 1780–1914* (London, 1981), pp. 87–91.

21 Wehler, *Bismarck*, pp. 480 ff.

22 I have considered the ramifications of this question in two additional essays: 'Defining social imperialism: use and abuse of an idea', *Social History*, vol. 1 (October 1976), pp. 265–90, and 'Social imperialism in Germany: reformist synthesis or reactionary sleight of hand?', in J. Radkau and I. Geiss (eds), *Imperialismus im 20. Jahrhundert. Gedenkschrift für Georg W. F. Hallgarten* (Munich, 1976), pp. 71–86.

23 For example, this is tendentiously present in H.-U. Wehler, 'Der Aufstieg des Organisierten Kapitalismus und Interventionsstaates in Deutschland', in H. A. Winkler (ed.), *Organisierter Kapitalismus. Voraussetzungen und Anfänge* (Göttingen, 1974), p. 51.

24 Of course, this is not peculiar to this or any other period of German historiography as such. For a sharp critique of the tendency in general see E. P. Thompson, 'The moral economy of the English crowd in the eighteenth century', *Past and Present*, no. 50 (February, 1971), pp. 76 ff.

25 S. Volkov, *The Rise of Popular Antimodernism in Germany. The Urban Master Artisans 1873–1896* (Princeton, NJ, 1978). Volkov was a student with Hans Rosenberg at Berkeley.

26 ibid., p. 7. Here Volkov draws explicitly if perfunctorily on conceptual and methodological protocols established in the social history writings of Edward Thompson and Eric Hobsbawm. The reference is purely rhetorical, however, as she never returns to this kind of analysis in the body of her book.

27 ibid., pp. 10 ff. The question is also begged in S. Pollard's *Peaceful Conquest. The Industrialisation of Europe 1760–1970* (Oxford, 1981), p. 254: the 'Great Depression' as an economic concept has become problematic; but important political changes occurred; therefore the concept can be retained for the period. Very odd.

28 Volkov, *Rise*, pp. 16–31.

29 ibid., p. 7.

30 D. F. Crew, *Town in the Ruhr. A Social History of Bochum 1860–1914* (New York, 1979), pp. 103–45.

31 I have put this case in detail in *Reshaping the German Right. Radical Nationalism and Political Change after Bismark* (New Haven, Conn. and London, 1980).

32 I have examined this idea of 'incompleteness' and the accompanying concept of 'failed bourgeois revolution' at length in my contribution to D. Blackbourn and G. Eley, *The Peculiarities of German History. Bourgeois Society and Politics in Nineteenth-Century Germany* (Oxford, 1984), pp. 39–155.

33 There is also a reasonably extensive discussion of the economic importance and effects of tariffs on the various large-scale and peasant-farming sectors of German agriculture, begun unobtrusively by Karl Hardach at the very time of Rosenberg's publication: K. W. Hardach, *Die Bedeutung wirtschaftlicher Faktoren bei der Wiedereinführung der Eisen- und Getreidezölle in Deutschland 1879* (West Berlin, 1967); H.-G. Reuter, 'Schutz-zollpolitik und Zolltarife für Getreide 1880–1900', *Zeitschrift für Agrargeschichte und Agrarsoziologie*, vol. 25 (1977), pp. 199–213; J. C. Hunt, 'Peasants, grain tariffs, and meat quotas: imperial German protectionism re-examined', *Central European History*, vol. 7 (1974), pp. 311–31; R. G. Moeller, 'Peasants and tariffs in the *Kaiserreich*: how backward were the *Bauern*?', *Agricultural History*, vol. 55 (1981), pp. 370–84; S. B. Webb, 'Agricultural protection in Wilhelminian Germany: forging an empire with pork and rye', *Journal of Economic History*, vol. 42 (1982), pp. 9–26.

34 Such a case would begin with the substantial literature on the Wilhelmine pressure groups and their relationship to the state. For a recent discussion see T. Nipperdey, 'Organisierter Kapitalismus, Verbände und die Krise des Kaiserreichs', *Geschichte und Gesellschaft*, vol. 5 (1979), pp. 418–33.

35 I have provided a brief preliminary sketch for part of such a project in another essay not collected for this volume: 'Zum Problem der Verbände im Kaiserreich', *SOWI (Sozialwissenschaftliche Informationen für Unterricht und Studium)*, vol. 11 (January 1982), pp. 22–8.

2

Capitalism and the Wilhelmine State: Industrial Growth and Political Backwardness, 1890–1918

This second essay in the volume had a similar purpose to the first and was an attempt to take stock of a major influence on recent German historiography, in this case Eckart Kehr. Kehr's writings were discovered by the post-Fischer generation in the 1960s in a process which began with the publication of his essays, *Der Primat der Innenpolitik*, edited by Hans-Ulrich Wehler in 1965, and continued with the assimilation of his book, *Schlachtflottenbau und Parteipolitik 1894–1901*, originally published in 1930. By the early 1970s the Kehr revival had gone so far that it became customary to refer to the 'Kehrites' as a distinctive school of current historiography, a term first used by Wolfgang J. Mommsen in 'Domestic factors in German foreign policy before 1914', *Central European History*, vol. 6 (1973), p. 8. The time of writing (1977, in response to books published between 1973 and 1976) was the last point at which this designation went largely undisputed. In the meantime the 'Kehrites' themselves have rejected the label and there now seems general agreement that it implies too exact and uncritical an identification with Kehr's own ideas and too much intellectual homogeneity amongst the people it describes. (For example, see Hans-Jürgen Puhle's angry disclaimer to this effect, in 'Zur Legende von der "Kehrschen Schule"', *Geschichte und Gesellschaft*, vol. 4 [1978], pp. 108–19).

On the other hand, none of the terms proposed as alternatives (such as the 'Bielefeld School', or 'critical historians') entirely escape the same strictures. My own view is that between the late 1960s and mid-1970s the term did capture a definite reality of interpretation and intellectual affiliation, which it becomes pedantic beyond a certain point to dispute. In the immediate wake of the Fischer Controversy it implied a common set of intellectual positions, which I have tried to describe sympathetically in the earlier part of the introduction to this volume. But by the later 1970s research was being pushed into new directions and differences were beginning to appear in what was previously a more united generational grouping. New intellectual alignments emerged, together with new sources of inspiration. At the same time, Kehr's original stimulus remains, as do a set of interpretations focused more specifically on the years 1897–1902, with a more extensive implication for the subsequent prewar decade. To my knowledge, these have not been seriously questioned by members of the original 'Kehrite' grouping.

In my own work this was the first time I grappled in print with the 'primacy of pre-industrial traditions' as the explanatory key to modern German history, which might be described as the central 'Kehrite' or 'Bielefelder' postulate. As such, it was something of a trial run for some of the arguments developed more extensively in *The Peculiarities of German History. Bourgeois Society and Politics in Nineteenth-Century Germany* (Oxford, 1984, especially pp. 91–143). It also marked my attempt to draw explicitly on Marxist discussions of the state. It appeared originally as a review essay in the *Historical Journal*, vol. 21 (1978), pp. 737–50, and is reprinted in an unrevised form. Two of the unpublished articles referred to in the footnotes have subsequently appeared in print: C. Medalen, 'State monopoly capitalism in Germany: the Hibernia affair', *Past and Present*, no. 78 (1978), pp. 82–112; and H. Pogge von Strandmann, 'Widersprüche im Modernisierungsprozess Deutschlands. Der Kampf der verarbeitenden Industrie gegen die Schwerindustrie', in D. Stegmann, B.-J. Wendt, and P.-C. Witt (eds), *Industrielle Gesellschaft und politisches System* (Bonn, 1978), pp. 225–40.

I

It is well known that recent Wilhelmine history has been heavily influenced by a revival of interest in Eckart Kehr, an innovating historian of rather indeterminate radical views, who died tragically in 1933 at the age of 30. Kehr is best known for his phrase 'the primacy of domestic policy' – an attempt to stand Ranke polemically on his head – and the belief that the analysis of a society's foreign policy can pinpoint the relations of domination in the class structure and the state. More generally, he was deeply influenced by Max Weber and his dissertation was for its time that comparative rarity amongst historians, an attempt to redefine political events in terms of their social and economic determinations. In both cases Kehr was consciously departing from the main traditions of his profession and when a newer generation of West German historians came to reopen certain methodological questions in the 1960s, it was natural that they should return to his work for guidance. Moreover, ideologically there is a further significance to the latter, which has likewise left its imprint on current historiography.

This concerns the belief that the *Kaiserreich* was a pre-capitalist state dominated by the landed aristocracy, in which the bourgeoisie played a subordinate role. By studying the Navy Laws of 1898 and 1900 Kehr uncovered a situation 'which turned over political power to the economically backward strata of agriculture and officialdom who were politically represented in the two Conservative Parties' (Kehr, p. 465). These tied their support for imperialism to high tariffs and fiscal immunities which 'deliberately repelled the masses of the proletariat, continuously angered the liberal bourgeoisie' and anchored government to a bloc of heavy industry and agriculture. The political tactic that resulted – *Sammlungspolitik* or the alliance of 'iron and rye' – proved an insuperable obstacle to progressive reforms before 1914. Strikingly, this double critique – of the aristocratic Prusso-German state and a supine bourgeoisie lacking the combative liberalism to challenge it – recalls almost exactly the position of Wilhelmine left liberals themselves. In this, as in other respects, Kehr provides an intellectual bridgehead linking the progressive wing of West German historians to an older critical tradition in history, social theory and politics.

This is a good starting-point for a review of recent literature. It is prompted partly by an English translation of Kehr's great work. But in general this is a good time to take stock of the 'Kehr revival', for the influence of those historians directly inspired by him in the 1960s has now been consolidated and a second wave of monographs is starting to appear. Not all the books under review are avowedly 'Kehrite', but all have been inserted into a discourse formed decisively by the discovery of Kehr's works and none seek to challenge it. Those of Saul, Mattheier, Guratzsch, Ullmann and Mielke deal with the organized involvement of industry in politics, whilst Gessner takes the agrarian equivalent; Feldman and Homburg, Zunkel and Kocka consider the impact of the war; Deist and White take aspects of the state and party politics; the Winkler collection displays the attempts at a general theory; and the East German essays edited by Klein provide a nice counterpoint to the whole operation. A single review cannot hope to do full justice to such a rich body of work, and both the strengths and weaknesses of the individual books will inevitably be neglected. Instead the following pages will focus on the general theme raised above, namely the claim that the *Kaiserreich* somehow lacked a 'modern' political system because a 'pre-industrial power élite' managed to preserve the 'anti-democratic bases of its power by successfully containing the bourgeoisie within the institutional and ideological structures of the traditional society. All the West German works concur in the view that the 'persistence of authoritarian structures in state and society' is to be explained primarily by reference to 'pre-industrial' or 'feudal' survivals into an 'industrial' era. The aim of this review is to see how convincingly their case is made.[1]

II

The tendency to explain Wilhelmine politics in terms of pre-industrial 'relations of domination' instead of the disposition of forces within Wilhelmine society itself is particularly marked in recent discussions of 'organized capitalism'.[2] For though committed to finding a single expression for 'essential structural changes in economy and society' in the modern epoch (Winkler, p. 8), the 'Kehrites' are equally convinced that Germany's specific political development during that period cannot be located in the same explanation. The weakness of German liberalism is explained not by the interior dynamics of the Wilhelmine conjuncture, but by ideological traditions surviving from a previous epoch which are thought to be out of phase with the 'normal' logic of industrial capitalism. Thus in his general definition of organized capitalism Jürgen Kocka finds no place for a consideration of specific political histories. Situating the transition to organized capitalism between the end of the Great Depression and the First World War, he proposes a check-list of eight factors for its definition: higher levels of concentration in the economy; separation of ownership from control; 'radical changes in social stratification' (managers, technocrats, white-collar workers); spread of collective organization; increasing state intervention, both to stabilize the economy and to regulate social conflicts; imperialism; higher levels of mobilization and changes in the state; and finally, changes in 'the sphere of ideas, ideologies and collective mentalities' (Winkler, pp. 20–3).

Kocka presents this as a tentative 'model' with a 'primarily heuristic function', but it also has a political dimension. This was already true of the original usage in the 1920s when Hilferding proposed it as a materialist theory of social democratic gradualism, and this clearly has its attractions for both Winkler and Kocka.[3] But the ideological motivations are more visible in the evident desire to find an alternative to the East German formula of *Stamokap* – 'state monopoly capitalism'. This is a theme both of the symposium itself and of Kocka's own monograph. For Kocka 'organized capitalism' has two advantages. First, it recognizes the relative autonomy of the state, whereas *Stamokap* insists on a fusion of the monopolies and the state as a distinguishing feature of the new period. Kocka argues that any definition of the state's relation to capital must contain the possibility of its functioning to the detriment as well as the advantage of the latter, for the range of its possible interventions was determined by other constraints as well. Secondly, Kocka also rejects the claim that state monopoly capitalism is a 'crisis-prone final phase' of capitalism. Specifically, he denies that the structural changes in the economy lead necessarily to a weakening of liberal democratic and a strengthening of authoritarian or proto-fascist possibilities. Instead such changes provide the common structural context of the respective national capitalisms within which variant political developments can take place. Kocka also argues these points through in his study of the war, and in a careful dissection of the Auxiliary Labour Law of December 1916 shows that the action of the state was determined by a more complicated set of pressures than the simple *Stamokap* thesis can apparently accommodate.

These are good points. Yet it is unclear what they owe to the concept of organised capitalism itself. The relative autonomy of the state could not be inferred from Kocka's check-list of factors. The definition of organized capitalism they produce is purely descriptive, and though causal relations are clearly attributed to the respective phenomena (for example, greater concentration leading to new managerial bureaucracies and changes in the class structure), Kocka specifically excludes the possibility of showing how they combine at the level of politics and the state. 'Typical processes of change' in this respect cannot be abstracted, because the political effects of organized capitalism varied 'strongly between countries' (Winkler, p. 23). Where the issue is broached at all, the terms used – 'entanglement' (Kocka),

45

'mutual dependence' (Wehler), 'inter-penetration' (Maier) – to character-ize the relations between monopolies and state are in themselves quite close to the East German idea of 'fusion', and Hilferding's talk of domination by 'the combined powers of the capitalist monopolies and the state' is even closer. Such terms are intentionally more open-ended, but to refute the idea of 'fusion' Kocka has to reach outside the concept of organized capitalism itself, either by appropriating a fresh set of concepts from Marx or the recent descendants of the Frankfurt School, or by the empirical discussion of particular events. Thus it is doubtful whether Kocka's concept properly measures up to the global claims he makes for it – namely, that it aims 'to grasp economic, social, political and ideological phenomena in their inter-connectedness' (ibid., p. 25). The most interesting questions – that is, the political ones, like the role of Charles Maier's 'corporatism' in redrawing the boundaries between state and civil society – are left out of the definition and made subject to other, external determinations. In the end Kocka's concept gives us only a general description of important economic changes and the functions they added to the state. Where their political impact is grasped at all this takes the form of an implied determinism, in which virtually everything from social darwinism to anti-semitism and psychoanalysis is somehow explained by the surrounding context of organized capitalism as a kind of materialist first cause.

The symposium rather leaves the impression – as Gerald Feldman argues in his contribution – that the concept of organized capitalism is just too general to be very helpful without building into the definition some concrete suggestions about the political level. As Maier observes, the idea 'only makes sense if the social incidence of influence and power is situated in relation to the given levels of progress in technology and productivity' (Winkler, p. 195). Otherwise it is only one term substituted for another ('state monopoly capitalism', 'corporate capitalism', 'political capitalism', 'collective capitalism', 'pluralist capitalism', and so on). At present the terms of the inquiry entail a certain arbitrariness of theory: a simple model of base and superstructure is maintained, with changes in the organization of capital leading to changes in the social structure and the forms of politics; but, at the same time, a dogmatic isolation of politics from economics is reintroduced. By constructing 'organized capitalism' as a universal category for basic structural changes common to all capitalist economies, Kocka renders it incapable of explaining their differential political development. For the latter we are forced back on to purely political, cultural and ideological factors – in the German case, 'pre-industrial' survivals. Thus it is no surprise to find both Kocka and Winkler stressing precisely this procedure.

In other words, there is no sense that 'Germany's persistent failure to give a home to democracy in its liberal sense' (Dahrendorf, cited by White, p. 199) may have lain in the conditions of capitalist reproduction themselves and not in the continuing domination of a 'pre-industrial power élite'. This is one vital area in which the 'Kehrite' emphasis on 'failed bourgeois revolution' has combined with a partisan belief in the possibility of 'a welfare-statist, liberal democratic variant of organised capitalism' (Kocka, in Winkler, p. 29) to confuse our understanding of the *Kaiserreich*. For unless the Wilhelmine polity is analyzed in the primary context of Wilhelmine capitalism and its interior relations, the perspective will be skewed. Wilhelmine society contained the most dynamic capitalism in Europe, and it is this rather than 'feudal' continuities which needs our primary attention.

III

The hostility of big industrialists to 'democratic' reform exemplifies the problem, for most of the authors under review explain this by the normal 'Kehrite' emphasis on the survival of 'pre-industrial' attitudes. 'Traditional patterns of authority' prevented the big employers from developing an enlightened view of their own self-interest by acknowledging the 'just' demands of the working class for 'equality of status in politics and society'; here as elsewhere 'the power élites . . . showed themselves neither willing nor able to introduce the transition to modern political and social relations in good time'.[4] Yet as Baldur Kaulisch remarks, this assumes a 'rational' form of industrial relations in a 'modern' society, representing a 'natural' equilibrium or 'partnership' between capital and labour, which is belied by the actual history of industrial capitalism in the last hundred years (Klein, p. 136 f.). Indeed, following Hans Medick's suggestion that welfare-statism resulted in Britain from the relative absence of an organized capitalism in Kocka's sense (Winkler, p. 59 f.), one might argue that it was precisely the advanced levels of concentration in Germany which first made possible the repressive labour relations described so exhaustively in the books by Saul and Mattheier.

This would make the intransigence of employers like Krupp, Gutehoff-nungshütte or MAN less the result of some surviving 'conservative-feudal notions of value'[5] than a specific form of capitalist rationality: it might just as easily be argued that some form of paternalism aimed at excluding trade unions is the 'natural' inclination of most employers when left to themselves, particularly in this period, but only becomes feasible when the productive units are sufficiently large. Under small-scale competitive capitalism with high labour mobility and little employer co-operation, the use of black-lists and company unions was impossible. Moreover, when these obstacles had gone, such devices became aids for rationalizing production. This was certainly true in the Ruhr coalmines, where the labour turnover in 1895–1907 rose from 84 per cent to 127 per cent: here the introduction of the black-list in 1908 was not just a means of victimizing militants but an aid to a stable work-force (Saul, pp. 87 ff.). Likewise, company housing was less an expression of some pre-industrial moral paternalism than a necessary means of attracting and keeping workers at a time of breathtaking urban growth and primitive amenities.

By permitting company paternalism, the tendency to monopoly conferred a distinct political advantage. By contrast the employers in the less concentrated industries (where unions were strongest) had been faced with the alternatives of calling in the state or of reaching some *modus vivendi* with the unions. Increasingly they chose the latter, as could be measured by the spread of wage agreements in those sectors of German industry. Once unions got established in certain industries this was easily converted into a demand for national recognition. Kocka, Zunkel and Feldman show that this effect was favoured by the war, but it had already started before 1914, as the more flexible social policies described by Mielke and Ullmann reveal. In other words, fewer and larger units of production made it easier to contain the antagonisms between capital and labour within the individual plant or industry without displacing the process into the political domain proper, where it became subject to far less predictable determinations. Moreover, big employers like Krupp had no need for a deal with the unions when the latter were virtually excluded from their own plants. They had no interest in social reform at the national level when they were already making adequate provision at the level of the individual firm. Indeed, as company paternalism was so sucessful, its practitioners had an active interest in opposing reform, for this would duplicate facilities, increase costs and by recognizing trade unions would cut the legal ground from practices like the black-list, compulsory membership of company schemes and simple intimidation.

This lends some weight to the view that Winkler and Kocka set out to deny, namely that what they describe as 'organized capitalism' *did* contain built-in tendencies towards authoritarian as against democratic politics. The option of intransigent anti-socialism was simply not on for smaller employers: it was too costly, laid them open to union retaliation and forced them into political dependence on the big monopolies. Conversely, it was only the latter that had the resources for a sustained offensive against the organizations of labour *per se*. This was a clear instance where the differential progress of monopoly organization created unequal opportunities for controlling the labour process and accordingly inscribed divergent political possibilities on the practice of German employers.

Moreover, this coincided with other differences stemming from monopoly capitalism's uneven development: briefly, new positions of strength for the monopolies entailed simultaneous difficulties for industries which were still fragmented, and conflicts over tariffs, cartels and price-fixing were the characteristic result. Thus the power of the monopolies not only obstructed reformist projects, it also directly damaged a range of capitalist interests – not just small and medium capital, but even larger manufacturers, shippers and some banks, who wanted cheaper access to raw materials and dismantlement of the protective tariffs supported by the Centralverband Deutscher Industrieller (CVDI) and its agrarian allies. Ullmann and Mielke are largely concerned with the combination of these positions into a firm political programme: the former with the efforts of smaller manufacturers in the Bund der Industriellen (BdI), the latter with the launching of the Hansabund as a broad anti-agrarian front in 1909.

These detailed studies enable a much clearer understanding of why that programme was never realized in any larger reformist grouping before 1914. For one thing it never made many inroads into the CVDI which was still dominated by the big heavy industrialists. But, in addition, the Hansabund found it hard to rally the rest of the business world for a campaign against the CVDI. After 1895–6 broad alliances had been possible over the tariffs, the *Zuchthausvorlage* or cartels. But by 1911–12 two things had happened. Advancing concentration in the engineering industries had detached key interests from this looser anti-monopoly front, whilst the chemicals industry preferred to straddle both the Hansabund and the CVDI. By 1914 the old antagonism of CVDI and BdI was becoming less important than the hidden relations amongst a small number of big monopolists. The pressure groups naturally remained something more than the mere instruments of the latter, but increasingly the crucial decisions – which then prescribed the terms of discussion in the pressure groups – were taken outside the formal structures of business opinion by informally constituted groups of concerns.

In commercial matters this had been promoted by mergers and cartelization, but in his useful study of the Hugenberg network Dankwart Guratzsch now shows that it was happening politically as well. The effect was to enmesh even the more 'liberal' employers, such as the two electrical engineering giants AEG and Siemens, in networks of monopoly decision-making which owed nothing to liberal reform of the state, and arguably made the latter redundant.[6] But, secondly, the SPD's victory in the 1912 elections made the more liberal employers less receptive to reform. These two factors reduced the anti-monopoly position to a rump of small and medium capitalists in the BdI and severed it from a democratic politics of *rapprochement* with labour. Moreover, reformism lacked an adequate party political articulation, for despite Gustav Stresemann it proved impossible to win the National Liberals as a whole for a new departure. This left the Hansabund in limbo – a programme devoid of solid industrial backing with no obvious political focus.

The economic power of the big concerns was a factor of the highest political importance in the failure of reform. It facilitated a closer control over the labour process and introduced a company paternalism going far beyond any 'pre-industrial' habits of authority. Indeed for heavy industry in Silesia and the Ruhr this was a vital condition of capitalist development – that is, not an external intrusion from a bygone feudal era which 'ought' to have been superseded, but a set of relations generated by capitalism itself. Naturally there were determinate effects at the political level, because such advanced managerial autonomy excited opposition both from trade unions and from smaller employers who were denied its benefits. Monopoly capitalism promoted an entrepreneurial ideology of company self help in the area of welfare, which worked against the adoption of more elaborate schemes by government. It both gave an impetus to progressivism by forcing opponents into new defensive alliances and then weakened the latter by drawing further branches of industry into its orbit. The greater the extent of the monopolies, the less likely became welfare-statist solutions on the British model, and the greater the need for embittered political conflict before the latter were extracted. Contrary to Winkler's and Kocka's disclaimer, the advance of 'organized capitalism' indubitably structured the political discourse on the eve of 1914 against the possibility of reform.

IV

The relation of the political to the economic is an abiding theoretical problem and one which has left a number of ambiguities in the 'Kehrite' position. As we have seen, the latter contains not so much a separation of the political level from the economic – which is a necessary analytical procedure preparatory to their careful and theoretically sophisticated reintegration – as their mutual isolation. It is true that 'restrictive conditions' are distinguished in the structures of organized capitalism that are thought to have broadly circumscribed the chances for reforming action.[7] But these are conceived very much as the general arena in which autonomous political factors then compete, and in the German case a series of 'pre-industrial' traditions (absolutism, military and bureaucratic autonomies, the power of the Junkers, deferential 'status' mentalities, and so on) are held to have obstructed a proper 'modernization' of the political system. This is to concede the 'relative autonomy' of the political process with one hand and to remove it with the other, for it is made subject not to the unpredictable outcomes of successive conjunctures and the complex interaction of political and economic factors, but to linear continuities from a previous era. In addition (and paradoxically), in practice the 'Kehrites' often reduce the political process to the interplay of corporate economic interests and their control over government policy: corporate bargaining became institutionalized, it is claimed, into a specific set of relations between the government and the pressure groups which narrowed the competence of Parliament and stifled any 'participant political culture'.[8] This is rarely theorized as a relationship between the economy and the state as such, but more often emerges from a particular empirical definition of the subject – for example, a particular pressure group as with Mielke or Ullmann, an individual businessman as with Guratzsch, or a set of practices towards labour as with Saul and Mattheier – which then structures the inquiry's field of vision to produce an extremely partial picture of the political process.

Altogether this is an area of theoretical ambiguity which needs some unravelling: on the one hand, the resistance of the 'power élites' to democratization is to be explained not by the logic of organized capitalism, but by the anachronistic survival of authoritarian ideologies of 'pre-industrial' origin; but, on the other hand, the agencies through which these continuities act are precisely the institutional products of the modern era of organized capitalism, namely the corporate pressure groups. The real conjuncture of Wilhelmine politics is the casualty of this confusion. The 'Kehrites' not only obscure monopoly capitalism's direct impact on the terms of politics, but also collapse the relative autonomy of the political process into an idealist determinism of linear continuities between the mid-nineteenth century and the 1930s.

This neglect of the political sphere proper is most serious perhaps in the discussion of the state. A number of difficulties may be isolated. Most obviously, the state can easily emerge as the simple repressive instrument of the 'ruling strata', and here the preoccupation with the Prussian 'military-bureaucratic state', and its aristocratic survivals plays a key role. Yet it is by no means clear that the *Kaiserreich* actually was a state dominated by the Junkers in the way normally implied, and empirical studies of the social origins of state personnel (for example, the well-known prominence of the aristocracy in the officer corps or the Junkers in the Prussian provincial administration) are not sufficient to delineate its character in this respect. Thus Klaus Saul's study of judicial repression (pp. 188–282), though a pioneering expedition into badly neglected territory, presents a one-sided view of state power: on his own evidence judicial rulings recurrently forced the government to devise fresh expedients of legal chicanery in order to harass the trade unions, and 1890–1914 was certainly a period in which the 'rule of law' steadily constrained the area of arbitrary bureaucratic intervention against trade union and civil rights. A similar comment may be made about the role of the state in industrial conflicts: though the government was fully prepared to throw the full weight of its police authority behind the employers in particular disputes, this should obscure neither the general tendency towards arbitration nor the comparability of government–employer relations else-where. A stronger comparative sense would diminish the belief in German exceptionalism: though Saul's evidence of official collusion with the employers in the coal strike of 1912 is very valuable (pp. 269–82), a knowledge of the British mining industry between the 1890s and 1926 would quickly indicate that such interventions are by no means confined to Germany.

Kocka has done most towards producing a more sophisticated understanding of the state, but even here there are problems. Kocka's understanding of the state, for instance, confines the latter to the formal agencies of government (reflecting perhaps the conventional Weberian distinction between class and power), whereas the actual boundaries of state power in this modern period are by no means as clear or simple as this would suggest. In general Kocka omits discussion of the state's relation to civil society, a problem theorized by Althusser in the concept of the 'ideological state apparatuses'.[9] When concepts like 'social imperialism', 'caesarism' and 'plebiscitary politics' are used by the 'Kehrites' to characterize the Wilhelmine system, this theoretical dimension ought perhaps not to be so neglected. The state's relation to the churches, schools, the family and the cultural domain is less relevant to the specific books under review, but areas like communications, the law and trade unionism are absolutely central.[10] From the 1890s the state was being redefined to embrace new consultative arrangements with corporate interests in the economy (for example, tariff commissions, the Colonial Council, the consular service), and during the war the *Verbände* and trade unions became closely enmeshed inside the structures of the state itself. Maier's concept of 'corporatism' is potentially useful here, and there is much relevant empirical material in Zunkel's and Feldman's discussions of the triangular relations between government, industry and labour in the latter stages of the war.[11]

Though Kocka is to be applauded for tackling these matters at the level of general theory, two further problems may be mentioned. For one thing it is not clear how his picture of a flexible, 'relatively autonomous' state mediating between the interests squares with the more familiar 'Kehrite' view of the Prusso-German state's 'autocratic, semi-absolutist sham-constitutionalism' before the war.[12] But secondly, his dismissal of a Marxist approach to the problem of the state appears rather strange in view of his stress on 'relative autonomy', because Marxists have themselves been stressing this idea for some years.[13] One feels that a vulgar Marxist straw-man has been constructed to enable the harder challenge of a more sophisticated Marxism to be evaded. Thus both Kocka and Feldman make much of industrial hostility to the new role of the state in the economy during the war, arguing that this refutes the so-called Marxist view of the state as an instrument of the ruling class. Yet the political conflicts over the forms of economic demobilisation in 1918 (like the earlier conflict in 1916 over the concessions to trade unionism) provide almost a textbook illustration of one recent Marxist formulation on this question, namely that 'the capitalist state has inscribed in its very structures a flexibility which concedes a certain guarantee to the economic interests of certain dominated classes, within the limits of the system'.[14] In this view the state appears 'as a relation, as being structurally shot through and constituted with and by class contradictions',[15] or as a framework of institutions for containing and negotiating antagonisms, that is, as being itself located inside a field of political conflict rather than existing independently above it. By comparison Kocka has not taken his insights far enough, for whilst rejecting the obvious error of seeing the state as a 'thing/instrument . . . a passive tool in the hands of a class or fraction' with 'no autonomy whatever', he then tends towards the opposite mistake of seeing it as 'subject', a view which elevates autonomy to an absolute, freed from all structural moorings.[16]

V

What other comments can be made about this 'Kehrite' historiography? Its main strengths are those of traditional empirical scholarship pushed to its furthest extreme. The coverage of archives is exhaustive, and the framework of interpretation is provided largely by the sources themselves. Thus Mielke contents himself with a conscientious but unimaginative organizational history, Ullmann has a similar focus, and Saul simply lets his massive empirical apparatus speak for itself. Guratzsch likewise allows the empirical limits of his inquiry to structure the form of his analysis, for by making Hugenberg the sole centre of his interlocking studies of business, pressure groups, press and state, he reduces complex relations to mere epiphenomena of a personal biography. Mattheier is more successful within the limitations of this positivist mode, mainly because his exposition is clearest and most systematic. Each of them firmly confines his generalizing or 'theoretical' statements to a formal preamble, whilst the main text proceeds in classic empiricist style.

Thus the new interest in 'theory' which the contributors to the symposium on 'organized capitalism' think so vital to the historian's enterprise has made little impact on the actual practice revealed by these monographs. Rather than exploring the usefulness of concepts (as Kocka has done in his book on the war), the tendency is to reaffirm preferred formulas as self-evident given quantities in no need of critical examination. The resolute abstention from all theoretical controversy, especially those areas mapped out in the 'organized capitalism' symposium, is disappointing, for each of the themes chosen by Saul, Mattheier, Guratzsch, Mielke and Ullmann provides ideal material for such an exercise. The most astonishing omission is any systematic discussion of the domestic crisis on the eve of the First World War, for this provides the formal climax to the works of Saul, Mielke and Ullmann. Yet unaccountably there is no attempt to define the character of the crisis and its meaning for the state. After posing this very question in the title of his final chapter – 'On the Eve of the Crisis?' – Saul tails off into nothing without even a formal conclusion.[17]

This review has been mainly critical in general perspective and it would be unfair to end without picking out some of the strengths in recent work. Most obviously, some enormous gaps in our knowledge are gradually being filled and the five studies mentioned above provide a wealth of empirical detail and some closely argued analysis of political decision-making, which together will make them indispensable texts for students of Wilhelmine Germany. Moreover, if despite themselves, they provide useful indications of how the discrete understanding of politics and economics exemplified in the 'organized capitalism' discussion might be re-combined to say something more specific about the nature of the capitalist state in Germany. Several of the books do much to advance our understanding of the petty bourgeoisie as an object of politics in this period,[18] and further exploration of this theme might clarify the dissipation of reformist possibilities on the eve of 1914.

In this way the new literature has important implications for our understanding of German liberalism. The failure of the National Liberal Party to commit itself to the left is normally attributed to the power of the CVDI lobby and the clash of industrial sectionalisms inside the party.[19] However, Dan White's enterprising study reminds us that the National Liberals were something more than an agency for co-ordinating the interests of German capital: they also had a popular constituency to consider, and more than anything else it was their efforts to halt the loss of rural support and simultaneously to build an alternative base amongst the new white-collar strata that inhibited a stronger commitment to a more democratic reformism.[20] Similarly, Ullmann's book is at its most interesting when describing Stresemann's formulation of these priorities (pp. 138-61), and when plotting the transition in the BdI from a 'liberal-capitalist' to a *mittelständisch* entrepreneurial ideology (pp. 88–109). The appeal to the new petty bourgeoisie was also a wager on its nationalist temper and, as Wilhelm Deist's valuable study of naval propaganda shows, a general analysis of radical nationalist ideology as a social and political factor would further illuminate these problems. In all of these ways the lifeline to the petty bourgeoisie ran away from the working class and increased the rightward pull on the National Liberals.

In general, therefore, a critical reworking of the material in these books rather contradicts the central 'Kehrite' thesis, namely that the absent 'modernisation of the political system' (Mielke, p. 186) resulted from 'pre-industrial' ideological survivals rather than German capitalism's specific conditions of development. The above remarks have tried to suggest that the characteristic hostility of the CVDI industrialists to social and political reform derived from tendencies immanent to the monopoly phase of

German capitalism. Of course, pre-capitalist traditions also played their part, but this was no *more* true than elsewhere: it was simply that the exact modalities of the transition to industrial capitalism had differed amongst national examples, not least through the paramount factor of uneven and combined development. Moreover, the normal view which sees the CVDI barons as the compliant consorts of the Junkers in the 'pre-industrial power élite' (Mielke, p. 186) mistakes the interior relations of the ruling class and falsely attributes a posture of rigid backwardness to its leading fractions.

In fact by international standards German capitalism was highly advanced, and the ability to exclude trade unions by a mixture of intimidation and company paternalism was just as much an index of this as sophisticated technologies and higher levels of concentration. That Siemens – in the usual view a more 'flexible' employer – should have pioneered company unionism after 1905 only emphasizes this point. This was not the primitive anti-socialism of a Stumm, but the application of sophisticated 'managerial' techniques for controlling the labour process, which owed nothing to any 'feudalized' bourgeois consciousness. Finally, Dieter Gessner's admirable monograph on the agrarian pressure groups, together with his shorter essay on agrarian ideology and conservative politics, demonstrate that terms like 'pre-industrial' and 'feudal' are scarcely appropriate even for the Junkers themselves, who had long been behaving like agrarian capitalists. This more than anything else suggests that the 'Kehrites' may perhaps be using the wrong categories of analysis. The most interesting 'continuity' in West German historiography is not that of the 'pre-industrial' survivals which allegedly blocked 'the long hard road to modernity' (Dahrendorf), but the familiar liberal fixation on such an idea. This ideological continuity runs from Max Weber's left liberal critique of the landed interest right down to the more recent 'critical history' of the 1970s. Eckart Kehr, preoccupied with that same supposed subordination of the bourgeoisie to the Junkers which was held to be the source of all Germany's ills, provides the vital link.

CHAPTER 2: NOTES

This essay originally appeared as a review article based on the following books: E. Kehr, *Battleship Building and Party Politics in Germany 1894–1901. A Cross Section of the Political, Social and Ideological Preconditions of German Imperialism*, ed. and trans. by P. R. and E. N. Anderson (Chicago and London, 1975); H. A. Winkler (ed.), *Organiserter Kapitalismus. Voraussetzungen und Anfänge* (Göttingen, 1974); K. Saul, *Staat, Industrie, Abeiterbewegung im Kaiserreich. Zur Innen- und Sozialpolitik des Wilhelminischen Deutschland 1903–1914* (Düsseldorf, 1974); K. Mattheier, *Die Gelben. Nationale Arbeiter zwischen Wirtschafts-frieden und Streik* (Düsseldorf, 1973); D. Guratzsch, *Macht durch Organisation. Die Grundlegung des Hugenbergschen Presseimperiums* (Düsseldorf, 1974); S. Mielke, *Der Hansa-Bund für Gewerbe, Handel und Industrie 1909–1914. Der gescheiterte Versuch einer antifeudalen Sammlungspolitik* (Göttingen, 1976); H.-P. Ullmann, *Der Bund der Indus-*

triellen. Organisation, Einfluss und Politik klein- und mittelbetrieblicher Industrieller im Deutschen Kaiserreich 1895–1914 (Göttingen, 1976); W. Deist, *Flottenpolitik und Flottenpropaganda. Das Nachrichtenbureau des Reichsmarineamtes 1897–1914* (Stuttgart, 1976); D. S. White, *The Splintered Party. National Liberalism in Hessen and the Reich 1867–1918* (Cambridge, Mass. and London, 1976); J. Kocka, *Klassengesellschaft im Krieg. Deutsche Sozialgeschichte 1914–1918* (Göttingen, 1973); F. Zunkel, *Industrie und Staatssozialismus. Der Kampf um die Wirtschaftsordnung in Deutschland 1914–1918* (Düsseldorf, 1974); G. Feldman and H. Homburg, *Industrie und Inflation. Studien und Dokumente zur Politik der deutschen Unternehmer 1916–1923* (Hamburg, 1977); D. Gessner, *Agrarverbände in der Weimarer Republik. Wirtschaftliche und soziale Voraussetzungen agrarkonservativer Politik vor 1933* (Düsseldorf, 1976); D. Gessner, *Agrardepression, Agrarideologie und konservative Politik in der Weimarer Republik. Zur Legitimationsproblematik konservativer Politik in der Zwischenkriegszeit* (Wiesbaden, 1976); F. Klein (ed.), *Studien zum deutschen Imperialismus vor 1914* (West Berlin, 1976).

1 The scope of the discussion has been strictly limited to this single theme, and the books under review have been considered with this specific purpose in mind. In some cases this clearly undervalues the book concerned, for the latter's problematic need not coincide exactly with the one defined here. I am thus very conscious of being unable to do some of the authors full justice. This is notably true of Kocka's fine study of the First World War and its impact on German society, which is one of the best achievements of the new history in West Germany, and of the individual essays edited by Fritz Klein, which are likewise amongst the best recent work from East Germany. The works of Deist and White also make major contributions which fall outside the review's terms of reference, whilst those by Feldman and Homburg and Gessner deal mainly with the period after 1918. Similarly, there are many areas of controversy (e.g. the debate over naval policy and social imperialism) which arise from the reception of Kehr's ideas which cannot be gone into here.

2 The essays edited by Winkler originated in a symposium at the Regensburg Historical Congress in 1972. Whilst Kocka handled the task of general definition of 'organized capitalism', others provided a series of national case studies: Hans-Ulrich Wehler on Germany, Hans Medick on Britain, Volker Sellin in Italy, and so on, with Gerald Feldman and Charles Maier exploring later German developments in the years after 1914. For a particularly useful response to the symposium, see: M. Geyer and A. Lüdtke, 'Krisenmanagement, Herrschaft und Protest im organisierten Monopol-Kapitalismus (1890–1939)', *Sozialwissenschaftliche Informationen für Unterricht und Studium (SOWI)*, vol. 4 (1975), pp. 12–23. I have also benefited from C. Medalen, 'State monopoly capitalism in Germany: the Hibernia affair', *Past and Present*, no. 78 (1978), pp. 82–112.

3 There is no space to explore these ideological implications, but Hilferding's theory as expounded by Winkler clearly anticipates more recent Social Democratic thinking. Winkler himself appears to be arguing the historical legitimacy of the SPD's practice in the 1920s, and explicitly upholds 'liberal democracy as a political principle' in his exposition (p. 15).

4 H.-U. Wehler, *Das deutsche Kaiserreich 1871–1918* (Göttingen, 1973), pp. 138 ff., 238.

5 D. Stegmann, 'Hugenberg contra Stresemann. Die Politik der Industrieverbände am Ende des Kaiserreichs', *Vierteljahrshefte für Zeitgeschichte*, vol. 24 (1976), p. 337.

6 In making this point I have benefited from a reading of H. Pogge von Strandmann, 'Widersprüche im Modernisierungsprozess Deutschlands. Der Kampf der verarbeitenden Industrie gegen die Schwerindustrie', in D. Stegmann, B.-J. Wendt and P. Chr. Witt (eds), *Industrielle Gesellschaft und politisches System* (Bonn, 1978), pp. 225–40. There is also an excellent conspectus of these developments in Willibald Gutsche's essay, in the Klein volume, pp. 33–84: 'Probleme des Verhältnisses zwischen Monopolkapital und Staat in Deutschland vom Ende des 19 Jahrhunderts bis zum Vorabend des ersten Weltkrieges'.

7 See Wehler in his contribution to Winkler (ed.), p. 52; also Kocka, pp. 210 ff.

8 Though his own understanding of politics was more subtle than this, Kehr's study of naval policy has given this approach much impetus. For three major examples, see: H. Böhme, *Deutschlands Weg zur Grossmacht: Studien zum Verhältnis von Wirtschaft und Staat während der Reichsgründungszeit 1848–1881* (Cologne, 1966); D. Stegmann, *Die*

Erben Bismarcks. Parteien und Verbände in der Spätphase des Wilhelminischen Deutschlands. Sammlungspolitik 1897-1918 (Cologne, 1970); V. R. Berghahn, Der Tirpitz-Plan. Genesis und Verfall einer innenpolitischen Krisenstrategie unter Wilhelm II (Düsseldorf, 1971). Moreover, it has been generalized into a series of influential essays: T. Nipperdey, 'Interessenverbände und Parteien in Deutschland vor dem Ersten Weltkrieg', in H.-U. Wehler (ed.), Moderne deutsche Sozialgeschichte (Cologne, 1966), pp. 369–88; G. Schultz, 'Über Entstehung und Formen von Interessengruppen in Deutschland seit Beginn der Industrialisierung', in H. J. Varain (ed.), Interessenverbände in Deutschland (Cologne, 1973), pp. 25–54; W. Fischer, 'Staatsverwaltung und Interessenverbände im Deutschen Reich 1871–1914', Wirtschaft und Gesellschaft im Zeitalter der Industrialisierung (Göttingen, 1972), pp. 194–213; H.-J. Puhle, 'Parlament, Parteien und Interessenverbände 1890–1914', in M. Stürmer (ed.), Das kaiserliche Deutschland. Politik und Gessellschaft 1870–1918 (Düsseldorf, 1970), pp. 340–77.

9 See L. Althusser, 'Ideology and ideological state apparatuses (notes towards an investigation)', Lenin and Philosophy and other Essays (London, 1971), pp. 121–76.

10 This is a general failing of the books under review, but is perhaps especially marked in the case of Guratzsch and Saul, whose discussions of respectively the press and the law totally lack such a theoretical dimension.

11 Apart from Maier's contribution to the Winkler essays, see his Recasting Bourgeois Europe (Princeton, NJ, 1975).

12 Wehler, Das deutsche Kaiserreich, p. 63.

13 In fact, it could be argued that Kocka's analysis of the state in his monograph on the First World War (which he presents as a critique of a 'Marxist' view) comes closer to a Marxist approach than his avowedly 'Marxist' general model of 'class society', which bears little correspondence to recent Marxist discussions of class. In general see the works of N. Poulantzas: Political Power and Social Classes (London, 1973); Classes in Contemporary Capitalism (London, 1975); 'The capitalist state: a reply to Miliband and Laclau', New Left Review, no. 95 (January–February 1976), pp. 63–83.

14 Poulantzas, Political Power and Social Classes, p. 190.

15 Poulantzas, 'The capitalist state', p. 75.

16 Poulantzas' characterizations of these two positions provides an accurate commentary on the false polarity which 'Kehrite' thinking has tended to produce: 'Either the dominant classes absorb the State by emptying it of its own specific power (the State as Thing in the thesis of the merger of the State and monopolies upheld in the orthodox communist conception of "State monopoly capitalism"); or else the State "resists", and deprives the dominant class of power to its own advantage (the State as Subject and "referee" between the contending classes, a conception dear to social democracy)'. See ibid., p. 74.

17 A number of serious technical criticisms can be levelled at these books as a whole. Thus as well as the absence of adequate conclusions, few of them possess a serviceable subject index on the English model. On the other hand, Saul, Guratzsch, Mielke, Ullmann, and to a lesser extent Zunkel and Kocka, all suffer from a ridiculous surfeit of source references. In Saul the references comprise some 200 pages as against 400 of text, in Mielke some 150 against 180, and in Ullmann some 200 against 230. On a typical page of Ullman (p. 146) there are a total of twenty-one references filling one and a half pages of small print at the back of the book. This makes the books impossible to read with any sense of continuity, let alone enjoyment. More seriously, it can signify a rather narrow positivist understanding of historical explanation. Yet curiously, in the Feldman-Homburg edition of documents, where an elaborate footnote apparatus becomes essential in order to make sense of the organizations, events and personalities, the references are kept down to a minimum. As an edition this compares rather badly with, say, the splendid Quellen zur Geschichte des Parlamentarismus und der politischen Parteien, published by the Kommission of the same name, which have set exacting standards for this kind of venture.

18 See Kocka, pp. 65–95, for a general discussion; Ullmann, pp. 138–60, and Mielke, pp. 95–101, for attempts by the BdI and Hansabund to woo white-collar workers; and Guratzsch, pp. 26–62, 88–95, 117–26, 363–78, for land reform and co-operative movements in the East.

19 See espec. Stegmann, Die Erben Bismarcks, pp. 26–8, 146–65, 219–31, 305–15.

20 White's study is the most valuable work dealing with the National Liberals to be published in recent years and deserves far more attention than I am able to give it in this context. It grasps more firmly and imaginatively than virtually any other recent work that the National Liberals were also an agrarian party at the turn of the century, and that the crisis of that party was in large part the crisis of its defecting rural constituency.

PART TWO

*The Social Foundations
of the* Kaissereich

3

State Formation, Nationalism, and Political Culture: Some Thoughts on the Unification of Germany

Despite the popularity of social history and the desire to get away from the older institutional and organizational approaches, it has still been extremely difficult to free nineteenth- and early-twentieth-century German political history from a deeply entrenched 'statist' perspective. On the one hand, all the familiar interests of recent social history are present – historical demography and the history of the family, social structure and social mobility, labour history and the working class, women's history, the history of crime, popular recreation, education, food and drink, and the history of everyday life. There is also a large amount of work on economic interest groups and the articulation of organized interests into political life. But, on the other hand, German political history is still concerned to an inordinate extent with the mechanics of a formal political process. In this respect the main effect of the post-Fischer revisionism has been to shift research from the parliamentary and party political arenas towards a 'corporative' sphere of pressure groups and powerful vested interests. As a result (and without exaggerating the extent of our ignorance), the history of the parties before 1914 has become rather under-developed. Even more, we remain extremely ill-informed about the nature of popular political involvement, whether in relation to the various political parties (with the palpable exception of the SPD), or the implementation of different kinds of government policy. We know far less than we should about the political grass roots or the social dynamics of political mobilization. We know far more about the 'state' than we do about 'civil society'.

This remains particularly true of the Bismarckian period between the 1860s and 1890. Despite the historiographical iconoclasm of the 1960s, when the familiar political milestones of German unification were exchanged for a new periodization based on the growth of the national market and a 'social refoundation of the Reich' in 1878–9, discussions of political history remained surprisingly focused on the person of Bismarck and events at the centre. Perceptions of German unification have remained remarkably Prussocentric, implicitly bounded by the historical 'small-German' (or greater Prussian) outcome of the state-building process. The aim of this essay was to dislodge the customary 'statism' of this account by emphasizing the unfinished character of the new nation-state, the 'indeterminacy' of national consciousness in the period of unification, and the origins of the 'nationalizing' impulse in the associational initiatives of the progressive German bourgeoisie. It suggested that with the foundation of the Reich in 1871 the real work of national unification only began. As such it sought to re-evaluate the contribution of the German liberals and placed the *Kulturkampf* at the centre of such a discussion. It tried to redress the balance from 'state' to 'civil society'.

The essay originally appeared in a Festschrift for Eric Hobsbawm (R. Samuel and

G. Stedman Jones [eds], *Culture, Ideology and Politics* [London, 1983], pp. 277–301) and sought to combine a discussion of Germany with a general argument concerning the relationship between nationalism, state formation and political culture. It reflected a more general interest in nationalism, which I am trying to convert into a general book. It was also a first sketch for a future project on the history of German liberalism.

'Families barely know what holds them to this state of which they are part, . . . They regard the exercise of authority in the collection of taxes, which serve to maintain order, as the law of the strongest, seeing no reason to yield to it other than their powerlessness to resist, and they believe in avoiding them whenever they can. There is no public spirit, because there is no common, known, visible interest.' (Anne-Robert-Jacques Turgot, cited by T. Zeldin, *France 1848–1945. Vol. II: Intellect, Taste and Anxiety* [Oxford, 1977], p. 5)

'While the period of reaction has made Germany an economic totality, while every day general law-making encroaches by means of treaties farther on the independence of the individual state, while extensions of authority by the federal diet and "internal constitutional developments" make this people every day more accustomed to a central administration, the petty, vulgar, self-centred, and greedy behaviour of the small states disgusts everybody more and more, the "hereditary" princely house becomes every day more burdensome, and the realization penetrates every cottage "that we must begin to clean up, first at home and then in Frankfurt".' (Johannes Miquel in 1857, cited by T. S. Hamerow, *The Social Foundations of German Unification 1858–1871. Vol. I: Ideas and Institutions* [Princeton, NJ, 1969], p. 145)

' . . . self-help and self responsibility, the two pillars of German nationality.' Max Wirth, *Die deutsche Nationaleinheit in ihrer volkswirtschaftlichen, geistigen und politischen Entwicklung an der Hand der Geschichte beleuchtet* [Frankfurt-on-Main, 1859], p. 454)

' . . . Hurrah Germania! The Reich is complete, the Ultramontanes and their adherents are defeated, the black night of spiritual brutalization is beginning to disperse and the dawn of German unity and freedom begins to gleam on the horizon of the Fatherland . . . ' (*Wochenschrift der Fortschrittspartei in Bayern*, no. 5, 1871, p. 57)

' . . . the masses have come of age (through elementary education, mass conscription, universal suffrage, and the cheap oil lamp).' (Hermann Rassow, in a letter to Admiral Alfred von Tirpitz, 12 April 1898, Bundesarchiv-Militärarchiv Freiburg, 2223, 94943)

I

The most satisfying accounts of nationalism have related it to the uneven development of European capitalism, or (in an alternative notation) to problems of 'modernization'. Much of the impetus for this perspective comes from work on the Third World, and the union of older approaches from intellectual and political history (which earlier tended to dominate the field) with different types of developmental sociology has produced some interesting results.[1] Of course, the formal ideology of nationalism has its own history, which seems to originate with the French Revolution.[2] But to explain the nature of the ideology's appeal, the changing content of nationalist ideas and the vitality of the nationalist tradition over the subsequent century, something more than a straightforward history of ideas is clearly needed. The European diffusion of nationalist ideology could not proceed by the intrinsic attractions of the ideas alone and required a definite set of historical circumstances to become possible, whether we think of crude economic development, a distinctive social structure and a strong sense of cultural (ethnic, religious, linguistic) identity, or developed communications, improved literacy and the spread of new levels of socio-political organization into previously isolated rural areas. It is here that developmental or sociological perspectives have shown their usefulness. The incidence of 'patriotic' activity in a society, first amongst the intelligentisia and then amongst the masses, can be convincingly related to some complex combination of the above conditions.[3]

Returning to the ideology as such, we might see nationalism at least in part as a conscious reflection on this developmental syndrome. In the concrete circumstances of the nineteenth century, in a world marked by the domination of French arms and English manufactures, it was the classic ideology of 'under-development' for societies seeking to overcome their political and economic backwardness and constitute themselves as unified territorial states. Originating in the democratic ambience of the French Revolution, nationalist ideas migrated eastwards in the first half of the nineteenth century, borne initially by the revolutionary armies, but accumulating contradiction as they went. East of the Rhine, nationalist commitments could be motivated as much by fear as veneration of Jacobin radicalism and, when lacking the sustenance of a democratically defined popular constituency, such nationalisms might fall easy prey to romantic populism, stressing the organic community of the uncorrupted folk rather than a political ideal of citizenship. Of course, the metropolitan ideal of progress remained the ultimate goal and in its British and French guise exercised a vital influence throughout the nineteenth century. But at the same time the nationalities of Central and Eastern Europe (or more accurately, some of their representatives) craved the legitimacy of the past, grounding their claims for self-determination in mystical notions of cultural continuity and the invariable myth of origins. This simultaneous celebration of future and past, progress and authenticity, became a hallmark of nationalist ideology.[4]

Clearly, all the implications of these assertions cannot be pursued here.[5] My aim is more modestly concerned with certain questions of German nationality in the last third of the nineteenth century and its forms of political definition. But for working purposes we might consider a three-way conceptual distinction centred on the experience of the French Revolution. First, there are definite processes of institutional growth within territorial states which allow specifically patriotic (as against parochial or cosmopolitan) loyalties to take shape. Secondly, there is a special type of ideological commitment (nationalism) which seeks to rationalize (or initiate) these processes in a particularly pointed way, normally through some democratic or populist conception of social and political order. Thirdly, there are further processes of cultural unification, normally but not necessarily consciously directed, which presuppose the nation's established existence as a territorial, linguistic, religious, or other type of community. These three phenomena – underlying processes of state formation, the elaboration of nationalist ideology, the drive for cultural conformity – are clearly not cleanly separated in time. They certainly may follow one another in a rough chronological sequence (France would be the strongest case). But things are usually more confused. Political independence can be either a condition or a consequence of the ideological and cultural activity, and the growth of nationalism can just as easily follow as precede the formation of territorial units of the nation-state type.

II

The relevance of these assertions may be clarified once we turn specifically to Germany. The Second Reich was a new state, of finite duration: though a 'united Germany' had some sort of continuity between 1870 and 1945, this was a remarkably short time by most standards and, in any case, the imperial state differed markedly from the republican one between 1918 and 1933, and from the Nazi one that began to take shape in the later 1930s. As for the period before 1870, it cannot be said too strongly that the foundation of the empire was a radical, even a revolutionary departure, with no convincing precedent in the political history of Central Europe. Indeed, it is doubtful whether Germany ever corresponded to the nationalist desideratum of the nation-state. At most times its boundaries have included large non-German and excluded equally significant German populations, and in the most recent period (1945–81), when the great postwar migrations have permitted an unprecedented degree of ethnic homogeneity, the German region of Central Europe has been securely divided into three distinct territorial states. Not surprisingly, the most consistent German nationalists have been perpetually dissatisfied with the established political arrangements which have only ever approximated to the postulated unity of territory, language, political institutions and wider culture. To this actual disharmony between state organization and cultural formation (as nationalists see it), we might add a diversity of constitutional forms which have run the full course between federalism and centralism, dictatorship, monarchy and republic.

In this case German history becomes something of a problematic concept, reproducing the contradictions of the nineteenth-century political discourse itself. Is it to include or exclude Austria? Is it to follow the shifting and often arbitrarily drawn political boundaries of states, or the linguistic frontiers of a cultural region? How are the national minorities to be dealt with, or for that matter the more dispersed German populations of Eastern Europe and the Baltic? Can German history in the conventional political sense be written at all without replicating the cultural preconceptions of the German nationalist tradition, or should the territorial state be exchanged for the region (either the larger cultural area cutting across political frontiers, or the smaller locality within a state), as the unit of analysis most suited for dealing with these complexities? This indeterminacy has been noted by a number of recent authors, who point to the enduring effects of the *kleindeutsch* perspective bequeathed by the Bismarckian unification and rapidly institutionalized into German historiography. In a valuable exercise in sustained scepticism, for example, James Sheehan identifies its residual primacy in the implicit assumptions of most German historians, and suggests that it needlessly limits the kind of questions that tend to be asked. Carefully distinguishing the outcome of unification from the diversity it subsumed – the aggrandizement of Prussia from the regional bases of political culture, the political foundations of the national market from alternative patterns of regional international trade, the growth of a national public from widespread parochial isolation, the polite from the popular culture – Sheehan stresses the *artificial* and *provisional* nature of the Bismarckian settlement, rather than its 'predetermined' character or rootedness in any deeper cultural or historic unity. As he says, 'as a singular process', German history had only really begun.[6]

This both emphasizes and qualifies the importance of political, as opposed to social, economic, or cultural determinations. On the one hand, for instance, it reminds us that German unification resulted from specific political decisions and a specific combination of political events in the 1860s, which were very far from being a logical correlate of the wider nationalist movement, let alone of any operative cultural solidarity amongst German-speaking people. As Robert Berdahl puts it: 'The

Bismarckian state was not "pre-determined", it was "self-determined", not by popular sovereignty or the *Volk*, but by its leading statesmen'.[7] Without falling into the naïve voluntarism of a dogmatic anti-determinism, this should redirect us to the relative openness of succeeding historical situations. The Bismarckian small-German solution was the largely unanticipated success of only one amongst a number of national programmes, which included not only the small-German/greater-German option, but also the full spectrum of possible constitutions, in various permutations. At the same time, on the other hand, we may note the relative narrowness of the political nation in the 1860s and the possibly limited resonance of unification beyond the small circles of the politically initiated. It is unclear how far the political manoeuvres of the 1860s entered the consciousness of most ordinary German-speakers, especially in the countryside, and in the future the new state faced a long-term problem of establishing its popular legitimacy. To this extent unification entailed a subsequent process of cultural coalescence which in theory it had already presupposed. In this fundamental sense the creation of the empire was the beginning rather than the end of unification.

The process had gone furthest by the early 1870s in the most basic area of all, the capitalist economy and its conditions of existence. Of course, German historians have hotly denied the bourgeois (let alone the liberal) character of the imperial state, pointing to the limited powers of the Reichstag under the 1871 Constitution, the executive authority of the monarchy and the Prusso-German dualism that guaranteed the special position of the Junkers. But whatever else it was, as Perry Anderson affirms, 'the fundamental structure of the new State was unmistakably *capitalist*.'[8] Between 1867 and 1873 liberal demands for national economic integration became the centrepiece of the constitutional settlement, which consummated the process begun by the Customs Union earlier in the century: freedom of movement for goods, capital and labour; freedom of enterprise from guild regulation; emancipation of credit; favourable conditions for company formation; the metric system of weights and measures, a single currency and unified laws of exchange; a federal consular service and a standardized postal and telegraph system; patent laws; and the general codification of commercial law. Central financial institutions soon followed. As industrialization proceeded, the state did much else to organize the environment for capital – by regulating rail and water transportation, by managing external relations through commercial treaties and tariffs, by colonies and the protection of markets, by contracts for army and navy, and by a host of social interventions (in welfare, education, labour legislation, and so on).[9] To this we might add the codification of criminal law, the standardization of judicial procedure and the eventual adoption of a new Civil Law Code (in 1896). All of this presupposed the achievements of unification. Disgruntled opponents of

Bismarck's settlement might speak disparagingly of 'a customs parliament, a postal parliament, and a telegraph parliament'.[10] But in precisely these respects (and the others mentioned above) the new Reichstag had helped reconstitute the legal basis of Germany's social order.[11]

Within limits these are functions common to any capitalist state, in the sense that the accumulation and centralization of capital within nation-states structurally requires a certain range of state interventions. As well as those already mentioned (the basic guaranteeing of property rights, liberalization of the economy, standardization, management of external relations, and so on), we might also include taxation, the development of technology and the general problem of legitimation.[12] Of course, the danger of this line of thought is an over-facile functionalism, where the activity of government is made to correspond to a series of structural imperatives, based on the 'needs of the economy' or the 'logic of capital'. Shifting focus, there is a similar tendency in much sociology, stressing the moral solidarities essential to a society's effective functioning or sense of stability. This is especially marked in the case of nationalism, which Ralph Miliband calls 'the "functional" creed *par excellence*', perfect for ensuring the overall cohesion of the social formation.[13] These are seductive ideas, as the functionalist argument appears to explain so much. German historians have certainly found it hard to resist the temptations. Recent work has combined nationalism's explanatory potential (in these functionalist senses) with the imperial state's prevailing authoritarianism, to suggest that nationalist ideology was essentially conservative, stabilizing, and integrative in its social effects.

As such, nationalism is thought to have been generally available for manipulation by the state. By stressing what united rather than what divided the citizenry, nationalist ideology placed a powerful weapon in the hands of a centralizing government, which could then de-legitimize and marginalize certain kinds of opposition or dissent. This was most easily accomplished (as 1914 was to confirm) in times of war, but a comparable sense of national solidarity might also arise in peacetime, by artfully manufacturing a 'moral equivalent of war'.[14] This might be done in a number of ways, from the use of war scares, diplomatic successes and aggressive foreign adventures, to the uncovering of domestic subversion (by isolating ethnic and religious minorities, immigrants, revolutionaries and anyone 'soft' on patriotic priorities), and the political exploitation of cultural achievements (in science, technology, the arts and sport). By careful ideological labour (through state apparatuses like schools or a conscript army, or through manipulating public employment), the nation might be solidified into a powerful ideological community, fortified by symbolism and ritual.[15] This could never eliminate political conflict, let alone social contradiction. But the tangible reality of 'the nation' gave appeals to the 'national interest' a seductive credibility. They could be skilfully used to moderate and even to suspend certain kinds of disagreement.

German historians have developed a particularly strong version of this argument. In the first place the new German state badly needed to consolidate its superior legitimacy over older regional, confessional and dynastic particularisms, whose disruptive potential was all the greater for coinciding in the south of the country. The *Mainlinie* amounted to a serious fracture in the nation's cultural unity. In the 1870s, moreover, the situation was quickly complicated by the rise of the SPD, with its radical challenge to the empire's undemocratic constitution. According to most German historians, the resolution of these problems was hampered by the narrowness of the *Kaiserreich*'s social base, which heavily privileged the Junkers and precluded the reformist option of limited democratic concessions and a pluralist political system. Consequently, to achieve an adequate consensus of defensive interests and maintain the stability of the status quo, Germany's rulers were forced into elaborate techniques of secondary integration, for which nationalist ideology provided the ideal materials. This was already anticipated in the *Kulturkampf* of the 1870s, but the possibilities only came to full fruition in the colonial agitation of the 1880s, which has been called 'the diversion outwards of internal tensions and forces of change in order to preserve the social and political status quo'.[16] This 'Machiavellian technique of rule' rapidly became institutionalized in the state's political, administrative and ideological practice. It was massively extended in the imperialist agitation of the 1890s. It was applied to the treatment of national minorities (especially the Poles), to the overall conduct of foreign policy, to the demands for greater military and naval armaments, and to the political isolation of the labour movement. All in all, this amounted to 'the manipulative application of nationalism for the purpose of stabilising the social power structures and of thereby internalising the sublimated power relations' which were characteristic of Imperial Germany.[17]

There is much to be said for this integrationist approach. There can be little doubt that German governments tried to undertake this kind of ideological offensive, and this can be clearly shown for the army and the schools (the obvious cases), where elaborate measures were taken for the inculcation of patriotic values in the interests of political conformity.[18] Whether they were successful or not is another matter. We know a great deal about the anti-socialist directives of the educational bureaucracy, for example, but far less about the daily practice of schools and teachers, not to speak of the real effects on children. There is no reason why the findings of much educational sociology, with their stress on the limited impact of schooling and the countervailing importance of family, neighbourhood and peers in the socialization of the young, should be inapplicable to this earlier society, particularly one which seemed to be as segmented along ethnic, religious and class-cultural lines as Imperial Germany. In some ways, given the relative sparseness of public education and the incompleteness of the educational apparatus before 1914, we should expect them to be more pertinent rather than less: in 1882 the average class size in Prussian elementary schools was 66, and by 1911 it had only been reduced to 51.[19] Besides, attempts to expand educational provision and increase its efficiency could easily meet with opposition. The Polish resistance to Germanization is perhaps an extreme example. But the peasantry, particularly in the Catholic south, put up determined opposition to the extension of schooling (enforcement of attendance, raising the school-leaving age, reforming the curriculum, and so on), which seemed to threaten the patriarchal authority of the peasant family and undermine the system of child labour.[20] At a time of growing secularization the clergy had an obvious interest in sustaining this kind of resistance. Moreover, not only the Catholic Centre Party but also the Social Democrats maintained impressive cultural organizations of their own, with high levels of educational activity. Each of these factors qualified the effectiveness of state educational interventions.[21]

None of this is to dispute the importance of public education (or conscription and other areas of state intervention) for the general dissemination of patriotic values. But the formation of nationalist consciousness in school students (or military recruits) could only result from very complicated processes of ideological negotiation, through which nationalist commitments (whether formal or unspoken) acquired a variable specific content. We can see this by looking at the example of the *Kulturkampf*. Without entering the discussion of Bismarck's motivation, which remains obscure, it is clear that for the German liberals this was a logical accompaniment of unification. The attack on the Catholic religion *per se* was less important than a positive ideal of how the future German society was to be constituted. In the abstract this amounted to a centralist drive for the primacy of the citizen–state relation in the organization of public life, with radical implications for both traditional ideas of social order and the Prusso-centric version of federalism. As such, it was both inimical to Prussian Conservatives and a dangerous game for Bismarck to play, with potential consequences going far beyond the disastrous counter-mobilization of Catholics in the Centre Party. For liberals the *Kulturkampf* meant exactly what the term said, a struggle to unlock the potential for social progress, freeing the dynamism of German society from the dead hand of archaic institutions. This was clearest in the localities, where clerical control of charities, poorhouses and schools tied up capital resources, kept the poor in dependent ignorance and shackled the chances for social and economic development.[22]

In other words, the unification of Germany had a specific social logic, which partially determined the character of the new state and infused

69

German nationalism in the 1860s and 1870s with a particular content. The *Kulturkampf* articulated this specificity perfectly. At one level, of course, it was a natural extension of the Bismarckian (Prussian, small-German) solution to the German question, by emphasizing the North German, Prussian and Protestant bias of the new state. It also had positive functions for state formation, by cutting back the independent public authority of the church and strengthening government control of education. But in other respects it strengthened the momentum of exactly those forces in civil society – the liberal movement for German unity – that in the 1860s Bismarck had sought to control. After the liberalization of the economy the *Kulturkampf* was the object of the greatest liberal effort in the 1870s, and also saw the liberals' maximum penetration into the state apparatus (under Adalbert Falk at the Prussian Ministry of Culture and his counterparts in the other states). In this sense it threatened to upset the uneasy compromise on which the empire had been founded. Liberals were engaged in a secular crusade against the very values, institutions and vested interests that Bismarck's constitution was meant to defend. 'Junkers and priests together/Put townsmen and peasants in tether', ran one liberal slogan, and having done with the one, they might well turn to the other.[23] The ideal of German-national citizenship disclosed by liberal campaigning implied both an attack on corporate particularism and a strengthening of local self-government, and neither were possible in the terms of the Bismarckian constitution. Consequently liberals found themselves pitted against a growing constellation of conservative social forces.

This was nothing new. Liberals came to power in most German states at the end of the 1860s through broad regional coalitions against aristocracy, particularism and reaction. This was especially true in the south – in Baden, Württemberg, the Grand Duchy of Hesse and more uncertainly Bavaria – but also applied to many parts of Prussia, particularly those annexed in 1866 (Hanover, Nassau and the Electorate of Hesse).[24] The liberal cause suffered momentary setbacks after 1866, but the events of 1870–1 rebounded massively to its advantage. In the Grand Duchy of Hesse, to give an example, unification swept the Progressives into office in 1872 with 41 of the 50 seats in the Landtag. Moreover, this political hegemony presupposed much deeper processes of institutional growth and cultural formation going right back to the start of the century, by which liberals staked out their claims to social leadership. Here the forms of associational life were crucial, providing the practical environment in which a self-conscious bourgeois public could gradually take shape. Normally centred on an exclusive social club, where the town's notables would consort for a mixture of business, relaxation and political discussion, this new public domain was textured by a rich variety of charitable, educational, cultural and economic activities, from fire service and rifle club, to choir, theatre and commercial society. Linked to press, petition and public meeting, it opened new possibilities for political mobilization which were a key feature of the unification years. The emergence of a public sphere in this sense – as 'a sphere which mediates between society and state, in which the public organises itself as the bearer of public opinion'[25] – was the essential foundation of liberal politics. The movement for national unification (which for liberals was a vital condition of 'progress') originated in the same coalescence of political culture.[26]

This emerges clearly from the character of the opposition. The critics of the new nation-state were often acutely uncomfortable with the new public opinion, its ideology of citizenship and demand for civil freedoms. There were naturally elements to whom this does not apply – the democrats of central and south-west Germany, or a variety of special interests (like the financial oligarchy in Frankfurt) which benefited directly from the prevailing conditions of decentralization and political fragmentation – who opposed the Prussian solution from the same cultural and institutional resources of a flourishing civil society. But the conservative opponents of the Bismarckian settlement, the supporters of Austria and upholders of particularism, inhabited a much older institutional world, one dominated by courts, the church and aristocratic society. In opposing unification, they opposed the forces of change and reform.[27] The main supporters of the Guelph cause in Hanover, for instance, were noble landowners, the Lutheran clergy, sections of the Hanoverian administration and officer corps, and all those whose livelihood was linked to the royal household and the court. Of course, their resentment was directed as much at the particular form of unification – Prussian annexation – as the general principle. But the supporters of annexation (a majority of the Hanoverians who went to the polls for the North German Confederation in 1867) were probably no less conscious of Hanoverian traditions. They simply had a different conception of where they were to be found and of which institutions were to be preserved. In transferring their formal allegiance to the Prussian monarchy, for example, the citizens of Hanover were mainly concerned to maintain the levels of civic achievement – 'the rich installations, collections, and institutions for art and science, for the education and the instruction of youth, and training for trade and technology' – in which they had come to feel proud. Hanoverian liberals pushed for greater self-government in precisely the same areas, meaning principally public works and social welfare. It was no accident that the Guelph Fund was used for much the same purpose after 1869, to subsidize road-building, railway construction, educational installations like the Hanover Polytechnic, public monuments, cultural institutions like museums, the Natural History Society, and the Hanover Botanical Gardens, and the royal resort at Nordeney. This was a shrewd use of resources, emphasizing the Hanoverian contribution to German culture and pandering to civic pride, to build the cultural no less than the economic infrastructure of the new nation-state.[28]

Where does this leave us? Basically it returns us to the three-way distinction suggested above, between processes of state formation, the emergence of nationalist ideology and processes of cultural unification. It would clearly make little sense to discuss German nationalism without recognizing the important contribution of the Prussian state to the incremental definition of German nationality during the nineteenth century, particularly in the period of Bismarck after 1862. In this first sense, therefore, German nationalism was a complex effect of unification from above, beginning with the Napoleonic occupation, continuing through the Austrian-Prussian condominium, and finishing in the successive realignments of the 1860s, during which the German governments generated a new institutional framework for the formation of public consciousness. Within limits, as we saw, nationalist ideology could then function within the institutions of the *Kaiserreich* to solidify the new social and political status quo. But at the same time, German governments (and certainly not Bismarck) seldom acted with specifically nationalist intentions, rationalized by a coherent ideological commitment to the overriding legitimacy of national sovereignty. In this second sense – the formation of nationalist ideology – the German nation was conceived in the minds of intellectuals and realized in a political movement. That movement was principally liberal, though it contained a democratic left wing and defined itself before 1867–71 through opposition to the already constituted governments.

The contradiction between state and civil society ran through the centre of the national question in Germany. By contrast with the core states of Western Europe, nationalities east of the Rhine lacked the advantage of an early acquired statehood. Of necessity the real labour of constituting the 'nation' had to be conducted by private rather than public bodies, by individual intellectuals and voluntary associations rather than governments, though the latter could seriously affect the terms under which it was done. Accordingly, the process of 'proposing and elaborating the category of the nation' was to a great extent identical with the growth of a public sphere, with the 'nation' conceived simultaneously as a political community of citizens.[29] The interpenetration of these two terms – nation and citizenry – in the discourse of both liberals and democrats in the mid-nineteenth century was extremely close and complex. Thus when it came to defining the obligations of national citizenship, the boundaries of the private and the public, and the distribution of sovereignty in the new German state, divisions quickly opened between the state authorities and the various political tendencies, especially given the absence of direct parliamentary government. The labour movement and the left liberals pushed the disagreements furthest. But National Liberals (as most German nationalists became after 1867) also had their positive objectives. Essentially this was what the *Kulturkampf* was all about.

This brings us to the third facet of definition, concerning processes of cultural unification and the 'nationalization of consciousness' in society. Here the transition to statehood – in Germany between 1864 and 1871 – is crucial. As the realization of nationality in its strongest political form, this transforms the conditions of existence for nationalist movements and their ideas. It immeasurably simplifies the process of manufacturing, strengthening or imposing a set of shared political loyalties on the putative national population. Moreover, once political independence has been attained, the nation comes to represent an ideological and institutional structure of immense power, which begins to set limits on the possible forms of political action and belief. Almost imperceptibly nationalism loses its character as a sectional creed articulating the aspirations of liberal and other tendencies within the bourgeoisie, and passes into the common heritage of a political culture – becoming, as Tom Nairn puts it, 'a name for the general condition of the modern body politic, more like the climate of political and social thought than just another doctrine'.[30] The process of national integration simultaneously, gradually and subtly transforms the content of the national idea, universalizing its legitimacy, while endowing it with a vital plasticity. Thus, though drives for cultural uniformity within nations (Germanization, Russification, the imposition of Parisian culture on provincial France, and so on) may be vigorously state-directed, they are also subject to private initiative and political contestation, involving protracted struggles for leadership and control. Though open to functionalist interpretation, therefore, stressing the need for social solidarity, the initiating role of the state, and the conservative or stabilizing effects of nationalist propaganda, this can only be a part of the picture.

III

If we problematize the concept of the German nation, therefore, by converting unspoken assumptions into a very basic question (that is, what was the German nation, and how did the answer vary?), some fundamental issues come into view. Overall these concern what we might call the definition of an individual's political identity (or in a current idiom the constitution of political subjects), for if national consciousness was very low in the 1860s, other kinds of allegiance clearly functioned in its stead (for example, family, kin, village, locality, region, state, church, religion), and any attempt to strengthen loyalty to the nation almost certainly implied moderation, subordination, or active suppression of its rivals: how exactly individuals came to think of themselves primarily as citizens of Germany (or Britain, France, Italy, and so on), as opposed to the members of some smaller community, or the participants in some larger cultural enterprise like the Catholic Church, is a very under-researched problem. Moreover, as this essay has begun to suggest, it is a mistake to assume that in pursuing the goal of national solidarity the state had things all its own way – or even that the state was the most active agent in the process. So far from simply imposing its own definitions of the national interest, in fact, government entered some bitterly contested terrain, on which socialists and Catholics, liberals and democrats, radical agrarians, anti-semites and Pan-Germans, had all entered their claims. In this sense the national interest was open to widely conflicting interpretations, amongst which the official view of the Prusso-German state was just one example. Once this is grasped, an excessively functionalist account of nationalism's place in the maintenance of an authoritarian dominant culture (the most influential analysis of German nationalism under the *Kaiserreich*) is more easily avoided.

This is a salutary observation. Mere control of the socializing institutions (the schools system, the church, the conscript army, the organs of opinion, and so on) cannot guarantee ideological conformity or national integration, however authoritarian the political system. Efforts at ideological incorporation can always be contested, from a wide variety of positions. This insight was grasped by the French philosopher Ernest Renan, in his classic lecture of 1882 *What Is a Nation?*.[31] Voicing an extreme scepticism regarding objective criteria for the existence of nations, Renan emphasized the elements of cultural invention and historical process. Nations were 'the result of a long history of effort, sacrifice and devotion', requiring both 'a rich legacy of memories from the past and consent in the present'. They stood for 'a great solidarity', but one in constant need of creative renewal. Once created, a sense of national identity had to be continuously reaffirmed, by a difficult, unpredictable, and time-consuming labour of ideological reproduction. This is what, in a striking phrase, Renan called a silent 'daily plebiscite'. But it proceeded not simply by an unmediated interaction between governments and subject populations. By the state/civil society couplet we postulate a field of ideological negotiation, in which organized agencies of one kind or another (political, religious, cultural, economic) are necessarily present. That being the case, the content of nationalist ideology, the meaning of national loyalty and the very category of the nation itself, were all open to alternative definitions.

This was becoming clear by the end of the 1870s. As suggested, the basic work of constituting the nation (by proposing a German nationality and propagating a German-national view) originated in the growth of civil society as a public arena of freely associating citizens, distinct from the state and beyond its arbitrary supervision. In Germany, as elsewhere in the nineteenth century, this process had a self-consciously liberal coloration and the buoyancy of the liberal movement formed the context in which the demand for nation-states became a realistic proposition. After unification – a political act, which necessarily left the nation's social and cultural consolidation incomplete – liberals continued to press for the same ideals of progress and unity, initially with the state's resources behind them. The *Kulturkampf* dramatized their commitment and in this respect resembled the drive for republican consolidation in France in the 1870s and 1880s.[32] But the brief period of liberal dominance only really lasted from the early 1860s to the end of the 1870s, with a further decade or so in many of the regions. By the end of the empire's first decade the liberals were just one sectional tendency amongst others, no longer hegemonic in the political culture, without privileged access to government, and (ironically for the party of national unification) potentially factionalized on a wide variety of issues on an increasingly regional basis.

From this point on it becomes impossible to speak of a single national movement. If National Liberals still claimed the leading voice over specifically national questions, this was no longer undisputed. Moreover, liberal nationalism became less and less of a dynamic social force, taking more and more of a refuge in older ideological themes like the *Kulturkampf*, which sputtered on in the liberal heartlands of the Rhineland and the south-west as an impoverished and more straightforward anti-clericalism, a German version of waving the bloody shirt. Otherwise, apart from the passage of the Civil Law Code and an amended law of association between 1896 and 1900, which in liberal minds belatedly completed the legal side of unification, National Liberals put most of their energies into foreign policy, on matters like colonies, the navy and the promotion of foreign trade. Even here they were outflanked in innovative thinking, because between 1892 and 1907 left liberals readdressed the same questions and emerged with a more challenging programme of imperialism and social reform. More seriously, the Catholic Centre Party began affirming its own nationalist credentials in the 1890s, as a new generation of bourgeois Catholics displaced the clerics and aristocrats from the leadership and demanded civic equality within the German nation rather than simply defence of the church. It was no accident that the national achievements most prized by National Liberals in the 1980s – the Code of Civil Law and the two Navy Laws – were realized through parliamentary coalitions with the Centre. Over to the right Prussian Conservatives were also discovering the virtues of nationalist argumentation in their campaigns for agricultural protection.[33]

In other words, nationalism had ceased to be the prerogative of a particular group in German society and had entered the universal currency of political debate. The parties increasingly clothed themselves in the modern legitimacy of the 'national interest'. In effect they vied for the general will, claiming for their primary constituency (whether bourgeois, peasant, *mittelständisch*, or working class) the real embodiment of national virtue. Even the Social Democrats had their conception of the German nation, drawn from the experience of 1848, the democratic patriotism of the 1860s and the popular democratic vision of a socialist electoral majority, against which the emotional resonances of the Second International proved to be no impediment.[34] This multiplicity of nationalist conceptions – which was virtually inevitable given the structured ideological context of the nation and the territorial boundedness of the nation-state and its institutions – made nationalist appeals as much a source of conflict as unity. Despite its own elevated sense of classless cultural solidarity, nationalist ideology could never escape the contradictions of German society before the First World War.

This is the central paradox of the post-unification period, namely the indisputable suffusion of national values in a society where the exact content of the national tradition and its future direction were a matter of bitter dispute. This divisiveness – the fissiparity of the national idea – was highlighted in the 1890s by the rather turbulent popular mobilizations of that decade, which collectively redrew the boundaries of the political nation. Not only the working class in the towns, but also the *Mittelstand* and smallholding peasantry in the countryside showed new levels of political interest, activating themselves through new types of economic and political organization, and generally invading the public sphere. But this was not some unproblematic process of national integration, as the state and its metropolitan culture penetrated more deeply into the recesses of rural society, obliterating difference and homogenizing political identity. On the contrary, the Catholic farmers and small tradesmen of south-west Germany, their anti-semitic counterparts in Hesse, and the radical *Bauernbündler* of Bavaria, all bitterly resented the processes of national penetration, which seemed to further progress and integration mainly at their own expense (for example, through the new economic and fiscal legislation, the unfavourable siting of railway branch lines, the extension and reform of schooling, the imposition of conscription, and so on).[35] Yet nor, in most cases, did these mobilizations take place under narrowly particularist or localist auspices which dealt with the new national context by refusing its legitimacy altogether. At the grass roots there was much sentiment of this kind, but most of the discontent (certainly over the longer term) was articulated through organizations with an aggressively national presence (the Centre Party, the Anti-Semites, the Agrarian League). From this point of view the modalities of mobilization (the different ways in which people became inducted into the political system) could have a crucial effect on the form and the content of the nationalist orientation.

In this respect the contradiction between centre and periphery resembles the conflicts between dominant and small nationalities, particularly in regions with a distinctive culture, institutional history, or social structure (like the backward Catholic parts of Germany, or the areas annexed by Prussia in 1866). Indeed, the 'progressive' case for the assimilation of small 'backward' peoples by large 'developed' or 'advanced' nations was simultaneously an argument for metropolitan over provincial or local cultures, and this 'was directed as much against the regional languages and cultures of the nation itself as against outsiders'.[36] As Eugen Weber has reminded us, the impact of a dominant metropolitan culture on a parochial village world could be just as traumatic and alienating within a particular nation as any encounter between separate nationalities.[37] At the same time, the penetration of a centralizing nationalism into the countryside was neither always nor simply a process of destructive repression. Induction into the dominant culture was also a potential passport to mobility, new experiences and self-improvement. When things went well (for example, at times of general prosperity and expanding employment, without blatant national discrimination or dramatic inequalities between the economies of region and metropolis), assimilation could easily work. At all levels, a particularist sense of regional identity, cultural nationalism, or ethnicity is not, by definition, incompatible with willing participation in a larger nation and its state. In fact, the twentieth-century ideology of 'Americanism' in the USA is predicated on precisely this type of contention.[38]

The point of these observations is to stress the different effects of being socialized or educated into a sense of national awareness. We can see this very clearly if we consider the attempts of the imperial state to equip itself with a patriotic public tradition which was distinct from the existing paraphernalia of princely ceremonial, and which could foster a form of patriotism specific to itself. Commemoration of unification was the obvious form for this to take and while celebration of Sedan Day began immediately in the 1870s, the most concentrated period of innovation seems to have begun with the later 1890s.[39] Its principal form was the building of the great national monuments (the ones on the Kyffhäuser mountain and the Deutsches Eck, both finished in 1897, and the Siegesallee built in Berlin between 1898 and 1901), which were carefully laden 'with specific ideological-historical associations'. As well as the major public festivals like Sedan Day and the Kaiser's birthday, we should also mention the extended repertoire of ceremonial and ritual observed in public institutions like the army and the schools. Superficially this confirms the functionalist account of nationalism, with its stress on the latter's unifying potential, as a force for cohesion and solidarity in an otherwise divided society. As Hobsbawn says 'these systematically planned ceremonial campaigns' promulgated not only 'a particular version of German history' for use in the schools, but also 'the ritual practices, badges and symbols through which identification with the new Germany (as distinct from any other kind of Germany or any other German state) was internalised.'[40]

Yet this can be easily exaggerated. The imperial cult competed with the older pageantry of the individual states, which kept a vigorous existence down to the turn of the century and derived much legitimacy from the federal nature of the constitution.[41] Similarly, the agrarian mobilizations of the 1890s made great play of local political traditions often with a particularist and heavily anti-Prussian emphasis (again particularly in the annexed territories of Hanover and Hesse), appropriating the forms of popular Lutheranism and the iconography of 1848.[42] More seriously in the longer term, the SPD made a systematic attempt to challenge the hegemony of the official nationalism, counter-posing its own carefully articulated version of the national tradition with a rich variety of symbolism and ritual expression. May Day and other political festivals, the commemoration of dead leaders and great events, and a rich texture of symbolic forms (banners, portraits, badges, tableaux vivants, radical iconography, and other emblematic devices), all helped cement the cohesion of the SPD's subculture. A counter-mythology of the past was an important aspect of this activity, stressing the European revolutionary tradition, German popular resistance and the SPD's inheritance of the democratic past. A populist view of 1848 as the thwarted uprising of the democratic nation was a central feature of this historical imagery, whether in the successful popular history of Wilhelm Blos, or the public discussion accompanying the Revolution's fiftieth anniversary in 1898.[43]

Moreover, not all the patriotic inventiveness stemmed from the state. To a great extent the commemoration of German unity (no less than the process of unification itself) originated in civil society. The Hermanns-denkmal (1841–75), the Niederwalddenkmal (1874–85), the Kyffhäusser Memorial (1896–97), and the Völkerschlachtdenkmal (1894–1913) were all launched by private initiative and kept alive by various kinds of voluntary effort and public subscription, with a minimum of direct subsidy from the state. On a smaller scale but a similar basis, some 500 of Wilhelm Kreis's Bismarck towers were built between 1900 and 1910, normally with some sort of civic support, but owing little to the initiative of the state as such. Most of the impetus for the holding of patriotic festivals came originally from non-official sources. To promote the general idea a National Festival Society was formed in 1897, growing out of the earlier Central Commission for People's and Youth Sports set up in 1889, and closely linked locally to the choral and gymnastic movements. Though the actual occasions of patriotic celebration were inevitably dominated by dignitaries and officialdom, therefore, much of the drive and imagination came from private individuals or associations. Furthermore, at a certain point this meshed with the activities of the nationalist pressure groups (Pan-Germans, Navy League, Colonial Society, Eastern Marches Society, Defence League, Society for Germandom Abroad, and a number of lesser organizations), which often formed themselves into local patriotic coalitions and had their own strong views about how nationalist propaganda should be conducted.[44]

This revealed the contradictory, centrifugal effects of nationalist ideology most pointedly of all. In certain respects the activity of such nationalist associations was obviously conjoint with that of the government – for example, the general propaganda for colonies, navy and military spending, the anti-Polish activities in the east, or the promotion of patriotic values through the schools (as in the rewriting of textbooks, or the organization of school trips to colonial and naval exhibitions). Moreover, at the local level they busied themselves with much the sort of patriotic manifestations which the imperial state desired, as with the patriotic evenings which formed the high point in the Navy League branches' annual calendar, or the organization of film shows which exposed the importance of the navy to the maximum possible audience.[45] But while sharing the same general aims, the *nationale Verbände* also diverged sharply from the government on a number of issues. This was partly because their demands were more extreme (for more ships, faster development of the colonies, harsher treatment of the Poles, a much more 'German' foreign policy). But they also developed searching criticisms of the government's general political practice, demanding an end to parliamentary conciliation (particularly of the Centre Party), a full-scale assault on particularism and a patriotic mobilization of the people against the Reichstag. Most fundamentally of all, they questioned the government's own patriotic credentials (and by extension those of the right-wing party establishments), accusing it of neglecting Germany's interests in the world, surrendering to the pressures of special interests in the Reichstag and ignoring the threat from the left. In 1907–8, during a crisis in the Navy League and the Daily Telegraph Affair, this broadened into an attack on the monarchy itself. Though these tendencies towards national opposition were only partly realized before the First World War, a radical nationalist politics to the right of the government had definitely taken shape.[46]

This, perhaps better than anything else, demonstrates the complexity of the national question in Imperial Germany and the dangers of an overly functionalist account. National integration was certainly an urgent priority for the imperial government, given the difficulties of constructing a stable governing consensus while basic questions of national identity remained unresolved. The new government had to deal with strong particularisms in eastern Prussia, Bavaria and elsewhere, a potential liberal–democratic opposition, religious divisions and a rising labour movement, without the benefit of a centralized state apparatus (given the entrenched federalism of the constitution) or national cultural institutions. In the circumstances a strong emphasis on national unity was clearly some sort of functional necessity. But, in the event, the strengthening of the national framework did little to solve the problems of integration in anything but a formal and very general sense: by universalizing the legitimacy of the nation or national values, it simply transferred the contradictions from the margins to the very centre of the national idea. Though the contextual reality of the nation-state and its institutions increasingly structured the possible limits of dissent, conflicts now took place over how the nation was to be represented. Moreover, not only did Catholics, radical agrarians, Junkers and even Social Democrats add their own national conceptions to the older one of the liberals. Radical nationalists also entered the fray (Pan-Germans, anti-semites, Navy Leaguers, and all sorts of independent patriots), attacking the government's official nationalism with a new populism of the right.

Nowhere was this clearer than in the centenary celebrations of 1913, organized to commemorate Germany's war of liberation against Napoleon. In conjunction with Wilhelm II's silver jubilee this seemed to afford a golden opportunity to enhance the prestige of the empire and to tighten the moral bonds of public solidarity and identification. Events proceeded throughout the year, centring on the double climax of civic festivities in March and the opening of the Völkerschlachtdenkmal in Leipzig in November. Yet the national consensus revealed itself fractured by disagreements. Not only were the official celebrations attacked by the SPD, who reminded the enthusiasts of Germany's national liberation that the Prussian people were still awaiting their civic and political emancipation. The transmutation of the history of 1813 into a glorification of dynastic traditions was attacked from many other quarters too: the left liberal press, sections of the cultural intelligentsia, parts of the youth movement, but most importantly of all, the Pan-German right, who charged the government with falsifying the popular nature of the struggle against Napoleon.[47]

IV

There are many aspects of German nationalism which this essay has not discussed. Several of the problems raised during the previous section might have received more extensive treatment – for example, the process of popular mobilization in the 1890s and its reconstitution of the political nation; the nature of radical agrarianism; the complex interactions between rural society, particularism and political Catholicism in the formation of the Centre Party's secular patriotism; the Social Democratic conception of the German nation; the radical nationalist critique of official patriotism and conventional conservative politics; or the role of symbolism, ritual and invented tradition. Other questions have not been mentioned – for example, the treatment of the national minorities, racialist and social darwinist definitions of the nation, anti-semitism, the impact of colonialism and the idea of a big navy, the new economic nationalism of the protectionist period after 1879, or the forms of anti-socialism. By concentrating on the period of unification and the problems of national integration I have said nothing about two later conjunctures – the imperialist upturn after the end of the Great Depression in 1895–6, and the vital climacteric of the First World War – which profoundly affected the terms of the national question and the place of nationalist ideology. This is partly because I have discussed these matters elsewhere.[48] But my object in this essay has been more modest. It has been to abstract some general points of definition from the general literature on nationalism, to deploy these insights in the context of pre-1914 German history and to suggest some new lines of discussion for the future.

To conclude we can do far worse than quote Eric Hobsbawm. In his most concise statement he has called nationalism

a dual phenomenon, or rather an interaction of two phenomena, each of which help to give shape to the other. It consists of a 'civic religion' for the modern territorial-centralised state, and of a mode of confronting social changes which appear to threaten and disrupt certain aspects of the complex of social relationships. The former reflects a specific historic situation, a characteristic of Europe since the French Revolution, and of most of the non-European world in the twentieth century: the combination of economic development . . . with the mass participation in politics of a mobilised population . . . The latter is in principle not confined to any particular historic period or society, though it only acquired the full features of 'nationalism' as we know it in the specific historical era since 1789, and would probably not have done so in another setting.[49]

Arguably, this is precisely the point, between the formation and impact of states and the social determination of political culture, where the most interesting questions of nineteenth-century European history begin.

CHAPTER 3: NOTES

1 See, in particular, the following: A. D. Smith, *Theories of Nationalism*, (London, 1971); M. Hechter, *Internal Colonialism. The Celtic Fringe in British National Development, 1536–1966* (London, 1975); C. Tilly (ed.), *The Formation of National States in Western Europe* (Princeton, NJ, 1975); T. Nairn, *The Break-Up of Britain. Crisis and Neo-Nationalism* (London, 1977). See also the following works by Eric Hobsbawm: *The Age of Revolution* (New York, 1962), pp. 163–77; 'The attitude of popular classes towards national movements for independence', in *Mouvements nationaux d'indépendance et classes populaires aux XIXᵉ et XXᵉ siècles en occident et en orient* (Paris, 1971), pp. 34–44; 'Some reflections on nationalism', in T. J. Nossiter, S. Rokkan and A. H. Hanson (eds), *Imagination and Precision in the Social Sciences* (London, 1972), pp. 386–406; *The Age of Capital* (London, 1975), pp. 82–97; 'Inventing traditions in 19th century Europe', in Past and Present Society (ed.), *The Invention of Tradition* (London, 1977), pp. 1–24; 'Some reflections on "The Break-Up of Britain"', *New Left Review*, no. 105 (1977), pp. 3–24.

2   See J. Godechot, 'Nation, patrie, nationalisme et patriotisme en France au XVIIIᵉ siècle', *Annales historiques de la Révolution Française*, 206 (1971), pp. 481–501.

3   The most important analysis of this kind is M. Hroch, *Die Vorkämpfer der nationalen Bewegung bei den kleinen Völkern Europas* (Prague, 1968).Unfortunately, due to the limited currency of German and East European languages in the English-speaking world and the general ignorance about historical work in the socialist countries, Hroch's work is badly neglected. Eric Hobsbawm, who has introduced the latter into English-language discussion, is an important exception. Otherwise see J.-P. Himka, *Socialism in Galicia. The Emergence of Polish Social Democracy and Ukrainian Radicalism (1860–1890)* (Cambridge, Mass., 1983), and J. Chlebowczyk, *Procesy narodotworcze we wschodniej Europie srodkowej w dobie kapitalizmu: Od schylku XVIII do poczatkow XX w.* (Warsaw, 1975). Mention should also be made of a seminal work of sociology, K. Deutsch, *Nationalism and Social Communication* (Cambridge, Mass., 1966).

4   See Nairn, *The Break-Up of Britain*, pp. 92 ff., 329 ff., for the most eloquent defence of this view.

5   I have tried to discuss them in G. Eley, 'Nationalism and social history', *Social History*, vol. 6 (1981), pp. 83–107.

6   J. J. Sheehan, 'What is German history? Reflections on the role of the *nation* in German history and historiography', *Journal of Modern History*, vol. 53 (1981), p. 10. See also the following: R. M. Berdahl, 'New thoughts on German nationalism', *American Historical Review*, vol. 77 (1972), pp. 65–80; W. Real, 'Die Ereignisse von 1866–67 im Lichte unserer Zeit', *Historisches Jahrbuch*, vol. 95 (1975), pp. 342–73; N. M. Hope, *The Alternative to German Unification. The Anti-Prussian Party: Frankfurt, Nassau, and the Two Hessen 1859–1867* (Wiesbaden, 1973); R. Austensen, 'Austria and the struggle for supremacy in Germany, 1848–1864', *Journal of Modern History*, vol. 52 (1980), pp. 195–225.

7   Berdahl, 'New thoughts on German nationalism', p. 70.

8   P. Anderson, *Lineages of the Absolutist State* (London, 1974), p. 276.

9   See here H.-U. Wehler, 'Der Aufstieg des Organisierten Kapitalismus und Interventionsstaates in Deutschland', in H. A. Winkler (ed.), *Organisierter Kapitalismus. Voraussetzungen und Anfange* (Göttingen, 1974), pp. 36–57.

10 Benedikt Waldeck of the Progressive Party, cited by T. S. Hamerow, *The Social Foundations of German Unification 1858–1871. Vol. II: Struggles and Accomplishments* (Princeton, NJ, 1972), p. 330.

11 ibid., pp. 337 ff., for the best brief description of the specific changes brought by unification in this respect.

12 See R. Murray, 'The internationalization of capital and the nation-state', *New Left Review*, no. 67 (1971), pp. 84–109.

13 R. Miliband, *The State in Capitalist Society* (London, 1969), p. 185.

14 The phrase 'moral equivalent of war' comes from William James's essay of the same name, *Memories and Studies* (New York, 1917), pp. 267–306.

15 Hobsbawm had discussed these processes directly in 'Inventing traditions in 19th century Europe', cit. at n. 1 above.

16 H.-U. Wehler, *Bismarck und der Imperialismus* (Cologne, 1969), p. 115.

17 H.-U. Wehler, *Das deutsche Kaiserreich 1871–1918* (Göttingen, 1973), p. 126.

18 For an introduction to these problems: M. Kitchen, *The German Officer Corps 1890–1914* (Oxford, 1968), pp. 143–86; W. C. Langsam, 'Nationalism and history in the Prussian elementary schools under William II', in E. M. Earle (ed.), *Nationalism and Internationalism. Essays inscribed to Carlton J. H. Hayes* (New York, 1950), pp. 241–61; F. Wenzel, 'Sicherung von Massenloyalität und Qualifikation der Arbeitskraft als Aufgabe der Volksschule', in K. Hartmann, F. Nyssen and H. Waldeyer (eds), *Schule und Staat im 18. und 19. Jahrhundert*, (Frankfurt-on-Main, 1974), pp. 323-86; H.-J. Heydorn and G. Koneffke, *Studien zur Sozialgeschichte und Philosophie der Bildung. II. Aspekte des 19. Jahrhunderts in Deutschland* (Munich, 1973), pp. 179–238.

19 G. Hohorst, J. Kocka and G. A. Ritter, *Sozialgeschichtliches Arbeitsbuch. Materialien zur Statistik des Kaiserreichs 1870–1914* (Munich, 1975), p. 157.

20 In 1904 in Württemberg something like a fifth of all school-age children worked in some kind of paid employment, nearly half of them as domestic servants, not to speak of the still larger numbers whose unpaid family labour was crucial to the viability of

smallholdings. See D. G. Blackbourn, *Class, Religion and Local Politics in Wilhelmine Germany. The Centre Party in Württemberg before 1914* (New Haven, Conn. and London, 1980), pp. 139.

21 For an exemplary discussion, ibid., pp. 136–40; for the Polish school strikes, R. Korth, *Die preussische Schulpolitik und die polnischen Schulstreiks. Ein Beitrag zur Preussischen Polenpolitik der Ära Bulow* (Würzburg, 1963).

22 See the splendid analyses in G. Zang (ed.), *Provinzialisierung einer Region. Zur Entstehung der bürgerlichen Gesellschaft in der Provinz* (Frankfurt-on-Main, 1978), especially those by D. Bellmann, 'Der Liberalismus im Seekreis (1860–1870)', pp. 183–264; W. Trapp, 'Volksschulreform und liberales Bürgertum in Konstanz. Die Durchsetzung des Schulzwangs als Voraussetzung der Massendisziplinierung und -qualifikation', pp. 375–434; and Zang himself, 'Die Bedeutung der Auseinandersetzung um die Stiftungsverwaltung in Konstanz (1830–1870) für die ökonomische und gesellschaftliche Entwicklung der lokalen Gesellschaft. Ein Beitrag zur Analyse der materiellen Hintergründe des Kulturkampfes', pp. 307–79.

23 The slogan comes from a Progessive election leaflet in Hanau-Gelnhausen-Bockenheim (Hesse) in 1881, cited by D.S. White, *The Splintered Party. National Liberalism in Hessen and the Reich 1867–1918* Cambridge, Mass. and London, 1976), p. 100.

24 To be more exact we are dealing here with the National Liberals and their different regional equivalents – that is, that majority tendency of German liberalism which accepted the Bismarckian solution in 1866–7. The best introduction to German liberalism is now J. J. Sheehan, *German Liberalism in the Nineteenth Century* (Chicago, 1978), but there is little detail on regional politics in the 1860s.

25 J. Habermas, 'The public sphere', *New German Critique*, vol. 3 (1974), p. 49. Habermas developed the idea in full in *Strukturwandel der Öffentlichkeit* (Neuwied, 1962).

26 For the importance of voluntary association: T. Nipperdey, 'Verein als soziale Struktur in Deutschland im späten 18. und fruhen 19. Jahrhundert', in *Gesellschaft, Kultur, Theorie. Gesammelte Aufsätze zur neueren Geschichte* (Göttingen, 1976), pp. 176–205; O. Dann, Die Anfänge politischer Vereinsbildung in Deutschland', in U. Engelhardt, V. Sellin and H. Stuke (eds), *Soziale Bewegung und politische Verfassung* (Stuttgart, 1976), pp. 297-343. I have tried to explore the process in G. Eley, *Reshaping the German Right. Radical Nationalism and Political Change after Bismarck* (New Haven, Conn. and London, 1980), pp. 30 ff., 150 ff., and Eley, 'Re-thinking the political: social history and political culture in 18th and 19th century Britain', *Archiv für Sozialgeschichte*, vol. 21 (1981), pp. 427–57.

27 See especially Hope's fine monograph, *Alternative to German Unification*.

28 See S. A. Stechlin, *Bismarck and the Guelph Problem 1866–1890. A Study in Particularist Opposition to National Unity* (The Hague, 1973), pp. 159–93. The Guelph Fund was created from the sequestrated possessions of the Hanoverian royal family.

29 W. J. Argyle, 'Size and scale as factors in the development of nationalist movements', in A. D. Smith (ed.), *Nationalist Movements* (London, 1976), pp. 31–53.

30 Nairn, *The Break-Up of Britain*, p. 94.

31 E. Renan, 'What is a nation', in A. Zimmern (ed.), *Modern Political Doctrines* (Oxford, 1939), pp. 190 ff.

32 See S. Elwitt, *The Making of the Third Republic. Class and Politics in France, 1868–1884* (Baton Rouge, La, 1975).

33 See D. G. Blackbourn, 'The problem of democratization: German Catholics and the role of the Centre Party', in R. J. Evans (ed.), *Society and Politics in Wilhelmine Germany* (London, 1978), pp. 160–85, and *Class, Religion and Local Politics*, pp. 23-69; H.-J. Puhle, *Agrarische Interessenpolitik und preussischer Konservatismus im wilhelminischen Reich 1893–1914* (Hanover, 1966).

34 See especially: H.-U. Wehler, *Sozialdemokratie und Nationalstaat. Nationalitätenfragen in Deutschland 1840–1914* (Göttingen, 1971); W. Conze and D. Groh, *Die Arbeiterbewegung in der nationalen Bewegung* (Stuttgart, 1966).

35 Blackbourn, *Class, Religion and Local Politics*, pp. 141-64; I. Farr, 'Populism in the countryside: the peasant leagues in Bavaria in the 1890s', in Evans (ed.), *Society and Politics*, pp. 136–59.

36 Hobsbawm, *Age of Capital*, p. 87.

37 E. Weber, *Peasants into Frenchmen. The Modernization of Rural France 1870–1914* (London, 1977).

38 Hobsbawm's discussion of Welsh and Scottish nationalism provides a good example to this effect. Until recently the successful articulation of popular aspirations into British national parties since the 1860s (first the Liberals and then Labour) effectively pre-empted the emergence of Scottish or Welsh separatism as a serious political force. At the same time 'Scottishness' and 'Welshness' were far from negligible factors in the constitution of popular political identity. For example, since the 1920s the militants of the South Wales Miners Federation have been at once a mainstay of the *British* Labour movement, fervently *internationalist* and proudly *Welsh*. There is no reason for any one to preclude the others. See Hobsbawm, 'The attitude of popular classes', cit. at n. 1 above. See also H. Francis and D. Smith, *The Fed. A History of the South Wales Miners in the Twentieth Century* (London, 1980).

39 The reasons for the timing are complex. For a general discussion, see Eley, *Reshaping the German Right*, pp. 41 ff.

40 Hobsbawm, 'Inventing traditions in 19th century Europe', cit. at n. 1 above, pp. 5 f. See also: G. L. Mosse, *The Nationalization of the Masses. Political Symbolism and Mass Movements in Germany from the Napoleonic Wars through the Third Reich* (New York, 1975); T. Nipperdey, 'Nationalidee und Nationaldenkmal in Deutschland im 19. Jahrhundert', *Historische Zeitschrift*, no. 206 (1968), pp. 529–85; E. Fehrenbach, *Wandlungen des deutschen Kaisergedankens 1871–1918* (Munich, 1969), and 'Uber die Bedeutung der politischen Symbole im Nationalstaat', *Historiche Zeitschrift*, no. 213 (1971), pp. 296–357; W. K. Blessing, 'The cult of monarchy, political loyalty and the workers' movement in Imperial Germany', *Journal of Contemporary History*, vol. 13 (1978), pp. 357–76. Hobsbawm, in article above, pp. 5 f., cites the example of the Prinz-Heinrichs-Gymnasium in Schöneberg, where ten substantial ceremonies were held between August 1895 and March 1896, 'including ample commemorations of battles in the war, celebrations of the Emperor's birthday, the official handing-over of the portrait of an imperial Prince, illuminations and public addresses on the war of 1870–1, on the development of the imperial idea (*Kaiseridee*) during the war, the character of the Hohenzollern dynasty, etc.'.

41 See Blessing's valuable article on Bavaria, 'The cult of monarchy', cit. above. The late 1890s again seem to have been some sort of watershed. Blessing notes that the twenty-fifth anniversary of the Franco-Prussian War and Wilhelm I's centenary in 1897 saw a progressive displacement of Bavarian by imperial symbolism. By 1912–13, with the centenary of 1813, Wilhelm II's silver jubilee, and (ironically) the Prince Regent's funeral, the imperial motifs were clearly on top.

42 For general discussion: Eley, *Reshaping the German Right*, pp. 19 ff.

43 Hobsbawm, 'Inventing traditions in 19th century Europe', cit. at n. 1 above, pp. 7–9; W. Blos, *Die Deutsche Revolution: Geschichte der deutschen Bewegung von 1848 und 1849* (Bonn, 1978); H. Hartwig and K. Riha, *Politische Ästhetik und Öffentlichkeit. 1848 im Spaltungsprozess des historischen Bewusstseins* (Giessen, 1974), esp. pp. 23–32, 141–71.

44 For the building of monuments, see Mosse, *Nationalization of the Masses*, pp. 36–8, 58–67, 93–7. For the character of the nationalist pressure groups, see Eley, *Reshaping the German Right*, pp. 41–98, 147–60, 160–235, I have tried to summarize the argument in Eley, 'Some thoughts on the nationalist pressure groups in Imperial Germany', in P. Kennedy and A. J. Nicholls (eds), *Nationalist and Racialist Movements in Britain and Germany before 1914* (London, 1981), pp. 68–87.

45 Eley, *Reshaping the German Right*, pp. 133–9, 206–35.

46 ibid., pp. 239–90.

47 See K. Stenkewitz, *Gegen Bajonett und Dividende, Die politische Krise in Deutschland am Vorabend des ersten Weltkrieges* (East Berlin, 1960), pp. 77–95.

48 Apart from *Reshaping the German Right*, and 'Some thoughts on the nationalist pressure groups', cit. at n. 44 above, see the following: 'Defining social imperialism: use and abuse of an idea', *Social History*, vol. 1 (1976), pp. 269–90; 'Social imperialism in Germany: reformist synthesis or reactionary sleight of hand?', in J. Radkau and I. Geiss (eds), *Imperialismus im 20. Jahrhundert. Gedenkschrift für Georg W. F. Hallgarten* (Munich, 1976), pp. 71–86.

49 Hobsbawm, 'Some reflections on nationalism', cit. at n. 1 above, p. 404.

4

Army, State and
Civil Society:
Revisiting the
Problem of German Militarism

'Militarism' is central to the common sense of German historiography. From Frederick the Great to the Second World War it has dominated Anglo-American perceptions of the German past. In Western popular consciousness the imagery of 'Germanness' exudes such militarist associations. For many years after the war explanations for the fall of the Weimar Republic commonly stressed the anti-democratic machinations of the army and their roots in a deeper authoritarian tradition, from J. W. Wheeler-Bennett's *The Nemesis of Power* (London, 1954) and Gordon Craig's *The Politics of the Prussian Army 1640–1945* (Oxford, 1955), to F. L. Carsten's *The Reichswehr and Politics 1918–1933* (Oxford, 1966). The same literature stressed the role of the army in manipulating the circumstances of the republic's foundation to compromise the SPD with the odium of Germany's military defeat and to delegitimize the republican and parliamentary mode of government, while a longstanding obsession with evidence of aristocratic and military opposition to Hitler after 1933 reflects a similarly exaggerated view of the German officer corps as the decisive political arbiter. Inside Germany itself there has been a similar tradition of thought, which ultimately derives from liberal, democratic and socialist critiques of the Prussian army in the second half of the nineteenth century. In general, the Prussian army is thought to be the single most important institutional embodiment of all those aristocratic, authoritarian and pre-industrial traditions that proved so decisive in arresting Germany's political modernization. The social arrogance, reactionary narrow-mindedness and institutional power of the army in the state were the epitome of German backwardness.

This essay is an attempt to reconsider the usefulness of the above view. It originated in a paper I presented to an international symposium on 'Military and militarism in the Weimar Republic' in Hamburg in 1977 and which appeared in the resulting conference volume the following year (K.-J. Müller and E. Opitz [eds], *Militär und Militarismus in der Weimarer Republik* [Düsseldorf, 1978], pp. 223– 35). The same paper was also presented at a meeting of the Cambridge Historical Society in 1977 in a joint presentation with a paper by Jane Caplan on the tradition of the civil service (which was eventually published as ' "The imaginary universality of particular interests": The "tradition" of the civil service in German history', *Social History*, vol. 4 [1979], pp. 299–317). The general issue of militarism was very much in the forefront of my thinking at that time, but it was not until February 1983 that I returned to the subject directly, when I presented a longer and much rethought version of the paper to the War and Society Seminar at the Shelby Cullom Davis Center in Princeton. I am extremely grateful to the members of that seminar for an opportunity to expose the ideas, as I am to John Shy and the other members of the military history group at the University of Michigan, who also read and discussed the same paper. Otherwise, my debt to Michael Geyer should be obvious from the essay's notes. These days, any discussion of the army, militarism, and war and peace in modern German history has to begin with his seminal works.

My aim in this paper is to explore the dimensions of militarism in Germany in the period between unification and the First World War. Although other national histories will not be directly addressed, the argument is implicitly comparative, because I want to suggest that the German political system was not quite as archaic or irredeemably 'backward' by comparison with the more 'modern' politics of the West as most historians seem ready to assume. As such, the aim of the paper is congruent with the argument in some of my other recent writings and is meant to be a modest contribution to the continuing discussions of German exceptionalism which the latter have helped to provoke.[1] My remarks are general, provisional and wide-ranging, and are offered strictly as a basis for discussion. While occasionally elaborative, the reference notes are not meant to provide a full or exhaustive guide to the literature.

I

The problem of defining militarism is complicated by certain present usages. Chief among these is that of the international peace movement and the associated anti-armaments lobby, where 'militarism' has come to signify a sinister hypertrophy of military, bureaucractic, technological, economic and ideological power at the centre of the state, no longer subject to the political control of democratically constituted authorities.[2] But this also presupposes the flourishing field of military sociology, which may be said to have emerged between the late 1950s/early 1960s (with the appearance of pioneering works by Huntington, Janowitz and Finer) and the constitution of a Working Group on Armed Forces and Society by the Sixth World Congress of Sociology in 1966.[3] In this burgeoning literature (as Berghahn points out, the 1979 issue of the *War and Society Newsletter* monitored some forty-six professional journals in this general field)[4] it is possible to distinguish a number of salient themes, with a varying relevance or connection to earlier discussions of militarism in late-nineteenth/early-twentieth-century Europe. The professionalization of the military has been one of these, with reference both to the sociology of recruitment and training and to the ascendancy of efficiency and expertise as the primary military virtues (as opposed to, say, the officers' traditional code of honour). Another theme has been the varying forms of civil-military relations which (together with the theme of professionalization) has functioned as an index of the degree of 'modernization' in political systems, particularly in the Third World. Both these concerns have been central to the literature on 'nation-building' since the early 1960s.[5] A third theme has concerned the so-called 'military-industrial complex' since 1945 and the tendency of the 'permanent arms economy' to collapse the traditional distinction between the 'military' and the 'civil' spheres into a new type of corporatist coalition of armed forces, armaments industries, research establishments, trade unions, regional lobbies and bureaucratic interests.[6] It is here that the present critique of the new arms race finds one of its main points of departure.

Now, each of these meanings may be deployed in the earlier context of Imperial Germany with some profit. But in the conceptual vocabulary of most German historians the idea of militarism has had a rather different connotation, and for this reason it is worth looking at the original usage too. From this point of view the term itself has normally been attributed to Pierre-Joseph Proudhon in the early 1860s – not the most auspicious of beginnings for a concept of political theory, it might be said. But Conze has found an earlier reference at the start of the nineteenth century and locates the concept's intellectual origins in later-seventeenth and eighteenth-century Anglo-French criticisms of military absolutism. At all events, the term was properly coined during the 1860s and quickly entered the general currency of political debate, functioning prominently in the distinctive political discourse of mid-nineteenth century radicalism. Here it figures as a rather imprecise polemical watchword for the absolutist monarchical state, with its centralized military and bureaucratic apparatus, and was also applied to the regime of Napoleon III in France. During the 1860s 'militarism' seems to have been used virtually interchangeably with other pejoratives, like 'military state', 'military despotism', 'caesarism', 'corporatism', and so on.[7]

In Germany especially it is impossible to separate the term from a certain radical critique of the Prussian state. During the conflicts over German unification in the middle to later 1860s this provided the ground on which a miscellaneous coalition of anti-Prussian forces could meet – as Geyer says, ' "particularists", South German greater-German liberals, workingmen's associations, and Catholics', essentially the heterogeneous coalition of forces described by Nicholas Hope in his monograph on the 'anti-Prussian party' in Frankfurt, Nassau and the two Hessen, *The Alternative to German Unification* (Wiesbaden, 1973). As Bismarck's Prussian solution to the German question took shape during the wars with Austria and France, a specifically Catholic version of the argument became important, centring on a critique of 'Borussianism' and deriving extra impetus from the *Kulturkampf* in the 1870s. But despite the portmanteau qualities of the concept, so to speak, the main drift of this early usage was radical and democratic, and as Geyer argues, 'the idea of "militarism" achieved its general currency' in the popular movement against the Prussian state: 'In the brief period between 1867 and 1871 the struggle against "militarism" generated an effectively democratic mass movement, in which a disparate assortment of immediate discontents became translated into pre-dominantly democratic and pacifist demands'. For the period of the *Kaiserreich* proper these origins are important, because although there developed some variation across the political spectrum in the precise notation of 'militarism', the political fire of the critique was concentrated pretty consistently on the same institutional and ideological symptoms – that is, the special constitutional status and overbearing social prestige of the Prussian officer corps and the social power of the Junkers to which they were linked.

The strategic assumption which united liberal, radical democratic and many socialist critics of militarism was the belief that the power of the Prussian army was an archaic survival of a vanishing pre-bourgeois era which would eventually wither before the impact of progress. In the 1870s and 1880s this thinking was largely focused on the issue of military spending, since this both exemplified the relative independence of the army from public accountability and legislative control and yet seemed, through careful parliamentary coalitioning and steadfast application of the Reichstag's budgetary powers, to hold out possibilities for improvement. As is well-known, the periodic submission of the military estimates to the Reichstag was the occasion of recurrent political crises during Bismarck's chancellorship, and this remained the case in the period that followed, in 1892–3, 1899, and then again on the eve of the war in 1912–13. Moreover, while left liberals tended to make the running, this stress on high military spending and the associated taxation – a 'political and social calamity' that 'endangers peace instead of ensuring it', as the Centre Party's programme put it[8] – enabled the parliamentary leadership of the Catholic Centre Party to align their predominantly peasant constituency behind the same essentially liberal critique. Thus Philipp Wasserburg, the Hessian Centre leader and a self-styled 'clerico-democrat', explicitly counterposed 'militarism' to 'constitutionalism' in this sense, on the grounds that a 'constitutional state' and a 'military state' were mutually exclusive categories.[9] To this extent in the period following unification the problem of militarism was subsumed within the 'constitutional question' in the formal sense, while liberal and Catholic parliamentarians worked off their residual opposition to the Bismarckian settlement.

In other words, the later-nineteenth century concept of militarism rested on a strong contrast between authoritarian and liberal socio-political orders, so that militarism in this sense was held to be incompatible in the long run with the rise of a 'modern industrial society' (as it would come to be known). This was very definitely the view that took root in Britain and the USA, where militarism was regarded quite straightforwardly as the subordination of civilian to military considerations in the conduct of government, in a way which obstructed the growth of representative institutions. As Berghahn says, Prussia-Germany gave Anglo-American commentators 'the negative image of the political system that had taken root in England and the United States in the eighteenth century'.[10] Militarism in this sense was thought to have pernicious effects on the spiritual health and moral fibre of a nation, stifling individuality and initiative. This argument was elaborated in Spencer's distinction between 'militant' and 'industrial' types of society, and here the argument begins to shift from the character of the state to the suffusion of military values in society — to what Lasswell calls 'the permeation of an entire society by the self-serving ideology of the officer and soldier'.[11] In the words of the American liberal Joseph O. Miller: 'the military spirit is always on the side of reaction – always allied with the non-progressive and anti-liberal movements of the time. Militarism is the propagating source of every anti-social infection'.[12]

At the risk of stating the obvious, therefore, the concept of militarism was always polemically critical of the phenomenon it was meant to describe. Bearing these origins in mind, and taking the imperial period as a whole, we can make the following observations about the term's subsequent usage:

(1) The demand for parliamentary accountability of the army was originally a centrepiece of liberal constitutional rhetoric, reaching its climax in the debates over the military budget in 1874, when the imperial government demanded the so-called *Aeternat* for military expenditure, before compromising with the National Liberal-dominated Reichstag majority on a seven-year cycle of budgetary accountability, the so-called *Septennat*. At this point the National Liberal leader Rudolf von Bennigsen was still quite forthright, calling control over the army the backbone of a state's constitution, and arguing that Germany's new constitution could not become a reality until military affairs were properly incorporated into its provisions. His left liberal counterpart Eugen Richter denounced the *Septennat* as a 'reserve of absolutism against the parliamentary system', which could only have a 'cancerous' effect on the vitality of the latter. Completing the chorus of bourgeois parliamentarians, Hermann von Mallinckrodt, the leader of the Centre, attacked the seven-year budget as the 'flesh and blood' of militarism.[13]

Yet by the 1890s this impressive constitutionalist front had largely dissolved. The military estimates continued to be the occasion of parliamentary difficulty, as did the newer government commitment to the big navy. But the maximal position of liberal constitutional principle (annual budgets and full accountability) was practically exchanged for more limited goals of a tactical nature, secured through the classic modalities of parliamentary brokerage and manœuvre (for example, concessions on the legal status of Catholics, or a willingness to undertake policies that were more pro-industry than pro-agrarian, or simply a tacit recognition that government had to be conducted with the practical consent of a parliamentary majority). The National Liberals and the Centre ceased to worry about the 'constitutional question' in the stronger sense (Bennigsen and Ernst Lieber, Ludwig Windthorst's successor at the head of the Centre, were the masters of this parliamentary game), while between 1892 and 1907 the left liberals also withdrew from their strong anti-militarist stance.

(2) As this process of parliamentary accommodation proceeded (on both sides), roughly between 1897–1900 and 1912-13, liberal anti-militarism became mainly refocused on what were taken to be anomalies and archaisms in the conduct of the army's own internal affairs. This meant, above all, the survival of independent military jurisdictions, practices and codes of behaviour, beyond the purview of the civil and criminal law as that was coming to be consolidated by the 1890s (for example, in the final codification of the civil law, which for the National Liberals completed the legal work of unification). The courts martial procedure, the courts of honour and duelling were all examples of this concern, as were the problem of rank-and-file discipline, brutality and maltreatment, anti-semitic and social discrimination in the officer corps, and later the excesses of the colonial troops in Africa. Despite the importance of these specific issues, Geyer rightly calls this a significant 'contraction' of the concept. For it became increasingly confined in liberal circles to the symptomatic expressions of a decadent aristocratic preponderance, which were allegedly inhibiting the emergence of a genuine popular nationalism and the effective harnessing of Germany's new industrial energies.

This was true, above all, of the generation of liberals who succeeded the grand old men of the Bismarckian era (for example, Bennigsen and Richter) around the turn of the century, ranging from Friedrich Naumann on the left to Gustav Stresemann on the right. In these circles the critique of militarism became finally divorced from the earlier pacifist and democratic connotations and became little more than a plea for national efficiency (to adapt a contemporary term from Britain). That is, it became a demand for 'the adjustment of the rigidified and "atavistic" structures of state and society to the dynamism of an expansive and industrialised *Kaiserreich*'. As Geyer says, this was a new liberal-imperialist version of the anti-militarist critique, which was less interested in reducing the nation-state's military capability than in raising it to higher levels of professional and rationalized efficiency, freed of the traditional aristocratic encumbrances, vitalized by new levels of popular nationalist mobilization.[14] By contrast, the purer anti-militarist tradition, with its radical pacifist commitment to international conciliation and a demilitarized Europe, was reduced to the marginalized dissent of a few isolated individuals, whose most famous representative was probably Ludwig Quidde.[15]

(3) What happened to the specifically Catholic anti-militarism? Citing the work of Georg Michael Pachtler (a Jesuit writing in the 1870s under the

pseudonym of Annuarius Osseg), Geyer credits Catholic publicists during the *Kulturkampf* with the first serious recognition of 'the connection between the national movement, industrialisation and militarisation', so that militarism 'no longer appeared just as the Junker-aristocratic antipode to a bourgeois industrial society, but as the consequence of a positively "modern" bourgeois and capitalist social order'.[16] This is an interesting point. Under the terrible pressure of the *Kulturkampf*, Catholic intellectuals correctly perceived the relationship between the attack on the Catholic Church and National Liberal strivings for a strong nationalist conception of German citizenship unmediated by more 'traditional' loyalties of a religious, corporate, or particularist kind. Practically strengthening the North German, Prussian and Protestant biases of the new nation-state, liberal commitments to the primacy of the citizen–state relation threatened in the longer run simply to strengthen the aggressive proclivities of the Prussian military-bureaucratic establishment by placing new possibilities of popular nationalist mobilization at its disposal, and between the 1890s and the First World War National Liberals were indeed the most consistent exponents of an aggressive German presence in the European and wider worlds. But, on the other hand, Geyer's judgement probably overestimates the coherence and farsightedness of Catholic publicity in this respect, and the militarist connection was much more of an incidental feature of the Catholic anti-liberal discourse.

Moreover, by the 1890s under Lieber the Centre Party was busily affirming its own nationalist credentials, as a new generation of bourgeois Catholics displaced the clerics and aristocrats from their remaining positions in the parliamentary leadership and demanded civic equality within the German nation rather than simply defence of the Catholic Church. It was no accident that the national achievements most prized by National Liberals in the 1890s – the Code of Civil Law and the two Navy Laws – were realized through parliamentary coalitions with the Centre. At the same time, this metropolitan parliamentary leadership still contended with a Catholic parochialism of some popular power, and it was from the latter that most of the surviving anti-militarist sentiment now came, voicing the traditional resentments of peasants and small tradesmen against the human and financial exactions which high military spending and mass conscription involved. Both the Army Bills of 1892–3 and 1899 and the Navy Bills of 1897–8 and 1899–1900 were accompanied by significant backbench revolts of this kind, based in the rural and small-town *Mittelstand* and peasantry of the Catholic periphery (Bavaria, southern Württemberg, Baden, Hesse and the Palatinate, to a lesser extent Trier and Rhineland-Westphalia). The inner circle of the parliamentary fraction devoted much effort to neutralizing this opposition, but there were always elements who were willing to take demagogic advantage of it, of whom Matthias Erzberger became the most prominent representative. Of course, the specifically anti-militarist element can be hard to distinguish in the general anti-Prussian, anti-plutocratic, anti-bureaucratic and anti-capitalist cast of this radical Catholic ideology. The campaign against colonial expenditures and colonial abuses between 1904 and 1907, orchestrated by Erzberger from the back benches against the express wishes of the parliamentary leadership, was perhaps the last gasp of this populist anti-militarist tradition.[17]

(4)   It is unclear how far there was a distinctive *socialist* anti-militarism On the whole, most Social Democrats remained squarely within the earlier tradition from the 1860s (hardly surprising, since August Bebel, Wilhelm Liebknecht and other grand old men of the movement were formed in the democratic patriotism of that period), aiming their fire at what were thought to be the survivials of an aristocratic-monarchical social order which had become irrational and anachronistic. Of course, Social Democrats differed from liberals in regarding the military autonomies and aristocratic traditions of the Prussian army as perfectly compatible with capitalist development (or 'modernization'), and the linkage between 'militarism' and the special interests of the armaments industries (particularly Krupp and Stumm, who were greatly demonized in SPD propaganda) was an axiomatic feature of socialist polemics, particularly at the time of the two Navy Laws in 1897–1900. But the connections which the SPD drew between militarism and capitalism were ultimately largely rhetorical, certainly in the case of Karl Liebknecht, the best-known agitator on the issue in the decade before 1914. Kautsky, for instance, while conceding (as any good Marxist of the Second International would) that militarism and imperialism had economic *causes*, denied that the international arms race was an inevitable feature of capitalist development, and tended to attribute Germany's more aggressive pursuit of expansionist policies to the peculiarities of the political culture – the 'particular predominance of militarism and bureaucratism in Germany and the relative lack of developed bourgeois-democratic institutions'.[18]

This stress on the Junkers-in-uniform as the real villains of the piece is particularly apparent from the SPD press, notably the famous caricatures in *Simplicissimus* and *Der wahre Jakob*. With it went a radical overestimate of the Prussian army's repressive capability in the event of a genuine confrontation with the labour movement (for example, a general strike against war), and the belief that the Prussian state was peculiarly reactionary in its willingness to resort to military intervention against the democratic opposition (by comparison, that is, with the British, French or American parliamentary states).[19] A definite shift in the SPD's official position in the aftermath of the 1907 elections (which had been fought very successfully against the party on the basis of stridently patriotic slogans), involving public recognition of the legitimacy of national defence, further illustrated the attenuated character of the party's militarism concept. On

92

the whole it is only with Rosa Luxemburg that we encounter a more serious effort to anchor the idea in a theoretical critique of capitalism.[20] What can we say to pull these different usages together? Despite certain weak tendencies towards a theory of the military under capitalism (which, with the exception of Luxemburg, usually amounted to the dogmatic assumption that large military establishments, arms expenditure and imperialist foreign policies were an inevitable feature of any society short of socialism), most discussions of militarism proceeded from an observable historical circumstance: that is, the military forms of the absolutist state in Eastern Europe and their partial survival into the nineteenth century. 'Militarism' was taken to mean the institutional excrescence of a feudal society in the process of reluctant dissolution. Of course, there is a definite teleology at work in this conception, hinging on ideologies of progress (whether liberal or socialist) and the widespread belief that societies moved historically through lower to higher forms of political development. More specifically, late-nineteenth century references to 'militarism' invoked the persistence of coercive or repressive practices at a time when government was expected to rest increasingly on mechanisms of mediation and consent, for which parliamentary representative institutions were thought to provide the logical framework.

In terms of the teleology, 'militarism' acquired its meaning from the unevenness of the developmental process. Putting this strongly, we might say that in this 'classical' usage 'militarism' refers to the 'feudal ancestry' of the Prussian state (in Perry Anderson's phrase) and its effects on the new Bismarckian constitution. It refers to the surviving autonomies of the army during the final stages of the transition from feudalism to capitalism, when the legitimacy of the new society was still being consolidated. Indeed, it was precisely the encroachment of a parliamentary mode of politics on the old monarchical jurisdictions in the half-century after the 1860s that gave life to the concept. As the above discussion has tried to suggest, military autonomies at the level of the state drew such polemical fire because they were felt to be out of line with the dictates of progress, violating the canon of modernity, compromising the integrity of liberalism, impeding the efficiency of a dynamic capitalist society. If we follow the logic of the argument to its destination, moreover, the liberal (and probably the socialist) critique of militarism clearly implies a 'normal' form of state power adequate to conditions of relative stability under mature capitalism, in which the army's behaviour, internal affairs and relationship to the civil powers were made the object of due constitutional regularity. Borrowing a formula of Eric Hobsbawm's (after Gramsci) we might describe that normality as an 'equilibrium of coercive and hegemonic institutions'.[21] That being the case, 'militarism' becomes a transitional phenomenon of the period when the 'equilibrium' was still under construction. In this sense it was simultaneously a structural and an ideological phenomenon, *both* an actual characteristic of the German state after 1871 *and* a distinctive ideological tradition of thinking about it.

II

The question now arises: how far is this an accurate, useful or interesting description of the imperial state? At one level the special position of the army in the state is beyond controversy. Article 63 of the constitution stated flatly that 'the Emperor determines the peacetime strength, the structure, and the distribution of the army'. This was backed up by the historic doctrine of the *Kommandogewalt*, the right to command in military and naval matters (what Messerschmidt calls 'this core of late-absolutist rule'),[22] which was not susceptible to strict constitutional definition. The royal military prerogative was guaranteed by a series of institutional arrangements, ranging from the Kaiser's own Military Cabinet (which controlled all army personnel matters) to the so-called *Immediat-System*, which gave individual commanders and military chiefs direct access to the Kaiser, and the Kaiser's personal headquarters or immediate entourage. All of these were devices for circumventing the previous responsibility of the War Minister which had been created by the reforms of 1807–13 to unify the military administration, but which under the new constitutional conditions of the Reich threatened to expose the army to parliamentary surveillance and even control. In a similar way the General Staff were gradually emancipated from the War Ministry's nominal authority and acquired direct access to the Kaiser.

These processes were greatly assisted by the army's role in unification and the resulting prestige of the elder Moltke and by Bismarck's willingness to undercut the authority of the War Minister in order to immunize the army from the scrutiny of the Reichstag. But they were also actively connived at by Albedyll, Chief of the Military Cabinet from 1871 to 1887, and Waldersee, who became Moltke's Quartermaster-General in 1882. Things were brought to a head in the formal reorganisation of 1883, when the powers of the War Minister were diminished and the Military Cabinet and General Staff elevated 'to the status of independent agencies responsible only to the King-Emperor'.[23] As Craig has argued, this also strengthened the army's independence from the civil authority of the Chancellor. Moltke had already claimed in 1870 (with indeterminate success) that 'the Chief of the General Staff and the Federal Chancellor are equally competent and mutually independent agencies under the direct command of Your Royal Majesty', and when Waldersee succeeded him as Chief of the General Staff in 1888 he made a concerted effort to use the new post-1883 dispensation to convert this claim into a reality.[24] One way of doing this was to use the military attachés of foreign capitals for the assertion of an independent foreign policy, and Bismarck and Caprivi defeated this offensive only with much difficulty (and no lasting resolution) between 1887 and 1891.

After 1891, of course, under Schlieffen's tenure as Chief of the General Staff, the army's definitive option for a two-front war strategy against France and Russia, while not formally subordinating the conduct of Germany's foreign policy, none the less structured the framework of possibilities the latter had to observe. The elaboration of the Schlieffen Plan between 1895 and 1906, with its implicit warranty for conceptions of preventive war against France, led to that narrowing of political options which permitted Ritter's celebrated contrast between *Staatskunst* and *Kriegshandwerk:* 'The onesided determination of political decisions by military-technical considerations replacing a comprehensive examination of what is required by *raison d'état'*.[25] Pursuing this argument, Wehler has related the predominance of such 'military-technical thinking' to two developments. On the one hand, 'the militarisation of Prussian society since the eighteenth century had placed the military at the peak of the pyramid of prestige, so that military thinking, behaviour and norms became increasingly prevalent in civil society too'. On the other hand, he distinguishes a 'parallel development' after the fall of Bismarck by which 'the politicians capitulated before military arguments masquerading as objective necessity'. This amounted to 'an abdication before the military, a betrayal of the responsibility for political coordination, a denial of political priorities', which for both Bismarck and Clausewitz were the 'inalienable right of the political leadership'.[26]

These arguments reflect a general interpretation of German history, in which the army appears as the most powerful institutional embodiment of pre-industrial authoritarian traditions (which elsewhere in the West had been swept away by a process of successful 'bourgeois revolution', it is usually argued), as the major source of resistance to democratization of the constitution, and as a powerful agency of socio-cultural conformity in German society at large. In most German historiography, discussion of militarism is linked to a class analysis of the Prusso-German state and the traditional power of the East Elbian landowning aristocracy. In one especially forthright formulation, 'Prussian militarism' was 'the means by which that nobility preserved its own privileged position against the demands of the new age of industrialism, capitalism and the rights of man. Thus it held together an authoritarian and increasingly antiquated social order. It helped to create a powerful state, but one which was increasingly incapable of overcoming its internal problems and contradictions'.[27] This echoes the thesis of Gordon Craig's classic work on *The Politics of the Prussian Army*, which represented nineteenth and twentieth century German history as 'one long constitutional struggle', in which 'progress towards democracy was blocked by the army's ability to resist parliamentary or popular control'. For Craig, the army was 'the strongest supporter of the monarchical state and the most effective and inveterate opponent of political change'. It was the centrepiece (as he put it, quoting Franz Neumann) 'of a structure which vitiated the attempts to create a viable democracy'.[28]

If we take the army's position in the imperial state, therefore, the prevailing uses of the concept of militarism certainly seem very apposite. Some historians make no bones about this, and simply describe the system of the *Kaiserreich* as 'feudal'.[29] At all events great pains seem to have been taken to preserve the integrity of the army against civilian interference or control, as 'an insulated body into which no one dare peer with critical eyes', as Hahnke (Chief of the Military Cabinet 1888–1901) put it.[30] At the same time, a number of qualifying comments might also be made:

(1) First, the argument from Prussian traditions can be all too facile. It is important to remember just how 'modern' the phenomenon of the mass conscript army actually *was*. In 1861 the peacetime strength of the Prussian army was 212,650, rising to around 300,000 on the eve of the war with France. Under the *Septennat* of 1874 it was 401,659; by the Army Law of 1893 it was 589,000; and after the increases of 1911–13 it was around 800,000. A military establishment of this size presupposed a bureaucratic organization capable of sustaining its efficiency and cohesion, and the Prussian army acquired such a structure in the reshaped General Staff under Moltke after 1857. Michael Howard argues persuasively that this was a distinctive strength of the Prussian army as it emerged from the contentious reform of the 1860s, so that '1870 was as much a victory for Prussian bureaucratic method as it was for Prussian arms'.[31] While the General Staff originated in the Scharnhorst era after Jena, its refashioning under Moltke was really quite a new departure. The rationalization was essentially a response to the incipient industrialization of warfare and the new dependence of military effectiveness on *Railroads and Rifles*, to use the title of Showalter's useful book.[32] The Prussian army harnessed the new technology of capitalism (railway transportation, the telegraph, heavy artillery, mass-produced rifled firearms, modern explosives) with exemplary speed and efficiency, and as the best general writers have argued (Howard, Hobsbawm, Best), the wars of German unification were the first fully 'technological wars' of the nineteenth century.[33] The new railways section of the General Staff was dramatic evidence of the Prussian army's capacity for innovation and, as Best says, in the war of 1870 'gave the world its first lesson in the time-tabled rapid mobilisation (only fifteen days) of a mass army'.

This is a salutary reminder. In 1960, after two monstrous episodes of German expansionist aggression when Western perceptions of the past became heavily impregnated with mythologies of German exceptionalism, the wars of unification looked like the triumph of all that was retrograde and archaic in the Prussian tradition – feudal, absolutist, reactionary, authoritarian, *militarist* in that original polemical sense of the term. At the time, the victory of Prussianism seemed different: modern, dynamic, powerfully attuned to the potentialities of the new industrial-technological era, the coming wave of the future. In Howard's view, the traditional military ethic of 'romantic heroism' had been 'steam-rolled into oblivion by a system which made war a matter of scientific calculation, administrative planning, and professional expertise', backed by a new machinery of mass conscription and one of the most comprehensive systems of elementary education in Europe. In these ways the Prussian conflict of the 1860s was as much between these new 'principles of industrialised warfare' (as Geyer calls them) and the integrity of the older Prussian military tradition (but which had itself been newly constituted only fifty years before), as it was between liberal constitutionalism and the aristocratic-monarchical Prussian state. For our present purposes we should note that in 1866–71 the decisive Prussian military institutions – 'conscription, strategic railways, mobilisation techniques, above all the General Staff' – were all innovations rather than traditional strengths.[34]

If this is so, we should be prepared to think again about exactly how appropriate a vocabulary of 'pre-industrial traditions' and 'feudalization' is for characterizing the army in the imperial period. As I have argued elsewhere, 'a "tradition" is only as old as the practices and relations which embody and transform its meanings', and in this sense the German army was formed more in the 1860s than in the Scharnhorst era, let alone in the mid-eighteenth or later-seventeenth centuries.[35] In fact, once we start demystifying the 'Prussian military tradition' in this way (if only as a heuristic exercise), it is interesting how many of its manifestations turn out to be innovations of the modern period. The rise of the General Staff has already been mentioned. We might also cite the strengthening of the General Staff and the Military Cabinet at the expense of the War Ministry (ratified in the 1883 rearrangement), the creation of the Kaiser's personal headquarters (in 1888 on Wilhelm II's accession), and the general extension of the *Immediat-System* over the period as a whole. This is pre-eminently true of conscription itself in its modern form, both as a machinery for delivering the enormous quantities of manpower now required by mass warfare (a new development again dating from the 1860s), and as a vehicle for social discipline, cultural homogeneity and ideological conformity in the new German society.

Of course, some of these developments had more to do with military efficiency and modernization than others. The *Immediat-System* and the post-1888 importance of the *Flügeladjutanten* were far more bound up with the vexed question of Wilhelm II's personal rule. This is not the place to discuss the latter, and it should be said that to a great extent (and despite the enormous residual powers available to the Kaiser through the

Kommandogewalt) the positions of the army and Wilhelm II in the state are separate questions. Thus it is clear that the imperial entourage was a very specific grouping, with radical differences in background and mentality from the officer corps at large, let alone the technical elite who attended the War Academy and joined the General Staff. Furthermore, Wilhelm II was an immensely volatile and ambiguous personality, reproducing in his prejudices and enthusiasms many of the cultural contradictions of turn-of-the-century Germany, and it is far from clear that he should be seen principally as a bearer of archaic Prussian traditions rather than, say, *sui generis*, an authentic child of his Wilhelmine time.[36]

In short, I am arguing for an experimental shift of perspective. For instance: it is at least worth considering whether some of the Wilhelmine army's classic archaisms, like the effort to maintain the 'aristocratic' élan of the officer corps, were less the linear or spontaneous persistence of a traditional or feudal mentality than a *deliberate* and *innovative* response to a new situation, one in which greater heterogeneity of recruitment, growth of technical specialization, complex divisions of administrative labour, the command of new technology, criteria of efficiency and managerial expertise, and so on, were all ensuring that the earlier and natural solidarities of Junker officers could no longer be automatically relied upon. In 1867 the officer corps was already split evenly between nobles and bourgeois, and by 1913 the proportion of bourgeois officers had risen to 70 per cent. Predictably the latter were unevenly spread across the army's different sections. Wholly unsurprisingly, the entourage and the Guards were bastions of aristocratic exclusiveness. On the other hand, by 1913 there was a bourgeois strength of 50 per cent in the General Staff, where one might have expected aristocratic preferment also to prevail, especially given the Military Cabinet's post-1883 control over appointments. The army's changing functional needs were also reflected in the numbers of officers with the Abitur, which for Prussia, Saxony and Württemberg rose from 35 per cent to 65 per cent between 1890 and 1912. Finally, in the years 1888–1913 only 10 per cent of War Academy entrants were the sons of landowners with another 29 per cent the sons of officers, while 33 per cent came from higher civil service families, and 15 per cent from a background in industry or trade.[37]

Now, when the 'social and professional homogeneity' of the officer corps no longer existed in the *classical* (early-nineteenth century) Prussian sense, its cohesion had to be actively worked at. Arguably, it had to be *manufactured* by regulations, codes of behaviour and ideological norms, and self-consciously 'aristocratic' values, which emphasized the separateness of the officers from civil society, were the materials most readily at hand. Given the *actual* existence of a titled aristocracy committed to the defence of certain institutional privileges in German society, therefore, the interior culture of the officer corps then took shape through a shifting combination of aristocratic and professional modes. So it is certainly not my intention to go to the opposite extreme by presenting the Prusso-German army as an unambiguously modern, bourgeois, and technocratic institution. It is more a matter of recognizing the existence of contradictory potentials and of tracing their dynamic interaction through the developing present of Wilhelmine time. What we can say is that the army was a major institution in a society increasingly dominated by the capitalist mode of production and experiencing a breathtaking industrial expansion. This not only created a new environment of cities and a more complex social structure, but also determined (broadly speaking) a new structure of politics. Given this changing context (invoked here admittedly only in the barest of terms), it would be surprising if the army's situation and conception of itself were not affected. Perhaps it is here, in the interior dynamics of the imperial period itself, rather than in the legacies of deep-rooted Prussian traditions, that the analysis should properly begin.

(2) In fact, some of the most frequently cited instances of military/militarist excess during the Wilhelmine period provide a good illustration of this ambiguity. For example: the Courts Martial issue in the 1890s is superficially impressive for what it reveals of the army's ability, acting through the Kaiser and his personal entourage, to defeat moves to bring it under civilian control.[38] Yet if we set aside our assumptions about the peculiarly reactionary qualities of the Prussian military, and concede the Kaiser's special interest in preserving his *Bestätigungsrecht* (the right to confirm verdicts of the military courts or not) as part of the *Kommandogewalt*, the striking thing becomes the radicalism of the proposed reforms. By the standards of most contemporary armies the Bavarian Code of 1869 was extraordinarily liberal, with its provision for public proceedings, rights of defence, civilian participation and independent due process. That elements in the Prussian army should have resisted the application of these principles to its own internal affairs was not surprising; that an intensive public discussion should occur, mobilizing a majority of the Reichstag, the Chancellor and the Ministry of State, and a sizeable bloc in the Bundesrat for a reform which was ultimately passed in a modified form, perhaps is. Armies in general, and particularly in this period, do not have a good record of respect for the rule of law in the liberal sense (German historians should not need reminding that the Courts Martial crisis reached its climax in 1897–8 as the Dreyfus Affair entered its most dramatic phase), and that a Prussian Minister of War should have initiated such a reform was an interesting departure.

Symbolically speaking, exposure of the issue (rendering military procedure, discipline and jurisdiction accountable to the standards legally established in civil society) was more important than the modified final outcome (passage of the reform, with limitations on publicity and preservation of the Kaiser's rights). Much the same could be said of the

Zabern Affair, normally taken as a major confirmation of the anti-militarist critique of the Wilhelmine power structure. Yet the actions of the military, the rallying of the High Command and the court circle, the knee-jerk reactions of Wilhelm II, and the unwillingness of Bethmann Hollweg and his allies to go public in their opposition, are perhaps less important than the general public storm, the no-confidence vote of the Reichstag and Valentini's private admission of 'flaws in the constitutional structure and in the world of ideas of our military'. To say, as Berghahn does, that the Reichstag vote was simply 'a scrap of paper' is a simplistic reduction of a more volatile and complex political situation.[39]

(3) There is a specific version of the anti-militarist argument which has to be taken seriously. Essentially, the argument is that as the domestic and international crises deepened after 1911, the isolation of state from society increased, and government became reduced to the brute realities of the constitution. In this view a key trend on the eve of the war (to which the Zabern Affair made an important contribution) was the strengthening of 'the army's position *within* the decision-making machinery', a trend whose sinister potential was fully exposed in the July Crisis and the German decision for war.[40] The so-called War Council of 8 December 1912 has a vital evidentiary place in this argument, for whether one takes the stronger view of its significance (Wilhelm II and the army took a firm decision for war which was implemented as planned aggression eighteen months later) or the weaker one (henceforth war was thought to be inevitable), the subordination of political to military considerations remains a central part of the interpretation.[41]

Now, one of the interesting features of this meeting was the absence of the appropriate civil heads (Bethmann Hollweg as Chancellor, Kiderlen as Foreign Secretary); it was attended by only Moltke (Chief of the General Staff), Müller (Chief of the Naval Cabinet), Tirpitz (Navy Secretary), and Heeringen (Chief of Naval Staff). But there are two ways of interpreting this fact: either it shows the ultimate primacy of the service heads in the decision-making machinery and thereby exposed the *real* power structure of the imperial state (the view of Fischer, Röhl, and implicitly Berghahn); or else the absence of Bethmann and Kiderlen shows precisely the opposite, namely the relative unimportance of the *meeting* (on the whole the view of Mommsen and Jarausch). At this point the published evidence is inconclusive, and the case for the meeting's formative impact on policy seems to be largely circumstantial.[42]

But even if we concede the army's growing dominance over foreign policy between 1911 and 1914, we still have to judge its position amongst the overall configuration of state apparatuses and their range of interventions in society. One answer to this larger question, the social-imperialist one which sees the decision for war partly as an intended solution to domestic problems, should probably be regarded as non-proven, at least in relation to the specifics of decision-making in the July Crisis itself. Belief in the inevitability and desirability of war were certainly linked in military minds to definite conceptions of social and political order, normally of a fairly right-wing kind, whether these were given a racist, anti-liberal, anti-socialist, or some other formulation. But to show how these ideologies became articulated into domestic politics in very concrete ways is no easy matter, and aside from general efforts to immunize conscripts against Social Democratic and other subversive agitation, *ad hoc* interventions against trade union or SPD actions, or more general (but apparently non-systematic) counter-insurgency preparations, we remain surprisingly ignorant about these matters. Of course, the latent powers of the army also functioned as a kind of general constraint on the political culture, to the extent that political actors internalized the anticipation of a repressive response to certain kinds of political opposition.

The most extreme forms of such a repressive response involved some kind of exceptional legislation against the labour movement (either a new Anti-Socialist Law or something practically similar) or the last resort of a *Staatsstreich*, a coup d'état, suspension of the Reichstag and reactionary revision of the Constitution. Much has been made of the latter by certain historians, suggesting that the 'permanent threat of *Staatsstreich*' in effect structured the actual political framework against certain kinds of consistent constitutional politics. This is an interesting idea. But most of the argument is again circumstantial, hinging upon the interpretation of somewhat cryptic evidence in a series of specific cases (Bismarck's barely articulated threats against the federal nature of the constitution in 1878–9, Bismarck's complicated manœuvring in the conflict with the kaiser in 1889–90, and the Pan-German initiative with the crown prince in 1913). My own view is that a limited form of the *Staatsstreich* fear persisted into the 1890s, reaching a sort of climax in the summer of 1897, before passing into abeyance for the next decade and a half. Between the significant watershed of 1897–8 and the aftermath of the 1912 elections there was a definite stabilization of political life within the given parliamentary forms. On the eve of the war, provoked by the party-political right's unprecedented political weakness, there was a limited resurgence of reactionary designs against the constitution, but it is not clear that they would ever have come to anything. To describe the threat of *Staatsstreich* as a permanent presence in Wilhelmine public life is almost certainly a dramatic exaggeration.

(4) In other words, to assess the position of the army in the state it is not enough to show its influence on foreign policy and its ability to keep civilians out of its affairs. It has to be considered in relation to the full range of things that German governments found themselves having to do. It is only then that the anti-militarist critique, with its intimations of feudalism,

pre-industrial traditions and late-absolutist survivals, can be ultimately judged. But, at the same time, it is also here that the least tractable conceptual problems arise. Not the least of the problems in discussing German militarism is the difficulty of defining what kind of state exactly the imperial state was. This is not the place to begin resolving this question, however, as it would take the discussion far beyond the reasonable bounds of the present account.

My own view, which I have tried to argue elsewhere, is that the strictly reactionary elements were considerably more isolated and less powerful in the political system, that the constitution was considerably more flexible, and that modernizing forces had achieved considerably less penetration – indeed that the traditional elements were considerably less 'traditional' – than most historians have tended to believe. In particular, the common equation between authoritarian social and political structures, right-wing politics and imperialist foreign policies on the one side, and backwardness, archaism and pre-industrial traditions on the other, is potentially extremely misleading. It may be, in fact, that precisely the most vigorous modernizing tendencies in the *Kaiserreich* were the most pugnacious and consistent in their pursuit of imperialist and anti-democratic policies at home and abroad. If this is so (or at least worthy of discussion), then perhaps we should think again about what exactly the 'traditional' and the 'modern' mean, both in general and in the specific context of the *Kaiserreich*. In that case the most vigorous militarists (both inside the army and out) might appear as less the upholders of cloistered aristocratic traditions than the energetic exponents of modern military practice.[43]

III

It remains to say something briefly about the social dimension of militarism, what the *Shorter Oxford Dictionary* calls 'the prevalence of military sentiment and ideals among the people', or as Endres put it, the 'state of mind of the non-military'.[44] The ways in which military values were transmitted in Wilhelmine Germany are well known, and are conveniently itemized in Liebknecht's famous pamphlet of 1907.[45] Conscription was the most obvious of these and most thoughts of propagating military values aimed at extending the scope of this direct surveillance, both before and after the brief period of military service itself. Contact with ex-soldiers was kept through the *Kriegervereine*, with some 2,837,000 members in 1913 in 31,915 clubs.[46] At the other end, every effort was made to use the schools. Moreover, on the eve of war plans were afoot for some form of compulsory military instruction for 14-20 year-olds to bridge the gap between school and army, and the launching of the *Jungdeutschlandbund* in 1911 was linked to this aspiration.[47] Less tangibly, military virtues might be promoted by organizations like the *Turnvereine* (gymnastic clubs), and support for a strong army by the nationalist pressure groups. Otherwise, the state's public ceremonial was heavily military, exemplified in the twin festivals of Sedan Day and the Kaiser's Birthday. There is a good atmospheric account of this official culture in Karl Retzlaw's memoir of the West Prussian railway and garrison town of Schneidemühl. Retzlaw's elementary school was the *Moltkeschule*. Mornings began with patriotic and martial songs, and Retzlaw called the brutal system of corporal punishment 'a training (*Dressur*) by the military state for the military state'. His class teacher ritually asked each pupil 'What do you want to be?', to which the obligatory reply was 'Soldier, Sir!'. The Kaiser's Birthday and Sedan Day were the high points of the year: weeks of preparation would culminate in huge military display and a grand choral extravaganza. The military presence was visible and obtrusive: drilling spilled across the streets and squares. Social precedence was symbolized by a narrow footbridge with room for one person to pass, where civilians customarily gave way to officers.[48]

To explore the questions raised by this abbreviated description would require another long paper in itself. Before 1914 (but not before the 1860s or after 1918) a combination of circumstances allowed the army to serve as an extremely potent socializing institution for the inculcation of various kinds of social discipline and ideological conformity, 'a school of national virtue', as Kiernan puts it.[49] But, without disputing the formative potential, we remain very ignorant about conscription's exact effects. Moreover, we would have to look very closely at the practice of schooling before generalizing from accounts like Retzlaw's, and our findings will vary enormously across the country. The domineering militarist presence in Schneidemühl owed a lot to the town's East Elbian location and strategic importance, not to speak of the Junker-dominated socio-political structures of the region; the army's presence would look less imposing elsewhere, say in the more liberal south or in the new industrial conurbations in the Rhine-Ruhr and Central Germany.[50] Each of these themes and others could be pursued with a great deal of profit. But here I shall confine myself to two observations.

(1) The first concerns an alternative military tradition, that of the citizens' militia or the volunteer army. In its early versions (in the English Revolution and the 'No Standing Armies' ideology) this was the very antithesis of militarism in its aristocratic sense. In seventeenth-century England and later in the French Revolution and early-nineteenth-century Europe, the citizens' militia was an antidote to the aristocratic-monarchical state, a way of *confining* the command of force within strictly defined limits. It remained popular in the labour movements before 1914, finding new expression in the SPD idea of the *Volksheer* or 'People's Army', and

Jaurès' idea of *L'Armée nouvelle*,[51] But it would also be interesting to explore the relationship of other voluntary formations (for example, the *Schutzvereine, Turnvereine* and early *Kriegervereine* in Germany, or the Volunteer Force in Britain) to the same tradition, given their origins in an explicitly liberal politics of local citizens' initiatives (in Germany between the 1840s and 1860s, in Britain in the invasion scare of 1859). In Germany, of course, such clubs mostly lost their early liberal affiliations. But, as Saul comments, the expansion of organized social militarism around 1900 under the auspices of the *Deutscher Kriegerbund* was partly a centralization and rationalization of these already existing foundations – 'the reconstitution of spontaneously created social, friendly and burial societies'.[52]

What we may be seeing in the Wilhelmine period is, in effect, a confluence of two distinct military traditions: that of the Prussian state with its connotations of aristocratic power and that of the independent citizenry with its earlier connotations of liberalism and local initiative. In that case, approaches which subsume the patriotic clubs within the Prussian army's aristocratic tradition (which in any case, as I have argued, was perhaps not quite as aristocratic as we think) should perhaps be rethought. For instance: in February 1903 the executive of the Prussian *Landeskriegerverband* issued a circular urging members to fulfil their duties as citizens in four key areas – members' welfare, general charity, patriotic propaganda and voting in elections. Now, when we find an organization of *this* kind affirming the value of voting as 'the most important activation of civil rights', we are dealing with something more interesting and complicated than just the old aristocratic tradition.[53]

(2) It is also worth mentioning a special aspect of this Wilhelmine civil militarism, so to speak, namely the mass propaganda of the Navy League and later the Defence League. Again, it seems to me that such organizations' popular appeal had less to do with any desire to follow aristocratic military models than with social and political aspirations which were impeccably bourgeois. We can see this in their social composition, in the character of their leadership, in the sort of ideology they generated, in their extreme disrespect for the traditional political establishment (which they regarded as effete and lacking in nationalist commitment), and most of all perhaps in their relationship to an earlier mode of liberal politics. Once more, there is no space to pursue this argument in the necessary detail here, and I have explored the subject extensively in my other writings.[54]

IV

So in the end, therefore, the original nineteenth-century usages of the concept of militarism may have entrapped our imagination in an unhelpful tissue of meanings. Liberal and radical critics (including most socialists) remained fixated on a phenomenon ('aristocratic', 'feudal' and 'late-absolutist survivals') which if I am right had already been greatly superseded before 1914. These dominant perceptions none the less persisted well into the 1920s (witness the satires and polemics of Kurt von Tucholsky and Carl Ossietsky), and have continued to structure our understanding of the imperial army and its place in state and society. Clearly, certain objective features of both the 1871 Constitution and the Wilhelmine polity provided a strong licence for this sort of analysis, and my wish is not to question the *existence* of 'authoritarian and anti-democratic structures in state and society' (Bracher). My aim (here as elsewhere) is simply to ask how else they might be understood, with a view to generating some new and interesting questions. It may be that the specific characteristics of the Wilhelmine military will otherwise be missed. Between the pre-industrial past and the Nazi future, the rather interesting Wilhelmine present has tended to get lost.

CHAPTER 4: NOTES

1   I am referring to G. Eley, 'The British model and the German road: Rethinking the course of German history before 1914', in D. Blackbourn and G. Eley, *The Peculiarities of German History. Bourgeois Society and Politics in Nineteenth-Century Germany* (Oxford, 1984), pp. 39–155. See also: Eley, 'Capitalism and the Wilhelmine state: industrial growth and political backwardness in recent German historiography, 1890–1918', *Historical Journal*, vol. 21 (1978), pp. 737–50; Eley, 'James Sheehan and the German Liberals: a critical appreciation', *Central European History*, vol. 14, no. 3 (September 1981), pp. 273–88; Eley, 'What produces fascism: pre-industrial traditions or a crisis of the capitalist state?', *Politics and Society*, vol. 12 (1983), pp. 53–82.

2   The literature here is already enormous. For representative examples: A. Eide and M. Thee (eds), *Problems of Contemporary Militarism* (New York, 1980); E. P. Thompson and D. Smith (eds), *Protest and Survive* (New York, 1981); New Left Review (eds), *Exterminism and Cold War* (London, 1982).

3   S. P. Huntington, *The Soldier and the State* (Cambridge, Mass., 1957); S. E. Finer, *The Man on Horseback* (London, 1962); M. Janowitz, *The Professional Soldier* (Glencoe, Ill., 1961); J. van Doorn (ed.), *Armed Forces and Society* (The Hague and Paris, 1968). There is a useful survey of the growth of the field in A. Abdel-Malek, 'The army in the nation: a contribution to the theory of power', in *Nation and Revolution* (Albany, NY, 1981), pp. 33–68. See also V. R. Berghahn, *Militarism. The History of an International Debate 1861–1979* (New York, 1982).

4   Berghahn, *Militarism*, p. 6.

5   See esp. J. J. Johnson (ed.), *The Role of the Military in Under Developed Countries* (Princeton, NJ, 1962); A. Perlmutter, *The Military and Politics in Modern Times. On Professionals, Praetorians and Revolutionary Soldiers* (New Haven, Conn., 1977); S. E. Finer, 'State and nation-building in Europe: the role of the military', in C. Tilly (ed.), *The Formation of National States in Western Europe* (Princeton, NJ, 1975), pp. 84–163. There is a good conspectus of this literature in Berghahn, *Militarism*, pp. 67–84.

6   There is again a useful survey of the literature in Berghahn, *Militarism*, pp. 85–103. See also D. Senghaas, *Rüstung und Militarismus* (Frankfurt-on-Main, 1972).

7   This paragraph is based on W. Conze's entry on 'Militarismus' in O. Brunner, W. Conze and R. Koselleck (eds), *Geschichtliche Grundbegriffe*, Vol. 4 (Stuttgart, 1978), pp. 7–22. Berghahn's discussion in *Militarism* is drawn directly from this. The main source for older discussions is E. Assmuss, 'Die publizistische Diskussion um den Militarismus unter besonderer Berücksichtigung der Geschichte des Begriffes in Deutschland und

seiner Beziehung zu den politischen Ideen zwischen 1850 und 1950', PhD diss., University of Erlangen, 1951. The following paragraph is based mainly on M. Geyer's continuation of Conze's article, pp. 22 ff.

8   Cited by M. L. Anderson, *Windthorst. A Political Biography* (Oxford, 1981), p. 135.
9   P. Wasserberg, *Gedankenspähne über den Militarism* (Mainz, 1874), p. 1 f.
10 Berghahn, *Militarism*, p. 9.
11 In his revisiting of his own classic 1941 article, H. D. Lasswell, 'The garrison state hypothesis today', in S. P. Huntington (ed.), *Changing Patterns of Military Politics* (New York, 1962), pp. 51–70.
12 Cited by Berghahn in his introduction to V. R. Berghahn (ed.), *Militarismus* (Cologne, 1975), p. 10.
13 All three citations from H.-U. Wehler, *Das Deutsche Kaiserreich 1871–1918* (Göttingen, 1973), p. 150.
14 Geyer, 'Militarismus', p. 33 f.
15 See the recent edition of his writings, L. Quidde, *Caligula. Schriften über Militarismus und Pazifismus*, ed. by H.-U. Wehler (Frankfurt-on-Main, 1977), the most important of which were originally published in the 1890s. See also R. Chickering, *Imperial Germany and a World without War* (Princeton, NJ, 1975).
16 Geyer, 'Militarismus', cit. at n. 7 above, p. 29. Pachtler's pamphlet was *Der Europäische Militarismus* (Amberg, 1875).
17 We know far less about this tradition than we should. The real historian of popular Catholic politics is David Blackbourn, but he does not treat the question of militarism directly. See: D. G. Blackbourn, *Class, Religion and Local Politics in Wilhelmine Germany. The Centre Party in Wurttemberg before 1914* (New Haven, Conn., and London, 1980); I. Farr, 'Populism in the countryside: the peasant leagues in Bavaria in the 1890s', in R. J. Evans (ed.), *Society and Politics in Wilhelmine Germany* (London, 1978), pp. 136–59; L. M. Schneider, *Die populäre Kritik an Staat und Gesellschaft in München 1886–1914; Ein Beitrag zur Vorgeschichte der Münchner Revolution von 1918* (Munich, 1975), pp. 304–12.
18 M. Salvadori, *Karl Kautsky and the Socialist Revolution 1880–1938* (London, 1979), p. 174 f. By comparison Steenson's work is superficial and confused on this issue: G. P. Steenson, *Karl Kautsky, 1854–1938. Marxism in the Classical Years* (Pittsburgh, Pa, 1978), pp. 174–80.
19 See esp. H. Bley, *Bebel und die Strategie der Kriegsverhütung 1904–1913* (Göttingen, 1975), which is extremely revealing in this respect.
20 C. E. Schorske, *German Social Democracy 1905–1917* (New York, 1955), pp. 59–87, provides a good discussion of developments in the SPD on this issue after the 1907 elections. For the contribution of Gustav Noske, see H.-C. Schröder, *Gustav Noske und die Kolonialpolitik des Deutschen Kaiserreichs* (Berlin and Bonn, 1979). For a recent discussion of Luxemburg, see R. Rowthorn, 'Rosa Luxemburg and the political economy of militarism', in *Capitalism, Conflict and Inflation* (London, 1981).
21 E. J. Hobsbawm, 'The great Gramsci', *New York Review of Books*, vol. 16 (April 1974), p. 42.
22 M. Messerschmidt, *Die politische Geschichte der preussisch-deutschen Armee*, in *Handbuch zur deutschen Militärgeschichte*, vol. 2, pt IV/I (Munich, 1979). p. 167.
23 G. A. Craig, *Germany 1866–1945* (Oxford, 1978), p. 161.
24 The Moltke citation is from R. Stadelmann, *Moltke und der Staat* (Crefeld, 1950), pp. 434–8.
25 G. Ritter, 'Das Problem des Militarismus in Deutschland', *Historische Zeitschrift*, vol. 177 (1954), pp. 21–48. The phrase *Staatskunst und Kriegshandwerk* comes from the title of his major four-volume work, translated as *The Sword and the Sceptre* (London, 1972 ff.).
26 Wehler, *Das deutsche Kaiserreich*, p. 156.
27 M. Kitchen, *A Military History of Germany from the Eighteenth Century to the Present Day* (Bloomington, Ind., 1975), p. 5.
28 G. A. Craig, *The Politics of the Prussian Army 1640–1945* (Oxford, paperback edn, 1964), pp. xiii–xvi.
29 For example, H. H. Herwig, *The German Naval Officer Corps. A Social and Political*

History 1890–1918 (Oxford, 1973), p. ix: 'The German system under the Second Reich, despite the claims of naval officers that they adhered to "liberal" and "cosmopolitan" ideas and traditions, remained essentially "feudal".

30 Chl. zu Hohenloe-Schillingsfürst, *Denkwürdigkeiten der Reichskanzlerzeit* (Stuttgart and Berlin, 1931), p. 116.

31 M. Howard, *War in European History* (Oxford, 1976), p. 101.

32 D. E. Showalter, *Railroads and Rifles. Soldiers, Technology and the Unification of Germany* (London, 1975).

33 Howard, *War in European History*, pp. 97–107; E. J. Hobsbawm, *The Age of Capital* (London, 1975), p. 79; G. Best, *War and Society in Revolutionary Europe, 1770–1870* (New York, 1982), pp. 297–300.

34 M. Geyer, 'Die Geschichte des deutschen Militärs von 1860 bis 1945. Ein Bericht über die Forschungslage (1945–1975)', H.-U. Wehler (ed.), *Die moderne deutsche Geschichte in der internationalen Forschung 1945–1975* (Göttingen, 1978), pp. 277 f.; Howard, *War in European History*, p. 101.

35 G. Eley, *Reshaping the German Right. Radical Nationalism and Political Change after Bismarck* (New Haven, Conn. and London, 1980), p. 353.

36 The 'personal rule' thesis regarding the position of Wilhelm II in the political system of the empire was advanced by J. C. G. Röhl, *Germany without Bismarck* (London, 1967). See also: J. C. G. Röhl (ed.) *Kaiser Wilhelm II. New Interpretations* (Cambridge, 1982), esp. Röhl 'Introduction', pp. 1–22, and W. Deist, 'Kaiser Wilhelm II in the context of his military and naval entourage', pp. 169–92; I. V. Hull, *The Entourage of Kaiser Wilhelm II 1888–1918* (Cambridge, 1982).

37 The figures originate in a variety of sources: K. Demeter, *Das deutsche Offizierkorps in Gesellschaft und Staat 1650–1945* (Frankfurt-on-Main, 1962); F. C. Endres, 'soziolische Struktur und ihre entsprechende Ideologien des deutschen Offizierkorps vor dem ersten Weltkriege', in *Archiv für Sozialwissenschaft*, vol. 58 1927), pp. 282–319; D. J. Hughes, 'Occupational origins of Prussia's generals, 1841–1914', *Central European Entourage*, pp. 190 ff. For the same problem in the navy, Herwig, *German Naval Officer Corps*, is the main source.

38 The Courts Martial conflict centred on the attempt of the government to introduce a standardized reformed military code of justice, both to establish uniform procedures for the army as a whole (Prussia, Bavaria and Württemberg maintained their own codes at the time) and to reform the regulations in force in Prussia. The crisis extended between 1895, when the War Minister introduced the reform proposal to the Ministry of State, and 1898 when the modified Bill finally passed the Reichstag. Essentially, the military entourage mobilized general opposition in the Prussian officer corps and egged the Kaiser into a full-scale confrontation with an originally united Ministry of State. There is a good summary of the course of the conflict in Hull, *Entourage*, pp. 215–25.

39 The most recent account of the Zabern Affair is D. Schoenbaum, *Zabern 1913. Consensus Politics in Imperial Germany* (London, 1982). The Valentini citation is from H.-G. Zmarzlik, *Bethmann Hollweg als Reichskanzler 1909–1914* (Düsseldorf, 1957), p. 124; the Berghahn statement is from V. R. Berghahn, *Germany and the Approach of War in 1914* (London, 1973), p. 178.

40 Berghahn, *Germany and the Approach of War*, p. 180.

41 The main sources for the War Council are the following: F. Fischer, *War of Illusions* (London, 1974), pp. 161 ff.; K. H. Jarausch, *The Enigmatic Chancellor. Bethmann Hollweg and the Hubris of Imperial Germany* (New Haven, Conn., 1972), pp. 126 ff.; J. C. G. Röhl, 'An der Schwelle zum Weltkrieg: Eine Dokumentation über den "Kriegsrat" von 8 Dezember 1912', in *Militärgeschichtliche Mitteilungen*, no. 1 (1977), pp. 77–134; D. Groh, ' "Je eher, desto besser!" Innenpolitische Faktoren fur die Präventivkriegsbereitschaft des Deutschen Reiches 1913/14', in *Politische Vierteljahresschrift*, vol. 13 (1972). pp. 501–21; A. Gasser, 'Der deutsche Hegemonialkrieg von 1914', in I. Geiss and B.-J. Wendt (eds), *Deutschland in der Weltpolitik des 19. und 20. Jahrhunderts. Fritz Fischer zum 65. Geburstag* (Düsseldorf, 1973), pp. 307–39; W. J. Mommsen, 'Domestic factors in German foreign policy before 1914', *Central European History*, vol. 6 (1973), pp. 3–43. There is again a useful (if inconclusive) summary in Hull, *Entourage*, pp. 236–65.

42 Mommsen's latest contribution to this discussion is fairly persuasive in this sense: W. J. Mommsen, 'The topos of inevitable war in Germany in the decade before 1914', in V. R. Berghahn and M. Kitchen (eds), *Germany in the Age of Total War* (London, 1981), pp. 32 ff.

43 The debate in the army after 1911 over the implications of a new large-scale expansion of its establishment is well known to have involved a conflict of exactly this type, in which 'traditionalists' opposed a big army bill on the grounds that the resulting infusion of bourgeois officer recruits would compromise the officer corps' aristocratic integrity. Interestingly (in the light of what has been said about the long-term decline of the War Ministry in relation to both General Staff and Military Cabinet), it was the War Minister who articulated this concern, whereas the most insistent advocates of the technical and strategic necessity of the new bill were to be found in the General Staff. At the same time, the recently founded *Wehrverein* (Defence League) led a vigorous public agitation in support of the bill and its advocates. Who were the real militarists: the 'aristocrats' or the 'modernizers'? There is a good recent discussion of these matters in R. Chickering, 'Der "Deutsche Wehrverein" und die Reform der deutschen Armee 1912–1914', *Militärgeschichtliche Mitteilungen*, no. 1 (1979), pp.17–24. B. R. Schulte, *Die deutsche Armee 1900–1914. Zwischen Beharren und Verändern* (Düsseldorf, 1977), is disappointing in this respect. I have tried to develop an argument concerning the character of the imperial German state in my contribution to Blackbourn and Eley, *Peculiarities of German History*, pp. 127–44, from which the preceding paragraph is borrowed.

44 Howard, sensible as ever, defines militarism as 'an acceptance of the values of the military subculture as the dominant values of society: a stress on hierarchy and subordination in organisation, on physical courage and self-sacrifice in personal behaviour, on the need for heroic leadership in situations of extreme stress; all based on the acceptance of the inevitability of armed conflict within the states-system and the consequent need to develop the qualities necessary to conduct it'. See *War in European History*, p. 109 f.

45 K. Liebknecht, *Militarism and Anti-Militarism* (English edn, Glasgow, 1917).

46 See K. Saul, 'Der "Deutsche Kriegerbund". Zur innenpolitischen Funktion eines "nationalen" Verbandes im kaiserlichen Deutschland', *Militärgeschichtliche Mitteilungen*, no. 1 (1969), pp. 95–159; H. Henning, 'Kriegervereine in den preussischen Westprovinzen. Ein Beitrag zur preussischen Innenpolitik zwischen 1860 und 1914', *Rheinische Vierteljahresblatter*, vol. 32 (1968), pp. 430–75.

47 K. Saul, 'Der Kampf um die Jugend zwischen Volksschule und Kaserne. Ein Beitrag zur "Jugendpflege" im Wilhelminischen Reich 1890–1914', *Militärgeschichtliche Mitteilungen*, no. 1 (1971), pp. 97–143.

48 K. Retzlaw, *Spartakus: Aufstieg und Niedergang. Erinnerungen eines Parteiarbeiters* (Frankfurt-on-Main, 1971), pp. 13–15.

49 V. G. Kiernan, 'Conscription and society in Europe before the war of 1914–18', in M. R. D. Foot (ed.), *War and Society* (London, 1973), p. 147.

50 For an insight into the kind of environment in which such schooling might have to take place and the kind of circumstances which might militate against the straightforward 'social control' function, see the excellent cameo of the Ruhr town of Herne in J. Reulecke, 'Von der Dorfschule zum Schulsystem. Schulprobleme und Schulalltag in einer "jungen" Industriestadt vor dem Ersten Weltkrieg', in J. Reulecke and W. Weber eds, *Fabrik, Familie, Feierabend. Beiträge zur Sozialgeschichte des Alltags im Industriezeitalter* (Wuppertal, 1978), pp. 247–71.

51 A. Bebel, *Nicht stehendes Heer!* (Stuttgart, 1898); J. Jaurès, *L'Armée Nouvelle* (Paris, 1911).

52 Saul, 'Der "Deutsche Kriegerbund" ', cit. at n. 46 above, p. 96.

53 Cited ibid., p. 136. See also H. Henning, 'Kriegervereine in den preussischen Westprovinzen', cit. at n. 46 above. There has been some interesting discussion recently of 'social militarism' in British history. See especially: A. Summers, 'Militarism in Britain before the Great War', *History Workshop Journal*, vol. 2 (1976), pp. 104–23, and 'The character of Edwardian nationalism: three popular leagues' in P. Kennedy and A. J. Nicholls (eds), *Nationalist and Racialist Movements in Britain and Germany before 1914* (London, 1981), pp. 68–87; H. Cunningham, *The Volunteer Force* (London, 1976); J. Springhall, *Youth, Empire and Society. British Youth Movements. 1883–1940* (London, 1977); M. Blanch, 'Imperialism, nationalism and organised youth', in J. Clarke, C.

Critcher and R. Johnson (eds), *Working Class Culture. Studies in History and Theory* (London, 1979), pp. 102–20.

54 In general, see Eley, *Reshaping the German Right*. The argument is also summarized in Eley, 'Some thoughts on the nationalist pressure groups in Imperial Germany', in Kennedy and Nicholls (eds), *Nationalist and Racialist Movements*, pp. 40–67.

5

Sammlungspolitik, *Social Imperialism* and the Navy Law of 1898

The detailed historiographical setting for this essay has already been described in the introduction to the volume and little point would be served by repeating those osbervations here. It is the longest and most detailed in the collection and, as the reader will quickly discover, by far the most specifically focused on a short period of time and a compact series of events. It is – I hope in a good rather than a bad sense – a densely empirical piece. What it lacks in conceptual maturity (chronologically speaking, it is the earliest essay in this collection, and also the first article I published), it makes good in concrete analytical detail. It is still, I think, the most detailed, broadly researched and authoritative account of *Sammlungspolitik* at the time of its inception in 1897–8. A rash of relevant monographs were published immediately after its publication (essentially the ones discussed in Chapter 2 above), but they contributed little beyond the existing picture my own article was intended to revise. Several further monographs also appeared, including two on the Caprivi years (Peter Leibenguth, 'Modernisierungskrisis des Kaiserreichs an der Schwelle zum wilhelminischen Imperialismus: Politische Probleme der Ära Caprivi [1890–1894]' [PhD diss., University of Cologne, 1975]; Rolf Weitowitz, *Deutsche Politik und Handelspolitik unter Reichskanzler Leo von Caprivi 1890– 1894* [Düsseldorf, 1977]), and two on Bismarck's politics out of office (Wolfgang Stribrny, *Bismarck und die deutsche Politik nach seiner Entlassung (1890–1898)* [Paderborn, 1977]; Manfred Hank, *Kanzler ohne Amt. Fürst Bismarck nach seiner Entlassung 1890–1894* [Munich, 1977]). But while they contribute some vital circumstantial analysis, they have little to say about the immediate context of 1897–8.

Otherwise, the competing interpretations have remained pretty much the same, and as the exponents of the so-called 'Kehrite' approach to these events seem fairly unrepentant, I welcome this opportunity to revive my critique. The essay was originally published in *Militärgeschichtliche Mitteilungen*, vol. 15 (1974), pp. 29– 63, and is reprinted here in an unrevised form.

I

A mounting body of new research concerning the structure of German politics before 1914 is rapidly becoming available.[1] Having first defined itself by a vigorous critique of established interpretations, moreover, this new work itself now contains the seeds of an alternative orthodoxy, whose central thesis is the continuity of bourgeois politics between the 1870s and 1918 and, more ambitiously, from Bismarck to Hitler. For theoretical inspiration its exponents have drawn heavily on the writings of Eckart Kehr, a previously neglected radical democrat who stood firmly outside the mainstream of German historiography in the 1920s.[2] The key concept yielded by Kehr is that of *Sammlungspolitik*.[3] Put simply, this meant the attempt to unite all so-called 'national', anti-socialist forces in a common front against democratic reform. Historically, it became the rallying cry of a protectionist and anti-socialist bloc, the political expression of an economic alliance between heavy industry and agriculture. Kehr developed this concept in a detailed analysis of the two Navy Bills of 1897–8 and 1899–1900. By investigating the reactions of the classes, interests and parties to the government's naval programme, he hoped to reveal their basic attitudes towards the social status quo and the possibility of political change – to draw 'a cross-section through the domestic-political, social and ideological foundations of German imperialism', as he put it.[4] In using the naval question as the vehicle for a structural analysis rather than a chronological one, however, Kehr provides little conception of the dynamic events which initially generated the policy of *Sammlungspolitik* in the summer of 1897. *Sammlungspolitik* appears as a system of economic and political compensations, a symbiotic reciprocity of social forces, pragmatically determined by a succession of responses to the compulsion of entrenched interests, rather than the careful rationalization or creation of policy-makers. But despite the absence of detailed discussion of the particular political juncture of 1897 in Kehr's writings, this has not prevented a highly schematic version of these events from developing around certain of his statements.

The broad outlines of this interpretation can be easily stated. *Sammlungspolitik* is to be identified with the political position developed by the Prussian Finance Minister, Johannes von Miquel, in the summer of 1897. It emerged from two programmatic statements, one in Solingen on the 15 July 1897 and one in the Prussian Landtag on the 23 July 1897.[5] They were delivered as part of a far-reaching ministerial reconstruction and constituted a first official declaration of policy by the new government. Essentially, they asserted the 'great community of interest' between agriculture and industry and represented an obvious attempt to conciliate the agrarian demands for greater state protection. In this sense the changes in the executive marked a clear turn to the right and a decisive reaction against the liberal economic policies of the previous years. The government was to be supplied with a firm base in the Reichstag by re-forming the Bismarckian Cartel, the socio-economic precondition for which was a new *rapprochement* between heavy industry and agriculture. *Sammlungspolitik*, a term which seems to have been coined by Miquel in the second of his two speeches, was the slogan devised for this purpose. A crucial step in the realization of the objective was taken between July and September 1897 when a consultative committee was set up in the Reich Office of the Interior, in which representatives of industry, trade and agriculture could participate in the formulation of commercial policy. The co-operation of heavy industry and agriculture was facilitated by the offer of economic incentives (naval expansion and higher grain tariffs) and the fear of socialism (electoral advances by Social Democracy and increased unionization). This new alliance of the propertied classes was directed consciously at the working class, and new legal restrictions were to be placed on the Social Democrats and their unions. In order to increase the support of the Cartel parties (Conservatives, Free Conservatives and National Liberals) in the coming elections of 1898, the conventional view continues, an aggressive foreign policy was proclaimed through the construction of a large battlefleet and the slogan of *Weltpolitik*. This elaborate compromise culminated in the collaboration of the *Centralverband Deutscher Industrieller* (CVDI) and *Deutscher Landwirtschaftsrat* (DLR), together with the parties to which they were generally affiliated, for the passage of new grain tariffs in 1902.[6]

In the first instance, therefore, *Sammlungspolitik* was a governmental strategy, conceived in the summer of 1897 by the leading elements in the Prussian Ministry of State, pushed through in a series of ministerial discussions in the autumn, and implemented in the elections of 1898. Miquel did not, of course, bring his idea into a complete vacuum, and was able to draw upon a large body of existing ideas. The belief that a coalition of industrial and agrarian capital was the political constellation most appropriate to the preservation of the Prussian-German state drew its pedigree from Bismarck's political reconstruction of 1878–9, and the ideological content of *Sammlungspolitik* in 1897–8 was a product of this formative period.[7] Its rhetoric was derived quite consciously from Bismarckian precedents.[8] In this way Miquel's policy grew out of a previous historical experience and could relate to a large body of existing political doctrine. Moreover, if strong links existed with Bismarck's 'solidarity bloc' of 1878–9, then the recent work of Dirk Stegmann has demonstrated that a similar continuity may be identified between 1897 and a later *Sammlungspolitik* immediately before 1914. Not only was the political debate of 1913–14 couched in the vocabulary of 1897–8,[9] but the exponents of a new *Sammlung* also reached back beyond Miquel to Bismarck in their search for historical legitimacy and an allegedly unbroken right-wing tradition.[10] Stegmann argues that this lineage lends an overall unity to the entire epoch of the second Reich: 'The ideology of *Sammlung* appears, in fact, as the key concept of an understanding of the socio-historical development of the *Kaiserreich* after 1879. It describes, in striking form, a "model" of political self-understanding which defined the politics of the ruling social strata in complete continuity until the break of 1918.'[11] He defines *Sammlungspolitik*, therefore, as the 'compromise-ideology of the ruling strata of industry and agriculture, with its basis in the common . . . anti-liberal and anti-socialist calculation'.[12] A firm coalition of heavy industry and big agriculture, rigidly committed to the preservation of the authoritarian monarchical state as a necessary bulwark against democratic change, remained a constant in German politics from Bismarck until the Revolution of 1918.

Stegmann's work, therefore, contains a powerful statement of continuity. He argues, for instance, that after 1897, 'despite occasional differences, there was never any cause to renounce the alliance of interests' forged by Miquel.[13] Its 'solid phalanx' remained firm and unshaken throughout the following decades.[14] The stability was overriding, and stronger than all temporary tremors on its surface, such as the conflicts over the Canal Bill in 1899 and the tariffs in 1900–2. Thus, when describing the foundation of the Fatherland Party in 1917, Stegmann says: 'the old Cartel of 1897, newly formed in 1913, lived on unchanged'.[15] From these remarks it will be clear that the period between Miquel's proclamation of *Sammlungspolitik* in 1897 and the successful passage of the new tariff settlement in 1902 occupies a key position in the analysis. After the confusion following Bismarck's dismissal, during which Caprivi and certain of his ministers seemed to be questioning the primacy of the forces represented by the *Sammlung*, this period saw a definition of policy, a perfection of tactics and a coalescence of forces which then determined the course of German politics, Stegmann argues, 'in complete continuity until the break of 1918'.[16]

In the light of recent interest in the idea of *Sammlungspolitik*, it is surprising that not much detailed work has been done on the critical years of 1897–1902. Although several important monographs on problems of Wilhelmine history have recently appeared, most have examined the genesis and efficacy of Miquel's policy only incidentally.[17] Stegmann's own discussion of this period is little more than an extended introduction to the main body of his analysis, which relates to developments after 1909.[18] Other research has also concentrated on this later phase.[19]

What we now have, I would suggest, is a generalization concerning the nature of *Sammlungspolitik*, which has been developed from a detailed examination of two stages in its history, that of 1878–9 and that of 1909–18. This generalization has also been applied to a third period, that of 1897–1909, without a similar basis of detailed research. Nobody has tried, for instance, to examine *Sammlungspolitik* in the concrete – that is, in the movements of the political parties and in the election of 1898. This lack of substance becomes even more serious in view of the pivotal role of these years in the overall analysis. A paradoxical situation has emerged in which a concept developed in the study of one period has been utilized profitably for an understanding of events both before and after, and, correspondingly, refined and deepened, has been brought back to is original context as a more hardened generalization. A fuller understanding of Bismarckian politics and the domestic prelude to the First World War has thus created a propensity to diagnose problems in the intermediate period with more certainty than current understanding actually allows. Most discussions of the *Sammlung* of 1897 are based on a set of assumptions drawn mainly from the invaluable but incomplete work of Kehr and the detailed findings of research on other periods. In particular, Kehr's polemical use of the formula *Primat der Innenpolitik* has inspired the development of a concept of 'social imperialism' which has been loosely and uncritically applied to Miquel's *Sammlungspolitik*.[20]

II

A common misconception concerning the nature of *Sammlungspolitik* in 1897 resides in the role which is normally attributed to Tirpitz's naval programme in its inception. This is a classic example, in fact, of the way in which parts of Eckart Kehr's thesis have been hardened into a dogma. One of the points on which previous historians have been most insistent is that the inauguration of German *Weltpolitik* and the corollary of vastly increased naval armaments are to be considered as an integral part of the political system conceived by Miquel in 1897. In particular, the plans for a large navy have been described as the positive incentive which helped draw heavy industry into coalition with the agrarians. In this way *Sammlungspolitik* can be presented as a means of defending the structure of the state by setting up a framework of conciliation from which heavy industry and agriculture each derived necessary sectional benefits. The revival of Bismarck's alliance of 1879, after its period of recession under Caprivi, was made possible by a series of reciprocal compensations. In Kehr's classic formulation of this thesis, Miquel's *Sammlungspolitik* had a[21] '. . . three-fold tendency: for industry the fleet, *Weltpolitik* and expansion; for the agrarians the tariffs and the upholding of the social supremacy of the Conservatives; and a consequence of this social and economic compromise, for the Centre the political hegemony'.

Kehr goes further than this, in fact, and describes the naval programme as the leading weapon of the ruling class in warding off the demands of the working class for social and political emancipation. A large fleet was regarded both as a necessary instrument of further economic growth and as a potential source of popular support for the parties of the *Sammlung*. Subsequent commentary on the events of 1897–1902 has made little effort to reflect critically upon the validity of these insights, and Kehr's classic definition has provided the conceptual framework into which recent researchers have normally inserted their findings.

Following Kehr, therefore, an imperialist calculation of this kind has been described on many occasions as the dominant feature of the strategy proclaimed by Miquel in July 1897.[22] But if we move from these generalizations to a careful examination of the available evidence, it appears that the political function of the naval programme has been overstressed in

Miquel's thinking. If naval expansion was seen to possess this clear political function, for instance, or was demanded by the CVDI as the price of its co-operation with agriculture, or at least as an economic necessity in its own right, then this might naturally be expected to have appeared prominently in discussions of *Sammlungspolitik* in 1897 and 1898. Unfortunately, the evidence for this is slight. Miquel made no reference to the political utility of the naval question in his two speeches of the 15 and 25 July 1897 which must be taken as the twin texts for the proclamation of the new strategy.[23] In each major discussion of policy in the Ministry of State no such function was ascribed to the naval programme.[24] Far from wishing to incorporate an ambitious Navy Bill into his *Sammlungspolitik*, Miquel, after a period of equivocation, tried to exclude it from his plans as completely as possible.[25] In the critical discussions with Eduard Capelle in Wiesbaden in August 1897, Miquel constantly emphasized the dangers of introducing a large Bill before the next elections – scarcely evidence that such a Bill played any constructive role in his calculations.

In fact, Miquel raised two basic objections to the proposals advanced by Tirpitz. On the one hand, he argued that the Catholic Centre Party, which supplied the key to the Reichstag majority, would never accept a Bill which removed some of the latter's already limited budgetary controls and carried such large costs. The Reichstag majority would never agree to its own constitutional emasculation, and if matters came to a dissolution even candidates sympathetic to the navy might be compelled to oppose Tirpitz's financial proposals to secure re-election.[26] Capelle commented that Miquel constantly returned to this point.[27] When Tirpitz indicated that he stood or fell on the issue, Miquel still reiterated the argument. Moreover, if a dissolution failed to produce the necessary majority for the Bill, the government would be faced with a situation similar to the constitutional conflict of the 1860s. In such a deadlock there would be no choice but a *Staatsstreich* and a dangerous leap in the dark. As Miquel said: 'Nobody can say what would have come out of the Prussian conflict [of the 1860s] if the war had not arrived'.[28]

The second and more important source of opposition feared by Miquel, however, was that of the agrarians. This was the point at which Tirpitz's plans for a big Navy Bill threatened to clash with Miquel's own grand design for a reconciliation of industry and agriculture. An ambitious scheme for the growth of the navy, with its stress on the protection of foreign markets, keeping the trade routes open, accelerating industrial growth and helping food supplies to beat an enemy blockade, threatened to make it harder rather than easier for the government to win back the support of the embittered agrarian movement. An intensive naval propaganda stressing the value of a big fleet as a function of Germany's expanding industrial and commercial interests would play straight into the hands of agrarian demagogues anxious to exploit any suggestion that 'rural', 'traditional' or 'Prussian' values were being submerged in the process of industrialization. Miquel repeatedly emphasized to Capelle that Conservative support for the Bill would be secured only with great difficulty.[29] The most he would concede was that enthusiasm for the navy might help to integrate the popular base of the Cartel parties more tightly together. But Miquel was firmly behind the basic demand: the propaganda for the Bill must at all costs 'proceed with the utmost caution', and 'any suggestion of offence' to agrarian susceptibilities must be avoided. The 'broad economic arguments' in favour of the fleet were 'not opportune'.[30] In the forthcoming elections the Navy Bill would provide a 'decisive slogan under no circumstances', for 'economic demands override everything else'. 'Agriculture' and 'commercial treaties' were to provide the supreme issues, although the naval question might provide a 'useful national ferment'.[31]

There is little substance, therefore, to the often-repeated claim that Miquel's *Sammlungspolitik* represented an attempt to bind *Weltpolitik* and anti-socialism together in the policy of the government.[32] When set against the preoccupations of Miquel's Solingen speech and the idea of 'bringing the parties together in the economic field', a big Navy Bill was separate, foreign and potentially highly disruptive. In the Ministry of State on 29 July 1897, in the Wiesbaden talks with Capelle, and again in the ministry on 6 October 1897, Miquel tried to relegate the Bill to a small auxiliary role in the government's system of political priorities. The naval idea would find no echo amongst traditional Conservatives and the Navy Bill could expect little principled commitment from the agrarians. Tirpitz and his collaborators in the Navy Office themselves recognized that their most serious problem was how to convince agrarians 'that the development of the Navy does not necessarily entail disadvantages for agricultural interests'.[33] If the government went to the country on the naval issue, the already narrow framework of consensus between Conservatives and National Liberals, agriculture and industry, would contract still further. The Navy Bill entered Miquel's calculations only in so far as it might disturb his strategy of *Sammlung*. Any help it might give in securing the support of industrialists would be offset by countervailing reactions amongst agrarians who were, after all, the prime object of his attentions.

Accordingly, Miquel and his collaborators in the Ministry of State systematically excluded the naval issue from their preparations for the elections between the summer of 1897 and June 1898. Thus the naval issue went totally unmentioned in the detailed policy statement drawn up by the ministry at the end of December 1897 and in Arthur von Posadowsky's important statement to the press at the start of June 1898.[34] Similarly, the naval question was not mentioned in the *Wirtschaftlicher Aufruf* (Economic Manifesto) of March 1898, which was pivotal to the entire campaign for a new *Sammlung*.[35] The whole naval issue played a completely insignificant role in the election campaigning between April and June 1898, when it was dwarfed by the dominant preoccupations of tariff reform and a possible threat to the franchise.[36] The striking feature of virtually all discussion of the Navy Bill, in fact, especially in ministerial circles, was the absence of attempts to integrate it within a single political framework with Miquel's plans for the co-operation of industry and agriculture. The two questions – a new *Sammlungspolitik* and the implementation of the 'Tirpitz-Plan' – were kept formally and tactically quite separate. The conventional model of the interdependence of naval expansion and tariff settlement as the twin components of a tactical unity, therefore, does not seem to fit the facts in 1897–8.

However, the argument has recently been given a new twist by the work of Volker Berghahn. In the course of a long and illuminating analysis of Tirpitz's naval policy between 1897 and 1908, Berghahn has made some important comments on the nature of *Sammlungspolitik* in 1897–1902.[37] He has since repeated them and hardened their implications.[38] He criticizes existing work for placing too much emphasis on Miquel's role as the architect of *Sammlungspolitik* in 1897. He argues that the basis of Miquel's idea was too narrow as it rested on the co-operation of only one sector of industry and big agriculture, which could not command a majority in the Reichstag. Consequently, Tirpitz put forward an alternative proposal – an alliance with a larger base, which could take in the Centre, which Berghahn claims was explicitly excluded from consideration by Miquel, broader sections of the urban bourgeoisie than had previously been possible, and possibly even the working class in the distant future. To fulfil this goal, Tirpitz hoped to use the fleet 'as a positive integrative factor'.[39]

For Berghahn, therefore, *Sammlungspolitik* began 'at the same time with and through the construction of the fleet'.[40] He sees the policy of naval expansion as a response to a 'latent crisis' in the structure of the state after the fall of Bismarck, in which the traditional ruling groups tried to defend their power against rising social forces.[41] In a big navy policy the government found an ideal means of preventing a democratization of the system, for with its help it became possible to introduce a new *Sammlung* of agrarians and industrialists: 'in the fleet there finally seemed to have been found, after a long period of crisis, a vehicle for the introduction of a new period of stabilisation'.[42] Berghahn describes this alleged strategy as a more advanced form of *Sammlungspolitik*, brought forward in the summer of 1897 by Tirpitz and Hohenlohe in opposition to that of Miquel.[43] The idea had emerged by '1897 at the latest' and 'in the end won the upper hand over the "small" solution of Miquel and became superimposed upon it'.[44] Berghahn calls the resultant constellation, which appeared in two historical variants, the so-called Kardorff-majority of 1902 and the Bülow-Block, a 'large' *Sammlung*, as opposed to the 'small' *Sammlung* of Miquel.

This amounts to an important revision of the view presented by

Stegmann and most other historians of the period.[45] It also represents a rather unorthodox use of the term *Sammlungspolitik*, which has normally been identified exclusively with the particular policies announced by Miquel in July 1897 – namely, economic protection and reactionary anti-socialism. As indicated above, these policies were also part of a specific political tradition in Germany, that which received its baptism in Bismarck's settlement of 1878–9 and which was anchored in the class alliance of heavy industrial and agrarian capital. The term, as it was devised and used in 1897 and the following years, therefore, had a singular meaning and denoted a very specific set of demands. In June 1897 these were well articulated by Wilhelm II during a moment of demagogic clarity: 'Protection of the national labour of all productive estates, strengthening of a healthy *Mittelstand*, unconditional destruction of all revolution, and the heaviest punishment for anyone who tries to prevent a neighbour from giving his labour'.[46] This crucial specificity imposes important requirements on the manifestations which the term may legitimately be used to describe. In particular, the policy of *grosse Sammlung* which Berghahn attributes to Tirpitz must be shown to have clearly fitted the interests and needs of those forces which the concept of *Sammlung* alone connotes. Yet if we try to identify the political ambitions of Tirpitz in these critical years of 1897–1902, it becomes plain that the available evidence cannot support the far-reaching claims which have been made for them. Moreover, and more important, an examination of the actual operation of the naval policy, the actual forces to which it appealed and the actual energies it released, will reveal that a strategy basing itself primarily on the naval programme, far from serving to fortify the existing order, implied and partially realized an important challenge to its stability.

A preliminary comment, which must cast serious doubts on the strength of Berghahn's critique of Stegmann, concerns the role of the Centre in the attempts to reconstruct the *Sammlung*. The claim that Miquel explicitly excluded this party from his plans constitutes Berghahn's most important observation on the narrowness of his conception.[47] Any such attempt to build a majority without the Centre, either for the passage of the tariffs or for the elections of 1898, would have displayed a colossal political naïveté, and all the evidence, in fact, shows that Miquel fully appreciated this. The decision to reach an accommodation with the party, moreover, was a logical consequence of Miquel's policy in 1897–8, particularly of his decisive rejection of plans to revise the constitution.[48] A definitive decision against *Staatsstreich* determined one in favour of co-operation with the Centre, for the only alternative to the latter, given the balance of forces in the Reichstag, was an abandonment of the constitutional framework which made it necessary. These options encapsulated the political dilemma of the government in the spring and summer of 1897, when the conventional political process was heavily overshadowed by the threat of *Staatsstreich*.

The dilemma was united in the person of Miquel in June and July 1897, and was finally resolved by the decision 'to go with the Centre'.[49]

By June 1897 Miquel had decided that he could only co-operate in a new ministry 'if it was resolved to come to an arrangement with the Centre', for 'without the concurrence of the Centre I consider a successful domestic policy to be impossible'.[50] In his first meeting with Capelle in Wiesbaden Miquel stressed that the Centre would be 'decisive for the success of any plan.'[51] In the second meeting he was even more emphatic: 'The Centre is the master of the situation'.[52] Moreover, Miquel and his close ally, Posadowsky, together played a crucial role in ensuring the support of the party for the Navy Bill. He advised Tirpitz to consult closely with Lieber, and himself held two vital meetings with the latter on 10 and 16 August 1897.[53] He also suggested making contact with Cardinal Kopp, and himself conducted negotiations with him during the autumn.[54] In the Ministry of State on 6 October 1897 he proposed the abolition of paragraph 2 of the Jesuit Law to facilitate an understanding, and in February and March 1898 again played an important role in securing the passage of the Navy Bill.[55] Similarly, Miquel was careful to ensure that the key position of the Centre was taken account of in the government's guidelines for the elections.[56]

There is no doubt that Miquel's personal relationship with Lieber was a difficult one, but this must not obscure his recognition of the need for co-operation.[57] The limited success of his overtures in 1898 was a product of forces beyond his own, Tirpitz's or any other minister's control – namely, the complex and conflicting requirements of the party's diverse social base, and its opportunist pursuit of party-political advantage. Tirpitz could offer no alternative prescription for winning the party's support: a third of the Centre deputies voted against the first Navy Bill, and at the time of the second in 1899–1900 Tirpitz was similarly unable to exert a decisive influence over the tactical idiosyncracies of the fraction's politics.[58] Moreover, Miquel fell in 1901, not through the successful assertion of some alternative strategy by Tirpitz and Bülow,[59] but as the victim of the heightened contradictions of interest between industry and agriculture which he had been unable to overcome. After his departure Bülow brought forward no new strategy, but merely began reconstructing the old one. The Kardorff-majority which emerged from his efforts in 1902 was merely the logical realization of the goal formulated by Miquel in 1897 – namely, 'to establish the economic policies of Prince Bismarck from 1879, and therefore under all circumstances to win the Centre.[60]

Purely in terms of its party-political structure, therefore, the constellation advocated by Miquel seems indistinguishable from the one which Berghahn attributes to Tirpitz and Bülow: a reconstruction of the Cartel buttressed by a looser association with the Centre. Moreover, there appears little evidence to support the view that Tirpitz tried to advance his naval programme as a 'domestic political crisis-strategy' in Berghahn's

119

sense – that it acted as the 'vehicle' for the introduction of a new period of stability or, more concretely, that it paved the way consciously for the tariff settlement in 1902. Tirpitz himself gave no indication that he saw his plans as part of a larger political strategy or that he held any conception of the unity of industry and agriculture in the specific sense implied by the idea of *Sammlung*. The many discussions he conducted around the fortunes of the Navy Bill were all concerned with matters internal to the question of naval expansion. The aim of the Navy Office in 1897–8 was to construct a majority for the passage of the Bill; there is no evidence that Tirpitz wished to use that majority for other political purposes, such as the tariff settlement, or to institutionalize it in the manner suggested by Berghahn.[61]

There is little indication, in fact, that Tirpitz himself saw beyond the naval issue in any coherent way at all. In his own correspondence in the summer and autumn of 1897, where the Bill was discussed intensively in all its aspects, the possible function of the Navy Bill in a strategy of *Sammlung* played no role whatsoever. The discussion revolved exclusively around the tactics necessary to bring through the Navy Bill as such. At no point during the critical ministerial discussions, when Tirpitz had to defend his plans against the strong scepticism of his colleagues, did he suggest that these could lay the foundations for a broader long-term strategy.[62] It is certainly possible that Tirpitz held a strong belief in the social-imperialist potential of the naval programme, and Berghahn has gathered some evidence to suggest that this was so.[63] But we need far more than this to demonstrate that in 1897 Tirpitz saw this as the key to the construction of a stable political coalition for general purposes extending beyond his own departmental concerns. No evidence has been published to suggest that Tirpitz projected such an idea in discussions of high policy between 1897 and 1902 or that he advanced it consciously as an alternative to the strategy of Miquel.

Moreover, those political views which can be attributed to Tirpitz on the basis of the available evidence suggest that the ideological content of his naval plans was singularly unsuited to reunite the fragmented Bismarckian coalition. Tirpitz's entire philosophy was guided by a belief in a 'vitally necessary, worldwide expansion of German economic influence'.[64] This was the indispensable backcloth to his naval ideas, for which the 'interdependence of economy and sea-power'[65] was axiomatic: the navy had a vital interest in the development of overseas trade 'because its existence depends on the latter's prosperity'.[66] Tirpitz's undoubted commitment to the inevitability, the desirability and, above all, the actuality of Germany's transformation from an agricultural into an industrial nation had important implications.[67] For an invocation of large-scale societal change and the definition of the fleet as a function of this economic development would expose the tension which lay at the heart of the governmental coalition of heavy-industrial and agrarian interests – that between the exponents of a continuing process of industrialization and traditionalist conservatives who refused to accept the disappearance of pre-industrial values.[68] From those factors of German economic life which Tirpitz listed the navy as serving – sea trade, export industry, deep-sea fishing, colonies – agriculture was conspicuously absent.[69] For Tirpitz, 'Germany's development into an industrial and trading nation' was 'irresistable like a law of nature'. It was impossible 'to dam', for 'the process would flow on regardless'. Agriculture could be maintained if the chance arose, but it was 'not part of the great necessary development'.[70]

Such views contrasted starkly with those of agrarian conservatives. The latter easily grasped the implications of the naval programme which Tirpitz brought before the Reichstag in 1897. As one agrarian stated in opposing the Bill in its third reading: this was 'just one more step along the path trodden by the disastrous policy of commercial treaties'. Its passage would 'lead us still further along the path of development towards a state of industrialists and whosesale traders'. He ended: 'The decline of our German agriculture will be the decline of our German nation, of our fatherland; we don't want an industrial state, but want to remain what we were in olden times, an agricultural state'.[71]

The sources suggest that Tirpitz himself followed through the logic of his views in 1897–1900 by seeking the support of those groups with a strong ideological commitment to the concept of the *Industriestaat* and a corresponding hostility to that of the *Agrarstaat*. He voiced his mistrust of Miquel's economic policy – and therefore of the policy of *Sammlung* – at a very early stage. He pointed out that the decision 'to inaugurate a commercial policy which is likely to diminish our trade and export industry substantially' constituted 'a contradiction with this and for that matter with any other Navy Bill'. If Miquel's protectionist plans were implemented, 'any success' for the naval programme 'would appear to me to be impossible, for the fleet is after all a function of our sea interests'.[72] The tenuous compatibility of the naval programme with any genuine strategy of *Sammlung* between 1897 and 1902 could scarcely be more sharply stated.

Moreover, at this same time the anti-protectionist, anti-agrarian, anti-*Sammlung* tendencies which resided indisputably in Tirpitz's efforts to wring every ounce of propagandist value out of the economic motivation of the Navy Bill came clearly to the fore in the activities of his advisers. August von Heeringen, for instance, proposed the formation of an industrial-commercial pressure group to further the Bill under the name of Association for the Protection of Foreign Trade.[73] Shortly afterwards he urged Tirpitz that it was important to combine the campaign for the Bill with the movement in support of the existing commercial treaties.[74] The overall political context accentuates the meaning of these ideas. In August 1897 an attempt to organize economic opinion for the defence of the trading treaties actually materialized in the shape of the *Centralstelle zur*

Vorbereitung von Handelsverträgen.[75] It represented mainly the exporting industries fundamentally opposed to the reintroduction of high agricultural tariffs, was explicitly anti-agrarian and was boycotted by the CVDI.[76] This was the first appearance of an embryonic counter-coalition to that of the classic heavy-industrial-agrarian *Sammlung*. It documented adequately the convergence of the naval plans with the attempts to create a focus of opposition to the new *Sammlungspolitik*.

It is scarcely surprising, therefore, that the CVDI, which was in the process of committing itself to a revision of the commercial treaties, at first proved hard to engage for Heeringen's plans, which were finally realized in the Kaiserhof demonstration of January 1898.[77] This was the classic manifestation of those forces successfully mobilized by the Navy Bill, revealing both the apparent strength and the actual weakness of the naval issue as a leading instrument of government politics. On the one hand, it seemed capable of bringing together groups who were normally separated by deep divisions of interest – protectionists and free traders, large- and small-scale industry, heavy- and light-industrial interests, right- and left-wing liberals. In this way the naval issue seemed to offer a basis for the union of the bourgeois parties. As Adolph Woermann said in his address in the Kaiserhof, the fleet was a 'symbol of the future unity of Germany'.[78] But, on the other hand, it was equally clear that this was a juncture on one issue only, which could not be repeated on others. The problems which beset the organization of the meeting had been an indication of this and the bitter recriminations over tariff reform several months later, accentuated dramatically in the elections of June 1898, revealed that the much-vaunted 'unifying power' of the naval idea had a very tenuous reality. Above all, the spokesmen of organized agriculture had been conspicuously absent from the sponsors of a demonstration which they could hardly fail to view with suspicion. Indeed, the most enthusiastic patrons of the idea had been attracted not least by the possibilities of converting the naval issue into the vehicle for a strong anti-agrarian front.[79] The political constellation briefly glimpsed in the Kaiserhof meeting had a clear orientation, which 'threatened to tear apart the entire network' so carefully woven by Miquel.[80] One agrarian statement put this more sharply: 'A *Sammlung* around the naval demands is impossible. The *Sammelpunkt* [rallying point] lies elsewhere'.[81]

There is much evidence that both Tirpitz himself and his closest collaborators recognized and consciously cultivated the anti-agrarian potential of the naval issue. As Heeringen pointed out for the benefit of his successor, 'sea interests and the efforts of the agrarians' were incompatible, and this clash would inevitably grow worse during the debate over new tariffs.[82] As the central domestic-political contradiction between 'agrarianism and industrialism' became more acute the Navy Office must make a clear choice in favour of the 'industrial direction' and a strong effort to win the support of those 'leftist' forces in German industry which 'saw in all agrarian efforts something hostile to themselves'. Heeringen, like Tirpitz, believed in the desirable long-term necessity of the victory of industrialism. During 1901 his successor, Hollweg, went further and recommended the positive intervention of the Navy Office in the tariff question in order to strengthen the exporting interests in their struggle against the agrarians. He argued that the Navy Office must base itself increasingly and unequivocally on the side of the 'leftist' elements, for the key political question was whether 'we can become master of this opponent'.[83]

This was reflected in the specific negotiations conducted with the political parties for the passage of the two Navy Bills. In 1897–8 Tirpitz devoted special care to the cultivation of the *Freisinnige Vereinigung*.[84] The same concern was reflected in his relations with the trading communities of Hamburg and Bremen, and with individuals like Albert Ballin, Adolph Woermann, Fritz Hönig and, above all, Ernst von Halle.[85] In 1899–1900 this was even more marked. The second Bill was passed this time with the unreserved support of the *Freisinnige Vereinigung*, and the Navy Office had strengthened and broadened its contacts with the bourgeois left. To the older contacts, moreover, had been added new ones with social-reformist academics and individuals on the fringe of the *National-Sozialer Verein*.[86] There is much evidence of Tirpitz's close ideological affinity with the Barth–Rickert left liberals at this time, and this association must be defined as qualitatively different from that with the Centre. The latter was determined, above all, by parliamentary expedience: the naval programme held little attractive power for the party, and the ongoing use of threats and cajolery could not prevent between a quarter and a third of its deputies from opposing the Bills in both 1898 and 1900.[87]

In reality, however, Tirpitz left his own position ambiguous. Berghahn has pointed out very well, for instance, the anti-parliamentary, anti-democratic dynamic of his naval programme, and there is no doubt that he was a convinced supporter of monarchy and authoritarian rule.[88] But, on the other hand, he was equally clearly a firm supporter of industrial growth and argued that the agricultural sector could be protected only in subordination to this principle.[89] The tension between these two components in his ideological make-up made him reluctant to embrace the full implications of the proposition that 'everything which goes by sea is anti-agrarian and anti-Junker' – namely, a decisive break with the tradition of *Sammlung* and a radical overhaul of the state.[90] Tirpitz was thus a contradictory figure in many ways very similar to Caprivi, but unlike the latter was able to survive in office behind the shelter of his limited departmental preoccupations.

But while Tirpitz personally was able to evade the resolution of a certain ideological tension, this could not prevent the wider political reverberations of his policies, which posed an implicit threat to the cohesion of

Sammlung. The dynamic released by these in 1899–1900, for instance, was strong enough to force even Pan-Germans like Ernst Hasse into an anti-agrarian stance by submitting them to its political logic.[91] The tensions engendered by the campaign for the second Bill were worked out most dramatically in the crisis of the Navy League in November–December 1899, when an entrenched leadership closely observant of the dictates of *Sammlungspolitik* was unseated, with the deep complicity of Tirpitz, by a populist coalition of a strongly anti-agrarian hue.[92] On the resolution of this crisis one supporter of the *Sammlung* warned the partisans of 'national' policies to 'make sure that free-trading and socialist contraband is not smuggled in under the flag of the naval movement'.[93] This was echoed sarcastically by Viktor Schweinburg, the unseated secretary of the *Flottenverein:* 'It would have been so nice if in the shade of the Navy Bill free-trading weeds could be sown in the corn of the policy of *Schutz der nationalen Arbeit*'.[94] It was here that Tirpitz came closest to grasping the full import of his own policies.[95] The strength of these partially realized tendencies, moreover, was only the logical outcome of the principle evinced by Capelle in January 1898: 'Navy and liberal ideas belong together. A strong popular movement for the navy also strengthens the movement for the commercial treaties'.[96]

This discussion is important, for it helps to explain why the naval issue could never provide the rallying banner for a new *Sammlung* in 1897 and the following years and why Tirpitz could never become its high priest. Contrary to the conventional view, it appears to have been difficult to use *Weltpolitik* to build a new *Sammlung*, for it released energies and mobilized forces which were hostile to the essential principles of industrial-agrarian co-operation. Moreover, this discrepancy between the political reality of 1897–1902 and the received views concerning the function of the naval policy becomes all the more striking if we examine the concept which has normally been used to explain that function – namely, 'social imperialism'.

This has been defined by Hans-Ulrich Wehler as 'the diversion outwards of internal tensions and forces of change in order to preserve the social and political status quo', and a 'defensive ideology' against 'the disruptive effects of industrialisation on the social and economic structure of Germany'.[97] Using Bismarck's colonial policy as his model, Wehler describes a consistent attempt to use popular enthusiasm for foreign policy as 'a long-term integrative factor which helped stabilise an anachronistic social and power structure'. He has claimed that mass support for expansion abroad was successfully used to 'block domestic progress' and 'social and political emancipation'.[98] It was an effective 'technique of rule' applied by Bismarck, by Miquel, Bülow and Tirpitz, and later by Hitler to defeat 'the advancing forces of parliamentarisation and democratisation'.[99] It was responsible for reconciling the working class to the status quo and the victory of reformism in the SPD, and its consequences were so far-reaching that German history from Bismarck to Hitler may be defined in terms of a 'red thread of social imperialism'.[100] This definition has been accepted by Berghahn, Stegmann and most other historians.[101]

This definition of social imperialism, particularly when applied to the Navy Bill of 1898 and the inception of *Weltpolitik*, contains a serious confusion. It has been defined in terms of a reactionary attempt to stave off social and political reform. This determined a rigid hostility to both socialist and left liberal demands, to both workers' and parliamentary control. But in seeking to identify the idea with the perpetuation of authoritarian structures and an intransigent rejection of reform, Wehler has ignored the existence of a social imperialism which, on the contrary, willingly embraced the need for reform. In calling social imperialism the defence of 'an anachronistic social and power structure' against democratization and social reform, Wehler has obscured the fact that an extremely coherent social-imperialist impulse came from precisely those elements which were starting to demand such things. In the current discussion, in fact, the term has been used to describe two fundamentally separate conceptions of the domestic-political utility of imperialist expansion. This discussion has concealed two distinct variants of social imperialism in Germany – that described by Wehler and Berghahn in which expansion abroad was used to prevent reform at home; and a second form, in which the two went constructively together. As Ernst von Halle, a close adviser to Tirpitz and a powerful exponent of a reformist social imperialism, put it: 'one group wants to divert interest from the expansion of social legislation at home, while the other hopes to benefit its ambitious social policy at home precisely by means of a strong power politics abroad'.[102]

The existence of a social imperialism bound to reformist perspectives must introduce a serious qualification into the way in which the idea has previously been used. It is fundamentally mistaken, for instance, to define German history by a dichotomy between a 'social-imperialist' direction and a 'social-reformist' one, when the social reformists were themselves operating on the basis of a ruthlessly consistent social-imperialist synthesis of 'power abroad and reform at home'.[103] More concretely, this confusion of meanings has fostered a misinterpretation of the function of the naval programme. Previous historians have used the idea exclusively to characterize the ambitions of the defenders of the status quo and the exponents of *Sammlung*. It has already been suggested above that a political exploitation of the two Navy Bills stood at variance with such aims, however, and an exploration of the diverse sources of social-imperialist calculations between 1897 and 1902 will strengthen this proposition.

Volker Berghahn, for example, has suggested that

the naval policy was potentially suited also to manoeuvre the . . . fourth estate in the direction of the power-political status quo. With the help of a powerful fleet . . . the monarchy wanted to create a rising standard of living for all, through which the German workers would be better placed and satisfied materially. It was hoped that an economically contented working population could be led into the state without it being necessary to change the latter's received structures of rule.[104]

An early 'politics of economic growth' is a crucial feature of the political goals which Berghahn ascribes to Tirpitz. Yet an analysis of the real political context shows that the adoption of such a course would have determined forms of action and political alliances which Tirpitz, as the agent of 'Prussia-Germany and a strong monarchy,[105] could never have undertaken. The starting-point in Berghahn's whole analysis is the attempt to preserve an existing social order, an essential part of which was the special position of the Junker. Yet the attempt to advance the working class materially, which he attributes to the defenders of the status quo, threatened, in the form in which it may actually be found in 1897–1902, to bring that social order explicitly into question. Any genuine attempt by Tirpitz or Bülow to implement such a policy would have driven them into political dependence on those forces aiming at the destruction of the heavy-industrial-agrarian *Sammlung* rather than its perpetuation – that is, left liberals around Theodor Barth and Heinrich Rickert in the *Freisinnige Vereinigung*, and Naumann and the academic social reformers who stood close to his *National-Sozialer Verein*. Tirpitz may have realized this, Bülow certainly did. The latter was acutely aware of the conservative forces in the court, the bureaucracy and the army which precluded such a juncture. This fact has an overriding importance for an evaluation of Berghahn's analysis: the elements of 1897–1902 which actually espoused the 'exploitation of the expansionist forces of the industrial economy' were the bitter critics of the *Sammlung*.[106]

There was a fundamental political gulf between a belief in the utility of nationalist sentiments for increasing the popular support of the Cartel parties – that is, the concrete meaning of Wehler's notion of social imperialism in the conditions of 1897 – and the efforts of liberal imperialists to forge a novel programme of overseas expansion and far-reaching domestic reform. At the end of the 1890s a political grouping began to cohere, no less committed to the ideal of a *Weltpolitik* which could 'unite the entire impetus of the nation and all its layers and overcome the internal divisions which threaten it',[107] but convinced that any serious attempt to bind the working class to capitalist property relations presupposed a partial dismantlement of the repressive apparatus of the state and a genuine effort at social reform. These liberal imperialists at first comprised little more than a miscellany of intellectuals, engaged academics and political mavericks, but were able both to rationalize previous developments, anticipate later ones and provide a theoretical position around which political forces could begin to regroup. Friedrich Naumann argued that nationalist exhortations, or even rising material standards, might never seduce workers away from socialism by themselves; it might be necessary to combine them with a progressive social policy. Naumann and his co-thinkers began to develop an integrated programme of imperialist expansion and far-reaching domestic reforms: the first was projected as a necessity of national existence in the age of *Weltpolitik*, the second would help to win popular support. The systematic propagation of both would destroy the appeal of revolutionary socialism to the working class. As one exponent of this view put it: 'World policy and social policy are the two poles in which one and the same power manifests itself. The national drive abroad must be accompanied by social progress at home.'[108]

Naumann's particular achievement of the late 1890s was to develop a social-imperialist synthesis of 'power abroad and reform at home', which would act as an alternative to the conservative *Sammlungspolitik* to which the idea of social imperialism has recently been attached. The demand for tax reform was the salient feature of this programme, for it was axiomatic to Naumann's politics that the destruction of agrarian privileges in Prussia was a necessary precondition for both further economic growth and working-class support. His twin domestic aims – the cultivation of reformism in the labour movement and the dismantlement of the historically obsolete primacy of the Junker – led him into a decisive confrontation with the heavy-industrialist and agrarian supporters of Miquel's *Sammlungspolitik*. When he asserted that 'Our bread will depend on our ships', this general commitment to an expanding industrial economy also reflected a determination to pull down the tariff walls which protected the Junker's status and kept the bread prices high'.[109] Support of the fleet for Naumann and his supporters was predicated in this way on a larger view of Germany's future political development. As Max Weber, who decisively influenced Naumann's world view, put it: 'Not a policy of so-called "*Sammlung*" with its anti-capitalist slogans, but only a decisive pursuit of the consequences of our powerful bourgeois-industrial develop-ment can lend sense for the bourgeois class to the demand for sea-power. For the protection of ground-rents we need no fleet.'[110]

From this discussion it will become clearer why the Navy Bill was so unsuited to rally the forces of the *Sammlung*, and why Miquel was so suspicious of any attempt to make the issue the centre of the government's policies in 1897: the Bills were appropriated by liberal imperialists, with the partial complicity of the Navy Office, as the vehicle for an ongoing critique of the policies of *Sammlung*. The naval issue threatened to provide a broad platform for the liberal opponents of agrarian protection and the stimulus for an embittered political debate which might polarize the two wings of Miquel's nascent coalition. Too great an emphasis on the naval issue threatened in this way to canalize anti-agrarian sentiments. This was even more obvious in 1899–1900 than in 1897–8. The political alignments produced by the Navy Bills did not correspond to those required by a genuine *Sammlungspolitik*: they divided the Centre, sent a minority of agrarians into opposition, and proved attractive only to the *Freisinnige Vereinigung* amongst those forces not already embraced by Miquel's conception.

The real effect of the naval issue in 1897–1902 was not any unifying bond between heavy industry and agriculture but the definition of an embryonic alternative to this hegemonic coalition. It provided the context within which opposing prescriptions for Germany's future economic and political development worked out their points of conflict. In particular, it helped stimulate the first signs of a future juncture between rising industries, liberal imperialists and the reformist labour bureaucracy. The failure of these forces to assert themselves against the dominant coalition at this stage and their evident political fragmentation are no argument against their existence: the crucial point is that a coherent political alternative, basing itself on the experience of the Caprivi interlude, had now been posed. The exponents of this alternative were the only politicians in 1897–1902 consistently advocating the politics of economic growth which Berghahn claims to see in Tirpitz's naval plans. In the real circumstances of 1897–1902 an exploitation of the naval issue meant an alliance with these forces. But as Kehr said, *Sammlungspolitik* had nothing to do with such an alliance: it was the antithesis of a 'forward-looking policy which grasped the necessity of an industrialization of the Reich'.[111]

The point of these observations on the political function of the naval programme between 1897 and 1902 is to suggest that its importance for the development of a new *Sammlungspolitik* has been overestimated by previous historians. It is clear from the sources, for instance, that naval expansion was not a necessary and integral part of Miquel's policies in the way previously thought. In the evidence we may search in vain for any hint that ministers or politicians saw any constructive relationship between the Navy Bill and the tariff question in 1897–8, or that the former played any part in what they understood by the idea of *Sammlungspolitik*. Moreover, the political tendency which did draw the naval issue into a tactical unity with domestic policies tried also to make it contingent on a programme of reform fundamentally inimical to the survival of the class alliance enshrined in the *Sammlung*. In so far as Tirpitz had any wider political interests he appears to have identified himself with this incipient counter-coalition rather than the *Sammlung* itself.[112] The only factor which distinguished the naval coalition from the political bloc assembled by Miquel, in fact, was the presence in the former of the *Freisinnige Vereinigung*. This suggests the ultimate incompatibility of a vigorous naval propaganda with a reconstructed *Sammlung*, and the fundamental inexpediency of the naval issue for the supporters of the latter. Later, at the time of the second Navy Bill in 1899–1900, there is no doubt that the naval issue was brought into an important tactical relationship with the impending tariff settlement, in the sense that the agrarians were willing to make their consent for the former conditional on concessions over the latter. But the combination of navy and tariffs in 1900 resulted from a confrontation with reality rather than the conscious implementation of a political blueprint and, as such, constituted a disruption of the conception developed in 1897. Despite the problems created by the naval question, however, the forces of *Sammlung* still managed to survive and the Kardorff-majority of 1902 corresponded exactly to the political constellation envisaged by Miquel in 1897.

III

The concept of *Sammlungspolitik*, if it is to have any meaning at all, therefore, should be identified with the political position developed by Miquel in the summer of 1897. The formation of the *Wirtschaftlicher Ausschuss* under official auspices in September 1897 represented a first concrete success for his plans for 'bringing the parties together in the economic field.[113] This consisted of five nominees each from the DLR, the CVDI and the Deutscher Handelstag (DHT) as the three recognized economic corporations, and fifteen members nominated by the government. The CVDI delegates comprised one representative of the glass industry, one from the sugar industry and three from the protection-oriented textiles industry; the five heavy-industrialists appointed by the government were also supporters of protection. In combination with the representatives of agriculture, therefore, the CVDI was able to leave the exporting interests who wanted a continuation of the Caprivi commercial treaties in a clear minority on the committee.[114] But although this body provided a necessary institutional setting for political consultation between the twin partners of a revived *Sammlung* – the heavy industry of the Ruhr and Silesia, the big landowners of east and west Germany – the immediate impact of its foundation must not be overestimated.

A more cautious examination both of the corporate motivation of the CVDI and of the wide range of attitudes gathered within it is required. The CVDI's definition of an official attitude towards the existing commerical treaties was largely a pragmatic response to new world developments – the introduction of new American tariffs and the abrogation of the English commercial treaty. Moreover, the opening consultations with the DLR and the government over the formation of a joint committee was undertaken to forestall an earlier and potentially dangerous initiative from the *Chemieverein* and the DHT.[115] From this point of view the participation of the CVDI in the *Wirtschaftlicher Ausschuss* appears more as a defensive move than a grand design for the reconstruction of the old solidarity bloc of 1879. Miquel certainly had a more ambitious political function in mind for the committee, and this was no doubt shared by some heavy-industrialist politicians, but its mere foundation represented no decisive juncture of the interests of heavy industry and agriculture. At this stage it is difficult to detect a strong movement inside the CVDI for a new coalition with the agrarians on a political level. It is certainly misleading to talk in terms of a 'formal alliance'.[116]

It is clear that by the summer of 1897 a number of factors were combining to facilitate such a convergence. Well-established ideological affinities with the Conservatives, dissatisfaction with the disjointed pseudo-liberalism of the Hohenlohe administration, common antipathy to Social Democracy and, above all, a shared interest in protecting the home market, were all pushing the leading elements in the CVDI towards an agreement with the agrarians.[117] In the context this could only take the form of renegotiating the Caprivi commercial treaties on a basis more favourable to the interests of agriculture, and breaking politically with those sections of industry which had begun to identify their future prosperity with a continuation of the treaties. The hard political rationale behind such a coalition was the conviction that the only firm guarantee for the preservation of the iron tariff in the Reichstag was a coalescence of the twin movements of heavy-industrial and agrarian protection. This belief was reinforced by the fear that the light-industrial opponents of agrarian protection would also abolish the iron tariff if they had the chance. As the secretary of the CVDI, Henry Axel Bueck, pointed out, the economic interests most heavily committed to the existing commercial treaties were precisely the ones which were also calling for a gradual, systematic dismantlement of heavy industry's own tariffs.[118] But although a mixture of economic and ideological solidarity was bringing heavy-industrialists and agrarians together in the summer of 1897, the countervailing forces were still strong. At the general meeting of the *Langnamverein* in Düsseldorf at the end of May 1897, for instance, Bueck was careful to warn the *Bund der Landwirte* (BdL) that heavy industry could never accept their maximum demands published the previous day. Although the CVDI recognized the need for higher grain tariffs, it refused to support the demand for constantly rising state-guaranteed grain prices or to abandon its commitment to commercial treaties of long duration. Any genuine *rapprochement* must depend on concessions from both sides.[119]

A wide range of factors certainly created a propensity in heavy-industrialist circles to regard alliance with the agrarians as the natural expression of their interests: the dominant political and ideological climate under which German industrialization took place, a shared interest in

130

protecting the home market, above all the perception of a revolutionary threat from the organized working class. But this should not obscure the equally important points of conflict with the organized agrarian movement: the persistence in the latter of a strong anti-urban, anti-industrial and anti-capitalist ideology, different economic priorities, an opposing view of the labour market, and so on. In a period of accelerated industrialization and vast social changes the two interests were inevitably separated by a wide variety of economic and ideological incompatibilities. The stability and internal cohesion of the heavy-industrialist alliance with the agrarians, both across the period of time and at any one point within that period, have almost certainly been overestimated. In many ways, in fact, the most striking feature of attempts to re-create the Bismarckian coalition between 1897 and 1902 was the fragility of the relationship between the CVDI and the organs of agrarian opinion. Moreover, an examination of the efficacy of Miquel's call to unity will reveal that this was considerably less successful than has previously been supposed.

Although the long-term objective of a new *Sammlung* was clearly the formulation of common perspectives for a new tariff settlement, the immediate priority was the provision of a central rallying point for the forthcoming Reichstag elections, now set for June 1898. The continuing excesses of the BdL, however, and the angry response these inevitably provoked in liberal quarters, constituted a powerful obstacle to the realization of this goal. The embryonic *rapprochement* in the *Wirtschaftlicher Ausschuss* between the CVDI and the moderate agrarians of the DLR would be of little effect unless it could liquidate this mutual hostility and produce a similar convergence of the Conservative and National Liberal Parties. The hostility of those exporting and manufacturing interests committed to the existing commercial treaties was to be expected, as was that of their left liberal ideologists. But the deep antagonism between these forces and the BdL also cut across the historical barriers between majority and left liberalism and extended in many areas deep into the National Liberal Party.

One source of difficulty encountered by the *Sammlung*, therefore, was the reluctance of the National Liberal Party to endanger its own internal cohesion by adopting the so-called 'national' economic programme as the central plank in its election campaign. The failure to moderate the agitation of the BdL during the autumn and winter of 1897–8 only increased this reluctance, and the heavy-industrialist right-wing of the party was able to make little headway with its plans. When two spokesmen for the National Liberal national executive exhorted the delegates to a provincial conference in Magdeburg in February 1898 to give their support to higher grain tariffs, these tensions erupted into a series of bitter altercations throughout the entire party press.[120] The internal disquiet at the party leadership's apparent support for a dangerously ill-defined conciliation of the agrarians was threatening to become more serious. Accordingly, the tacticians of the heavy-industrialist right began to cover their rear. In mid-February Theodor von Möller, leading National Liberal and member of the CVDI *Ausschuss*, stated in the Landtag that the future of industry's exports depended on 'the binding of tariffs for a long period of time'. Bueck made the same point in a long programmatic article in the *Deutsche Industrie-Zeitung*. He argued that 'Industry will and must insist on the conclusion of tariff treaties, that is, on the binding of mutual tariff scales for the longest time possible'. He continued more ominously: 'Industry will have to consider carefully whether under the given circumstances its most vital interests allow it to ally with agriculture or to follow the call for *Sammlung* before absolutely unquestionable evidence is available that agriculture does not intend to follow the agrarian leaders further in their hostility to industry.'[121]

Moderate agrarians showed little success in restraining their extremist associates. Matters were complicated by the existence of a regionally important, independent anti-semitic movement beginning to define itself in opposition to the Conservative Party. Strong tendencies in the BdL towards a juncture with this movement created much disquiet in a Conservative leadership trying to make the aspirations of Miquel's *Sammlungspolitik* into a party-political reality. The more undisciplined Diederich Hahn was playing a more prominent role in the national leadership of the BdL, and the logic of their own agitation was leading other leaders, such as Berthold von Ploetz and Gustav Roesicke, to adopt a position on the tariff question far to the right of Conservative moderates like Schwerin-Löwitz, Limburg-Stirum and Manteuffel-Krossen.[122] In January 1898, for instance, Eduard Klapper, the BdL functionary, published an article in *Deutsche Agrar-Zeitung*, entitled Bund or Manteuffel?', which posed explicitly the question of continued loyalty to the Conservative leadership.[123] The Conservative conference in Dresden on 1–2 February 1898, the first since the Tivoli conference of 1893, brought little clarification.[124] Despite a show of unity, reports appeared a few days later that in the constituency of Minden-Lübbecke the BdL had decided to oppose the official Conservative candidate, Graf Roon, a known opponent of their extreme agitation, and had nominated their own man for the seat.[125] This was both a provocation and a clear warning to the Conservative leadership. It was confirmed at the BdL Congress when Hahn dealt another blow to hopes of a new *Sammlung*: after attacking the latter's programme as vague and general, with no concrete meaning, he declared that the BdL would negotiate with the parties only on the basis of its economic demands.[126] In the light of the individualist position aggressively projected by the BdL in mid-February the political reality behind *Sammlungspolitik* was proving fairly insubstantial. As *Vorwärts* commented with evident satisfaction: 'In the end one can only rally [*sammeln*] along a blurred middle line, which will always little suit the extreme wings on the right and left'.[127]

Sammlungspolitik, which emerged in 1897 as an attempt to reconstruct the fragmented links of the government with the Prussian Conservatives and to bring its policies back into consonance with the needs of the landowning class, was running into difficulties. Miquel's fundamental aim was a stabilization of government by re-embedding its priorities in that synthesis of interests which lay at the heart of the old Bismarckian coalition and the centre of the state – between East and West, agriculture and industry, feudal and bourgeois. The long-term focus of his efforts was the future tariff settlement, and the discussions between the CVDI and the DLR in 1897 were intended to lay the political foundations for a new protectionist front in the Reichstag. All alliances are forged from common efforts and mutual aid, however, and the first real test of the viability of such a parliamentary bloc was rapidly approaching in the elections of 1898. This realization was growing stronger by February 1898. Unless the whole strategy was merely to dissolve amidst the mutual recriminations of agrarian extremists and industrialists, right- and left-wing National Liberals, a formula was needed to embody the 'middle line' suggested by a *Politik der Sammlung* and to make possible the adherence of at least a section of the National Liberals without bringing the party's unity into question. The more perceptive of political observers were starting to argue that a 'positive programme' must be found.[128] The main obstacle to an effective *Sammlungspolitik*, it seemed, was the absence of a concrete programme around which to rally.[129]

On 25 February 1898 a meeting was convened in Berlin under the joint chairmanship of Richard von Vopelius and Hans von Schwerin-Löwitz.[130] Every member of the *Wirtschaftlicher Ausschuss* was invited except two – Wilhelm Herz ('the representative of the Berlin stock exchange') and Carl Ferdinand Laeisz ('the representative of Hamburg commerce') – since the chances of meaningful discussion with them were thought to be slight.[131] The meeting was attended by eighteen members of the *Wirtschaftlicher Ausschuss* and five further representatives of the CVDI. This confirmed the importance of the former in offering an institutional setting for the *rapprochement* between heavy industry and agriculture, and many bitter remarks were passed by the left liberal press about the political manipulation of the committee.[132] Vopelius, Schwein-Löwitz, Möller and Franz von Ballestrem met beforehand to draw up a manifesto – this was drafted by Möller and accepted by his colleagues with minor editorial revisions.[133]

In its original form this contained two salient features. First, it called for the discontinuation of the commercial treaties in their present form and the omission of the 'most-favoured-nation' clauses in any renegotiation. Secondly, it announced a commitment to the pursuit of a 'national' economic policy during the elections, 'by the elimination of party-political conflicts'. The aspiration to re-create the supraparty interest-coalition of the Bismarckian *Sammlung* was clearly present in this formula. However, an amendment tabled by three members of the Centre, objecting to the reference to the elimination of party-political differences, was accepted against the opposition of only three, who included both chairmen. This substituted a more orthodox statement – 'within the individual political parties'. The new formulation was, as Stegmann rightly comments, 'a clear dilution', and its adoption was symptomatic of both the strength of existing party loyalties and the need to accommodate the Centre in any reconstruction of the Cartel.[134] A second amendment, tabled apparently by a left liberal non-parliamentarian, proposed the deletion of the reference to the 'most-favoured-nation' clauses of the commercial treaties, but was defeated by nineteen votes against only three.

Both convenors then emphasized the purpose of the manifesto. It was not to set up 'a fixed system for our future commercial relations abroad', but 'merely . . . to bind more tightly together for the elections all supporters of the protection of the national labour [*Schutz der nationalen Arbeit*], who believe in the possibility of uniting the different productive estates, and who wish to further this in the country'.[135] Vopelius then asked who was willing to sign the manifesto on the spot. Eleven of those present agreed, including five agrarians. Of the remainder, one refused outright. The others made their signatures conditional on the assent of their parties, or reserved their decisions on general grounds. The meeting represented an obvious attempt to translate the limited *rapprochement* in the *Wirtschaftlicher Ausschuss* into a party-political practice, to convert Miquel's statement of principle into a hard prescription for electoral success.

Despite this new initiative, the passage of the *Sammlung* was still far from smooth. Difficulties emanated from the old sources – agrarian extremism and the resultant alienation of National Liberals. On 3 March 1898, for instance, in a provincial conference of the BdL in Königsberg, Hahn greeted the manifesto, or the *Wirtschaftlicher Aufruf* as it became known, as an accession to the BdL's own programme.[136] Nothing could be more calculated to alienate the left National Liberals, whose precondition for an electoral pact with the Conservatives was an unequivocal rejection of the agrarian demand for a *Sammlung* beneath the banner of the BdL. In these circumstances an attempt by left liberals to capitalize on National Liberal confusion was inevitable, and on 3 March 1898 the *Centralstelle zur Vorbereitung von Handelsverträgen* issued a public statement alleging that the *Wirtschaftlicher Ausschuss* had been manipulated for party-political purposes by the agrarians. In order to rebuff these overtures to the party's dissident left-wing, and to salvage the tactical progress achieved by the meeting of 25 February 1898, Möller issued a public statement which both firmly rejected the statement of the *Centralstelle* and attacked the continuing sectionalism of the BdL. He defended the meeting as an attempt to overcome unnecessary conflicts of interest in the name of common unity against the SPD. He attacked the BdL sharply and regretted that the efforts to call forth a conciliatory attitude on both sides had not yet born fruit. Though he had not given up hope, Möller could not append his signature to the manifesto unless firm guarantees were forthcoming from the BdL. On Hahn, Möller commented curtly: 'With men of this kind, whose existence depends on their agitation and its continuation in the sharpest possible manner, no policy of *Sammlung* is possible.'[137]   A more serious threat to the success of the manifesto came from within the very heart of west German heavy industry. On 3 March 1898 the joint executives of the *Langnamverein* and the North-West Group of the *Verein Deutscher Eisen-und Stahl-Industrieller* (VDEStI) met in Düsseldorf to consider their attitude to the manifesto.[138] Though they described it as 'self-evident' that they supported the principle of *Schutz der nationalen Arbeit*, the joint executives followed the example of Möller and refused to support the manifesto without explicit guarantees that agriculture was willing to recognize the interests of industry in the negotiation of new commercial treaties.[139] Moreover, they also warned that the CVDI could not give its official support until this had been approved by a Delegate Conference. This reaction carried critical implications for the efficacy of *Sammlungspolitik* in 1897–1902. Leading heavy-industrialist politicians such as Bueck, Vopelius, Theodor von Hassler, Hans Jencke and Wilhelm Beumer were clearly in the vanguard of a movement for an open alliance with moderate agrarians such as Schwerin-Löwitz and Limburg-Stirum. But it was equally plain that the resistance to this was not confined to the light-industrial and exporting interests with whom Stegmann identifies the opposition, but had also extended far into what he regards as the unyielding bastions of a Bismarckian *Sammlung*, namely the heavy industry of the Rhine-Ruhr.[140]

Naturally it is possible to detect a general sympathy for the aims of the manifesto in this area, but the controversy inside heavy industry over the signature of the document and later the election campaigning in the constituencies, suggest that the commitment of the CVDI to a political alliance with agriculture was not quite as monolithic as has been claimed. It was of great significance, for instance, that Beumer and Möller set up a series of consultations within the National Liberal Party in order to allay the fears of the *Langnamverein* and the VDEStI. The National Liberal Party and not a new form of organized collaboration with agrarian Conservatives was still accepted by a majority of heavy-industrialists as the most appropriate vehicle for their interests. The conscious association of the heavy-industrial interests with the party still reflected at this time basic antipathies towards both traditional and agrarian conservatism. As Bueck pointed out during a later discussion of political loyalties, many of industry's achievements had been won only after a long struggle against Conservative opposition and any attempt to attach the CVDI exclusively to either of the two Conservative parties would provoke a 'storm of indignation'. Thus, however unsatisfactory the existing liberal parties might be, Bueck argued, the CVDI must continue to recognize the strength of the 'old tried liberal philosophy on which the overwhelming majority of German industrialists stand'.[141] The old party loyalties, therefore, which themselves mediated important conflicts of ideology and interest amongst the dominant classes, placed heavy constraints upon the ability of the *Sammlungspolitiker* to realize their aspirations.

The concrete result of the disquiet expressed by the joint executives of the *Langnamverein* and the VDEStI was a meeting of the National Liberal executive on 7 March 1898, together with the Reichstag and Landtrag fraction committees and other leading party members, such as Möller and the leading exponents of its agrarian wing, Heyl zu Herrnsheim and Oriola. The formal object of the meeting was to remove public speculation concerning the party's attitude to the manifesto. The real aim, however, was the careful distancing of the party's position from any attempt to deny the need for long-term commercial treaties. Armed with an official declaration to this effect, that is, one which enshrined the principle which was missing from the manifesto, heavy-industrialists could sign the latter with a clear conscience. The heavy-industrialist politicians concentrated in the Landtag fraction, such as Möller, Bueck and Beumer, needed a formal statement by the party to stand as a rider to their signatures. This tactical reference-back to the central organs of the National Liberal Party revealed both the primacy of the old affiliations and the internal tensions which were beginning to upset the party's unity.

The scene was set at the very start of the meeting. Ernst von Eynern, a leading supporter of the existing treaties, proposed that an explicit reference to the necessity of 'most-favoured-nation' clauses in future commercial treaties be inserted in any party declaration.[142] Möller opposed this strongly, and then Heyl zu Herrnsheim intervened with Oriola to demand the total exclusion of any reference at all to long-term commercial treaties. A deadlock over details could only be avoided by confining the discussion and the ensuing declaration to a general statement of principle, and Rudolf Bennigsen, still the recognized authority in the leadership, saw this clearly. In a masterly exercise of tactical expertise, he converted what might have been an evasion of divisive issues into a statement of the general principles of National Liberalism, and succeeded, at least temporarily, in preserving the rather fragile unity of the party. In this way, he transformed a glaring source of weakness, the heterogenous interest base of the party, into an apparent souce of strength – namely, a claim to represent the national rather than any single sectional interest. Bennigsen began by recommending the withdrawal of Eynern's motion. He stressed 'the completely general principles for the co-operation' with agriculture, and argued that 'in this discussion it was dangerous to enter into details'. He continued:

We are a party which has so far excluded economic issues from its programme because from the very start we were, and hope to remain, a party which represented the most various of landscapes, in which first one and then the other interest would come more strongly to the fore. For this reason, therefore, we could not allow such matters to find a programmatic expression. Otherwise, we would lose sight of the principle that a large moderate liberal party can bring the differences among the people and their interests to a settlement more effectively than if they were represented by economic parties. We are against the domination of political life by economic issues. That would be the unhappiest of changes in our public life. Now we are representatives of the whole nation, then we would be the representatives of particular interests . . .

However, Bennigsen did concede that economic issues of such importance had now been raised that an official declaration had become 'unavoidable'. In these circumstances the party's role should be 'to apply a moderating influence and to reconcile'. It was 'in the sense that the question had been put to us by the *Wirtschaftlicher Aufruf* '. The demands of agriculture were justified, and it was wrong to attack the agrarians for organizing themselves. The government had taken a positive step in setting up the consultative committee as a forum for discussion. The manifesto was thus to be welcomed as an extension of the campaign for reconciliation, and many of the party's friends had already signed it. In accordance with Bennigsen's recommendations, which were decisive, a declaration was released that same day, expressing 'approval for the general aim' of the manifesto, but also carrying two important qualifications. First, it contained a clear refusal to allow 'the independence of our party and the national, idealist and liberal ideas from which our party has grown, to be forced into the background'. In other words, the National Liberal executive issued a clear statement that it would not allow the party to be supplanted by the kind of supraparty interest coalition implied by the Bismarckian protectionist front of 1879. Secondly, the statement pointed out that although the interests of agriculture should be better guaranteed in the renegotiation of the commercial treaties, the need of industry and trade for treaties of long duration must also be taken into account.[143] This National Liberal declaration was crucial for the heavy industry of the Rhine-Ruhr. On the day after its release Beumer and Bueck sent a copy to the executives of the *Langnamverein* and the North-West Group of the

VDEStI, expressing the belief that it had successfully removed the objections to signing the manifesto. The action had its effect, for on 10 March 1898 Beumer and August Servaes, respectively the secretary and chairman of the two organizations, informed their membership that the objections had disappeared, for the National Liberal declaration could in future be used as a point of reference in any discussions with the agrarians.[144] The manifesto was duly published on 11 March 1898.[145] In all it attracted about 1,500 signatures. They included every member of the CVDI Board except for Emil Russell. Most significant heavy-industrialists signed it. In general, those industries organized in the CVDI were strongly represented – iron, steel, coal, glass, sugar and textiles. The leading moderate agrarians were also present – Schwerin-Löwitz, Limburg-Stirum, Manteuffel-Krossen, Mirbach-Sorquitten, Roon, and so on. Hahn, Roesicke and Ploetz also signed, but in their political practice continued to contravene the terms of the manifesto. The manifesto performed its function most effectively in west Germany and Saxony.[146] However, these were also the regions in which a long-standing co-operation between industry and agriculture, National Liberals and Conservatives, made a rallying action least necessary.

In a purely formal sense, the manifesto fulfilled its objective, in that it was able to bring together on paper large numbers of representatives of industry, agriculture and the *Mittelstand*, from every region of the Reich, and from all political parties to the right of the left liberals. This front was apparently sealed in the Landtag on 4 March 1898, when Kanitz, Schwerin-Löwitz, Kardorff, Möller, Bueck and Ballestrem all joined hands to call for a co-operative approach to the problem of new commercial treaties, leaving the left liberals Rickert and Brömel to carry the torch for an expansive export policy.[147] The signature of Bismarck, moreover, conferred upon the new front an ultimate legitimacy.[148]

IV

The discussions around the *Wirtschaftlicher Aufruf*, therefore, revealed the difficulties of forming a new *Sammlung* in the face of conflicting economic needs, the tenacity of old party loyalties and the hostile ideologies of agrarians and industrial bourgeoisie. The greatest single obstacle to the elaboration of an effective *Sammlungspolitik* in 1897 and the following decade was the primacy of the existing party-political framework. One heavy-industrialist supporter of the manifesto had complained bitterly that the National Liberal Party was opposing a union of all 'national' forces from a 'fear of losing importance', and concluded that 'the political parties are opposed to reconciliation, for their very existence is dependent on the conflict of the parties'.[149] These remarks reflected an appreciation of the fact that, in the final resort, an effective *Sammlung* could only be built on the destruction of the existing party framework but, at the same time, displayed a militant refusal to admit that the party divisions represented actual conflicts of interest. A meaningful unity of the right would only be achieved within a unitary organizational framework but, at the same time, such a radical regrouping of forces could only take place once the old organizations had been left redundant by profound changes in the objective conditions. The reaction of National Liberals to the issue of the manifesto had shown this clearly. Of a total of 118 National Liberal Reichstag and Landtag deputies, moreover, only 55 signed the manifesto. Those who refused included Bennigsen, Brunck, Bueck, Clemm, Eynern, Hammacher, Hobrecht, Krause, Krawinkel, Osann and Schweckendieck. Stegmann identifies this group with the economic interests who felt themselves excluded and threatened by the nascent *Sammlung*, but to a great extent this misses the point.[150] As Bennigsen's address to the crucial meeting of 7 March 1898 had indicated, important groups of National Liberals perceived in the issue of the manifesto an attempt to convert the party into a political dependent of west German industry.[151] Stegmann has described the development of these fears after 1909 in considerable detail, but in 1897–8 they were equally strong and able, in fact, to animate individuals who would later dismiss them.[152]

A close analysis of the course of German politics between the ministerial changes of June–July 1897 and the elections of 1898, and even more clearly between 1898 and the elections of 1903, will reveal that a strategy of *Sammlung* had only limited success. The striking feature of the elections of 1898, in fact, was the disunity of the bourgeois parties rather than the existence of any 'solid phalanx',[153] of the mutual recriminations of agrarians and industrialists rather than their co-operation against the SPD. On the very day of the manifesto's publication wide cracks had appeared in the newly formed front. An agrarian resolution in the Reichstag calling for the exclusion of foreign textiles from subsidized shipping led to sharp exchanges. Posadowsky felt moved to warn the agrarians that they were endangering the success of the *rapprochement* by this threat to the textile industry, and Carl Ferdinand von Stumm became involved in an angry altercation with the supporters of the motion. The National Liberals were forced into a common front with the left liberals and Social Democrats in order to defeat the measure.[154]

Within a week fresh news of trouble was arriving. Stumm, one of the most consistent advocates of a new Cartel, was being opposed in his own constituency by Roesicke,[155] and the BdL had put up an independent candidate against the sitting National Liberal in Hamlin, where Hahn was already conducting an incontinent agitation.[156] Moreover, Graf Dohna-Wundlaken and Graf Dönhoff-Friedrichstein, both of whom had signed the manifesto, were opposing each other in the same constituency as

Conservative and BdL candidates.[157] As the election campaigning moved into full swing more extensive conflicts broke out. In two of the firmest National Liberal strongholds, the Palatinate and Hanover, the BdL intervened on a large scale and placed National Liberal candidates under massive pressure. Where the latter refused to commit themselves to the BdL programme, independent BdL candidates were nominated.[158] Similar interventions on a less dramatic scale occurred in Baden, Saxony and Schleswig-Holstein.[159] At the end of April the *Berliner Neueste Nachrichten*, normally the most vigorous defender of the *Sammlung*, attacked the leaders of the BdL for destroying the foundations of a united front, and complained that 'in many places the basic principle of the *Sammlung* has virtually disappeared in disputes over the details of economic policy'.[160]

The elections of 1898 were characterized by the BdL's ruthless pursuit of its own maximum demands, its disruption of previously stable National Liberal preserves, its frequent support of Anti-Semites against National Liberals and even Conservatives, and in general its subversion of a national *Sammlungspolitik* around the *Wirtschaftlicher Aufruf*. The only areas in which large-scale splitting was avoided were those where the hegemony of a particular party made intervention pointless – the Conservative strongholds east of the Elbe, the vast preserves of the Centre in Bavaria, Rhineland and Westphalia and a range of individual constituencies with local peculiarities. The only areas in which the protectionist axis proved strong enough to support meaningful co-operation between the Cartel parties were those such as the Ruhr or Saxony, where such unity was long established.[161] Moreover, one of the greatest failures of the strategy was its inability to strike up a form of co-operation with the Centre Party during the elections.[162] In the number of deputies actually returned, Miquel's policy was a demonstrable failure: the Conservative representation sank from 72 to 56, the Free Conservative from 28 to 23, the National Liberal from 53 to 46, and even these figures included a large number of deputies who had never fully committed themselves to the principle of *Sammlung*.

As suggested above, there are serious misunderstandings at large concerning both the nature of heavy industry's interest in a new *Sammlungspolitik* and its willingness to participate in one. Quite apart from the paucity of detailed evidence regarding the position of individuals and specific firms, one of the factors inhibiting an understanding of this question was the absence of any uniformity of response within the heavy-industrial interest. Even amongst relatively convinced exponents of the *Sammlung* there was still great disagreement over the precise form it should take and the sacrifices worth making to achieve it.

Theodor Reismann-Grone, for instance, stood at one extreme. Operating from within a Pan-German perspective, he wished to go far beyond the institutionalized *Sammlung* which already existed in Essen and other Ruhr constituencies, and tried to use this as the basis for a new mass movement and the demolition of the old party framework on the national level.[163] For many industrialists and their professional allies, however, this perspective was far too radical, and Reismann-Grone's efforts to gain control of the *Nationaler Verein* in Essen were strongly resisted.[164] Other industrialists were prepared to operate general co-operative arrangements with the Conservatives on a national level and forge a unitary organizational framework in their own constituencies.[165] But they were not willing to shackle their political fortunes to an agrarian chariot which might get seriously out of control, and for this reason the old affiliation with National Liberalism retained an important function. Some individuals might prefer to join the Free Conservatives, and in this way express their support for the principle of a more advanced form of political unity.[166] But the nature of the agrarian movement and the absence of a direct revolutionary threat consigned that unity to the future. Beyond the hard-core heavy-industrialist right, of course, there remained a powerful spectrum of opinion, strongly represented in the Ruhr as well as the Rhineland, which retained a stronger and more coherent ideological commitment to National Liberalism.

These comments have an important bearing on Stegmann's view of the constancy of heavy industry's links with the agrarians before the First World War. An appreciation of the strength of the contradictions between industry and agriculture is essential for a proper understanding of the precise nature of their collaboration. The mere pursuit of their respective interests in state protection certainly implied a high degree of political convergence, but the basic thrust of these twin sectionalisms remained at variance in several important ways. Although in the political arena they proved mutually reinforcing, economically they carried distinct disadvantages for each other. The iron tariff affected the needs of agriculture for cheap machinery and manufactures; food tariffs had adverse consequences for the industrial wages bill. The exclusion of foreign agricultural produce created the additional threat for industry of the retaliatory closure of important foreign markets. The dynamics of sectionalism, therefore, though conducive to a political framework of conciliation, left many conflicts of interest outstanding. As a pure coalition of interest the *Sammlung* was highly imperfect.[167] The factor which helped make this marriage of convenience into a functioning class alliance was a political one – namely, that of 'how the increasingly powerful labour movement could be held in check'.[168] The *Sammlung* was at its most cohesive when an immediate threat from the working class was perceived – after the 1903 elections during the intensification of the industrial struggle, in the artificially stimulated crisis of the 1907 elections, during the aftermath of the 1912 elections.

These two factors – the ambivalence in the economic relationship of heavy industry and agriculture and the fluctuation in the strength of the

socialist threat – are vital for an understanding of the instability of the
Sammlung. They illuminate, for instance, the limited success of Miquel's
policy in 1898 and the acute tensions in the summer and autumn of 1899.
They also explain why the apparent consummation of the *Sammlung* in the
Kardorff-majority of 1902 was followed almost immediately by the
chronic disunity of the bourgeois parties in the 1903 elections. The
economic dialogue between heavy industry and agriculture, therefore,
created tensions which could only be transcended under conditions of
social and political crisis.

An important distinction must be drawn between the ideal form of unity
expressed by the concept of *Sammlungspolitik* in 1897–8 and the political
reality of unresolved contradictions which prevented its realization. Any
appraisal of the term's meaning at this time must be based on an
understanding of the real constraints imposed by the situation, through the
current balance of class forces, the existing levels of class consciousness,
and the continued dominance of old institutions, organizations and
loyalties. There can be no doubt that the desire for a firmer unity can be
identified in important areas between 1897 and 1902, but conditions
consistently militated against this. The logic of *Sammlungspolitik* tended in
the direction of a complete refoundation of bourgeois politics and the
creation of a unitary organizational form for the expression of solidarity
and shared interests, but the trauma of 1918 proved necessary before such a
radical regrouping could take place. The very existence of independent
parties before 1918 was a reflection of real conflicts of interest and ideology
between heavy industry and agriculture. Even the Fatherland Party, the
closest approximation of such a refoundation, was forced to coexist
alongside the existing party framework and justified its existence only by
an exclusive concentration on foreign policy.[169]

The discussion of the *Wirtschaftlicher Aufruf* in 1898, especially in the
National Liberal Party, at once demonstrated where the boundaries would
have to be drawn in a new *Sammlung*. Only a limited degree of co-
operation was possible, and could take place only under the firm guarantee
of the partners' autonomy. This emphasized the nature of *Sammlungspolitik* in 1898: it was a call for unity, an expression of the principle of unity
and, at most, a set of tactics for the realization of that unity, in expressly
limited form, for concrete, immediate goals. There was no attempt to lay
out a detailed, long-term political programme, not even to define 'a fixed
system for our future commercial relations abroad', as Vopelius had
emphasized on 25 February 1898.[170] The basis for such an ambitious
programme of party co-operation did not exist. The problem was to lay the
foundations, in an elaboration of general principle and the provision of a
rallying point, for short-term alliances in the constituencies against the
SPD. As Reismann-Grone stressed: 'the important question is not the
wishes and intentions of the individual, but that a compromise should be

the product of future discussions'.[171] In the first instance *Sammlungspolitik* in 1897–8 was a mechanism for securing party alliances for these specific goals, 'the union of different interests along a middle line'.[172] There is no evidence that it saw beyond the impending tariff settlement, though aspirations for a more permanent co-operation were naturally present in some quarters.

If *Sammlungspolitik* is identified as a tactical mechanism of this kind, then the question of individual actors' divergent conceptions, which has received some attention recently, becomes less important.[173] It was, above all, an attempt to locate common ground for legislative and electoral co-operation. This common ground, and the terms in which both rhetoric and agreements were couched, remained inevitably general whilst the existing party-political framework survived. Whilst the parties insisted on their separate decision-making identity, their differences would continue to militate against comprehensive agreements over detailed, long-term prescriptions for action. As these differences were retained, and as they reflected genuine conflicts of interest within the *Sammlung*, it was scarcely surprising that the political conceptions of individuals also diverged. It would be misleading to call these divergent conceptions of *Sammlungspolitik*: this embodied the common ground and nothing more. In 1897–8 this ground was both narrow and unstable, as the discussions around the *Wirtschaftlicher Aufruf* and the disunity of the right in the elections amply illustrated. Significantly, the only tentative suggestion that a central office be set up to co-ordinate the campaigning of the Cartel parties was rejected out of hand.[174] *Sammlungspolitik* in 1897–8 reflected a recognition of the limited unity which already existed, but only an aspiration towards an advanced form of unity in the future. It was scarcely a success, and its failure was an accurate reflection upon the deep contradictions within the right.

The recent discussion of *Sammlungspolitik* has been extremely valuable in confronting the inadequacy of older analyses and in offering a new framework for discussion. The idea has tended to be used, however, to characterize political complexities for which its explanatory power is very limited.[175] To the extent that over a period of four decades it reflected an attempt to preserve a particular set of class interests, and a particular system of economic, social and political power, *Sammlungspolitik* could be said to have lent an element of continuity to the period as a whole. In this sense, it may be defined as the recurrent attempt of a part of the German right to overcome a prevailing system of political and ideological fragmentation. But this describes only an attempt and an aspiration to unite; it tells us little about the forms in which such unity could be created, and the factors which could facilitate it. In fact, there were, between 1879 and 1918, profound changes in the types of action *Sammlungspolitik* embodied, the ideological forms it embraced and the organizational expressions it sought.

The specific forms of unity available at any one time were obviously determined by the disposition of forces within that particular situation, and between the fall of Bismarck and the elections of 1912 the countervailing interests and allegiances were strong enough to ensure that such unity would be expressly limited in character.

V

Without wishing to discount the real achievements of previous historians, therefore, this study has tried to qualify the received interpretation of German politics between 1897 and 1902 in two ways. On the one hand, it has sought to demonstrate that the current notion of *Sammlungspolitik* contains a serious misinterpretation of the political significance of the Tirpitz-Plan. In the view of many historians the latter was integral to the development of *Sammlungspolitik*: it was a necessary part of a single package deal, a 'tit-for-tat' in which heavy-industrialists supported grain tariffs because the agrarians had put their name to the Navy Bill. But the culmination of long-standing plans for a big navy at the very time when the withered political bonds between heavy industry and agriculture were being aggressively tightened had misled historians into assuming that there was some positive, strategic relationship between the two processes. In fact, this was little more than a striking historical coincidence: it has allowed an arbitrary conceptual framework to become superimposed upon a complicated configuration of economic and political issues. The alliance of industry and agriculture came to fruition quite independently of the naval programme: far from helping it, the latter threatened to hold it back. By raising uncomfortable questions about the permanence of the *Agrarstaat* the naval issue disqualified itself as an effective vehicle for *Sammlungspolitik*. The architects of the *Sammlung* realized this and accordingly excluded it from their calculations. Tirpitz, who also understood the naval issue's implications for the stability of a new protectionist front, played no part in the negotiations from which this emerged. On the contrary, his few general statements of a political character tend to stress the anti-agrarian bias of the naval issue and his own separation from the political tradition which the idea of *Sammlungspolitik* denotes.

Secondly, this article has tried to emphasize the dangers of presenting an unbroken linear continuity between Böhme's 'refoundation of the Reich' in 1879 and the formation of the Fatherland Party. Although Stegmann acknowledges the partial break of the Caprivi years, for instance, he tends to present the following decades as the backcloth for the inexorable unfolding, strengthening and sharpening of a firm political alliance. Yet the most interesting factor revealed by a careful investigation of the efficacy of calls for *Sammlung* at any time between 1897 and 1912 is the resilience of the barrier such calls were meant to overcome. It is the disunity and fragmentation, the structural instability and inherent contradictions of the rightist bloc of industry and agriculture, rather than its monolithic permanence, which is the striking feature of these years. The imposition of a rigid framework of interpretation on to the events of 1897– 1902 has been made possible by the uncritical assimilation of a single historian's findings, those of Eckart Kehr, and a retroactive generalization of developments within a single period, that of 1909–1914/18. This is not to deny the general validity of the continuity thesis of the achievements of recent work, but merely to suggest the internal complexities of a historical epoch. The analytical utility of the concept of *Sammlungspolitik* will only be brought beneath a more accurate perspective when we realize that continuities of class interest are also the source of profound movements of historical change.

CHAPTER 5: NOTES

For critical advice on the preparation of this article, I would like to thank V. R. Berghahn, T. Mason, H. Pogge von Strandmann, M. Stürmer and P.-C. Witt.

1 Much of the momentum, of course, was provided by the pioneering work of F. Fischer, *Griff nach der Weltmacht* (Düsseldorf, 1961). For a comprehensive survey of the ensuing controversy and its literature, see I. Geiss, *Studien über Geschichte und Geschichtswissenschaft* (Frankfurt-on-Main, 1972), pp. 101–98. The most influential of recent works have been H. Böhme, *Deutschlands Weg zur Grossmacht: Studien zum Verhältnis von Wirtschaft und Staat während der Reichsgründungszeit 1848–1881* (Cologne, 1966); H. Rosenberg, *Grosse Depression und Bismarckzeit. Wirtschaftsablauf, Gesselschaft und Politik in Mitteleuropa* (West Berlin, 1967); H.-U. Wehler, *Bismarck und der Imperialismus* (Cologne, 1969). See also F. Fischer's successor volume, *Krieg der Illusionen. Die deutsche Politik von 1911–1914* (Düsseldorf, 1969), and three collections of essays: H. Böhme (ed.), *Probleme der Reichsgründungszeit 1848–1879* (Cologne and West Berlin, 1968); H.-U. Wehler (ed.), *Moderne deutsche Sozialgeschichte* (Cologne, 1966); M. Stürmer (ed.), *Das kaiserliche Deutschland. Politik und Gesellschaft 1870–1918* (Düsseldorf, 1970). These bibliographical notes, as throughout the article, are not meant to be exhaustive.

2 His most important work was E. Kehr, *Schlachtflottenbau und Parteipolitik 1894–1901* (Berlin, 1930); but his collected essays have now been edited by H.-U. Wehler, as *Der Primat der Innenpolitik* (West Berlin, 1965).

3 Literally, it means 'the politics of collection' or 'rallying-together'. I shall use the original throughout.

4 This was the subtitle of Kehr's *Schlachtflottenbau und Parteipolitik*.

5 J. von Miquel, *Reden*, Vol. 4 (Halle, 1914), pp. 279 ff.

6 The source of this interpretation is largely older works. In addition to those of Kehr, the following also adopted his thesis: G. W. F. Hallgarten, *Imperialismus vor 1914*, 2 vols (Munich, 1951); A. Vagts, *Deutschland und die Vereinigten Staaten in der Weltpolitik*, 2 vols (New York, 1935); P. R. Anderson, *The Background of Anti-English Feeling in Germany, 1890–1902* (Washington, DC, 1939). The interpretation has been developed further by J. C. G. Röhl, *Germany without Bismarck* (London, 1967), pp. 246 ff., and D. Stegmann, *Die Erben Bismarcks. Parteien und Verbände in der Spätphase des Wilhelminischen Deutschlands. Sammlungspolitik 1897–1918* (Cologne, 1970), pp. 63 ff. The insights have been incorporated into innumerable other works in a more incidental fashion.

7   See W. Sauer, 'Das Problem des deutschen Nationalstaats', in Wehler (ed.), *Sozialgeschichte*, pp. 407–36, and Rosenberg, *Grosse Depression*.

8   For example, *Schutz der nationalen Arbeit, Kräftigung eines gesunden Mittelstandes, Kampf gegen den Umsturz, Zusammenschluss aller nationalen Elemente, Gutgesinnter, Reichsfreunde*, etc.

9   See, for instance, the press discussion in the spring of 1914, cited by Stegmann, *Die Erben Bismarcks*, pp. 348 f.

10 See the press discussion of the *Kartell der schaffenden Stände* in 1913, cited ibid., pp. 387 f.

11 ibid., p. 13.

12 ibid.

13 ibid., p. 128.

14 ibid., p. 131.

15 ibid., p. 499.

16 ibid., p. 13.

17 See, for instance, H.-J. Puhle, *Agrarische Interessenpolitik und preussischer Konservatismus im wilhelminischen Reich 1893–1914* (Hanover, 1966); H, Kaelble, *Industrielle Interessenpolitik in der Wilhelmnschen Gesellschaft. Centralverband Deutscher Industrieller 1895–1914* (West Berlin, 1967). An exception is E. Böhm, *Überseehandel und Flottenbau. Hanseatische Kaufmannschaft und deutsche Seerüstung 1879–1902* (Düsseldorf, 1972).

18 His recent article has added to this, but is concerned mainly with the prelude to 1897. See D. Stegmann, 'Wirtschaft und Politik nach Bismarcks Sturz. Zur Genesis der Miquelschen Sammlungspolitik 1890–1897', in I. Geiss and B.-J. Wendt (eds), *Deutschland in der Weltpolitik des 19. und 20. Jahrhunderts. Fritz Fischer zum 65. Geburstag* (Düsseldorf, 1973), pp. 161–84.

19 The comments of P.-C. Witt, *Die Finanzpolitik des deutschen Reiches von 1903–1913* (Hamburg and Lübeck, 1970, pp. 58 ff., also have an introductory character, as do those of D. Groh, 'Negative Integration und revolutionärer Attentismus. Die Sozialdemokratie im Kaiserreich', in *Internationale Wissenschaftliche Korrespondenz*, no. 15 April 1972), pp. 1–18. The only detailed critique of Stegmann is also confined largely to the years 1909–14; see G. Schmidt, 'Innenpolitische Blockbildungen in Deutschland am Vorabend des Ersten Weltkrieges', in *Aus Politik und Zeitgeschichte*, 13 May 1972. V. R. Berghahn, *Der Tirpitz-Plan. Genesis und Berfall einer innenpolitischen Krisenstrategie unter Wilhelm II* (Düsseldorf, 1971), approaches the problem exclusively through the naval question.

20 For an example of this theoretical slackness, see Böhme, *Deutschlands Weg zur Grossmacht*, p. 316, where Miquel's policy in 1897 is described as 'the diversion of revolutionary elements into colonial policy'. The *Sammlung* of 1897 has often been described as the attempt to bind together *Weltpolitik* and anti-socialism in a single strategy. The sole basis of this view seems to be a letter from Tirpitz to Stosch in December 1895 (A. von Tirpitz, *Erinnerungen* [Berlin, 1927]), p. 52. This has been quoted many times in support of a simplistic theory of 'manipulated social imperialism' (e.g., Wehler, *Bismarck*, p. 498; Witt, *Finanzpolitik*, p. 59; Stegmann, *Die Erben Bismarcks*, p. 109). It certainly betrays an important train of thought, but cannot be used as the basis for a whole thesis concerning the nature of *Sammlungspolitik* in 1897. One important need in the current discussion is a detailed analysis of popular imperialism. But a considerable advance will not be achieved until the definition of social imperialism is taken beyond that of Wehler, *Bismarck*, pp. 112 ff.

21 Kehr, *Schlachtflottenbau*, p. 205.

22 See Stegmann, *Die Erben Bismarcks*, pp. 110 ff.; Böhme, *Deutschlands Weg zur Grossmacht*, p. 316; Witt, *Finanzpolitik*, p. 59; Röhl, *Germany without Bismarck*, pp. 251 ff.; G. A. Ritter (ed.), *Historisches Lesebuch. Bd 2: 1871–1914* (Frankfurt-on-Main, 1967), p. 20; I. Geiss, 'Kontinuitat und Tradition', in I. Geiss and V. Ullrich (eds), *Fünfzehn Millionen beleidigte Deutsche oder Woher kommt die CDU?* (Hamburg, 1970), p. 8; H. Pogge von Strandmann, 'The Kolonialrat, its significance and influence on German politics from 1890 to 1906' (D. Phil., Oxford University, 1970), pp. 257 ff. The same assertion is made, but with a different emphasis, by Wehler, *Bismarck*, p. 498; Berghahn, *Der Tirpitz-Plan*, p. 16; P. Kennedy, 'German colonial expansion. Has the

"manipulated social imperialism" been ante-dated?' in *Past and Present*, no. 54 (1972), pp. 134–41, here p. 137.

23 Miquel, *Reden*, Vol. 4, pp. 278 ff. The kaiser also made no reference to the Navy Bill in his much-quoted speech in Bielefeld on 18 June 1897, although he did deal with the subject in a speech in Cologne the next day. See *Vorwärts*, no. 141, 20 June 1897.

24 In particular, the meetings on 29 July 1897, 6 October 1897, 22 November 1897, 4 March 1898 and 19 April 1898.

25 Miquel's precise motivation in certain respects remains obscure. For a survey of the available sources, see Berghahn, *Der Tirpitz-Plan*, pp. 124 f., together with his fn. 94.

26 Capelle to Tirpitz, Wiesbaden, 6 August 1897, in Bundesarchiv-Militärarchiv Freiburg (Federal Military and Naval Archive), hereafter referred to as BA–MA, Nachlass Tirpitz, N. 253, 4.

27 Capelle to Tirpitz, Wiesbaden, 7 August 1897 (1st letter), ibid.

28 Capelle to Tirpitz, Wiesbaden, 7 August 1897 (2nd letter), ibid.

29 Capelle to Tirpitz, Wiesbaden, 7 August 1897 (1st letter), ibid. For a discussion of this problem, see Berghahn, *Der Tirpitz-Plan*, pp. 231 ff., and Böhm, *Überseehandel und Flottenbau*, pp. 246 ff.

30 Capelle to Tirpitz, Wiesbaden, 6 August 1897, in BA–MA, Nachlass Tirpitz, N. 253, 4.

31 Capelle to Tirpitz, Wiesbaden, 7 August 1897 (2nd letter), ibid.

32 See note 22.

33 Heeringen to Tirpitz, Berlin, 6 July 1897, in BA–MA, Nachlass Tirpitz, N. 253, 40.

34 For the texts, see Puhle, *Agrarische Interessenpolitik*, pp. 329–31; *Strassburger Post*, no. 461, 8 June 1898.

35 For the text, see *Rheinisch-Westfälische Zeitung*, no. 61, 3 March 1898.

36 This statement is based on a detailed analysis of the election campaigning in 1898.

37 See Berghahn, *Der Tirpitz-Plan*, pp. 151, n. 162, 15 ff., 592 ff. The comments in this article are concerned with Berghahn's view of *Sammlungspolitik* and are in no way meant to detract from the high value and importance of his analysis of the development of naval policy.

38 See his review of Stegmann (V. R. Berghahn, 'Das Kaiserreich in der Sackgasse,' in *Neue Politische Literatur*, vol. 16 [1971], pp. 497–501), and 'Der Tirpitz-Plan und die Krisis des preussisch-deutschen Herrschaftssystems', in H. Schottelius and W. Deist (eds), *Marine und Marinepolitik im kaiserlichen Deutschland 1871–1914* (Düsseldorf, 1972), p. 93; idem, *Rüstung und Machtpolitik. Zur Anatomie des 'Kalten Krieges' vor 1914* (Düsseldorf, 1973) pp. 12–18.

39 Berghahn, *Der Tirpitz-Plan*, p. 151, n. 162.

40 ibid., p. 236.

41 ibid., p. 592.

42 ibid., p. 157.

43 Berghahn, 'Der Tirpitz-Plan und die Krisis', cit. at n. 38 above, p. 93.

44 Berghahn, 'Das Kaiserreich', cit. at n. 38 above, p. 499.

45 See the works cited in note 23.

46 See *Vorwärts*, no. 141, 20 June 1897.

47 See Berghahn, *Der Tirpitz-Plan*, p. 151, n. 162; Berghahn, 'Das Kaiserreich', cit. at n. 38 above, p. 499.

48 See esp. Holstein to Eulenburg, 15 June 1897, in Bundesarchiv Coblenz (Federal Archive), hereafter referred to as BA, Nachlass Eulenburg, 47, pp. 339 f., and an undated note by Hohenlohe, June 1897, headed 'Miquel', in BA, Nachlass Hohenlohe, Rep. 100, XXII, A. 2; also H. Herzfeld, *Johannes von Miquel*, Vol. 2 (Detmold, 1938), pp. 462 f., and Chl. zu Hohenlohe-Schillingsfürst, *Denkwürdigkeiten der Reichskanzlerzeit* (Stuttgart and Berlin, 1931), pp. 352 ff.

49 Kiderlen-Wächter to Holstein, 3 July 1897, in N. Rich and M. H. Fischer (eds), *The Holstein Papers*, Vol. 4 (Cambridge, 1963), p. 46.

50 A. von Waldersee, *Denkwürdigkeiten*, Vol. 2 (Stuttgart and Berlin, 1922), p. 399; B. von Hutten-Czapski, *Sechzig Jahre Politik und Gesellschaft*, Vol. 1 (Berlin, 1936), p. 324.

51 Capelle to Tirpitz, Wiesbaden, 6 August 1897, in BA–MA, Nachlass Tirpitz, N. 253, 4.

52 Capelle to Tirpitz, Wiesbaden, 7 August 1897 (2nd letter), ibid.

53 ibid., and also H. Hallman, *Der Weg zum deutschen Schlachtflottenbau* (Stuttgart,

1933), p. 278.

54 Capelle to Tirpitz, Wiesbaden, 7 August 1897 (2nd letter), in BA–MA Nachlass Tirpitz, N. 253, 4; also Herzfeld, *Miquel*, Vol. 2, p. 550.

55 See esp. H. Gottwald, 'Centrum und Imperialismus' (Phil. diss. University of Jena, 1966), 176 ff., 195 ff. Once Tirpitz had used the Kaiser to force through his plans, of course, Miquel, Posadowsky and the other opponents were forced to operate on the given ground; this did not prevent them from trying to minimize the political consequences of the Bill.

56 See Puhle, *Agrarische. Interessenpolitik*, pp. 329–31.

57 See Hutten-Czapski, *Sechzig Jahre Politik und Gesellschaft*, Vol. I, p. 324.

58 See esp. the materials in StA Cologne, Nachlass Bachem, 112.

59 As claimed by Berghahn in 'Das Kaiserreich', cit.at n. 38 above, p. 499, n. 12.

60 Heeringen to Tirpitz, 6 August 1897, in BA–MA, Nachlass Tirpitz, N. 253, 4.

61 See, for instance, BA–MA, Nachlass Tirpitz, N. 253, 4, 5, 16, 40.

62 See esp. the Ministry of State on 6 October 1897; also Tirpitz's notes for the audience with the Kaiser on 15 June 1897, and his notes for a meeting with Hohenlohe on 15 September 1897, in BA–MA, Nachlass Tirpitz, N. 253, 4.

63 This seems to amount largely to the letter to Stosch cited in note 20.

64 Böhm, *Überseehandel und Flottenbau*, p. 196.

65 Berghahn, *Der Tirpitz-Plan*, p. 138.

66 Tirpitz to Senden, 12 February 1896, in BA–MA, Nachlass Senden, N. 160, 5.

67 See Tirpitz to Stosch, 21 December 1895, in Tirpitz, *Erinnerungen*, pp. 52 f. See also Tirpitz's memorandum of 16 June 1894, cited in F. Klein (ed.), *Deutschland im Ersten Weltkrieg* (East Berlin, 1970), p. 78; Tirpitz's notes for an audience with the Kaiser, 15 June 1897, in BA–MA, Nachlass Tirpitz, N. 253, 4; Tirpitz's notes for an audience with the Kaiser 28 September 1899, in BA–MA, Nachlass Tirpitz, N. 253, 5. In general see Berghahn, *Der Tirpitz-Plan*, pp. 135 ff.

68 See Kehr, *Schlachtflottenbau*, pp. 272–7; K. Barkin, *The Controversy over German Industrialization 1890–1902* (Chicago and London, 1970), pp. 131–86.

69 Tirpitz to Stosch, 21 December 1895, in Tirpitz, *Erinnerungen*, pp. 52 f.

70 Tirpitz's notes for an audience with the Kaiser, 28 September 1899, in BA–MA, Nachlass Tirpitz, N. 253, 5.

71 Bindewald, *Stenographische Berichte über die Verhandlungen des Reichstags* (Reichstag debates), hereafter referred to as RT, 28 March 1898, p. 1827. Lest these views be dismissed as extremist, compare the similar statement by Limburg-Stirum, RT, 6 December 1897, pp. 57 f.

72 Draft for a letter to Thielmann, 8 August 1897, in BA–MA, Nachlass Tirpitz, N. 253, 4.

73 Heeringen to Tirpitz, Berlin, 6 August 1897, ibid.

74 Heeringen to Tirpitz, Berlin, 10 September 1897, ibid.

75 *Vorwärts*, no. 196, 24 August 1897.

76 See Bueck's report to the general meeting of the VDEStI on 4 January 1898 in BA, R. 131, 163.

77 Schweinburg to Hassler, Berlin 2 October and 25 October 1897, in StA Augsburg, Hassler-Archiv, 10; Bueck to Hassler, Berlin, 27 October 1897, Hassler to Bueck, Augsburg, 26 October 1897, ibid., 13; Böhm, *Überseehandel und Flottenbau*, pp. 100 f., does not grasp this reluctance of important sections of heavy industry to participate in large-scale public actions for the Bill.

78 *Rheinisch-Westfälische Zeitung*, no. 13, 14 January 1898.

79 See Böhm, *Überseehandel und Flottenbau*, pp. 75–87, 91–102, 192–201.

80 Herzfeld, *Miquel*, Vol. 2, p. 526.

81 *Deutsche Tageszeitung*, no. 474, 9 October 1897.

82 Memorandum by Heeringen, 24 September 1900, in BA–MA, F. 2284, PG. 94272; also for the following.

83 Hollweg's annotations, 'Ergebnisse und Erfahrungen 1900–1901', probably early 1902, ibid.

84 See Capelle's notes on conversations with Barth, 6 October 1897, and Rickert, 12 January 1898, in BA–MA, Nachlass Tirpitz, N. 253, 4.

85 See Böhm, *Überseehandel und Flottenbau*, pp. 91–106, 196 ff.; Honig to Tirpitz, 6 December 1897, in BA–MA, Nachlass Tirpitz, N. 253, 4; note by Jacobsen, 21 June

1901, in BA–MA, Nachlass Tirpitz, N. 253, 4; F. 2284, PG. 94272; for Halle, see Witt, *Finanzpolitik*, pp. 217 ff.

86　See Hollweg, 'Ergebnisse und Erfahrungen 1900–1901', in BA–MA, F. 2284, PG. 94272; Heeringen for Tirpitz, 17 December 1899, in BA–MA F. 2223, PG. 93947; Heeringen for Tirpitz, 9 February 1900, in BA–MA, F. 2260, PG. 94151; Hollweg for Tirpitz, 19 June 1899, in BA–MA, F. 2233 PG. 93995; unsigned note, 26 January 1900, in BA–MA, F. 2286, PG. 94284; Wenckstern to Hollweg, 27 July 1899, in BA–MA, F. 2259, PG. 94146.

87　The Centre's final support for the Bill in 1898 proved of doubtful value for the *Sammlung*: the disruption of the Centre's unity by the Bill partially determined its opposition to co-operation with the Cartel parties in the elections.

88　See Berghahn, *Der Tirpitz-Plan*, pp. 23–45, 495 ff., 531 ff. This was nowhere more clear than in Tirpitz's association with the Fatherland Party and the German National People's Party after the war. See especially Tirpitz to Trotha, Berlin, 16 October 1916, in BA–MA, Nachlass Tirpitz, N. 253, 64; Tirpitz to Platen, 27 March 1918, Tirpitz to Johann Albrecht, 17 October 1918, ibid., 239.

89　For one of the clearest statements of this view, see his notes for an audience with the Kaiser, 28 September 1899, in BA–MA, Nachlass Tirpitz, N. 253, 5.

90　Barth to Brentano, 2 January 1900, cited by K. Wegner, *Theodor Barth und die Freisinnige Vereinigung* (Tübingen, 1968), p. 71. Hollweg observed this reluctance in 'Ergebnisse und Erfahrungen 1900–1901', in BA–MA, F. 2284, PG. 94272.

91　See his statements to a naval meeting on 18 November 1899, cited by *Tägliche Rundschau*, 20 November 1899.

92　See especially Tirpitz to an unnamed correspondent (probably Hollmann), 18 November 1899, in BA–MA, Nachlass Tirpitz, N. 253, 16.

93　*Die Post*, cited by *Freisinnige Zeitung*, no. 301, 23 December 1899.

94　*Berliner Politische Nachrichten*, cited by Böhm, *Überseehandel und Flottenbau*, p. 259.

95　See, for instance, the note by Carl Bachem on the second Navy Bill, in StA Cologne, Nachlass Bachem, 112: 'Tirpitz, who is said to be left liberal by political conviction, had at first thought to do the job by bypassing the Centre and by making up to the left liberals, notably the *Freisinnige Vereinigung*'.

96　Capelle's note on a conversation with Rickert, 12 January 1898, in BA–MA, Nachlass Tirpitz, N. 253, 4. Appropriately, the conversation took place on the day before the Kaiserhof demonstration.

97　Wehler, *Bismarck*, p. 115, also for the following.

98　H.-U. Wehler, 'Industrial growth and early German imperialism', in R. Owen and B. Sutcliffe (ed), *Studies in the Theory of Imperialism* (London, 1972), pp. 89, 87.

99　ibid., p. 88.

100　ibid., p 89.

101　See Berghahn, *Der Tirpitz-Plan*, pp. 18 f., Stegmann, *Die Erben Bismarcks*, pp. 105–13.

102　E. von Halle, 'Weltmachtpolitik und Sozialreform', in E. von Halle, *Volks- und Seewirtschaft. Reden und Aufsätze* (Berlin, 1902), Vol. 2, p. 212.

103　Programme adopted at the founding congress of the National-Sozialer Verein, Erfurt, 25 November 1896, cited by D. Fricke, 'National-Sozialer Verein 1896–1903', in D. Fricke (ed.), *Die bürgerlichen Parteien in Deutschland 1830–1945* (Leipzig, 1970), Vol. 2, p. 378. See Wehler, *Bismarck*, pp. 497 ff.

104　Berghahn, *Der Tirpitz-Plan*, pp. 592 f.

105　Tirpitz to Trotha, Berlin, 16 October 1916, in BA–MA, Nachlass Tirpitz, N. 253, 64.

106　Berghahn, *Der Tirpitz-Plan*, p. 593.

107　F. Meinecke, 'Sammlungspolitik und Liberalismus', in F. Meinecke, *Politische Schriften und Reden* (Darmstadt, 1958), p. 41.

108　E. Francke, 'Weltpolitik und Sozialreform', in G. Schmoller and M. Sering (eds), *Handels- und Machtpolitik* (Stuttgart, 1900), Vol. 1, p. 131.

109　Cited by Fricke in *Die bürgerlichen Parteien*, Vol. 2, p. 378.

110　Reply to the naval questionnaire of the *Allgemeine Zeitung*, published in full in W. J. Mommsen, *Max Weber und die deutsche Politik 1890–1920* (Tübingen, 1959), pp. 420 f.

111　Kehr, *Schlachtflottenbau*, p. 264.

112　The available evidence has been assembled by Böhm, *Überseehandel und Flottenbau*, pp. 196 ff.

113 The formation of the *Ausschuss* in Röhl, *Germany without Bismarck*, pp. 246 ff., and Stegmann, *Die Erben Bismarcks*, pp. 63 ff.

114 For a full list of the delegates, see Stegmann, *Die Erben Bismarcks*, p. 71.

115 For a detailed account of the negotiations, see Bueck's circular to the members of the CVDI Board, 10 August 1897 (StA Augsburg, Hassler-Archiv, 9 a). For further details, see the protocols of the board meetings on 1 April 1897 and 24 May 1897, and Bueck's memorandum of 13 June 1897 (ibid.). See also the circular of the CVDI to its membership informing them of the project (HA/GHH, 3001073/2), and Bueck's report to the general meeting of the VDEStI on 4 January 1898 (BA, R. 131, 163). The Chemieverein had proposed a joint committee of the CVDI and DHT which would have excluded the agrarians. The anti-agrarian implications of this move were realized in the foundation of the *Centralstelle zur Vorbereitung von Handelsverträgen* in August 1897, which was a direct continuation of the Chemieverein's proposal. For an earlier proposal, see the protocol of the CVDI board meeting of 29 October 1894 (StA Augsburg, Hassler-Archiv, 9 a).

116 Stegmann, 'Wirtschaft und Politik', cit. at n. 18 above, p. 179.

117 ibid., pp. 161 ff.

118 See Bueck's circular to the members of the CVDI Board 10 August 1897, in StA Augsburg, Hassler-Archiv, 9 a. That Bueck's fears were justified can be seen from any close analysis of the movement for the defence of the commercial treaties. In particular, the desire to knock the bottom out of the CVDI's protectionism was one of the most important ulterior motives behind left liberal attempts to detach heavy industry from the agrarian alliance between the 1890s and 1914. For a classic formulation of this calculation, see Georg Gothein to Gustav Williger, Berlin, 25 February 1908 in BA, Nachlass Gothein, 34. See also Kehr, *Schlachtflottenbau*, pp. 306 f. For a good example of heavy industry's dogmatic adhesion to the principle of protection, see the discussion in the *Vorstand* of the VDEStI on 3 October 1900 of an attempt to exempt ship-building materials from the iron tariffs, especially the comments of August Servaes (published proceedings, pp. 2–7, in BA, R. 131, 163).

119 See the report of the meeting in the *Deutsche Industrie-Zeitung*, 11 June 1897.

120 See the detailed reports in *Rheinisch-Westfälische Zeitung*, no. 55, 25 February 1898 and *Vorwärts*, no. 44, 22 February 1898. See also *Hamburgischer Correspondent*, no. 53, 2 February 1898.

121 For both citations, see *Vorwärts*, no. 42, 19 February 1898.

122 For good character sketches of Ploetz, Hahn, Roesicke and Wangenheim, see Puhle, *Agrarische Interessenpolitik*, pp. 295–7.

123 Cited in *Vorwärts*, no. 23, 28 January 1898.

124 See the reports in *Rheinisch-Westfälische Zeitung*, no. 32, 1 February 1898, and no. 33, 3 February 1898.

125 *Vorwärts*, no. 31, 6 February 1898.

126 *Vorwärts*, no. 38, 15 February 1898.

127 *Vorwärts*, no. 42, 19 February 1898.

128 See, for instance, Reismann-Grone's leading article in *Rheinisch-Westfälische Zeitung*, no. 52, 22 February 1898: 'The new elections to the Reichstag'.

129 The Ministry of State had drawn one up, but this was not for public consumption. See the discussion in the Ministry of State on 22 November 1897, and Puhle, *Agrarische Interessenpolitik*, pp. 329-31.

130 Both Vopelius and Schwerin-Löwitz were members of the *Wirtschaftlicher Ausschuss*, Vopelius as a representative of the CVDI, Schwerin-Löwitz as a government nominee for agriculture. Vopelius was a Saar glass industrialist, member of the CVDI board from 1893–1911 (chairman 1904–09) and a Free Conservative Reichstag deputy from 1876–1903, when he entered the Herrenhaus. Schwerin-Löwitz was a Conservative Reichstag deputy from 1893 to 1918 and a constituency chairman of the BdL in Pomerania. In 1901 he became chairman of the DLR.

131 *Rheinisch-Westfälische Zeitung*, no. 61, 3 March 1898. The description of the meeting which follows is drawn from a range of press reports at the start of March. No account of the proceedings was released to the press, but leakages and allegations in the left National Liberal press led to anonymous rebuttals by participants. The papers consulted in the account were basically: *National-Zeitung*, *Vorwärts*, *Kreuz-Zeitung* and

Rheinisch-Westfälische Zeitung. Specific references will be given only for direct quotations and citations, for most of the information is fragmented across several issues of several papers.

132 See *National-Zeitung*, no. 134, 27 February 1898, and for further quotations *Vorwärts*, no. 49, 27 February 1898.

133 Ballestrem was a large landowner with extensive industrial holdings and a leading member of the Centre Party right wing. See Gottwald, 'Centrum und Imperialismus', cit at n. 55, pp. 17–23.

134 Stegmann, *Die Erben Bismarcks*, p. 74. These two factors (the position of the Centre in the Reichstag and the existing party loyalties) were decisive in inhibiting the construction of an effective *Sammlungspolitik* in 1898. Neither receives attention from Stegmann.

135 See *Rheinisch-Westfälische Zeitung*, no. 63, 5 March 1898. This reprinted a statement given anonymously to *Kreuz-Zeitung* by a participant in the meeting.

136 See the detailed report in *Vorwärts*, no. 55, 6 March 1898.

137 *National-Zeitung*, no. 147, 4 March 1898.

138 Vopelius had sent out a circular on 1 March 1898 urging the affiliates and members of the CVDI to sign the manifesto, which was originally to be published on the 7 March 1898. For a copy of this circular, see Historisches Archiv der Gutehoffnungshütte (Historical Archive of the Gutehoffnungshütte), hereafter referred to as HA/GHH, 3001071/3.

139 Circular to the membership from Servaes and Beumer, Düsseldorf, 3 March 1898, copy ibid.

140 See Stegmann, *Die Erben Bismarcks*, p. 75.

141 Comments made in a discussion in the CVDI Board, 16–17 September 1908, cited by Stegmann, *Die Erben Bismarcks*, p. 160.

142 See the minutes of the meeting, in BA, Nachlass Friedberg, Kl. Erw., 303–309.

143 For a copy of this declaration, see HA/GHH, 3001071/3. It was published in the press on 9 March 1898.

144 For copies of these circulars, see ibid.

145 The text of the document appeared in the press at the start of March, but this was the first publication of a list of signatures. For a complete list, see BA–MA, F. 2222, PG. 93942, and BA, Nachlass Hohenlohe, Rep. 100, XXII, B. 14.

146 In West Germany, for instance, besides the leading representatives of heavy industry, the manifesto attracted the support of Summermann and Plettenburg-Mehrum, the two chairmen of the BdL in Westfalen and Rheinprovinz respectively, and the leadership of the Catholic *Bauernvereine* – Landsberg-Vehlen, Loe Wissen, Wilhelm Hoensbroech, Landsberg-Steinfurth and Winkelmann.

147 See the report in *Vorwärts*, no. 54, 5 March 1898.

148 *National-Zeitung*, no. 148, 4 March 1898.

149 Statement published anonymously in *Rheinisch-Westfälische Zeitung*, no. 62, 4 March 1898.

150 Stegmann, *Die Erben Bismarcks*, p. 75.

151 This same fear informed the discussion of election strategy in the National Liberal executive meeting of 20 March 1898. For a copy of the minutes, see BA, Nachlass Friedberg, Kl. Erw., 303–309.

152 See, for instance, the statements by Bassermann and Stresemann, cited by Stegmann, *Die Erben Bismarcks*, pp. 222, 307 f.

153 ibid., p. 131.

154 *Vorwärts*, no. 60, 12 March 1898.

155 ibid. Stumm was also involved in a clash with Mirbach-Sorquitten, normally a moderate agrarian, in the Herrenhaus at the end of April over an agrarian proposal for the introduction of wooden sleepers on the railways. See *Vortwärts*, no. 100, 30 April 1898.

156 *Vorwärts*, no. 61, 13 March 1898.

157 ibid.

158 For the situation in Hanover, see the detailed report in *National-Zeitung*, no. 295, 10 May 1898, and the running commentaries on events in the constituencies throughout May–July 1898. For the situation in the Palatinate, where the intervention of the BdL provoked particular bitterness from large numbers of National Liberals, both in the

region and in Berlin, see the detailed reports in *National Zeitung*, no. 324, 24 May 1898 and no. 369, 20 June 1898. On the 28 June 1898 the paper reported that the leader of the National Liberals in Ludwigshafen, Hecht, Justitiar of BASF, had shot himself as a result of the conflict with the BdL.

159 For Baden, see *National-Zeitung*, no. 338, 2 June 1898, and *Heidelberger Zeitung*, no. 128, 4 June 1898. For Saxony, *National-Zeitung*, no. 200, 2 April 1898, and for Schleswig-Holstein, no. 340, 3 June 1898.

160 Cited by *Vorwärts*, no. 98, 28 April 1898. A few days later *Berliner Neueste Nachrichten* launched a further attack on the BdL for demanding that candidates give unconditional support to 'a programme which conflicts in many points with the most important life-needs of German industry' (cited by *Volksstimme*, Mannheim, no. 51, 5 May 1898).

161 This unity was not enough to prevent the SPD from winning a further five seats in Saxony, including all three in Dresden.

162 There was little disagreement in the Centre leadership over the economic content of the *Wirtschaftlicher Aufruf*, and this was made clear by its subsequent support of the tariff settlement. The factors which inhibited the party's integration into a broadened Cartel after its support of the Navy Bill were many and varied: the need to observe the demands of its working-class and petty-bourgeois constituency alienated by fears of higher indirect taxation, the legacy of the *Kulturkampf*, the ideological exclusiveness of political Catholicism. The dominant motivation of the leadership, however, seems to have been heavily opportunist. A strong Cartel returned at the expense of the left liberals would weaken the Centre's primacy in the Reichstag. Consequently, the party's election tactics in west and central Germany, at least, were based upon a defensive coalition with the left liberal *Freisinnige Volkspartei*. For a candid statement of this motivation, see Carl Bachem to Müller-Fulda, 18 May 1898: 'In principle I am completely of your opinion. We will get a powerfully strengthened rightist Reichstag. All reasonable agrarian demands will therefore be easy to push through, but on tactical grounds it is desirable that the left liberals do not disappear, which is a possibility' (StA Cologne, Nachlass Bachem, 86 d).

163 See the many statements to this effect scattered throughout diaries. For example, at this time he still believed that 'the Pan-German League could and should become a powerful people's association' (StA Essen, Nachlass Reismann-Grone, 10, IX, 98, 12).

164 ibid., IV. 98.7, IX. 03.11 ff., IX. 04.2, IX 05.4 ff., IX. 08.7, etc. It is significant that one of Reismann-Grone's chief opponents in the Essen *Nationaler Verein* was Wilhelm Hirsch, an important spokesman of the *Sammlung* (see Stegmann, *Die Erben Bismarcks*, pp. 32, 227–30, 241, 354, 404 f., 424, 455). Whereas there is no doubt that Hirsch did operate within a broad perspective of this kind, the history of the *Nationaler Verein* in Essen and the factional conflicts within it point to the need for much more carefully differentiated analysis of the attitude of heavy-industrialists and their spokesmen to the concept of *Sammlung*.

165 The *Nationaler Verein* in Essen is one example, and similar organizations existed in many other constituencies in Rhineland-Westphalia. See, for instance, the material in HA/GHH, 300127/1.

166 The role of the Free Conservatives as agents of *Sammlungspolitik* deserves closer investigation. A beginning may be found in D. Fricke's article on the party in D. Fricke (ed.), *Die bürglichen Parteien*, Vol. 2, pp. 560–79, and in Stegmann, *Die Erben Bismarcks*, pp. 24–6, 232–9, 316–23.

167 This is not to deny the existence of many individuals who were able to see beyond these conflicts, or the crucial political role of an intermediate group of ennobled industrialists and agrarian capitalists in forming the hard core of the *Sammlung*. Therein lies the true function of the Free Conservatives.

168 M. Clemenz, *Gesellschaftliche Ursprünge des Faschismus* (Frankfurt-on-Main, 1972), p. 77.

169 See, for instance, the many statements to this effect in BA–MA, Nachlass Tirpitz, N. 253, 62, II: e.g. Tirpitz to Stenburg-Birstein, 23 January 1918; Stolberg to Jaeger, 20 October 1917; Tirpitz to Johann Albrecht, 1 November 1917; Wintzer to Johann Albrecht, 13 October 1917, etc.

170 *Rheinisch-Westfälische Zeitung*, no. 63, 5 March 1898.

171 *Rheinisch-Westfälische Zeitung*, no. 68, 10 March 1898.

172 *Neue Reichskorrespondenz*, no. 56, 27 July 1897.
173 See, for instance, Puhle, *Agrarische Interessenpolitik*, pp. 158 f., and *Von der Agrarkrise zum Präfaschismus* (Wiesbaden, 1972), pp. 58 f.
174 *Konservative Korrespondenz* proposed such an office at the start of April 1898, but the suggestion was immediately rejected by the *Nationalliberale Korrespondenz*. See *Rheinisch-Westfälische Zeitung*, no. 92, 3 April 1898.
175 Whereas the concepts themselves can be extremely valuable, the use of catching formulas, such as *Sammlungspolitik*, 'social imperialism', 'secondary integration', 'caesarism', and so on, has tended none the less to act too often as a substitute for a critical analysis of concrete problems.

6

Social Imperialism in Germany: Reformist Synthesis or Reactionary Sleight of Hand?

Like the previous one, this essay has already been placed into context by the introduction to the volume. Essentially, it grew immediately out of the discussion of *Sammlungspolitik*, because social imperialism had been one of the principal concepts used to define the political function of the big navy policy adopted in 1897–8. It also featured centrally in conventional treatments of the Navy League and the other nationalist pressure groups, and once I had finished my doctoral thesis in 1974 (on 'The German Navy League in German politics, 1898–1914', D.Phil., University of Sussex, 1974), it seemed a logical next step to sort out my thinking on the subject. In fact, I had already presented a paper on social imperialism to the thesis writers' Work in Progress Seminar in Sussex in the spring of 1973, and this gave a welcome opportunity to step back both from the highly particularized discussion of the *Sammlungspolitik* article (which was written during 1972–3) and from my materials on the Navy League (which I was then beginning to write up). In the event, the resulting essay became too large, and I split the text into two separate articles. One, the longer of the two, was published in *Social History*, vol. 1 (October 1976), pp. 265–90 as 'Defining social imperialism: use and abuse of an idea', and large parts of it were subsequently incorporated into *Reshaping the German Right: Radical Nationalism and Political Change after Bismarck* (New Haven, Conn. and London, 1980). The other, the one included here in an unrevised form, appeared in the memorial volume for Georg W. F. Hallgarten (originally conceived as a Festschrift) edited by Joachim Radkau and Imanuel Geiss, *Imperialismus im 20. Jahrhundert* (Munich, 1976), pp. 71–86.

Basically, once I had pursued the origins of the term through the political discourse of the earlier twentieth century it rapidly became clear that the usage developed by German historians since the late 1960s obscured a rich diversity of thinking about the relationship between imperialist expansion and domestic political mobilization. For one thing, government and other establishment attempts to utilize the popular enthusiasm generated by imperialist expansion were invariably outflanked by broader and more radical mobilizations further to their right, an argument I developed in 'Defining social imperialism' and more extensively in my book, and one which has unsettling implications for any manipulative conception of the relationship between government propaganda and popular opinion. But, as I discovered in my discussion of *Sammlungspolitik* and the 1898 Navy Law, imperialist agitation could also be linked ideologically to ambitious programmes of social and political reform. By tying discussion of social imperialism rigidly to a notion of diversionary and manipulative resistance to reform in the interests of an immobilist and traditional power structure, recent German historians were making it more difficult to see the importance of this reformist nexus, and in fact rather summarily dismissed its significance. My essay is an attempt to restore the liberal or reformist versions of social imperialism to the agenda, both to recover the full repertoire of thinking about the relationship between imperialism and domestic politics and to begin discussion of reformist potential in imperial society. It also reflects a longer-term interest in the possibilities for comparison between German and British liberalism, particularly between the 1890s and the First World War.

I

Historians, half embarrassed by the empiricist habits of their profession, tend to jump eagerly at an attractive concept. Add a genuine desire to repudiate the knowing condescension often shown to sociologists in the past and we have a state of mind particularly receptive to certain kinds of sociological theory. This basic disposition is all to the good. Areas of notable vitality in recent historical studies – population and the family, social protest and collective behaviour, work, leisure and crime, obsolescent patterns of belief like witchcraft and magic – have benefited tremendously from the adoption of new approaches and techniques. Similarly, quantification is no longer a fad but an essential part of the historian's professional equipment. However, this has its bad side too. Concepts are often used as a mere convenience, substitutes for critical thinking, filched from neighbouring disciplines by historians unwilling to spend time and energy in the more arduous process of perfecting – or more commonly adapting – their own ideas. They become mere code-words, symbols of an analysis whose validity is assumed rather than systematically explained. Recent German historiography is full of this. For instance: until recently 'modernization theory' had been taken up with a minimum of critical reflection, and even terms like '*Sammlungspolitik*', 'caesarism' and 'secondary integration', which Wilhelmine historians have in a real way made their own, have tended to meet a similar fate. All these have quickly petrified into unreflected conventions of habitual analysis.

'Social imperialism' is a classic instance. From being the polemical watchword of revolutionary Marxists in the First World War, who wished to discredit Social Democrats for their complicity in the latter, this was appropriated by a number of academic theorists, of whom Schumpeter and Franz Neumann were the most notable.[1] It was generally used to indicate popular support for imperialism, though Lenin's references to labour aristocrats were rather more precise than the statements of his academic successors, who preferred to speak of the 'masses' or the 'working class' as a whole. One of the problems with the idea is that it was scarcely used in any analytical way: Lenin's remarks have never been developed further, and neither Schumpeter nor Neumann make more than a passing descriptive reference to its uses. Moreover, though the existence of government attempts to 'incorporate the working classes into an imperialistic system'[2] is now recognized, historians have normally focused on the formulation of policy rather than its *effects*: they have rarely tried to establish the extent of imperialist sentiments in the populace, still less to explain their motivation. They continue patrolling the well-trodden corridors of power, rarely venturing into the streets outside, into the uncharted reaches of the committee room, the working-men's club, the recreational society, the public house, or the family. There is still little understanding of how socialist imperialist mechanisms might have acted on the consciousness of real people. Even Semmel, who provides by far the most thorough treatment of social imperialist thinking before 1914, defines the idea only by describing the sort of policies associated with it.[3]

This vagueness about matters of definition has made it easier for recent historians to tamper with the idea without doing obvious violence to an existing usage. It is important to recognize, in other words, that the meaning now current amongst German historians differs markedly from the original one, which is discarded somewhat cursorily as a political slogan of dubious analytical value.[4] The new emphasis is on 'modernization', 'status-anxiety' and the social-psychological consequences of the Great Depression, a situation in which German politicians sought 'to legitimate the social status quo and the political power structure by means of a successful imperialism'.[5] Hans-Ulrich Wehler, the architect of the new approach, sees social imperialism as an attempt to organize and manipulate the feelings of disorientation experienced by 'broad social strata', including 'the petty bourgeoisie of artisans and small businessmen, parts of the industrial labour force, of the rural *Mittelstand* and of the larger landowners', during a period of rapid but irregular industrialization.[6] Colonies were conceived partly as a form of 'anti-cyclical therapy', but partly also as propaganda objects, a means of focusing popular loyalties on the monarchy and of countering the appeal of the left. Social imperialism becomes 'the diversion outwards of the internal tensions and class contradictions arising from the process of industralization', a Machiavellian 'technique of rule' by which pressure for democratic change is diverted on to harmless foreign objects.[7] This function has been ascribed to Bismarck's colonial policy, to the naval policy of Tirpitz after 1898, and by extension to most forms of extreme nationalism in the Wilhelmine period.[8]

Two things have happened in the couse of this definition. First, it is no longer concerned primarily with the structural relationship of labour reformism and empire – the familiar theorem of imperialism, regular growth and social stability – but with a particular aspect of this, namely the action of government policy on popular consciousness. The surrounding context of the Great Depression, it is true, is axiomatic, and Wehler devotes much space to demonstrating its effects on the social thought of the time. But the original stress on the importance of higher wages, improved social conditions, the provision of welfare and ideologies of racial superiority in transmitting the benefits of empire to the masses and in translating the calculations of policy-makers into a tangible political reality of working-class quiescence has been lost.[9] The complex array of mechanisms, some consciously directed, others structurally determined, by which opposition was contained, modified and absorbed by the system, in short the process by which the disaffected convinced *themselves* that their interests could be pursued inside the given framework after all, is reduced to a single expedient: government manipulation of popular sentiments through pressure groups, the press and the educational system. Recent work has been concerned almost exclusively with the dynamics of the high-level decision-making process and with the methods of manipulation, whilst the popular reception of these efforts has been largely ignored.[10] Moreover, with this has gone a second shift in meaning, for social imperialism is now identified solely with *conservative* policies to the explicit exclusion of *reformist* ones. Together these two revisions narrow the idea's usefulness: they reduce it to the conscious manipulations of *some* politicians, to *particular* state actions and to *conservative* policies, whereas the original meaning encompassed the determinate *context* in which all politicians had to work, the changing forms of state power and the pressures which affect *all* politics, whether conservative, liberal, or socialist.

This narrowing of the idea in the course of its redefinition is the crux of the problem. For the equation of social imperialism with diversionary techniques of rule calculated to give 'permanence and stability to the status quo'[11] through the organized manipulation of popular nationalism begs many questions. When Wehler speaks of 'slowing down the process of social and political emancipation',[12] for example, the meaning is ambiguous. *Whose* emancipation is to be obstructed: that of the bourgeoisie, that of the working class, or that of German society as a whole in some obscure metaphysical sense? *What* did this emancipation entail: parliamentary representation and the classic liberal freedoms, or direct democracy and the socialization of the means of production? Moreover, *how* were the political 'energies' which liberals and socialists devoted to these demands actually diverted into support for colonies or the navy: by a dramatic apostasy which sent them straight from one extreme to another, or by a more partial and complicated rightward movement? These questions have scarcely even been posed by existing work let alone answered. 'Diversion of reformist energies' surely implies some success amongst those who were actually demanding 'emancipation' as well as those who were already hostile to democratic change. Wehler appears to think that the diversionary strategy not only drew the dissident left liberals into the imperialist consensus, but that the same climate of opinion also had the effect of moderating the SPD's practical revolutionary commitment.[13]

These are important implications. For recent works on social

157

imperialism also contain far-reaching claims concerning the weakness of Germany's liberal-democratic tradition. When Wehler speaks of the continuity of social imperialism from Bismarck to Hitler, he necessarily prefigures these larger issues.[14] His work constitutes an important statement about the reforming potential of Wilhelmine Germany and about the failure of the left to achieve significant parliamentary reform. Moreover, the failure to fracture the authoritarian modes of politics which had survived the process of industrialization compounded the problems of the SPD in 1918 and disastrously faulted the foundations of the Weimar Republic. In this way the years of Bismarck's colonialism constituted an authentic 'founding period' which largely determined the lines of future development.[15] According to Wehler, the popularly legitimated inauguration of a manipulated social imperialism in the 1880s situated Germany decisively in the camp of the 'authoritarian regimes' rather than that of the 'welfare state mass democracies'. 'Social imperialism' and 'social reform', in other words, are to be seen as a pair of polar opposites.[16]

This usage of social imperialism may be faulted on a number of accounts. There is no attempt, for instance, to examine how the manipulative strategy was actually received by the dissidents at whom it was aimed. There are no studies of how the working class itself reacted, as opposed to the socialist politicians and trade unionists who claimed to speak in its name, and the same is also true of the peasantry and *Mittelstand*.[17] The discussion of the policies described by Wehler cannot be separated from the problem of their impact in society, and of course Wehler makes all kinds of assumptions about the effectiveness of their appeal.[18] Yet there remains a striking imbalance in existing work: the conventional descriptions of Bismarck's aims and the nature of the 'ideological consensus' are backed up by a massive empirical apparatus; by contrast the sociology of the popular response is engaged only at the level of unverified generalization. Given the final claims of recent work – the system *was* 'stabilized', 'modernization' *was* obstructed – an analysis is badly required which not only unravels the threads of official motivation, but also considers the actual effectiveness of social imperialist initiatives in socializing dissident groups into the dominant political value system. Beyond this there is evidence to suggest that the prominence of 'manipulative' calculations in government practice was much less than has been supposed, and that when such ideas were indulged they did more harm than good by inflaming radical nationalist expectations which could not be satisfied.[19] There is, finally, a larger view of the German past in recent work, employing sub-Weberian categories of cultural change and proceeding from a supposed, 'deep discrepancy between the social structure and the political system', which must also be subjected to critical examination.[20] The brief comments which follow cannot hope to resolve these issues. But given the undoubted popularity of the idea of social imperialism and the general difficulties which arise when concepts are grafted too readily on to a basically empiricist historiographical tradition, they can at least clear some of the ground for such a project by clarifying the basic issue of definition.[21]

II

To understand how social imperialism acted on popular consciousness to displace feelings of discontent *two separate* processes must be distinguished. First, governments successfully activated people whose interests and values *already* disposed them to be deeply suspicious of democratic projects. This is the phenomenon Wehler and his contemporaries have identified. But secondly, independently and in spite of this, the dominant national context of action and the imperialist world economy to which this was linked were simultaneously enabling the gradual impoverishment of the labour movement's revolutionary potential. This was the vital shift in German politics before 1914 and involved the SPD's emergence from an exclusive labourist isolation. Unfortunately, although these two processes require separate treatment, they have been conflated by recent work into a single problem: explanations suitable for one are inappropriate when applied to the other. In particular, the 'diversionary model', with its stress on preserving the status quo *against* reform, provides little insight into why workers should exchange their democratic loyalties for imperial ones: once the older connection between imperialism and social reform is rejected we are left with nothing but unspecified generalizations about 'status-anxiety'.

We can go further. Diversionary expedients played into the hands of the left for they went together with all the worst features of domestic reaction: anti-strike legislation, the three-class franchise in Prussia, an iniquitous tax system, in general the left's systematic confinement within a strict moral ghetto.[22] This militated against the intended impact of a prestigious foreign policy, for the worker's subaltern status – as a trade unionist and a citizen – belied the claim that his or her interests lay with the status quo. Conservatives could never specify the benefits of empire: these were presumed to follow naturally from economic growth, a miraculous transmission of the surplus back to the pockets of the producer without the necessity of any redistributive mechanism.[23] This is the problem: trade unionists needed convincing evidence that support for imperialism would bring concrete improvements in wages and working conditions, social welfare, taxation, civil rights; yet diversionary techniques were intended precisely to shift public debate away from these issues.

Thus to establish the legitimacy of capitalist property relations presupposed some partial dismantlement of the repressive apparatus of the state, whilst the benefits of empire could be made more convincing by linking them to a programmatic reforming commitment.[24] By the mid-1890s a coherent political position was forming around this insight, whose advocates ranged from liberal bureaucrats like Hans von Berlepsch, acting from a curious mixture of humanitarian and pragmatic motives, to radicals like Friedrich Naumann, who proceeded from more systematic ideological premises. Between the two poles a shifting coalition of forces was able to gather on specific issues, including left and often National Liberal politicians, reforming academics, enlightened employers and labour bureaucrats, not only from the non-socialist unions but potentially from the *Freie Gewerkschaften* themselves. The Hamburg Dock Strike, the defeat of the Prussian *Vereinsgesetz* in 1897, the resistance to *Lex Heinze* and the *Zuchthausvorlage*, and the opposition to the tariffs were all the occasion of fleeting progressive coalitions.[25] Hans Delbrück drew out the implications: 'The party of the future would be one which grasped simultaneously . . . the great problems of foreign and domestic politics: appeasement of the fourth estate's just demands. At this juncture that means freedom of association and coalition, with preservation of the existing franchise and extension of Germany's power at sea'.[26]

Rationalizing industrial relations into a serviceable network of conciliatory mechanisms was the priority: replacing the 'system of industrial absolutism' with one of 'negotiations with the organizations of labour'. For

whoever studies the history of the English trade union movement knows very well that the English worker hasn't always been as mature as today, that decades were necessary before the trade unions had educated him accordingly. I would have thought it much cleverer of our employers – and much more in their own interest – if they wouldn't oppose every progress in the labour movement and would go some way to meet the latter instead. Trust awakens trust. But the worker won't have that trust if every concession has to be wrenched from the employers by legislation.[27]

Max Weber, adding an interesting theoretical gloss, argued that the object of reform was not the furtherance of human happiness, but a cultural disposition of self-improvement in key sections of the working class. British workers, whom Weber considered thoroughly 'aristocratic' by status and ideology were again a classic instance of what could be achieved.[28] Social engineering would separate 'the upper strata of the working population', and it was a measure of the inadequacy of Bismarck's social policy, he argued, that it had failed to conciliate these 'healthy and strong elements' in the early craft-based trade unions.[29] Commenting in 1905 on the idea of *Arbeiterkammern* (workers' chambers) in which all workers' unionized and non-unionized, would be represented, he insisted that 'the agreement of working conditions by the entire labour force would subject the skilled and generally more highly developed strata . . . to the control of the broad masses beneath them'. This 'would make the fixing of wage differentials according to the quality of the labour virtually impossible', and 'that upper stratum would lose its natural leadership' in the working class.[30] The moral was that 'trade unionism is a beneficent power, when it is wielded with discretion'.[31]

This was the terrain upon which imperialist agitation could make real headway in the working class. It was vital to treat the respectable workingman as a 'gentleman', to coax him gradually into nationalist views rather than stigmatizing his socialist leanings and patronizing him from above.[32] The way to prevent endemic labour unrest was 'to create strong credible labour organizations which are accepted by the employers' organizations as negotiating bodies of equivalent weight'.[33] Politically this required the 'incorporation of labour into the life of the state as an equal partner'.[34] This prefigured a new ideology of state intervention, social welfare and national solidarity for which the 1890s were especially conducive, since the entry into *Weltpolitik* seemed to impose fresh priorities on German liberals. On the one hand, it was vital in an age 'when the masses have come of age (through elementary education, mass conscription, universal suffrage and the cheap oil-lamp)' to legitimate imperialist policies by popular acclaim;[35] on the other hand, the popularity of the imperial myth might fracture existing fronts with a novel alliance of social reformers and defecting socialists. Imperialism and social reform seemed to fuse into a new dynamic unity: 'World policy and social policy are the two poles at which one and the same power manifests itself. The national drive abroad must be matched by social progress at home.'[36]

The outer limits of this bourgeois reformism were clearly demarcated. The concern was technocratic, only marginally democratic in any full sense, directed mainly at equipping the state for survival in the imperialist world economy, much as the attention of the Fabians in Britain turned around the same time to the problem of 'national efficiency'.[37] Friedrich Naumann's 'policy of power abroad and reform at home'[38] was neither an unrealistic project of disinterested social concilation nor the devaluation of reform to a mere function of an efficient *Weltpolitik*.[39] It was nothing less than an attempt to consolidate the legitimacy of the capitalist mode of production (and eliminate residual enclaves of feudal privilege), by providing basic social security, recognizing the organizations of labour and incorporating the latter in an enervating network of advisory bodies.[40] This, the most far-reaching attempt to rationalize the implications of imperialist expansion into a workable domestic strategy, was motivated not by the desire to *prevent* reform, but by the desire to *promote* it. Social imperialism is currently associated only with immobilist resistance to progress in the liberal as well as the socialist sense of that term. Yet there were actually two distinct variants of social imperialism: that described by Wehler as a conservative diversion from reform, and that which he explicitly excludes from consideration, which was linked unambiguously to the *need* for reform. On one side there is support

for an active policy of foreign power, with one group wanting to divert attention from the extension of welfare legislation, whilst another expects to boost its ambitious social policy from precisely the same source. On the other side the spokesmen of a 'little Germany' policy divide into those who hope to achieve healthy reforms more easily for the absence of militarism, and those who think that a great world empire must needs be democratic, whilst in a small state all the resources of the ruling classes can be marshalled for the protection of their power'.[41]

III

The distinction between a *conservative* and a *reformist* social imperialism makes more sense once the original meaning is recovered: winning the workers from socialism by the promise of higher wages and better welfare.[42] This might well mean a purely propagandist exercise of a 'diversionary' kind, the mere activation of nationalist emotions for narrowly conservative ends. The exploits of the national pressure groups were ample testimony to the popularity of such a policy. But it might also mean something much more sophisticated. By a varied repertoire of political tricks, from the manipulation of the press and the hustings to the gradual incorporation of the labour bureaucracy and the concession of limited social reform, it was possible to convince the workers by a systematic campaign of mystification that their wages, their jobs and their general well-being were all dependent on the continued existence of empire, colonies and overseas markets.[43] The key factor was calculated reform. As Austen Chamberlain put it: 'The democracy want two things: imperialism and social reform . . . We can only win by combining them again'.[44] Social imperialism always meant the combination of these two things. It was the attempt to demonstrate their interdependence, 'to say that the realisation of one was not possible without the realisation of the other'.[45]

By avoiding this older usage recent historians have confused the discussion. For it is one thing to connect social stability with material prosperity and to believe that the latter could only be secured by a vigorous drive for foreign markets. It is quite another to believe that the propagation of this idea could act as a total substitute for change at home. This was a possible stance. But the domestic programmes associated with imperialism ranged from far right to moderate left. The political imperatives which Bernhard von Bülow, Heinrich Class, Friedrich Naumann, or Hans Delbrück derived from their understanding of imperialism diverged as dramatically as those drawn by Joseph Chamberlain, Karl Pearson, Cecil Rhodes, or Sidney Webb. By eliding this critical diversity current usage fails to convey a full sense of the variety of imperialist thinking at the turn of the century. That diversity in a real sense supplied the motor of political conflict in general, for the response to imperialism became a crucial determinant of a party's overall direction. The debate about empire 'functioned as an element of fission, favouring the profound and fertile agitation of the period', imparting 'its vitality to the battle of ideas', and serving as 'a means of political, emotional and intellectual polarisation'.[46]

The recovery of social imperialism's original meaning is consequently not just a quibble over semantic consistency, for this described the changing *context* of political intervention, the common stimulus for both right- and left-wing policies.[47] All anti-socialist strategies were conservative to the extent that they aimed to maintain the integrity of the existing property relations. But this larger aim concealed vital differences of policy and practice, embracing not only entrenched reaction but also flexibility and tactical reform. To subsume this range of options beneath the single formula of 'preserving the status quo' effectively disqualifies one of the crucial political dialogues of the twentieth century. Moreover, the importance of the reformist alternative has been badly underestimated by previous historians. Liberal imperialists played a vital part in redefining the limits of legitimate intervention by the state in economic and social life, while the new technocratic ideology quickly permeated through the state bureaucracy.[48] As left liberals began to flirt with a deradicalized labour movement and the right moved inexorably closer to the Pan-German panacea of the national Volksgemeinschaft, the bureaucratic pragmatists moved in to fill the gap. The key development after the fall of Bülow's Conservative-Liberal Bloc in 1909 was not so much the reconstruction of the old industrial-agrarian *Sammlung* on a broader footing (that is, the locus of Wehler's social imperialism) as the efforts of men like Theobald von Bethmann Hollweg and Clemens von Delbrück to build bridges to the reformist left.[49] Above all, liberal imperialists made their own distinctive contribution to the abortion of Germany's democratic republic, for the victory of their collaborationist perspective in the SPD, which moved swiftly after 1914 from acquiescence in German imperialism to active complicity, decisively inhibited the party in the revolution of 1918. The historical impact of reformist social imperialism cannot be measured in the electoral fiasco of Naumann's *National-Sozialen* between 1896 and 1903. Its real vindication came with 4 August 1914 and 19 July 1917, with the November agreement between trade unions and employers in 1918, and with the bloody events of January 1919.

163

IV

In summary, three layers of meaning may be distinguished. First, there is a general sense in which social imperialism expresses the dominant features of the relationship between imperialism as a system of power in the world and the social structure of the metropolis: a process, a dynamic system of economic and political pressures, some consciously directed, some built into the evolving structures of capitalist society in the imperialist epoch. Secondly, there is the sense emerging from the Marxist polemics of the First World War: the attempt to rationalize these pressures into a coherent political strategy, involving at its most sophisticated a synthesis of imperialism and social reform, which seemed to afford the best chance of reconciling the working class to the capitalist social order. In this sense social imperialism was an 'ideology which sought to combine protectionist defence of the "national interest" with social reformist attempts to improve the condition of the working class in the imperial metropolis'.[50] Finally, there is the current sense, in which governments try to divert and appease social unrest by compensatory success abroad. This is really an abridged version of the second sense, in which mere propaganda is made to do the job of tactical reform: a timeless reality, common to most social systems, with little to do with imperialism as such. But since this facet has now been isolated in recent work, it can scarcely be ignored.

These reflections somewhat invalidate the larger scenario associated with current work on social imperialism. This makes great play with a formal dichotomy of 'social imperialism and social reform' which stamped the whole future development of Germany 'from Bismarck to Hitler'.[51] But social reform was never an exclusive , unequivocal alternative to social imperialism in this way. Almost without exception Wilhelmine reformists – unlike their revolutionary opponents – were also committed to the continuation of imperialist policies. The touchstone of reformism in the SPD was a willingness to accommodate party policy to the requirements of the imperialist world system, and apart from a few pacifists it was only the revolutionary left which successfully resisted the latter. When reformists themselves accepted the aggrandizement of the nation-state the dichotomy of 'social imperialism and social reform' loses its explanatory value. Rather than polar opposites these were two faces of a single coin.

CHAPTER 6: NOTES

This paper was first presented to two seminars in Sussex and London (February 1973, October 1974), and benefited greatly from the resulting discussions. I have already discussed this matter in my unpublished thesis: 'The German Navy League in German politics, 1898–

1914' (D. Phil., University of Sussex, 1974), and in two articles: 'Sammlungspolitik, social imperialism and the Navy Law of 1898', *Militärgeschichtliche Mitteilungen*, no. 1 (1974), pp.33–48; 'Defining social imperialism: use and abuse of an idea', *Social History*, vol. 1 (1976), pp. 269–90. I would like to give special thanks to Hartmut Pogge von Strandmann, Volker Berghahn and Imanuel Geiss for their criticisms.

1 The earliest recorded use of the term social imperialism seems to have been by Trotsky in autumn 1914. See I. Deutscher (ed.), *The Age of Permanent Revolution. A Trotsky Anthology* (New York, 1964), p. 78. Lenin was using it by 1916: e.g. *Imperialism and the Split in Socialism* (Moscow, 1972), p. 11. The precise authorship is less important than the term's rapid assimilation to the general vocabulary of the left. It was interchangeable with 'social chauvinism' and 'social patriotism' at this stage, and the latter may be found much earlier: e.g. Rosa Luxemburg, 'Der Sozialpatriotismus in Polen', *Gesammelte Werke*, vol. 1, pt 1 (East Berlin, 1970), pp. 37–51. For its later academic use: J. A. Schumpeter, *Imperialism and Social Classes* (Oxford, 1951), pp. 114 f.; F. Neumann, *Behemoth* (London, 1944); B. Semmel, *Imperialism and Social Reform* (London, 1960), pp. 13–28.

2 Neumann, *Behemoth*, p. 153.

3 Significantly the term social imperialism is not even mentioned by the two most systematic works on imperialism as a concept: T. Kemp, *Theories of Imperialism* (London, 1967), and R. Koebner and H. Schmidt, *Imperialism* (Cambridge, 1964).

4 H.-U. Wehler, *Bismarck und der Imperialismus* (Cologne, 1969), p. 116, n. 5; also H.-C. Schröder, *Sozialistische Imperialismusdeutung* (Göttingen, 1973), pp. 57–77.

5 H.-U. Wehler, *Das deutsche Kaiserreich 1871–1918* (Göttingen, 1973), p. 173. See also: H. Rosenberg, *Grosse Depression und Bismarckzeit. Wirtschaftsablauf, Gesellschaft und Politik in Mitteleuropa* (West Berlin, 1967).

6 Wehler, *Bismarck*, pp. 480 f.

7 ibid., p. 115.

8 Wehler has established this usage in the following works: *Bismarck*, pp. 112–26; 'Bismarck's imperialism 1862–1890', *Past and Present*, no. 48 (1970), pp. 119–55; 'Industrial growth and early German imperialism', in R. Owen and B. Sutcliffe (eds), *Studies in the Theory of Imperialism* (London, 1972), pp. 71–92; *Das deutsche Kaiserreich*, pp. 172 ff. His exchange with G. W. F. Hallgarten is also illuminating: *Geschichte in Wissenschaft und Unterricht*, vol. 22 (1971), pp. 257–65; vol. 23 (1972), pp. 226–35, 296–303; vol. 24 (1973), pp. 116 f. See also: V. R. Berghahn, *Der Tirpitz-Plan. Genesis und Berfall einer innenpolitischen Krisenstrategie unter Wilhelm II* (Düsseldorf, 1971), and the same author's *Germany and the Approach of War in 1914* (London, 1973); D. Stegmann, *Die Erben Bismarcks. Parteien und Verbände in der Spätphase des Wilhelminischen Deutschlands. Sammlungspolitik 1897–1918* (Cologne, 1970). The following critique would be incomplete without some acknowledgement of Wehler's achievement, for methodologically and theoretically his work on imperialism was a moment of rare intellectual excitement.

9 See Semmel, *Imperialism and Social Reform*, pp. 13–28, and in general.

10 See Wehler, *Bismarck*, p. 116: he is concerned 'more with the intentions of the ruling strata than with the collaboration of the working population'.

11 K. Hildebrand, *The Foreign Policy of the Third Reich* (London, 1975), p. 137.

12 Wehler, 'Industrial growth and early German imperialism', cit. at n. 8 above, p. 89.

13 ibid., p. 92: 'for whatever reason, the Bismarckian policy of seeking to contain the power of the Social Democrats by an emphasis on overseas expansion had been fatally successful', for by 1900 'most of the Social Democrats' had made their peace with imperialism. On the other hand, some authors specifically deny the impact of diversionary strategies on the labour movement. See: H.-C. Schröder, *Sozialismus und Imperialismus* (Hanover, 1968), p. 16; D. Groh, *Negative Integration und revolutionäre Attentismus* (Frankfurt-on-Main, 1973), pp. 32 f.

14 H.-U. Wehler, *Krisenherde des Kaiserreichs 1871–1918* (Göttingen, 1970), p. 131; *Bismarck*, pp. 498, 19. It should also be said that Wehler regards his version of social imperialism as a universal phenomenon, generalizing his conclusions with alacrity across space as well as time. See: ibid., pp. 112–26; 'Industrial growth and early German imperialism', cit. at n. 8 above, pp. 90 f.; 'Der amerikanische Imperialismus vor 1914', in W. J. Mommsen (ed.), *Der moderne Imperialismus* (Stuttgart, 1971), pp. 172–92; *Der Aufstieg des amerikanischen Imperialismus* (Göttingen, 1972).

15 Wehler, 'Bismarck's imperialism', cit. at n. 8 above, p. 150.
16 Wehler, *Krisenherde*, p. 131, and Bismarck, p. 498; D. Stegmann, 'Wirtschaft und Politik nach Bismarcks Sturz. Zur Genesis der Miquelschen Sammlungspolitik 1890–1897', in I. Geiss and B.-J. Wendt (eds), *Deutschland in der Weltpolitik des 19. und 20. Jahrhunderts. Fritz Fischer zum 65. Geburstag* (Düsseldorf, 1973), p. 172.
17 Of recent works on the SPD and imperialism, the most notable are: Schröder, *Sozialismus und Imperialismus*; G. Kruschet, 'Ein Brief Konrad Haenischs an Karl Radek. Zur Politik des 4. August', *Internationale Wissenschaftliche Korrespondenz*, no. 14 (December 1971), pp. 1–17; H. Bley, *Bebel und die Strategie der Kriegsverhütung 1904–1913* (Göttingen, 1975); H.-U. Wehler, *Sozialdemokratie und Nationalstaat. Nationalitätenfragen in Deutschland 1840–1914* (Göttingen, 1971). German labour history has an institutional bias superseded elsewhere. See e.g., the issues of the *Bulletin* of the Society for the Study of Labour History (London). There is no German work to match R. Price, *An Imperial War and the British Working Class. Working-Class Attitudes and Reactions to the Boer War 1899–1902* (London, 1972), which examines the attitudes of working people themselves rather than those of their public spokesmen. For agrarian and *Mittelstand* suspicion of *Weltpolitik*, see E. Böhm, *Überseehandel und Flottenbau. Hanseatische Kaufmannschaft und deutsche Seerüstung 1879–1902* (Düssldorf, 1972), pp. 183–263; Eley, 'German Navy League', cited in introductory note above, pp. 22–89; R. Gellately, *The Politics of Economic Despair. Shopkeepers and German Politics, 1890–1914* (London, 1974), pp. 92 f., 96.
18 Wehler, *Bismarck*, pp. 480 f.; 'Industrial growth and early German imperialism', cit. at n. 8 above, pp. 89–92; 'Bismarck's imperialism', cit. at n. 8 above, p. 152.
19 See my work on the naval question and on the *nationale Verbande: 'Sammlungspolitik*, social imperialism and the Navy Law of 1898', pp. 29–48, 63; 'German Navy League', pp. 260–326; 'Defining social imperialism', pp. 269–90. All cited in introductory note above.
20 K. D. Bracher, 'Kaiser Wilhelm's Germany', *History of the 20th Century*, vol. 5 (1968), p. 119. The reliance of recent German historians on 'modernization theory' to make sense of their past requires a thoroughgoing critique which cannot be attempted here. See T. W. Mason, 'Zur Entstehung des Gesetzes zur Ordnung der nationalen Arbeit vom 20. Januar 1934: Ein Versuch über das Verhältnis "archäischer" und "moderner" Momente in der neuesten deutschen Geschichte', in H. Mommsen, D. Petzina and B. Weisbrod (eds), *Industrielles System und politische Entwicklung in der Weimarer Republik* (Düsseldorf, 1972), pp. 322–51.
21 This discussion should be regarded as a preliminary sketch for more detailed work on the problem of Wilhelmine reformism at some future date. Its main aim is to point out some of the problems in applying the idea of social imperialism as currently defined.
22 This connection was especially clear in the case of Victor Schweinburg, first secretary of the Flottenverein who was also the confidant of *Sammlungspolitik*'s most entrenched supporters. See Eley, 'German Navy League', pp. 64–89, cited in introductory note above.
23 Typical examples: G. A. Erdmann, *Meister Thesen* (Berlin, 1904), and H. Rassow, *Auf dem Elbdampfer* (Berlin, 1904), both commissioned by the Flottenverein for distribution amongst the working class; also the entry under 'Flotte' in *Handbuch fur nichtsozialdemokratische Wähler*, ed. Riechsverband gegen die Sozialdemokratie (Berlin, 1911).
24 See Hermann Wagener's critique of Bismarck's labour policy: Wehler, *Bismarck*, p. 460.
25 For reasons of space detailed verification of this point must await a future occasion.
26 *Preussische Jahrbücher*, vol. 83 (1896), p. 593.
27 Gothein to Williger, 25 February 1908, Bundesarchiv Koblenz, Nachlass Gothein, 34. Georg Gothein was a leading left liberal parliamentarian based in Silesia; Gustav Williger was a Silesian heavy-industrialist.
28 W. J. Mommsen, *Max Weber und die deutsche Politik 1890–1920* (Tübingen, 1959), p. 115.
29 ibid., p. 116. In 1918 Weber described the formal co-operation of employers and unions as the 'only valuable achievement of the revolution in social policy': *Gesammelte Politische Schriften* (Tübingen, 1958), p. 474.
30 Mommsen, *Max Weber*, pp. 130 f.
31 E. E. Williams, *Made in Germany* (London, 1897), p. 174.
32 Rassow to Reichsmarineamt, 8 August 1902, Bundesarchiv-Militärarchiv Freiburg,

2257, 94136. Hermann Rassow was a gymnasium headmaster and a tirelessly imaginative naval propagandist.

33 Gothein to Williger, 25 February 1908, Bundesarchiv Koblenz, Nachlass Gothein, 34.

34 E. Francke, 'Reichsmacht und Reichsreform', *Soziale Praxis*, vol. 29, 17 April 1913. Ernst Francke was an academic proponent of liberal social policy.

35 Rassow to Tirpitz, 12 April 1898, Bundesarchiv-Militärarchiv Freiburg, 2223, 94943.

36 E. Francke, 'Weltpolitik und Sozialreform', in G. Schmoller and M. Sering (eds), *Handels- und Machtpolitik* (Stuttgart, 1900), Vol. 1, p. 131.

37 For the British case: Semmel, *Imperialism and Social Reform*; G. R. Searle, *The Quest for National Efficiency 1899–1914* (London, 1971); A. M. MacBriar, *Fabian Socialism and English Politics 1884–1918* (Cambridge, 1962); E. J. T. Brennan, *Education for National Efficiency: The Contribution of Sidney and Beatrice Webb* (London, 1975); and above all, E. J. Hobsbawm, 'The Fabians reconsidered', in *Labouring Men* (London, 1964). pp. 250–71. In Germany, Weber typifies the technocratic commitment to reform: D. Beetham, *Max Weber and the Theory of Modern Politics* (London, 1974), pp. 95–118, 151–82, 215–49; W. Struve, *Elites Against Democracy* (Princeton, NJ, 1973), pp. 114–18.

38 Founding programme of National-Sozialer Verein: D. Fricke, 'National-Sozialer-Verein 1896–1903', *Die Bürgerlichen Parteien in Deutschland 1830–1945* (Leipzig, 1970), Vol. 2, p. 378.

39 These have been the commonest verdicts, with the most recent study, D. Düding, *Der National-Soziale Verein 1896–1903* (Munich, 1972), opting largely for the former, and Wehler, *Bismarck*, p. 497, for the latter.

40 This was functional of *Weltpolitik* in that social conciliation was viewed as necessary for an efficient imperialism. But this worked both ways: imperialism was also seen as an essential means to social conciliation. The two were never separate in Naumann's mind.

41 E. von Halle, 'Weltmachtpolitik und Sozialreform' in. E. von Halle, *Volks-und Seewirtschaft. Reden und Aufsätze* (Berlin, 1902), Vol. 2, p. 212. The quotation gives a succinct summary of the complex political function of the debate over imperialism. Ernst Levy von Halle orchestrated much of the official naval propaganda in the early years of the Tirpitz-Plan. Later he performed a similar function during the campaign for the abortive finance reform in 1908–9, a key measure of technocratic and liberalizing progress.

42 Lenin, *Imperialism, the Highest Stage of Capitalism* (Moscow, 1968), pp. 118, 73 f.; Schumpeter, *Imperialism and Social Classes*, pp. 114 f.; Semmel, *Imperialism and Social Reform*, pp. 13–28.

43 Lenin called this 'Lloyd-Georgism'.

44 Semmel, *Imperialism and Social Reform*, pp. 25 f.

45 ibid., p. 26.

46 T. Nairn, *The Left Against Europe?* (Hardmondsworth, Middx. 1973), p. 8.

47 Wehler and his contemporaries are not unaware of this changing context, but seem unable to see its reformist as well as its conservative or 'stabilizing' possibilities. See H. A. Winkler (ed.), *Organisierter Kapitalismus. Voraussetzungen und Anfänge* (Göttingen, 1974).

48 For some suggestions in this connection, see: G. Schmidt, 'Parlamentarisierung oder "Präventive Konterrevolution"?', in G. A. Ritter (ed.), *Gesellschaft, Parlament und Regierung* (Düsseldorf, 1974), pp. 149–278; C. Maier, 'Between Taylorism and technocracy', *Journal of Contemporary History*, vol. 5 (1970).

49 See Groh, *Negative Integration und revolutionäre Attentismus*, pp. 577–730.

50 G. Lichtheim, *Imperialism* (London, 1971), p. 10. As Lichtheim's definition suggests, British historians still use the older meaning of social imperialism unaffected by Wehler's redefinition.

51 Wehler, *Krisenherde*, p. 131, and *Bismarck*, p. 19; Stegmann, 'Wirtschaft und Politik nach Bismarcks Sturz', cit.at n. 16 p. 172.

PART THREE

'Enemies of the Reich'

7

Joining Two Histories: The SPD and the German Working Class, 1860–1914

Aside from my immediate research interests in Germany, I have also maintained a continuing interest in the history of the left. Indeed, when I started thinking about graduate work, my initial preference would have been for research on the SPD or some other aspect of the German labour movement, and it was mainly the sense that left-wing historians were enticed too easily into essentially internalist histories of their own political tradition, combined with a strong political desire to understand the sources of fascism, that led me to study the politics of the right instead. But, in fact, the late 1960s were also a time when focus was shifting strongly from the intellectual and institutional history of the labour movement to the social history of the working class. These trends registered earlier in Britain, France and the USA, but by the second half of the 1970s they had definitely captured the imagination of historians in Germany too. During the last ten years the more interesting research has been produced on aspects of work, working-class culture and the history of everyday life, together with pioneering studies of trade unionism and strikes, rather than on the history of the SPD *per se*. This is far less true perhaps of work on the war and the Weimar Republic, but the same trends have also made their influence felt there. They are especially marked in research on the Nazi period, because the suppression of the legally organized institutions of the labour movement has forced historians to think more seriously about how else the working class is to be studied.

Though in itself an unqualified good, this turn to the social history of the working class itself has sometimes been accompanied by a certain lack of interest in the implications of such research for our understanding of the SPD. When I was asked by *Radical History Review* to review Molly Nolan's book on the SPD in Düsseldorf, therefore, it seemed a good opportunity to consider how the two fields – history of the working class, history of the SPD – might be brought back together. It also seemed a useful occasion for bringing the vast riches of research in Germany to the attention of an English-speaking public, because usually very little of the German work gets to enter the English-language discussion outside the circles of German historians themselves. The result was a long historiographical essay, which tried to draw the contours of the field as a whole, both to distinguish the salient emphases of work on the prewar SPD and to suggest how the recent social history might take discussion of the latter further on.

The argument of the essay built directly on the argument of an earlier essay which I wrote jointly with Keith Nield ('Why does social history ignore politics?', *Social History*, vol. 5 [1980], pp. 249–72), and which in its turn tried to build on discussions in the SSRC German Social History Seminar at Norwich in January 1979. Those discussions were continued at a subsequent meeting of the Norwich Seminar in the summer of 1980, and found a certain reflection in a volume of essays edited from the proceedings of the two meetings by Richard Evans, *The German Working Class 1888–1933* (London, 1982). My own thinking owes a special debt to

171

the participants in those seminars, and especially to Jane Caplan, David Crew, Dick Geary, Tim Mason, Keith Nield and Eve Rosenhaft. The essay originally appeared in *Radical History Review*, nos 28–30 (1984), pp. 13–44.

I

The SPD (Sozialdemokratische Partei Deutschlands) was the pride of the Second International. It was the earliest, largest and best-organized of the European socialist parties. In Karl Kautsky it possessed the International's most prestigious theoretician. It faced serious competition from neither popular liberalism nor anarcho-syndicalism, and its primacy on the German left was unchallenged before 1914. It was a powerful electoral force (by 1880 it had more votes than any other German party and by 1912 more parliamentary seats, and claimed to integrate both parliamentary and trade union struggle. Its organized presence within the working class, across the entire front of political, economic, social and cultural activities, was exceptionally well developed. Most of all, it was officially committed to the revolutionary overthrow of capitalist society and upheld the legitimacy and overriding historical necessity of social transformation. Yet, at the successive moments of general crisis in 1914 and 1918, it failed the revolutionary test. In retrospect, of course, this could be made consistent with the party's previous formation. Reformism, a disposition to compromise and a tendency to pull back from a full-scale confrontation with the capitalist order were all explicable in terms of the SPD's pre-1914 experience. But the question remained. How did such a party, which always proclaimed itself revolutionary, come to renounce its original commitment?

For many years there were basically two answers to this question. One, that of the left, played variations on a theme of betrayal, taking its cue from the polemics of the First World War and Lenin's denunciations of the 'renegade Kautsky'. The SPD's fall from revolutionary grace is attributed to labour bureaucrats (sometimes elided with a 'labour aristocracy'), co-opted parliamentarians and incorporated trade unionists who exchanged their principles for the illusion of immediate reform and eventually turned on the left. Conversely, Rosa Luxemburg and the party radicals appear as the defenders of the revolutionary tradition, upholding the purity of the programme against Revisionists, practical reformists and leadership centrists alike. At the root is the belief in a working class which is essentially revolutionary, or at least potentially available for revolutionary politics if certain conditions of crisis are met and the 'correct' strategy could only be found. Given the teleology of class consciousness, which informs the orthodox Leninist accounts of the pre-1914 SPD, the failure of revolution to occur can only be explained by more or less sophisticated arguments of 'betrayal', which locate responsibility outside the authentic structures and aspirations of the 'class itself' – in processes of corruption, bureaucratization, parliamentary reformism and trade union incorporation, or in the social imperialist manipulations of the ruling class, the repressive power of the state, and so on. The main locus of this analysis is East German official historiography, but the few Marxist accounts in West Germany have tended to follow the same line too.[1]

A second answer, which has long dominated the academic historiography of the SPD, is that the party was never *really* revolutionary in the first place. This view has several components. The students of Werner Conze at Heidelberg (the single most important school of nineeenth-century German labour historians) have stressed the period between *Vormärz* (pre-1848) and unification as a critical founding moment, when German labour acquired its lasting ideological characteristics. The analysis begins with the crystallization of a separate workers' interest in the 1830s and 1840s (originally amongst the clubs of emigrant artisans in England, France and Switzerland), articulated through a new vocabulary of class and consummated in the heroic democracy of 1848.[2] After the repression of the 1850s, politically active working men regrouped in the context of the liberal resurgence of the early 1860s. Social Democracy was conceived amidst the recriminations of the nationalist movement, in which the labour movement was an integral part. The initial complementarity between the workers' social and patriotic goals ('emancipation' on the one side, the democratic *Volksstaat* [People's State] on the other) was sundered by the actual form of Germany's unification, in which the liberal majority compromised with greater Prussian aggrandizement for an extremely imperfect constitution. Seeing their democratic aspirations spurned, the labour movement retreated into revolutionary rhetoric and class-based isolation.[3]

This is a coherent and well-developed interpretation. It placed some burden on the *theoretical* possibility of a lasting juncture between liberal and social democracy, whose chances were actually stifled by the specific circumstances of the 1860s – the fact that 'the industrial revolution entered its critical phase at a time when neither national consolidation nor political democratization had been forced through', as one of Conze's earliest students puts it.[4] In other words, it was the divisive domestic effects of Germany's national unification – a moment of *political* fission, as opposed to an irreducible social contradiction between capital and labour – that led to the 'separation of the proletarian from the bourgeois democracy' (in Gustav Mayer's classic formulation) and the ascendancy of a combative class analysis amongst working-class socialist politicians. For 'until 1870 the labour movement in Germany was part of the national movement'.[5] This has a direct bearing on one's view of later developments. As Conze says, the SPD's rightful place was in the democratic wing of an integrated national consensus, as 'an independent party of labour, allied with the

173

Democrats but organizationally distinct, without revolutionary hostility to the state, and committed to participating in a generally accepted democratic-monarchical constitution'.[6] Instead we have a story of unrequited democratic aspirations, in which the workers' demand for citizenship and their 'readiness for co-operation in state and society' were pre-empted by an unimaginitive and dogmatic liberalism.[7]

After 1870 the labour movement's isolation was strengthened by the repressive hostility of Bismarck's authoritarian state, of which the Anti-Socialist Law (1878–90) was the most extreme manifestation. In effect, the Social Democrats were driven into a political ghetto. Revolutionary ideology was adopted as a mask of self-preservation, a defensive posture against the hostile environment that withheld the movement's legitimacy, an unintended consequence of the persecution. It was only under the abnormal circumstances of virtual illegality, when the public activities and democratic associational life of the labour movement were severely constricted, that Marxism could be imposed as the SPD's official ideology. It was the achievement of a small clique around August Bebel, who ruthlessly asserted their control of the party's organs in the 1880s and purged the existing socialist tradition of its rich eclecticism, laying the foundations for the adoption of a new programme in 1891.[8] The 'Erfurt synthesis' of that year, which became the jealously guarded front of orthodoxy for the next two decades, was thus an extremely artificial concoction, grafted insensitively on to a far richer existing tradition.[9] But beneath the revolutionary gloss, it is argued, the movement's authentic preference was still for the older democratic values of citizenship, fraternity, self-improvement and patriotism. Given the chance, that is, the labour movement would have gladly rejoined the national consensus, as the events of August 1914 demonstrated only too well.[10]

Moreover, after the abolition of the Anti-Socialist Law the entire thrust of the labour movement's practical experience was towards integration. This is the theme of Gerhard A. Ritter's pioneering study of the 1890s, which draws a detailed cross-section through the SPD's second founding period when its qualities as a mass movement were properly established.[11] For Ritter the SPD's 'ultimate admission to the given framework of economic and political relationships' was its 'inescapable fate' after 1890, and this could be seen in 'the workers' involvement in ever greater areas of practical effectiveness, for which there were thousands of individual manifestations'.[12] This was true, above all, of the trade unions whose mass growth after the economic upswing of 1895–6 amounted to a vital 'shift in the centre of gravity' of the overall movement. Increasingly after the turn of the century the unions sought to free themselves from the political leadership of the party and rapidly established themselves as a major force for political moderation.[13] Compared with the process of practical integration, Ritter argues, the party leadership's obsession with 'correct' revolutionary strategy was so much rhetoric and hot air, 'theoretical humbug' which simply held up the inevitable victory of reformism. The real substance of the movement was in the sensible pragmatism of the trade unions, the service activities of the labour secretariats and the moderate parliamentary socialism of the south German sections. On this basis by 1900 the SPD had become 'essentially a practical labour party with a few revolutionary phrases that were no longer taken seriously'.[14]

If this is so, why did the SPD insist on retaining its revolutionary credentials? The scholarly literature proposes three reasons. The first relates to the hold of Marxist ideology on the party, already described above, Once the orthodoxy was in place, it proved extraordinarily resilient, and the Erfurt Programme remained the fixed point in the leadership's public statements of principle, consistently defended against criticisms from both right (Bernstein and other revisionists) and left (Luxemburg and other radicals). For the party executive it was a necessary 'ideology of integration' capable of holding divergent tendencies within the same party, an essential mechanism of ultimate solidarity during the frequently bitter debates over policy and a final court of ideological appeal. The integrative function of the Marxist tradition, which supplied the ideological basis of the SPD's cohesion before 1914, was dubbed 'Kautskyism' by Erich Matthias, after Karl Kautsky's role as the party's official ideologist in the post-Erfurt era. This Marxist centrism proved an effective means of containing the divisions within the movement, but only at the expense of de-legitimizing discussions that smacked of reformist contamination and complicating the party's integration within existing society.[15] Moreover, it is now conventional to question the effective meaning of the official ideology for the mass of the ordinary members, who are thought to have had little understanding of Marxist theory and certainly little interest. In this judgement the 'logic of reformism' argument re-enters as a familar dichotomy of theory and practice – between the esoteric concerns of party intellectuals out of touch with the 'real' interests of ordinary workers, and the practical realism of the honest functionaries, labouring for the tangible benefits of immediate amelioration.[16] The formality and artificial character of the SPD's revolutionary posture is thus re-emphasized.

Secondly, SPD failures are connected to the Social Democratic subculture. Originating also in the heroic isolation of the illegal years, when the SPD's clandestine organization could only subsist on a dense undergrowth of politicized sociability, the movement's famous socio-cultural apparatus powerfully buttressed the primary trade union and political activities and rendered its working-class constituency imperme-able to the surrounding society, a world within a world or a state within the state. As the movement grew, its organizations expanded 'to include almost the whole of social life':

A member of the party could read Social Democratic newspapers and borrow from a Social Democratic library books which covered every aspect of life from a Social Democratic point of view; he could spend his leisure in Social Democratic pubs, or gymnastic clubs, choirs or cycling societies, he could enrich his life through Social Democratic cultural and artistic associations; his wife could enlist in the Social Democratic Women's Movement and his son in the Social Democratic Youth Movement; if he was injured or fell ill, he could call upon the Working Men's Samaritan Federation to help him; if he died, there were Social Democratic burial clubs to see he received a decent funeral.[17]

The implications of this situation were systematically laid out by Gunther Roth in a study that proved paradigmatic for later discussions. The argument has the same double edge. On the one hand, the subculture reinforced the movement's isolation, by reducing supporters' dependence on the authoritarian dominant culture, by promoting their self-reliance and by creating a sense of pride and confidence in working-class cultural endeavour. In this framework the SPD's Marxism again takes its place as an ideology of integration. But, on the other hand, the subculture was both defensive and increasingly complacent. There was little attempt to develop a revolutionary practice and, on the whole, the SPD's cultural organizations broadly reproduced the values of the dominant culture. Ultimately, they sustained a political immobilism in which maintaining the movement became its own justification, divorced from any activist revolutionary ambition. In Roth's paradoxical and widely accepted phrase, the SPD became 'negatively' integrated into the dominant system. It both expressed the aspirations of the excluded workers and contained their revolutionary potential, dissipating the full force of their resentment against the existing society. This belied the SPD's revolutionary rhetoric. Objectively, the subculture functioned as a force for stability.[18]

Given the functionalist overtones of this account and the attempt to minimize the real as opposed to the formal radicalism of the SPD's presence in society, the burden is increased on a third explanation, namely the attitude of the state. Ultimately, the SPD remained 'revolutionary' because the system left it no choice. In effect, the party's retention of Marxist perspectives is reduced to a political exigency beyond its control, namely the repressive and reactionary policies of an imperial state which refused to accept its admission to the political system. It was this that finally prevented all the tendencies to integration from coming to fruition. As Evans says,

The SPD is portrayed in this interpretation as having been a pre-dominantly non-revolutionary party from the beginning ... What prevented the SPD from realising its potential as a broadly based

176

movement of social reform . . . was above all the hostility of the authorities. By subjecting the party to constant police harassment . . . the authorities manoeuvered the SPD into a ghetto. It was thus impossible for the party to make the politically crucial transition from a labour movement [*Arbeiterbewegung*] to a broadly based democratic party [*Volkspartei*]. The verbal radicalism of the party, taken seriously only by its intellectuals, served as a rhetorical fig leaf for its political impotence. Had the state offered the SPD full participation, the pseudo-Marxism of the party's programme would soon have been dispensed with.[19]

This returns us to the starting-point. As I have argued elsewhere,

the complex ideological formation of the Social Democratic sub-sulture, at least in its politicised radical and oppositional form, is conceptualised as an *unnatural* development, because it both inhibited the proper integration of the working class into the institutional framework of a modern bourgeois society (which in the long run is assumed to be inevitable), and yet was *imposed* on the labour movement from the outside by the irredeemably entrenched backwardness of the Imperial political system.[20]

This framework of interpretation now has an enormous weight of opinion behind it. Resting on the solid foundations of the Conze school, it was elaborated in Ritter's pioneering text, Matthias's commentary on Kautsky and Susanne Miller's more general exegesis, and anchored in a detailed sociology by Gunther Roth. It was no accident that this scholarly activity (1957–64) spanned the adoption of the Godesberg Programme in 1959, which officially ratified the SPD's long march through the existing institutions and realized the aspirations which the new historian attributed to the movement before 1914. This confluence of a new academic historiography with the SPD's impending legitimation as a party of government was strikingly revealed in the literary celebration of the labour movement's centenary in 1963.[21] The intellectual departures were con-solidated by a series of institutional developments: the appearance of the splendid *Archiv für Sozialgeschichte* in 1961; the launching of the *Internationale wissenschaftliche Korrespondenz zur Geschichte der Deutschen Arbeiterbewegung* (IWK) in 1965; and the opening of the SPD's official archive, the *Archiv für soziale Demokratie*, in Bad Godesburg in 1969. Under the auspices of the *Friedrich-Ebert Stiftung*, an enormous apparatus of publication and research has unfolded, most of it firmly situated within the interpretive perspectives sketched above. The teleology of class consciousness has subsided before a teleology of integration. The SPD's destiny as a 'responsible party of government', taking its stand resolutely on the ground of a modified welfare capitalism, has increasingly structured perceptions of its earlier history. Most work has tacitly accepted this perspective and some has been self-consciously affirmative.[22]

Thus when the second wave of scholarly research started to appear in the later 1960s a definite problematic was strongly in place. The question was not why the SPD reneged on its original revolutionary commitment, but why an artificial revolutionism took so long to fall away, revealing the authentic reformism of the labour movement beneath. On the whole a fixed conception of the possible limits of radical reform in an 'industrial society' (involving belief in the permanence of the capitalist economy, qualified by the welfare-statist allayment of distributive injustice and the political constraint of rational parliamentary authority, with strong assumptions about the 'natural' place of trade unions and pluralist scepticism about the relevance of a class-based workers' party to a 'modern' political system) have made German labour historians relatively uninterested in certain kinds of analysis. There is no need for concepts of the labour aristocracy, bureaucratization, incorporation and other theories of reformism, as the mass of the working class is assumed to have been essentially reformist in the first place. The hold of an outwardly revolutionary ideology on the SPD is explained by specific political processes of factional control facilitated by the abnormal conditions of the Anti-Socialist Law. Once the party graduated into a genuine mass movement after 1890, an inevitable process of 'deradicalization' set in, or the 'emancipation from theory as such'.[23] That this failed to dislodge the dominant Marxist perspectives was partly caused by the dynamics of inner-party factionalism, the need of the party centre for a serviceable 'ideology of integration'. But it was above all a function of Imperial Germany's political system which confined the SPD in its radical ghetto. This political determination – the complex reciprocity between isolation and self-isolation – was ultimately decisive.

II

This, broadly speaking, is where the discussion has remained. The three major general studies of the pre-1914 SPD published in the late 1960s and early 1970s – by Hans-Josef Steinberg, Hans-Christoph Schröder and Dieter Groh – deepen our understanding by careful argument and a wealth of research, but do not overstep the bounds defined above.[24] Steinberg's book in particular now stands as the authoritative account of the party's ideological physiognomy, presenting a far more nuanced analysis of the official Marxism and the position of Kautsky, and introducing the concept of *Praktizisus* to describe the practical reformism of the party apparatus. Since then detailed research has accumulated on particular aspects of the SPD's development – the structure of its ideology, its relationship to particular issues, biographies, regional and local studies and, above all, aspects of the subculture.[25]

Measured against the extensive literature in German, treatments of the SPD in English have a much sparser appearance. However, there are several distinguished exceptions to this generalization. Gunther Roth's work has already been mentioned, and the contributions by Carl Schorske, Vernon Lidtke and Peter Nettl should also be singled out.[26] Yet each of these latter three authors is hard to place in relation to the broad tendencies of interpretation I have been trying to identify. Nettl's now classic essay defies ready classification in this respect, and despite the promise of its title never properly explicates the nature of the 'political model' the SPD is being made to represent. Lidtke's conclusions concerning the impact of the Anti-Socialist Law are not inconsistent with the arguments advanced by Miller, Matthias and Steinberg, but his stress on the 'heritage of ambivalent parliamentarism' and the party's growing reliance on the 'certainties of Marxist economic theory' is notably more circumspect than the Germans' interpretation, and he modestly abstains from any general evaluations of the period after 1890. Schorske's work remains in a class of its own, tracing the inner-party alignments with an unsurpassed lucidity, and richly combining intellectual, political and sociological discussions in its account of the left–right split after 1905. But all three of these contributions are ultimately extremely 'political' in their historical approach and achieve the power of their analysis mainly by the meticulousness and density of their empirical illustrations.

Otherwise, the subsequent literature in English is largely derivative and reinforces rather than supersedes the older general accounts. Moreover, the English-speaking left has surprisingly shown no interest in the SPD. There are no Marxist historians of the party in the English language. There is some exegetical literature, sometimes of a high quality – for example, Norman Geras's essays on Rosa Luxemburg, or Lucio Colletti's 'Bernstein and the Marxism of the Second International'. But such works remain essentially uninterested in history *per se*, as opposed to its usefulness for current theoretical debates.[27]

This makes the appearance of Molly Nolan's new book on Düsseldorf, *Social Democracy and Society. Working Class Radicalism in Dusseldorf, 1890–1920* (Cambridge, 1981) extremely welcome. It is easy to forget how little we have known until very recently about the local character of the SPD. There were few contemporary chronicles of major cities and a handful of rather orthodox political narratives. But it is only since the 1970s that efforts have been made to relate the party's activities to the local socio-economic environment and its political culture.[28] It is here that

Nolan's own ambitions are directed. Quoting the talismanic sentences from Edward Thompson's famous preface ('Class is a relationship, and not a thing . . . Class is defined by men as they live their own history . . .'), she sets out to plot the making of the working class in Düsseldorf, by describing its forms of self-activity as these were expressed through its trade union and socialist organizations, and by tracing the actions upon it of the dominant classes, political Catholicism and the state.[29] Düsseldorf is a well-chosen setting for this account. As one of the industrial West's new cities, it combined three of Wilhelmine Germany's striking particularities in a way that condensed the complex strategic problems facing a mass socialist party of the working class like the SPD (itself a striking particularity of the German situation): an economy dominated by technically advanced and highly concentrated metal and machine-building industries, with an extremely effective political representation; an authoritarian political system, which was effectively closed against the working class; and the powerful cultural presence of organized Catholicism, which was permanently implanted amongst the predominantly Catholic population of the city (70 per cent in 1900).

Each of these characteristics presented itself to the local SPD as a serious obstacle. The big plants in heavy industry (iron, steel, pipes, wire, heavy machinery, machine tools) were notoriously hard to organize, and in Düsseldorf firms like Rheinmetall, Haniel & Lueg, Oberbilkerstahlwerk and Springorum reproduced the familiar pattern of their sector: ruthless paternalism, effective exclusion of trade unions, blacklists, company welfare schemes, a highly rationalized labour process, draconian factory ordinances and tight co-operation amongst the employers.[30] Consequently, although metal industries employed almost a third of the Düsseldorf workers by 1907 and metalworkers had come to form the largest group of the city's organized workers (in both the union cartel and the party membership), the rate of unionization was disproportionately low (only 4,035 out of 20,443 metalworkers in 1907). As in the rest of Germany, most of the organized metalworkers came from the most skilled trades (fitters, turners, moulders) in the small- and medium-sized firms. Otherwise, the party and unions recruited mainly from the numerous artisanal trades in construction and woodworking, with smaller contingents at different times from the skilled tailors, brewers and shoemakers. This meant that the unskilled proletariat, large numbers of whom of course were women (in the advanced factory sector of chemicals, paper, and fats and oils, in the food and clothing trades, and in catering), remained untouched. Obviously, this gave the organized working class a specific profile: 'primarily skilled construction, wood, and metal workers, who had an advantageous position in the labour-market and division of labour'. As Nolan says: 'They had received artisan training and absorbed the culture of the skilled trades. They regarded themselves and were regarded as full-fledged and permanent members of the urban, industrial working class' (p. 112).

They were also more likely to be Protestant than Catholic (though less so as time went on), and in-migrants than natives. Like the cities of the Ruhr, Düsseldorf recruited its massively expanding population (from some 70,000 in 1871 to 213,711 by 1900, with another 96,559 in the surrounding county) from newcomers. Many of these were transients (youths, foreigners and especially peasants), whose expectations of industrial work were frequently instrumental and temporary, and who were quite prepared to change jobs and residences both inside the city and out. For example, by the end of 1905 'one-third of those who had come since January and two-thirds of those who had arrived in 1904 had departed' (p. 115). On the whole the labour movement had little success in organizing this unskilled and mobile mass and was dependent for support mainly on the smaller pool of migrant artisans, skilled factory workers and others with some prior experience of urban living or industrial work. At first this strongly re-emphasized the social profile mentioned above, which confined the socialist working class predominantly to its more skilled, male, German-speaking and Protestant fractions. Later, 'the ever-growing number of skilled Catholic migrants also found their way into the movement', with enormous political implications (p. 117). The bastion of political Catholicism in Düsseldorf was the 'native-born working class', whose religious and associational culture proved obstinately resistant to the SPD's agitation and was enough to keep the city's Reichstag seat in the Centre Party until 1911–12. It was only very gradually, as the in-migrants swamped the natives and the adaptive capacities of the Catholic Centre's politico-cultural apparatus, that the SPD partially overcame the religious divisions and established its broader leadership within the Düsseldorf working class.[31]

Finally, the SPD ran up against the power of the state, ramified through its local manifestations. Aside from the obvious facts of the Prussian three-class franchise and the limited powers of the Reichstag, and hence the limited significance of the SPD's parliamentary representation, this took a powerful local form. As Nolan says, 'In Prussia, unlike the more liberal South German states, provincial and municipal institutions reinforced the authoritarian character and narrow class base of politics' (p. 26). The city council was elected on an extraordinarily restrictive three-class suffrage which placed municipal affairs in the hands of a tightly knit bourgeois oligarchy, organized informally through the so-called 'Middle Party' (the characteristic local forum for the predominantly National Liberal urban property-owners in western Germany) in collusion with the local Centre. Other things followed from this, for example, control of police, education, health, sanitation, public utilities, local taxation and the growing municipal labour force (1,600 in 1900, doubling within the decade). The local SPD made little impact on this structure, which in certain situations of crisis (such as strikes and popular demonstrations) could be turned brutally against it. It is true that the party achieved higher turnouts in municipal elections (so that 49 per cent of the third-class voters were going to the polls by 1910, against only 18 per cent in 1900), which were quite impressive given the practical immunity of the city's oligarchy to popular democratic pressure. It is also clear that the SPD's agitation galvanised the local Centre into minimal reformist demands and elicited minor concessions from the council, for example, a social commission in 1906, a labour exchange by 1905–6, and limited public works in 1901–3 and 1907–9. But as far as concrete material or social advances were concerned, there was very little to show. The main outcome of the local political process was actually the powerlessness of the SPD and the exclusion of the working class.

Nolan argues strongly that these factors – the intransigence of heavy industry, the resilience of the native Catholic subculture, above all the unbending authoritarianism of the local state – were the determinants of radicalism. This contention hinges essentially on the absence of real opportunities for reformism in the local setting. As Nolan shows, the local Social Democrats (who at that time were an isolated and marginal minority within the working class) emerged from the 1890s profoundly mistrustful of 'parliamentarism, class collaboration and political alliances', because these seemed 'either unfeasible or unproductive in the Düsseldorf context' (p. 303). After intensive involvement in both local and national inner-party controversy at the turn of the century, they began a successful process of 'movement building' firmly committed to an orthodox revolutionary Marxism as that was understood at the time. Contrary to the popular bureaucratization theses of Robert Michels and others, the construction of a centralized city apparatus for political, ideological and cultural purposes was not a recipe for conservatism and inertia, but a means of fuelling the leadership's radical commitments.[32] Repeatedly, experience showed the activists and their supporters that reformism would simply not work, whether in the trade union, municipal, or electoral arenas of their agitation. Gradually, as the Centre compromised its popular credibility on the issues of taxes and tariffs, as the employers set their faces against trade union concessions, and as the local state demonstrated its rigidity, larger and larger sections of the popular classes in Düsseldorf came to agree. Here Nolan basically follows Dick Geary's argument in a number of recent publications: the German working class was no more 'uniformly reformist' than it was 'monolithically revolutionary'; each orientation depended on the precise combinations of local social, economic and political conditions that different party organizations had to face; there were important sections of the SPD, including Düsseldorf, which either retained or developed a strong radical direction before 1914.[33]

Much of this analysis carries conviction. At her chosen level of generality (in parallel accounts of the working class and the SPD, the one structural, the other mainly narrative) Nolan successfully combines 'the history of the working class with the history of the workers' movement' (p. ix). The pivotal chapter is the one called 'Skilled migrants, peasant workers, and native Catholics', where the complex socio-cultural topography of the Düsseldorf working class is juxtaposed with the potential organizing problems faced by the local party. On this Nolan predicates an argument regarding the role of centralizing political institutions in unifying the disparate interests and experiences of the class: 'In order to organise, educate and integrate these highly mobile workers, it was, as we shall see, absolutely essential for the party and unions to have a stable core of functionaries. A certain irreducible level of bureaucratisation was dictated by the unalterable facts of working-class life' (p. 118). At the centre was the SPD subculture which afforded the organizational resources for contesting the unconscionably propagandist content of the dominant culture and the associated efforts of the Catholic Church. It provided a bridge to the more transient, unskilled, Catholic, female and youthful workers who were otherwise so difficult to organize. It helped politicize everyday life. In general, it 'strengthened members' identity with their class by emphasizing the centrality of class to all aspects of workers' lives and enabling them to define all their activities consciously in terms of their class position' (p. 143).

However, the stronger version of this argument is more problematic. Nolan believes that 'political organisations and ideologies' are 'a crucial – but not exclusive – determinant of class formation and class relations' (pp. ix ff.).

In 1890 there were workers in Düsseldorf, tens of thousands of them, ranging from skilled cabinetmakers through semiskilled metalworkers and unskilled construction helpers to female domestics. There were Catholics and Protestants, natives and migrants, permanent city dwellers and temporary peasant workers. But there was not a working class, united by shared traditions, experiences and consciousness. In the ensuing three decades an increasingly articulate and organised working class, aware of its interests and striving to assert them against others, emerged in Düsseldorf (p. 1).

The key contribution was that of the SPD. It was decisive in 'forging those diverse and divided workers into a cohesive class with a shared political outlook, cultural experiences and goals'. It 'provided a common language and created a dissenting tradition where none had existed'. Consequently, it 'not only created a powerful movement but a working class as well' (p. 223). This is strong stuff. Edward Thompson's conception in *The Making of the English Working Class* – of a class consciousness forged in the crucible of shared experienced and embodied in culture – resonates through Nolan's account. In Thompson's book the working class is 'made' not just from its experience of exploitation, but from a long encounter with political repression, and Nolan clearly intends a similar sort of argument for Düsseldorf.

But in practice Thompson's 'working class' is a formation heavily dominated by skilled artisanal sections and its 'class consciousness' is defined mainly by a specific configuration of organizations (what he calls 'strongly-based and self-conscious working-class institutions – trade unions, friendly societies, education and religious movements, political organisation, periodicals – working-class intellectual traditions, working-class community-patterns, and a working-class structure of feeling'), whose lines of representation to the working class as a whole are anything but clear.[34] In other words, Thompson's conception of a working class which is already 'made' by the 1830s tends to fudge the question of the relationship between the radical culture of the 1820s (which was largely artisanal) and the mass of the workers (a more general category of direct producers working for a wage) in a way that suppresses a vital area of difficulty concerning the economic formation of the working class and its internal divisions of trade, skill, nationality, age and sex.[35] *Mutatis mutandis*, much the same might be addressed to Molly Nolan's account. There is a sort of substitutionism at work in a large part of her book through which the party militants imperceptibly stand in for the ordinary rank-and-file workers. Now, in fact, this is a latent contradiction as opposed to a straightforward weakness, because as we have seen she spends a lot of time precisely discussing the proletariat's internal fragmentation. But in the extremely positive evaluations of the SPD's political achievement, this dimension tends to get lost. To talk of the SPD *creating* 'a working class' (p. 223) or (more qualified but more powerful) 'a cohesive working class' (p. 225), to attribute to the party the central role in the process of class formation – in effect to say that politics is *constitutive* of class – is a doubtful theoretical procedure. After all, the class was still just as divided sociologically after the SPD had achieved its barely 50 per cent of the votes in the 1912 election, and by 1919 the combined total of the SPD and the USPD (Unabhängige Sozialdemokratische Partei Deutschland – Independent Social Democratic Party) had dropped to only 39.3 per cent. To talk of 'the making and the unmaking of the Dusseldorf working class' (p. 301) in this context (with its affirmative implication of completeness and resolution, of achieved class consciousness, of authenticity gained and lost) is arguably not the best way of capturing the socialist movement's complex and contradictory relationship to the working class.

Part of the problem is that Nolan presents the SPD as if it were external to the working class, acting upon the processes of class formation to shape them. She speaks of the Social Democrats 'mediating between workers on the one hand and the state and society on the other' (p. 223). But (as Nolan would surely agree) the party was itself situated in a field of antagonistic social relations, given its uneven recruitment from the working class as a whole, and participated in the very contradictions (of 'occupation and skill, culture and religion, age and sex, birthplace and commitment to urban life and industrial work' [p. 301]) it was pledged to overcome. One would like to know far more about the activist cadre which dominated the Düsseldorf party and which Nolan describes so well. What did they think of apprenticeship and seniority rules? Did they have a conception of the 'lumpenproletariat'? How did they distinguish between the 'respectable' working class (to use a British category) and the criminal, feckless, drunken and undeserving poor? What priority exactly (ideologically and in the practice of the movement's agitation) did they give to the casual labourer and factory unskilled? Did they look down on the Poles and other Easterners? What did they think of blacklegs? Where did they live, and what were the patterns of residential segregation (between classes, between religions, between nationalities, between different in-migrant groups, between trades)? What was their conception of 'proletarian morality'? And last but not least, how did they treat their wives and daughters? Some of these questions are easier than others, and some may not be answerable in terms of the available sources. But to pose them is the best way of getting at the SPD's adversary relationship to significant sections of the German working class.

There has been some attention recently to the question of fragmentation and sectionalism within the working class, which so far from disappearing with the progressive development of capitalism are continuously reproduced in ever-new forms, usually complicated by additional divisions of a cultural and sexual kind. That being so, the 'active unity' of the working class will depend on an 'area of conscious manoeuvre, choice, negotiation and compromise between working-class sections, whether in the arenas of local and national politics, in the building of united industrial movements or in the development of cultural and social institutions'.[36] This insight forms the starting-point for Nolan's book, and she rightly sees the key questions as being the SPD's ability to handle the dialectic of unifying and fragmenting tendencies within the working class to achieve the maximum degree of political solidarity.[37] But in the body of the book, carried away by the discovery of the Düsseldorf movement's organic radicalism, she seems to close the circuit by collapsing the party's partial status into too straightforward an identity with the class as a whole. In the end she is too impressed with the party's political achievement. Not that this was insignificant – quite the contrary, in fact, as I have tried to argue elsewhere.[38] But it was uneven, incomplete and transitory, defined by the specific circumstances of the Wilhelmine conjuncture. As the events of 1918–19 confirmed, the SPD was both too proletarian (because it failed to rally other groupings lastingly to the Socialist flag) and not proletarian enough (because it failed to establish a stable leadership over the whole working class). In this sense the radicalism of the party in Düsseldorf was just as sectionally grounded as its moderation in certain cities elsewhere.

III

Where does this leave us in terms of the historiography outlined at the start of this essay? In conclusion it is worth situating Nolan's work in relation to current trends in the literature. In this respect I have four points to make.

First, taken on its own terms Nolan's study is a timely contribution to the discussion of the pre-1914 SPD. By stressing the homegrown nature of the SPD's Marxist radicalism in Düsseldorf – its organic relatedness to the local conditions – she supplies an important corrective to the main drift of the scholarly literature. As suggested above, the latter postulates a sharp disjunction between the revolutionary ideology of the 'intellectuals' and a section of the leadership (including the post-1900 centrism of Kautsky) and the essentially humble, quotidian and economistic concerns of the rank and file. Into this space are then inserted the 'practical men' of the movement, the local functionaries and trade union officials, the real 'soul' of the SPD, who quietly get on with improving the lot of the workers, publicly indulgent but privately scathing about the inflammatory and maximalist rhetoric of the revolutionaries. As argued above, this view is common to both the early accounts of the SPD (especially Ritter, Miller, Matthias and Roth) and the more recent research, mediated through Steinberg's much more sophisticated discussion. Its *locus classicus* is in discussions of the subculture, where it has long been conventional to stress the membership's indifference to socialist theory and the essential escapism of its leisure-time pursuits, and where the preference of workers for adventure stories over *Das Kapital* becomes conclusive evidence against the existence of a socialist consciousness.[39] By going against the grain of this conventional wisdom Nolan has performed a valuable service, though her account of the subculture would have been strengthened by some detailed textual analysis of party literature, by close explorations of particular events and by a more 'Gramscian' perspective on the nature of the party.[40] This would allow us to test Geary's suggestive reference to 'a Social Democratic consciousness at the base of the party which transcended the ideological divisions at the level of the leadership'.[41] But none the less, by taking its appeal seriously Nolan registers a definite advance in the discussion of the SPD ideology. As she says, the Düsseldorf Social Democrats 'found the Kautskyan synthesis of revolutionary theory, reformist tactics and isolation appealing not because it served as an "integrating ideology" that unified the party, but rather

186

because it offered an analysis of and means to deal with the ambiguous, stalemated society that was Imperial Germany' (p. 89).

Secondly, the most interesting question about the SPD is how far it *really* challenged the bases of social order in Germany – its ability, that is, to organize German society into a genuine counter-hegemonic potential in Gramsci's sense. In Germany this presupposed a concerted effort to establish the SPD's moral leadership across a broad social coalition, so that its credibility as an agency of progressive change could be properly established. Unfortunately, while the catastrophic theory of capitalist breakdown still reigned (with the associated ideas of working-class immiseration and the polarization of society into two classes), the political problems of building such a front were never faced, because it was assumed that intermediate groupings like the peasantry, petty bourgeoisie and intelligentsia would either disappear through the logic of capitalist development or be attracted to the workers' movement by the contestable force of its moral authority. The people who *were* to raise the issue did so in a *reformist* light – revisionists following Bernstein's example, 'practicists' like the party secretary Ignas Auer, trade union pragmatists like Karl Legien or Otto Hué, or the south German parliamentarians in Bavaria, Baden and Württemberg – and that was enough to disqualify the question from the left's agenda. The problem of building broad popular-democratic unities behind *revolutionary* socialist policies – of recognizing the complexities of Germany's advanced capitalist social formation (as it was already becoming after 1900) while preserving the movement's funda-mental commitments to social transformation – were always evaded by different affirmations of orthodoxy or doctrinal purity, whether on the Luxemburgist left or in the Kautskyan centre. In other words, the problem of class alliances was never openly faced.[42]

Yet, at the same time, the SPD's practice necessarily tended in this direction. The moments of maximum electoral success (1898, when the party penetrated certain parts of the countryside; 1903, after the high tariffs of the previous year; and finally in 1912), for instance, included a vital 'non-proletarian' component, whether from the peasantry, white-collar categories, or sections of the traditional petty bourgeoisie.[43] Even in Düsseldorf the SPD's appeal almost certainly extended beyond the industrial workers proper, though Nolan is quite right to stress the self-consciously proletarian character of the local party's adopted self-image. The interesting question is how far the local party qualified this stance in its everyday practice, as for instance in the efforts to form a tenant's association in the 1890s (p. 67), or the municipal electioneering behind egalitarian rather than specifically socialist demands (pp. 201–14). A more meticulous analysis of the SPD's local ideological profile would have helped in evaluating the labour movement's broader popular-democratic potential in these respects.[44] For example, Nolan makes rather light of the party's efforts to tackle the question of religion after 1903 by trying to break the hold of popular Catholicism on the Düsseldorf working class, arguing that it went over the workers' heads. It did not 'speak to a felt working-class need or offer an interpretation of a significant experience', and consequently 'it fell on deaf ears' (p. 165). But there is no attempt to justify these assertions about working-class religious preference. There is no discussion of the details of the campaign, and Nolan's own figures for party membership suggest that it certainly did not harm the progress of recruitment, which increased membership by 55.4 per cent in 1905–6 and 66.8 per cent in 1906–7. Given her comments on the self-isolating effects of the party's situation in Düsseldorf and the sloth of its expansion elsewhere in the Catholic Rhine-Ruhr, this attempt to work with and through the contradictions of Christianity, by seeking to disarticulate the progressive elements in popular religiosity from their current ideological location, arguably deserved a more developed treatment.[45]

Thirdly, despite the strengths of Nolan's account, we are not really much further in understanding the bases of radicalism and moderation in different sections of the SPD, or more generally in different working-class movements. It is hard to fault the basic procedure of Nolan's approach – identifying the specificities in the recruitment, employment, culture and overall situation of the Düsseldorf working class as a basis for interpreting the problems faced by the SPD and the forms of its response. But her particular explanation for the Düsseldorf party's radicalism – essentially that the local situation left no scope for reformism – is not entirely satisfactory. For one thing, similar situations elsewhere culminated not in radicalism but in reformism and moderation. At the risk of oversimplifying, this seems to have been true of most of the Ruhr before 1914, for example, where the SPD and trade unions confronted much the same local difficulties as in Düsseldorf. Often, if we look at the homogeneity of local industry, its structure of ownership and control, the tightness of the local power structure, the power of Catholicism, and the religious and ethnic divisions in the working class, these could even be more extreme. But such conditions could be used to justify more than one kind of politics. Indeed, Stephen Hickey argues that 'in trying to meet effectively the challenges of the social and industrial conditions of the Ruhr the labour movement thus adopted a gradualist, cautious and non-political stance, with a strong emphasis on the need for organisation and discipline'. His argument is just as carefully and structurally 'determinist' as Nolan's, with the policies of the miners' union and the region's Social Democrats squarely juxtaposed to the conditions that made them intelligible, a 'direct response to the divisions and contradictions within working-class society'. But where Nolan has her local party leaders responding with radicalism, Hickey has his miners' leaders reacting with cautious moderation.[46]

How do we go from here? Clearly we need more local studies of particular working classes (particular cities, particular industries, particular firms) and their forms of trade union and political representation. In one way Nolan does not tell us enough about how the bonds of solidarity amongst and between different groups of workers were created. In his exemplary comparison of miners and metalworkers in Bochum, David Crew proposes the concept of occupational community (defined by interlocking structures of work and neighbourhood) for this purpose, and its application to Düsseldorf might well shed light on the greater propensity of certain categories of workers (for example, skilled metalworkers in small- and medium-sized industry, or construction workers) for trade union and party radicalism.[47] At all events, we need more detail – and more thought – about the concrete material circumstances of working-class experience (at home, in the neighbourhood, on the job) and their conscious, organized manifestation in working-class culture. Moreover, the latter means looking not just at the institutions of the SPD subculture, but at the *full range of working-class activities*, including (in the Düsseldorf case) those of popular Catholicism. Only by leaving the reassuring surroundings of the SPD committee rooms for the wider worlds of the working class, to view the impact of the teacher, priest, poor commissioner, policeman, philanthropist and others, will we bring the SPD's influence properly into perspective. If we are to claim that the party was crucial in creating a relatively cohesive working-class identity in Düsseldorf and elsewhere, or (to put it more modestly) that it achieved a high degree of solidarity amongst a wage-earning population which was otherwise heavily fragmented along sectional, religious, ethnic, sexual and cultural lines, then we have to be much more explicit about its relationship to the working class as a whole. In other words, we have to look at the overall field of relations in which the SPD had to operate, conceding its contradictions with the subordinate as well as with the dominant classes.

This provokes a general observation. There are perhaps three general approaches to the study of comparative labour protest and its conditions of possibility. One stresses the importance of leaderships and the formative interventions of a labour movement in the narrower institutional sense; another stresses the sociology of protest, seeing it as 'the product of certain shared conditions of working-class life', such as (most commonly) 'geographic and social uprooting', 'economic misery' or the effects of 'social and technological change';[48] a third looks to the actions of government and the dominant classes for the decisive influence on the willingness of popular forces to take collective political action. Each of these approaches has its uses. The first has the advantage of avoiding economic or sociological reductionism, treating the possibility of radicalism as more of an empirical question, concerning the ability of leaderships to mobilize different degrees of solidarity from situation to situation. It reminds us of the contingency of political outcomes, the complex mediations between movements and their support, and the frequent disjunctions between formal ideology and rank-and-file beliefs.[49] But is can also make the emergence of racialism seem arbitrary, dependent on the preferences of local activists and whoever happens to be in control at the time.[50] Similarly, while the sociological approach sensitizes us to the importance of social determinations, it must be said that by this time the interpretations referred to above look pretty threadbare ('social and technological change' no less so than the others). As Crew says, 'misery, uprooting, and change can all create grievances experienced individually by workers, but there is no guarantee that these grievances will be expressed collectively if they are all that binds the group together'.[51]

By far the most compelling of these approaches, to judge from the current literature, is the third. Dick Geary has advanced its virtues in a number of recent texts, both as a general description of European labour protest ('the European working class turned to independent politics only in certain cases and in cases in which the state intervened in the daily lives of workers in both the factory and the home') and as a particular explanation of the SPD's predicament before 1914.[52] Specifically, Geary argues that 'certain kinds of governmental interference in industrial relations' transformed 'what began as economic protest into political action', and that most major working-class mobilizations have been a defensive radicalization against repressive actions by the state.[53] As we have seen, this is also the generally preferred explanation of the SPD's adoption and subsequent retention of a Marxist revolutionary ideology under Bismarck and Wilhelm II, and it is consistent with the position adopted by Molly Nolan in her book. Its corollary (though not, it should be noted, for Nolan) is a rather disparaging scepticism about the practical relevance of the SPD's public ideology, which is thought to have played little part in the activation of working-class protest. Either working-class life proceeded 'beneath' the level of formal socialist activity according to its own quotidian rhythms, motivated by its own 'inherited values', or else, on occasion, it was jolted into radicalism by the provocations of the state and the dominant classes. The effectiveness of 'formal organisation and theory' (that is, socialism, in this case the SPD) is inscribed in the latter, not the former.[54]

In a previous article Keith Nield and I argued against this downgrading of ideology.[55] This is not to dispute the importance of the overall political context: the state, the political representation of capital and the institutions of the dominant classes are clearly decisive in structuring the possible forms of working-class politics, in both a limiting and a provocative way. Given the prevailing authoritarianism of the Wilhelmine system before 1914, this was especially clear in Germany. Yet, it is far from clear why this view should rule out a serious consideration of the SPD and its cultural impact on the working class. In fact, Geary draws a rather sharp distinction between 'an intellectual system imported into working-class ranks by an outside intelligentsia' (that is, 'the Leninist theory of "consciousness from without", which ascribes the determining role to professional revolutionaries') and the spontaneous culture of the working class itself ('a set of perceptions and values into which individual workers are socialised through innumerable agencies, through their backgrounds, work and home environment').[56] Now apart from leaving the Leninist dichotomy of spontaneity and revolutionary consciousness intact while simply reversing the positive evaluation, this presents a needlessly restrictive view of how working-class consciousness gets formed. In other words, it is not made clear why we should exclude the institutions of the SPD and its subculture from the range of influences, the 'innumerable agencies', which help to form and reproduce the native culture of the working class. If we are to stress the tangible material presence of *the state* in the everyday lives of German workers we should at least *consider* the efforts of the SPD to implant itself in a similar style, instead of confining it to some 'superstructure' largely removed, it is suggested, from the real preoccupations of the workers themselves. If we were to take something like David Crew's concept of occupational community, combine it with some sensitive and imaginative investigations of everyday life, and consider the full range of institutional and ideological influences acting on workers' lives, then there is no reason why 'imported political theory' and 'ideology in the more general sense of a received or changing set of ideas and values' should be mutually exclusive categories.[57]

Finally – this is the fourth of my concluding observations – it becomes terribly important to find ways of reintegrating the history of the SPD with the developing preoccupations of current German social history. On the whole, as in other national historiographies, the turn to social history has been simultaneously a turn against the study of formal organizations, so that the recently proliferating research (for example, the quantitative analyses of migratory labour markets, family and industrialization, or social structure, and the interpretive investigations of *Alltag*, 'everyday life') has rarely anything to say very directly about the SPD, public ideology, or the political representation of the working class.[58] In this respect it is instructive to compare the account of Düsseldorf in Nolan with that of Bochum in Crew. While Nolan builds on a fine analysis of economy, social structure and composition of the working class, her book becomes essentially a political history of the SPD, in which the material circumstances of working-class life and the class relations of Düsseldorf society are certainly present, but in a general contextualizing way. Crew, on the other hand, builds up a meticulously layered analysis, beginning with geographic and social mobility and ending with the 'foundations of worker protest' and the actual progress of industrial conflict in the great miners' strikes of 1889, 1905 and 1912; his account hinges on a dynamic presentation of Bochum's class structure and class relations. But the character of the SPD in the town, as a concrete material presence within the working class, is almost completely omitted.[59] As a consequence the two labours of the more-political and the more-social historian never completely intersect and what should be a fruitful complementarity of approaches is never properly reached.

It is important to find ways of remedying this situation. Of course, to have the new research on the social history of the working class is in itself an unqualified good. We now have a much clearer sense of the patterns of working-class sociability; we possess many of the materials for a deeper and more sophisticated conception of class formation and for the first time we have an adequate general history of the German trade unions.[60] Certain individuals – Alf Lüdtke and Dieter Groh among them – are posing the question of politics in quite challenging and openly theorized ways.[61] The time is very auspicious. Thus in his introduction to *The German Working Class*, Richard Evans announces the need 'to re-integrate social and political history, the history of the working-class and the labour movement, which the rapid development of social-historical research in German labour history is threatening to tear asunder'. And, in fact, most contributors to his volume discharge this task with great distinction and imagination (in Eve Rosenhaft's case, even with brilliance.) Yet there is still a tendency for social historians to raise the subject of the SPD (and formal socialist ideology) mainly to minimize its importance, and the salutary distinction between 'Social Democratic values' and 'working class values' (with the associated stress on 'the growing gulf between proletarian culture and Social Democratic culture') creates some important problems of its own. There is a nagging feeling, ratified by Dick Geary's essay referred to earlier, that the SPD may be sold too short, that the social history of the German working class may too easily become history with the SPD left out, as Trevelyan might have said.[62] There are no simple answers to these questions, and my own remarks have clearly tended in a similar direction, towards problematizing the SPD's relationship to the working class. But for an ambitious history, certainly for a Marxist one, the new social history will only fully realize its value by reinvigorating discussion of the SPD on a shrewder and more sophisticated basis.

CHAPTER 7: NOTES

1   East German literature may be approached through the official *Geschichte der deutschen Arbeiterbewegung* published by the Institute for Marxism-Leninism of the Central Committee of the SED in eight or fifteen volumes, depending on the edition (East Berlin, 1966), and Dieter Fricke's indispensable compilation. *Die deutsche Arbeiterbewegung 1869–1914* (East Berlin, 1976). Amongst the many monographs the following are still very valuable: E. Engelberg, *Revolutionäre Politik und Rote Feldpost 1878–1890* (East Berlin, 1959); D. Fricke, *Bismarcks Pratorianer. Die Berliner politische Polizei im Kampf*

gegen *die deutsche Arbeiterbewegung 1871–1898* (East Berlin, 1962) H. Hesselbarth, *Revolutionäre Sozialdemokraten, Opportunisten und die Bauern am Vorabend des Imperialismus* (East Berlin, 1968). Otherwise, the periodical dealing with labour history is *Beiträge zur Geschichte der Arbeiterbewegung*. It must be said that the limits of permissible interpretation in the labour history field are quite tightly drawn for East German historians and dissenting perspectives have been quite rare. But see J. Kuczynski, *Der Ausbruch des ersten Weltkrieges und die deutsche Sozialdemokratie. Chronik und Analyse* (East Berlin, 1957). Moreover, this has not prevented some individuals from producing social history which is methodologically extremely challenging: see esp. H. Zwahr, *Zur Konstituierung des Proletariats als Klasse. Strukturuntersuchung über da Leipziger Proletariat während det industriellen Revolution* (East Berlin, 1978), reviewed by Sidney Pollard in *Social History*, vol. 5 (May 1980), pp. 320–3. For an example of West German orthodoxy: G. Fülberth and J. Harrer, *Arbeiterbewegung und SPD. Band I. Die deutsche Sozialidemokratie 1890–1933* (Darmstadt, 1974).

2 See Conze's classic essay, 'Vom "Pöbel" zum "Proletariat". Sozialgeschichtliche Voraussetzung für den Sozialismus in Deutschland', *Vierteljahresschrift für Sozial- und Wirtschaftsgeschichte*, vol. 41 (1954), pp. 33–64; and the early monographs by W. Schieder, *Anfänge der deutschen Arbeiterbewegung* (Stuttgart, 1963), and F. Balser, *Sozial-Demokratie 1848–1863*, 2 vols (Stuttgart, 1963).

3 Other works in the Heidelberg School include the following: H. Soell, 'Die deutsche Arbeiterbewegung im Reichsland Elsass-Lothringen, 1871–1918', (PhD diss., University of Heidelberg, 1963); W. Schmierer, *Von der Arbeiterbildung zur Arbeiterpolitik. Die Anfänge der Arbeiterbewegung in Württemberg 1862–1878* (Hanover, 1969); J. Schadt, *Die Sozialdemokratische Partei in Baden 1868–1900* (Hanover, 1971); H. Eckert, *Liberal-oder Sozialdemokratie? Frühgeschichte der Nürnberger Arbeiterbewegung* (Stuttgart, 1968); U. Engelhardt, *Nur vereinigt sind wir stark. Die Anfänge der deutschen Gewerkschaften 1862–3 bis 1869–70*, 2 vols (Stuttgart, 1977). Summary accounts may be found in the following: D. Groh, 'Hundert Jahre deutsche Arbeiterbewegung?' *Der Staat*, vol. 2 (1963), pp. 351–66; W. Conze, 'Der Beginn der deutschen Arbeiterbewegung,' in W. Besson and F. von Gaetringen (eds), *Festschrift fur Hans Rothfels* (Göttingen, 1963), pp. 323–38; W. Conze, *Möglichkeiten und Grenzen der liberalen Arbeiterbewegung in Deutschland. Das Beispiel Schulze-Delitzschs* (Heidelberg, 1965); W. Conze and D. Groh, *Die Arbeiterbewegung in der nationalen Bewegung* (Stuttgart, 1966).

4 W. Schieder, 'Das Scheitern des bürgerlichen Radikalismus und die sozialistische Parteibildung in Deutschland', in H. Mommsen (ed.), *Sozialdemokratie zwischen Klassenbewegung und Volkspartei* (Frankfurt-on-Main, 1974), p. 21.

5 Conze and Groh, *Die Arbeiterbewegung in der nationalen Bewegung*, p. 124. See also G. Mayer, 'Die Trennung der proletarischen von der bürgerlichen Demokratie in Deutschland, 1863–1870', H.-U. Wehler (ed.), in *Radikalismus, Sozialismus und bürgerliche Demokratie* (Frankfurt-on-Main, 1969), pp. 108–78 (originally published in 1912).

6 Conze, 'Der Beginn der deutschen Arbeiterbewegung', cit. at n. 3 above, pp. 337 ff. What exactly Conze means by 'Democrats' in this context is not clear. Liberal unwillingness to undertake specifically democratic commitments in the 1860s was what pushed labour politicians into independent positions in the first place, and outside the South-West it is unclear how far there was ever a distinct democratic option within the liberal coalitions. The elision of liberalism and democracy (under the impact of the post-1945 liberal-democratic consensus) is a weakness in Conze's argument.

7 Schieder, 'Scheitern des bürgerlichen Radikalismus', cit. at n. above, p. 21. The most recent detailed accounts are in Engelhardt, 'Nur vereinigt sind wir stark', cit. at n. 3 above, and T. Offermann, *Arbeiterbewegung und liberales Burgertum in Deutschland 1850–1863* (Bonn, 1979). The works of Shlomo Na'aman are also consonant with this. See: *Lassalle* (Hanover, 1970); *Demokratische und soziale Impulse in der Frühgeschichte der deutschen Arbeiterbewegung der Jahre 1862–3* (Wiesbaden, 1969) (ed.), *Die Konstituierung der deutschen Arbeiterbewegung 1862–63* (Assen, 1975); *Zur Entstehung der deutschen Arbeiterbewegung. Lernprozesse und Vergesellschaftung 1830–1868* (Hanover, 1978).

8 This process has been described by Susanne Miller, *Das Problem der Freiheit im Sozialismus* (Frankfurt-on-Main, 1964), and H.-J. Steinberg, *Sozialismus und deutsche Sozialdemokratie. Zur Ideologie der Partei vor dem 1. Weltkrieg* (Bonn and Bad-Godesberg, 1976; 1st edn., 1967). See also E. Matthias, 'Kautsky und der Kautsky-anismus: Die Funktion der Ideologie in der deutschen Sozialdemokratie vor dem ersten Weltkriege', *Marxismusstudien*, 2nd ser. (1957), pp. 151–97.

9 For the process leading to the adoption of the Erfurt Programme, see Miller, *Problem der Freiheit*, pp. 199ff.; G. P. Steenson, *Karl Kautsky, 1854–1938. Marxism in the Classical Years* (Pittsburgh, Pa 1978), pp. 93 ff. For subsequent debates around the new orthodoxy, see C. E. Schorske, *German Social Deomocracy 1905–1917* (New York, 1955) and P. Gay, *The Dilemma of Democratic Socialism: Eduard Bernstein's Challenge to Marx* (New York, 1962). Schorske, whose account is still by far the best narrative history of the years after 1900, does not share the general belittlement of the SPD's Marxist tradition.

10 See esp. Miller, *Problem der Freiheit*, but this is also a common theme of the Heidelberg works.

11 G. A. Ritter, *Die Arbeiterbewegung im Wilhelminischen Reich 1890–1900* (West Berlin, 1959). Ritter's book has still not been superseded as an account of the movement's second founding period, and is the equivalent in German historiography of Henry Pelling's classic *Origins of the Labour Party 1880–1900* (London, 1954).

12 Ritter, *Die Arbeiterbewegung im Wilhelminischen Reich*, pp. 149, 208, 187.

13 This is one of Ritter's principal arguments, e.g., see his heavily loaded recommendations of the key trade union leaders Karl Legien and Theodor Leipart, ibid., p. 166. The formal subordination of the trade unions to the party's political leadership was a hallmark of the Continental Social Democratic tradition in the last third of the nineteenth century, in contrast to Britain where the independent political representation of labour originated from an initiative of the pre-established trade union movement. The revision of this arrangement, particularly through intensive debates in 1905–6, is a major theme of Schorske's book. For the best accounts of the German trade union movement see G. A. Ritter and K. Tenfelde, 'Der Durchbruch der Freien Gewerkschaften Deutschlands zur Massenbewegung im letzten Viertel des 19. Jahrhunderts', in Ritter, *Arbeiterbewegung, Parteien und Parlamentarismus* (Göttingen, 1976), pp. 55–101; K. Schönhoven, *Expansion und Konzentration. Studien zur Entwicklung der Freien Gewerkschaften im Wilhelminischen Deutschland 1890–1914* (Stuttgart, 1980); J. A. Moses, *Trade Unionism in Germany from Bismarck to Hitler 1869–1933. Vol. 1: 1869–1918* (London, 1982).

14 Ritter, *Die Arbeiterbewegung im Wilhelminischen Reich*, pp. 127, 187. Ritter's approach is essentially a pluralist one; it conceives the labour movement as just 'one grouping of forces amongst others' in German society, constituted by certain common sectional interests with neither more nor less legitimacy than any others, and not by more fundamental class antagonisms. In this respect and in the central stress on the trade unions, Ritter's thinking reflects an idealized version of the British experience. It is no accident that he is also one of West Germany's leading authorities on British constitutional history. Here his writings strongly affirm the Whig romance of parliamentary evolution. For example, Ritter (ed.), *Das britische Regierungssystem. Quellenbuch* (Opladen, 1958); Ritter, *Deutscher und britischer Parlamentarismus* (Tübingen, 1962).

15 Matthias, 'Kautsky und der Kautskyanismus', cit. at n. 8 above. Matthias's view of Kautsky has been enormously influential on the academic historiography of the SPD. A number of more satisfactory Marxist discussions are now available: R. J. Geary, 'Karl Kautsky and the development of Marxism' (PhD, University of Cambridge, 1971); M. Salvadori, *Karl Kautsky and the Socialist Revolution 1880–1938* (London, 1979); W. Holzheuer, *Karl Kautskys Werk als Weltanschauung* (Munich, 1972); R. Walter, ' . . . aber nach der Sundflut kommen wir und nur wir', 'Zusammenbruchstheorie', *Marxismus und politisches Defizit in der SPD, 1890–1914* (Frankfurt-on-Main, 1981), pp. 84 ff. For a useful statement of the state of discussion, see R. J. Geary, 'Karl Kautsky and "Scientific Marxism" ', *Radical Science Journal*, vol. 11(1981), pp. 130–5.

16 See esp. Steinberg, *Sozialismus und deutsche Sozialdemokratie*, pp. 129–42, and D. Langewiesche and K. Schönhoven, 'Arbeiterbibliotheken und Arbeiterlektüre im Wilhelminischen Deutschland', *Archiv für Sozialgeschichte*, vol. 16 (1976), pp. 135–204.

17 R. J. Evans, 'Introduction: the sociological interpretation of German labour history', in Evans (ed.), *The German Working Class 1888–1933* (London, 1982), p. 19.

18 G. Roth, *The Social Democrats in Imperial Germany. A Study in Working-Class Isolation and National Integration* (Ottowa, 1963), esp. p. 315. Evans, 'Sociological interpretation', contains a valuable if possibly exaggerated critique of this view. Some of the wider implications are discussed in G. Eley and K. Nield, 'Why does social history ignore politics?' *Social History*, vol. 5 (1980), pp. 249–71.

19 Evans, 'Sociological interpretation', cit. at n. 17 above, pp. 23 ff.

20 Eley and Nield, 'Why does social history ignore politics?', pp. 255 ff.

21 G. Eckert (ed.), *1863–1963. Hundert Jahr deutsche Sozialdemokratie. Bilder und Dokumente* (Hanover, 1963). The responsible authors of this magnificent compilation were Frolinde Balser, Werner Conze, Ulrich Dubber, Willi Eichler, Susanne Miller, Otto-Ernst Schüddekopf, Wilhelm Wehner and Gerhard Wuthe. The Conze school were the most important academic grouping stressing the labour movement's historic affinities with the 'national movement', but while less concerned directly with the SPD, the influence of Theodor Schieder in Cologne has been cognate to this concern. See Schieder, *Das deutsche Kaiserreich von 1871 als Nationalstaat* (Cologne, 1961), and H.-U. Wehler, *Sozialdemokratie und Nationalstaat. Nationalitätenfragen im Deutschland 1840–1914* (Würzburg, 1962; rev. edn, Göttingen, 1971).

22 The temptation to speak of an official SPD historiography is very great, especially given the growing institutional importance of SPD research sponsorship from the later 1960s and the general shifting of ideological fronts in West Germany from that time. But a simplistic correlation should be resisted. There is certainly a body of work conceived directly as historical justification for the SPD's post-1945 evolution: e.g. W. Eichler, *Hundert Jahre Sozialdemokratie* (Bonn, 1962); K. Anders, *Die ersten hundert Jahre. Zur Geschichte einer demokratischen Partei* (Hanover, 1963); P.-C. Witt, *Friedrich Ebert – Parteiführer, Reichskanzler, Volksbeauftragter, Reichspräsident* (Bonn, 1971). Some other works also come very close: e.g. Miller, *Problem der Freiheit;* H. A. Winkler, *Die Sozialdemokratie und die Revolution von 1918/19* (Berlin and Bonn, 1979).

23 Steinberg, *Sozialismus und deutsche Sozialdemokratie*, p. 124. For the concept of 'deradicalization', see R. C. Tucker, *The Marxian Revolutionary Idea* (New York, 1969), pp. 172–214.

24 Steinberg, *Sozialismus und deutsche Sozialdemokratie;* H.-C. Schröder, *Sozialismus und Imperialismus* (Hanover, 1968); D. Groh, *Negative Integration und revolutionäre Attentismus. Die deutsche Sozialdemokratie am Vorabend des Ersten Weltkrieges* (Frankfurt-on-Main, 1973). A chapter of Steinberg's book was translated as 'Workers' libraries in Germany before 1914', in *History Workshop*, vol. 1 (1976, pp. 166–80.

25 An exhaustive bibliography would be inappropriate here. Gary Steenson provides a good introduction in his 'Suggestions for further reading', in *'Not One Man! Not One Penny!' German Social Democracy, 1867–1914* (Pittsburgh, Pa, 1981), pp. 265–73. Otherwise consult the footnotes in Evans, 'Sociological interpretation', cit. at. n. 17 above.

26 Schorske, *German Social Democracy;* V. Lidtke, *The Outlawed Party: Social Democracy in Germany, 1878–1890* (Princeton, NJ, 1966); P. Nettl, 'The German Social Democratic Party, 1890–1914 as a political model', *Past and Present*, no. 30 (April 1965), pp. 65–95; P. Nettl, *Rosa Luxemburg*, 2 vols (Oxford, 1969).

27 N. Geras, *The Legacy of Rosa Luxemburg* (London, 1976); L. Colletti, 'Bernstein and the Marxism of the Second International', in *From Rousseau to Lenin. Studies in Ideology and Society* (London, 1972), pp. 45–108. Salvadori, *Karl Kautsky*, is another example of first-class exegesis. Unfortunately most work on Luxemburg, Kautsky and other representatives of the SPD's Marxist tradition has been preoccupied with defining their relationship to post-1917 Leninism, not the most auspicious of beginnings for a well-contextualized historical understanding. It should not be thought from these remarks that I am assuming a familiar dichotomy between 'history' and 'theory'. It is more a case of locating particular theoreticians in the specific historical circumstances that lent coherence to their ideas. But this (an elementary principle for any materialist sociology of knowledge, one might have thought) is all too frequently absent from Marxist discussions of their own tradition. For a suggestive, if abbreviated, example of how an analysis might be conducted: P. Anderson, *Considerations on Western Marxism*

(London, 1976). For my own comments: 'The legacy of Rosa Luxemburg', in *Critique*, no. 12 (Autumn–Winter 1979–80), pp. 139–50.

28 The chronicles include E. Bernstein's *Geschichte der Berliner Arbeiterbewegung*, 3 vols (Berlin, 1907–11); H. Laufenberg, *Geschichte der Arbeiterbewegung in Hamburg, Altona und Umgebung*, 2 vols (Hamburg, 1931); E. Heilman, *Geschichte der Arbeiterbewegung in Chemnitz und dem Erzgebirge* (Chemnitz, 1912); H. Müller, *Geschichte der Arbeiterbewegung in Sachsen-Altenburg* (Jena, 1923). For a while Ralf Lützenkirchen's able study of Dortmund, *Der Sozialdemokratische Verein für den Reichstagswahlkreis Dortmund-Hörde* (Dortmund, 1970), was virtually the only recent study to offer a well-rounded account of a local SPD's sociology and politics in the imperial period. K.-E. Moring, *Die Sozialdemokratische Partei in Bremen 1890–1914* (Hanover, 1968), was by comparison a very straightforward political chronicle, and otherwise there was an entire genre of constituency studies (many of them unpublished) which offered little more than some useful electoral details. But recently a number of substantial works have left the situation much improved: V. Ullrich, *Die Hamburger Arbeiterbewegung vom Vorabend des Ersten Weltkriegs bis zur Revolution 1918–19* (Hamburg, 1976); E. Lucas, *Zwei Formen von Radikalismus in der deutschen Arbeiterbewegung* (Frankfurt-on-Main, 1976); D. Rossmeissl, *Arbeiterschaft und Sozialdemokratie in Nürnberg 1890–1914* (Nuremberg, 1977); F. Boll, *Massenbewegungen in Niedersachsen 1906–1920* (Bonn 1981); K. Ditt, *Industrialisierung, Arbeiterschaft und Arbeiterbewegung in Bielefeld 1850–1914* (Dortmund, 1982). See also the excellent series, *Die Arbeiterbewegung in den Rheinlanden*, ed. G. Bers and M. Klöcker (Wentorf bei Hamburg, 1974), which has published materials mainly on Aachen and Cologne.

29 The Edward Thompson quotes are taken from *The Making of the English Working Class* (London, 1963), p. 11.

30 For some further discussion of this point see my 'Capitalism and the Wilhelmine state: industrial growth and political backwardness in recent German historiography, 1890–1918', *Historical Journal*, vol. 21 (1978), pp. 737–50, and 'Deutscher Sonderweg und englisches Vorbild', in D. Blackbourn and G. Eley, *Mythen deutscher Geschichtsschreibung: Die gescheiterte burgerliche Revolution von 1848* (Frankfurt-on-Main, 1980), pp. 37–53 (English edn, *The Peculiarities of German History, Bourgeois Society and Politics in Nineteenth-Century Germany* (Oxford, 1984).

31 The SPD carried the Reichstag seat in a by-election in 1911 and kept it in the general election of 1912 several months later. The core of Nolan's analysis in this regard is the chapter on 'Skilled migrants, peasant workers, and native Catholics', (pp. 99–125) as I shall argue further below. However, I do not intend to imply that the argument concerning the shift from Centre to SPD rests solely on a kind of demographic determinism, because the analysis is far more complex than that. The demographic argument is combined with a strong stress on political determinations, including the Centre's diminished credibility after its support for the 1902 tariffs, the consequences of the intensified labour struggles in 1904–6, the suffrage agitations of 1908–10 and the positive attractions of the SPD's subculture. For the larger problematic of migration and mobility, see the following: D. F. Crew, *Town in the Ruhr. A Social History of Bochum 1860–1914* (New York, 1979), pp. 59–101; D. Langewiesche, 'Wanderungsbewegungen in der Hochindustrialisierungsperiode. Regionale, interstadtische und innerstadtische Mobilitat in Deutschland 1880–1914', in *Vierteljahresschrift für Sozial-und Wirtschaftsgeschichte*, vol. 64 (1977), pp. 1–40; K. J. Bade, 'Massen wanderung und Arbeitsmarkt im deutschen Nordosten von 1880 bis zum Ersten Weltkrieg', *Archiv für Sozialgeschichte*, vol. 20 (1980), pp. 265–323.

32 R. Michels, *Political Parties* (New York, 1962).

33 See the following works by R. J. Geary: 'The German labour movement, 1848–1919', *European Studies Review*, vol. 6 (1977), pp. 297–330; 'Radicalism and the worker: metalworkers and revolution, 1914–23', in R. J. Evans (ed.), *Society and Politics in Wilhelmine Germany* (London, 1978), pp. 267–86; 'Identifying militancy: the assessment of working-class attitudes towards state and society', in Evans (ed.), *German Working Class*, pp. 220–46; *European Labour Protest 1848–1939* (London, 1981).

34 Thompson, *Making of the English Working Class*, p. 194. I have developed this argument in full in 'Re-thinking the political: social history and political culture in 18th and 19th

century Britain', *Archiv für Sozialgeschichte*, vol. 21 (1981), pp. 443 ff., 454–7.

35 Thompson certainly considers non-artisanal groups at some length (e.g. the chapters on agricultural labourers or the Irish immigration). But the crucial final section of the book (on 'The working-class presence', which carries the narrative of the class's formation, and occupies almost half the total text) deals overwhelmingly with artisans. This is notably true of the generalizing final chapter on 'Class consciousness', esp. p. 774. These comments (which are necessarily elliptical) should not be read as a dismissive criticism of Thompson's great book. They merely state a problem which is arguably worth discussing, not least because of the pervasive influence of Thompson's account on subsequent social historians of the European and North American working class.

36 A. Reid, 'Politics and economics in the formation of the British working class: a response to H. F. Moorhouse', *Social History*, vol. 3 (October 1978), pp. 359–61. Nolan herself cites C. F. Sabel, *Industrial Conflict and the Sociology of the Labour Market* (Cambridge, 1982) on this point.

37 See her statement on pp. 2 ff.: 'This study is based on certain premises about the formation of the working class and the role of workers' organisations in that process. The working class is by no means created once and for all at the beginning of industrialisation. Rather, it must re-create itself at each stage of industrial capitalism, as the economy and labour force are restructured, political institutions and forms of hegemony change, and old cultural forms give way to new ones. That process of class formation is as difficult in more advanced industrial capitalist societies as in less developed ones. The diversity and divisions within the working class – be they occupational, cultural, religious or sexual – far from diminishing, recur in ever new guises'.

38 With K. Nield, 'Why does social history ignore politics?', cit. at n. 18 above, 264 ff.

39 There is a good catalogue of such arguments in Evans, 'Sociological interpretation', cit. at n. 17 above, pp. 18–24. Though he provides an admirably condensed discussion of the issues, Guttsman ultimately toes the same line. W. L. Guttsman, *The German Social Democratic Party 1875–1933. From Ghetto to Government* (London, 1981), pp. 167–218.

40 I cannot elaborate on these rather cryptic statements due to lack of space. But see my discussion of Chartism in 'Re-thinking the political', cit. at n. 34 above, pp. 446–54, and the polemical advocacy of a 'Gramscian' perspective in Eley and Nield, 'Why does social history ignore politics?', cit. at n. 18 above, pp. 264–9.

41 Geary, *European Labour Protest*, p. 119.

42 The *aficionado* will recognize in these formulations the contemporary 'left-Eurocommunist' problematic currently influential in British Marxism. However, this particular way of posing the strategic problem facing the SPD is not the only one, and I am more concerned to raise the issue than to push the virtues of my own preferred resolution.

43 Most of the existing literature tends to play this down, stressing instead the party's failure to win support from the intermediate strata and the drift of the latter to the right. This is quite in conformity with another received opinion, which sees the disproportionate support of these quarters for the Nazis as evidence of their long-term rightward disposition, originating in the period before 1914. My own view is that this underestimates the volatility of the peasantry and petty bourgeoisie (old and new), certainly before 1914, and probably in the early years of Weimar too. One may accept in general that the party's inability to mobilize a stable petty-bourgeois and peasant constituency held it back from achieving the much desired majority status while reserving judgement on the SPD's uneven successes among these groups at different times and in different places before 1914.

44 Nolan quotes a leaflet from the 1912 municipal elections, for instance, which argues from a general contradiction between 'the class interests of the propertied, of big capitalists, large landlords, and speculators', and 'the interests of the broad mass of the population, of the poor, the worker, and the little man' (p. 213). In other contexts (like the Labour Party) this essentially populist dichotomy has usually been the basis for an intentional and fairly successful appeal to a larger-than-working-class constituency, and it would be interesting to know how far this applied in Düsseldorf too. I am using the term 'populist' here in a technical and not a pejorative sense.

45 For an interesting discussion in this light: D. I. Kertzer, *Comrades and Christians. Religion and Political Struggle in Communist Italy* (Cambridge, 1980).

46 S. Hickey, 'The shaping of the German labour movement: miners in the Ruhr', in Evans (ed.), *Society and Politics in Wilhelmine Germany*, pp. 236 ff. See also Boll's excellent comparative study of Hanover and Brunswick, *Massenbewegungen in Niedersachsen*, where the moderate reformism of the Hanover SPD is explained in much the same terms used to characterize its radicalism in Düsseldorf. Although the factors of migration and religious division were much less important, the structure of Hanover's industry showed some marked similarities. The base of the trade unions was again in the woodworking and construction industries, together with the smaller and medium-sized engineering firms. Moreover, as in Düsseldorf, the larger-scale metalworking industries were virtually closed to the trade unions by employer paternalism. In Düsseldorf, Nolan argues that this made for radicalism, but in Hanover it was used to justify an extremely defensive politics which was then strengthened (just as the party's radicalism in Düsseldorf was) by the processes of bureaucratic centralization and subcultural introspection. Furthermore, in Brunswick, by contrast, it was the strength of trade union organization *vis-à-vis* the employers that provided the foundation for a vigorous political radicalism both before and during the war.

47 Crew, *Town in the Ruhr*, esp. pp. 186–94, together with the preceding argumentation, pp. 159–86.

48 ibid., pp. 163–86, which provides an excellent critical survey of these options, as does Geary, *European Labour Protest*, pp. 37–80.

49 See esp. Reid, 'Politics and economics in the formation of the British working class', cit. at n. 36 above.

50 The SPD before 1914 lends a certain amount of support to this view, given the largely self-perpetuating nature of the national and many local leaderships and their increasing removal from effective accountability to the membership. Local leaderships were often unrepresentative and undemocratic in their behaviour: e.g., Lützenkirchen's account of the party in Dortmund, *Der sozialdemokratische Verein für den Reichstagwahlkreis Dortmund-Hörde*. The question of functioning inner-party democracy is not really dealt with in Molly Nolan's book. There is a tendency simply to assume that a left-wing leadership presumes a democratically organized constituency, but there is no reason for this to be so.

51 Crew, *Town in the Ruhr*, p. 185.

52 Geary, *European Labour Protest*, pp. 58 ff., 'Identifying militancy', cit. at n. 33 above, 240 ff. (the source for the quote). For a particularly strong statement, see *European Labour Protest*, p. 60; 'the major determinant of the forms of political action adopted by the different national labour movements was the role of the state and of the social groups it claimed to represent'.

53 ibid.

54 The phrases are taken from Geary, 'Identifying militancy', cit. at n. 33 above, pp. 242, 241.

55 'Why does social history ignore politics?', cit. at n. 18 above.

56 Geary, 'Identifying militancy', p. 241; *European Labour Protest*, p. 52.

57 'Identifying militancy', p. 241.

58 Examples of this new literature include the following: H. Schomerus, *Die Arbeiter der Maschinenfabrik Esslingen. Forschungen zur Lage der Arbeiterschaft im 19. Jahrhundert* (Stuttgart, 1977); H. Pohl (ed.), *Forschungen zur Lage der Arbeiter im Industrialisierungsprozess* (Stuttgart, 1978); P. Borscheid, *Textilarbeiterschaft in der Industrialisierung* (Stuttgart, 1978); W. Conze and U. Engelhardt (eds), *Arbeiter im Industrialisierungsprozess. Herkunft, Lage und Verhalten* (Stuttgart, 1979); J. Reulecke and W. Weber (eds), *Fabrik – Familie – Feierabend* (Wuppertal, 1978); G. Huck (ed.), *Sozialgeschichte der Freizeit* (Wuppertal, 1980); D. Puls (ed.), *Wahrnehmungsformen und Protestverhalten. Studien zur Lage der Unterschichten im 18. und 19. Jahrhundert* (Frankfurt-on-Main, 1979). These remarks should not be misunderstood. They are not meant to disparage the qualities or contributions of this work, still less to suggest that it should not be done. But ultimately the questions of class domination and class consciousness, in which political matters have a central place, will need to be readdressed. The best recent work is sensitive to this priority. See for instance: D. Groh, 'Base-processes and the problems of organization: outline of a social history research project', *Social History*, vol. 4 (May 1979), pp. 265–83; K. Tenfelde, *Sozialgeschichte der*

Bergarbeiterschaft an der Ruhr im 19. Jahrhundert (Bonn and Bad Godesburg, 1977); A. Lüdtke, 'Alltagswirklichkeit, Lebensweise und Bedürfnisartikulation', *Gesellschaft. Beiträge zur Marxschen Theorie*, vol. 11 (Frankfurt-on-Main, 1978), pp. 311–50; A. Lüdtke, 'Rekonstruktion von Alltagswirklichkeit – Entpolitisierung der Sozialgeschichte?', in R. Berdahl *et al.*, *Klassen und Kultur. Sozialanthropologische Perspektiven in der Geschichtsschreibung* (Frankfurt–on–Main, 1982), pp. 321–53; D. Groh, 'Preliminary remarks on the making of the German working class', forthcoming.

59 Subsequently Crew has addressed the problem of the SPD more directly, but his comments are too cryptic to derive a clear sense of his general views on the party. See 'Steel, sabotage and socialism: the strike at the Dortmund "Union" Steel Works in 1911', in Evans (ed.), *German Working Class*, pp. 108–41.

60 As well as the works listed in n. 58, the following works referred to earlier should be given special mention: Zwahr, *Zur Konstituierung des Proletariats als Klasse* (which unlike the others is by an East German historian); the work on migration by Langewiesche and Bade referred to in n. 31; the local studies listed in n. 28, particularly those by Lucas and Boll; and Schönhoven's study of the trade unions mentioned in n. 13. Beyond this, important work is also being produced in Britain and the USA, though much of it is mainly relevant to the Weimar and Nazi periods (e.g. pre-eminently the work of Tim Mason, and that of Eve Rosenhaft and James Wickham referred to below). It is worth singling out Stephen Hickey's unpublished Oxford D.Phil dissertation on the Ruhr miners (see his summary essay, 'Shaping of the German labour movement' mentioned in n. 46) and David Crew's *Town in the Ruhr* which pioneered North American social history approaches in the German context. Otherwise, a good sense of current work may be gained from two collections of essays: Evans (ed.), *German Working Class*, and R. J. Evans and W. R. Lee (eds), *The German Family. Essays on the Social History of the Family in Nineteenth- and Twentieth-Century Germany* (London, 1981). Both collections originated in meetings of the British SSRC Research Seminar Group in Modern German Social History, which has been assembling regularly at the University of East Anglia in Norwich since 1978, and which has made possible a rare degree of vitality and coherence in the discussions of German historians in Britain.

61 See the essays mentioned in n. 58 above. The works by Lucas, *Zwei Formen von Radikalismus*, and Boll, *Massenbewegungen in Niedersachsen*, may also be specially commended in this respect. Finally, two texts on a later period may be cited for the imagination and originality of their attempts to produce a well-integrated social history of politics: E. Rosenhaft, 'Organizing the "lumpenproletariat": cliques and communists in Berlin during the Weimar Republic', in Evans (ed.), *German Working Class*, pp. 174–219; and J. Wickham, 'Working-class movement and working-class life: Frankfurt am Main during the Weimar Republic', *Social History*, vol. 8 (October 1983), pp. 315–44. It may be no accident that most light appears to be shed on the Wilhelmine SPD by works which allow the experience of 1914–23 to structure their prewar problematic, or more obliquely by works on the later period altogether.

62 The essays in the Evans volume are on different aspects of working-class 'roughness' – pilfering at work (M. Gruttner on the Hamburg docks), drinking (J. A. Roberts on the 'Schnaps boycott' of 1909), industrial sabotage (D. Crew on the Dortmund steel strike of 1911), illegitimate motherhood (S. Bajohr on Brunswick), and adolescent gangs in late-Weimar Berlin (E. Rosenhaft) – sandwiched between Evans's own critique of existing approaches ('The sociological interpretation of German labour history') and D. Geary's provocative Conclusion ('Identifying militancy'). The volume's sub-title is 'The politics of everyday life', which is simultaneously an affirmation and implied critique of recent trends in West German social history. The quotations in my final paragraph are taken from Evans's Introduction, p. 45, and Preface, p. 11. It should be noted that the essay by Eley and Nield referred to several times above ('Why does social history ignore politics?') was originally conceived as a response to the meeting of the SSRC Research Seminar in Norwich at which three of the essays (by Evans, Rosenhaft and Geary) were first presented, in January 1979, and that both Evans and Geary comment on this essay in their turn (*German Working Class*, pp. 41, 45, 229, 240, 242 n. 6). There is an important sense, in other words, in which this current text is an attempt to continue that dialogue.

8

German Politics and
Polish Nationality:
The Dialectic of Nation Forming
in the East of Prussia

We can sometimes forget that the *Kaiserreich*, like the Romanov and Habsburg empires, was a multinational state. The dominant German nationality was demographically far more preponderant than either the Russians or the Austro-Germans and Hungarians in their respective empires, and the national minorities constituted far less of a threat to the integrity and survival of the existing state, but the 'internal colonialism' of the official nationalism was no less of a significant force in the social and political history of the years between German unification and the end of the First World War. During the war, in fact, the German government, the military High Command, the politicians of the right, and the industrial agrarian spokesmen of the dominant classes all showed themselves more than willing to incur precisely the larger imperial responsibilities in Central and Eastern Europe which had been causing so much trouble for the Habsburg and Romanov governments before 1914. Germany's expanionist drive to the east, which by 1918 had established German arms from the Baltic to the Caucasus, revealed a nationalist logic which was capable of emulating the worst excesses of Habsburg and Romanov national exploitation and oppression. This has obvious implications for the character of the German political culture. Not the least of the weaknesses of German liberalism, and for that matter of German Social Democracy too, was its inability to embrace a co-operative political framework which was capable of accommodating the legitimate social, cultural and political interests of the various national minorities within German borders.

The largest of these minorities were the Poles, but after the 1860s there were also significant French and Danish populations, too, as well as smaller ethnic populations like the Masurians, Kashubians and Lusatian Sorbs. West German historiography since 1945 has not been unmindful of the problem this poses, even before the liberating effects of the Fischer Controversy. But until recently, most discussion has approached the question from the German point of view, or at least from the aspect of the problems it posed for the newly united nation-state in a mainly administrative sense. (As paradigmatic in this sense we might cite Theodor Schieder's *Das deutsche Kaiserreich von 1871 als Nationalstaat* [Cologne, 1961]). Virtually nobody bothered to use sources in Polish or other relevant languages. Moreover, by 1900 the national question had acquired a wholly new dimension with the massive migration of Polish and other peasant peoples from the rural east and south to Berlin, Saxony and the exploding urban environment of the Ruhr. There is rich scope here for comparative studies of ethnicity and popular culture of the kind which has become more familiar in North America, but which might also connect with other experiences of ethnic labour migration, such as Algerians in France, Italians in Switzerland, or Irish in Britain. (For an extremely important

move in this direction, see Klaus J. Bade [ed.], *Auswanderer, Wanderarbeiter, Gastarbeiter* [Ostfildern, 1984]).
Like a number of the other essays in this collection, this discussion of the Poles in Prussia originated as a review essay, in the *East European Quarterly*, vol. 18 (1984), pp. 335–64. It speaks as much to my larger interest in nationalism as to my specifically German one. It was written at the instigation of my colleague Roman Szporluk, from whom my appreciation of Polish history mostly comes.

The East, once a land of German hope and German work, which fell to the good of all peoples and united them to a Western community of fate, is shattered. It has become a foreground of Asia. (F. Gause, *Deutsch-slawische Schicksalgemeinschaft*, Veröffentlichung des Göttinger Arbeitskreis, no. 50 [Wurzburg, 2nd edn, 1953], p. 291, cit. G. Berndt, 'Polen ein Schauermarchen – Das Polenbild der Deutschen', in *Polen ein Schauermarchen oder Gehirnwasche für Generationen*, ed. G. Berndt and R. Strecker [Hamburg, 1971], p. 13)

This movement [the movement for a Greater Poland] strove for the establishment of an independent state at the expense of German territory and in violation of the rights of German men and women. Its agitators made the Polish language into a sold wall shutting them off from the German-speaking population, even inciting school-children to resist all authority, boycotting their German fellow-citizens socially and economically, declaring as traitors all citizens of Polish origin who entered into any kind of trade relationship with their German neighbours. They founded exclusively Polish clubs and co-operatives to the exclusion of all Germans and pursued a policy of exclusive Polish colonization. This was the enemy within the German frontiers, 200 km (120 miles) from Berlin. The danger did not lie in a possible violent secession of the Poles from the German Reich, but in the dangerous situation in the event of war. Bismarck's defensive measures were directed not against the individual Polish-speaking member of the community – as such a neighbour – but against the Greater Poland movement. His measures were in the interest of the eastern provinces themselves. These were German lands won by industry, civilization, order, custom, and a state welfare policy. The peaceful coexistence of the citizens was being threatened by the efforts of the agitators for Greater Poland, directed as they were towards dividing the population and sowing hatred. It was a disastrous but inescapable turn of fate that this Polish–German conflict was answered by an increased feeling of German national-ism, an attitude which was always foreign to Bismarck. (W. Frauen-dienst, 'Prussian civic consciousness and Polish nationalism. Prussian and German policy towards Poland 1815–1890', in *Eastern*

Germany. A Handbook, ed. Göttingen Research Committee Würzburg, 1961), 168 f.

A critical historiography of the German–Polish relationship is one of the unqualified goods to come out of the Brandt government's *Ostpolitik*. Until quite recently, the historical literature on the subject issuing from the Federal Republic of Germany was indelibly marked by deeply rooted ideological traditions, going back at the very least to the period of German unification between the 1860s and 1880s, and more subtly to the founding years of German nationalism between the French Revolution and *Vormärz*. The treatment of Imperial Germany's Polish policy reflected a range of attitudes for which the above quotations are entirely typical – a residual conception of the Germans' civilizing mission in the East, an arrogant disregard for the culture of Slav peoples, a certain reverence for the vaunted civic 'universalism' of the Prussian state and an associated indifference to the rights of subject nationalities, the familiar mythology of disinterested Bismarckian statecraft, and an obstinate adherence to the 'defensive' interpretation of Germany policy, as something that was imposed on the Prussian government by the unreasonable behaviour of the Poles. These attitudes had been incomparably radicalized during the Nazi dictatorship, of course, but despite the latter's military defeat they received a powerful new lease of life from the German refugee movements and the Eastern expulsions, the new identification of the East with Soviet communism, and the drawing of the Iron Curtain. Throughout the 1950s discussion was dominated by these perspectives, so that certain 'classic' works of a *deutschnational* and Nazi provenance (primarily those of Hans Rothfels and Manfred Laubert) were never dislodged from their strategic place in the field.[1] Historical work remained enmeshed in the cultural and intellectual apparatus of the Adenauer era's Eastern Revisionism and with certain honourable exceptions – liberal conservatives like Theodor Schieder and Werner Conze who went on to publish or sponsor significant research – little new was produced.[2]

It was not until the 1960s that things began to change. The *Institut für Zeitgeschichte* played an important role here, by ensuring that the most harrowing chapter in the German–Polish relationship would be properly confronted (as in Martin Broszat's *Nationalsozialistische Polenpolitik 1939–1945*, Stuttgart, 1961). Broszat's *Zweihundert Jahre deutsche Polenpolitik* (Munich, 1963) marked something of a watershed in the emergence of an avowedly non-nationalist historiography in West Germany. Probably more important, in retrospect, was the impact of Hans-Ulrich Wehler. This was partly because of Wehler's own immediate work. His early monograph, *Sozialdemokratie und Nationalstaat. Nationalitäten-fragen in Deutschland 1840–1914* (2nd edn, Göttingen, 1971; originally published with a slightly different subtitle, Würzburg, 1962), which contained extensive discussion of the Polish question, was one of the first works in the West to exploit archival holdings from the former German territories in Poland, and this was followed by a series of essays on Imperial Germany's Polish policy, Polish–German relations more generally and Polish migrants in the Ruhr.[3] But, equally importantly, Wehler's trenchant critique of Bismarck's imperialism, an extraordinarily influential textbook, and an imposing array of other works, opened the way for a comprehensive re-examination of pre-1914 history.[4] This harnessed the impetus of the celebrated Fischer Controversy and set in motion a current of historical reinterpretation which has still not spent its force.[5] The growing propensity to be critical of Germany's nationalist past acquired extra legitimacy from the *Ostpolitik* of the early 1970s, and in the wake of the latter contacts between West German and Polish historians gradually became more extensive. Finally, in 1978 the first official conference of West German and Polish historians took place in Freiburg. As the editors of the resulting volume said, it was finally possible for historians from the two countries to group themselves by thematic and methodological interests rather than in separate and hostile national camps.[6]

It is against this background that the four works under review must be set. All, as it happens, are by Americans, begun as dissertations in the late 1960s when the historiographical openings referred to above were at their most novel and exciting. Blanke, Hagen and Kulczycki explore different aspects of the nationality conflict in the east of Prussia, while Murphy deals with the experience of Polish migrant workers in the Ruhr. Each is based on hitherto unexploited sources (that is, by historians in the West) – on a wide range of state, church, local and private records, together with an impressive listing of statistical, newspaper and other printed materials, in the cases of Blanke, Hagen and Kulczycki; on the records of the Prussian provincial administration, local statistical and printed sources, and on the records of the Bottrop residential registration office in particular, in the case of Murphy. None of the three authors working on the East, regrettably, were able to use sources in the German Democratic Republic (leading to a certain peevishness on the part of Blanke), although Hagen and Kulczycki were given access to copies of some key documents by Witold Jacobczyk, one of their Polish advisers and a leading specialist in this field.[7] All three laboured prodigiously in the Polish-language sources.

Taken together these books amount to a major step forward in historical understanding. For the first time in the recent literature on the nationality conflict in the East *both* German *and* Polish sources are systematically and comprehensively evaluated.[8] Blanke and Hagen, and to a lesser extent Kulczycki, are genuinely binational studies. Hagen is the most rounded of the three, considering the economics, sociology and demographics of Polish–German relations as well as their politics, and paying equal attention to the changing dynamics of the Polish nationalist movement and to the respective roles of the Prussian state, the Eastern landowners, and the independent German nationalist movement. As an additional strength he plots the nationality conflict in a triangular relationship of Germans, Poles and Jews, and devotes some detail to the role of the Eastern Prussian liberals. As a consequence he is able to present both the unfolding of the Prussian Polish policy as a set of ideological and administrative practices *and* the complex field of social, ethnic and political forces which the latter sought to affect. Blanke has more of an administrative focus on the decision-making of the Prussian government and the implementation of its policies, but he also delineates the formation of public opinion on both sides of the national divide, and devotes much space to the successive reconfiguration of Polish nationalist politics between the 1860s and the end of the century. Kulczycki's is the most particularized of the three analyses, offering 'the first complete history of the struggle over bilingual education in Prussian Poland from 1815 to its climax in the general school strike of 1906–07' (p. xi).

On the whole Blanke and Hagen confirm each other's accounts. Both agree that German unification, through the North German Confederation of 1867 and the Imperial Constitution of 1871, created a new situation, because it introduced a far more stringent interpretation of the obligations of citizenship in a German (as opposed to a Prussian) state. In fact, since the first Partition of 1772 there had always been an oscillation in Prussian policy between a more conciliatory and a more adversary approach to the Polish nobility, exemplified in the successive Poznanian regimes of Anton Radziwill and Josef von Zerboni (as *Statthalter* and *Oberpräsident*) between 1815 and 1830 and Eduard Flottwell (*Oberpräsident*, 1830–41). Of course, most features of the harsher anti-Polish offensives under the empire were presaged in the previous century, and Bismarck's measures of the 1870s and 1880s stand in a distinct tradition with Flottwell's policies, going back to the memoranda of Justus Gruner in the aftermath of Jena and the South Prussian rising of 1806–7 (Hagen, p. 76). But there was also a more enlightened line of development represented by the ministerial memorandum of 1798, the language policy of Karl von Altenstein, and the Stein–Hardenburg reform era, and partially resumed under Frederick William IV in the 1840s (Hagen, pp. 59, 77 ff., 91 ff.). As Frederick William III had said in his Poznanian Proclamation of May 1815: 'You too have a fatherland and therewith a demonstration of my respect for your devotion to it. You are being incorporated into My Monarchy *without having to deny your nationality* . . . Your language is to be used along with German in all public transactions' (Blanke, p. 1). (My emphasis).

This was made possible by what Blanke calls 'a political rather than an ethnic' definition of the Prussian 'nation' (p. 12). Or to put it another way, it made the basis of Prussian citizenship loyalty to the Frederician state and not the principle of nationality as a complex of ethnic-linguistic and cultural solidarities. As Hagen says, Poles were required to 'locate their political identity in the Prussian state' and to that end to acquire proficiency in the German language (p. 61). In fact, this process of Prussianization was also thought to involve 'a "transformation" (*Umbildung*) of the Polish character along Prussian–German lines, not only in a political, but also in a socioeconomic and cultural sense', and to this extent the nineteenth-century concept of nationality was present in Prussian policies, but embryonically, or in a practical state.[9] In the early nineteenth century there was a certain indeterminacy in official Prussian thinking, for in the absence of a fully mobilized civil society (the socio-cultural precondition for a securely founded liberal politics and the associated ideas of sovereignty and representation), but at a time when such advanced thinking was available from elsewhere in Britain and France (that is, classically during the Prussian reform era), the bureaucracy was able 'arbitrarily' to explore different modes of legitimacy for its actions. This explains the coexistence of the brutal geopolitical realism and cultural chauvinism of a Flottwell or his teacher Theodor von Schön (*Oberpräsident* of West Prussia 1816–42) and the 'pedagogically enlightened and humane stand' (Kulczycki, p. 4) of an Altenstein. On the one hand, Flottwell could demand 'the complete fusion of both nationalities . . . through the decisive prominence of German culture' (ibid., p. 6). But, on the other, Altenstein could call 'religion and language . . . the highest treasures of a nation, in which its whole sentimental and conceptual world is grounded', and on these grounds oppose any attempt to 'Germanize' or 'denationalize' the Poles by the 'open extirpation of their language' (ibid., p. 4). Both stances were possible during the first two-thirds of the nineteenth century, although circumstances militated increasingly against the second (the Polish insurrections of 1831 and 1863, the Revolutions of 1848, the need for good relations with Russia). With the unification of Germany things changed. For one thing, the new imperial (or Prussian-German) government felt the need for cultural uniformity and a unitary conception of citizenship far more acutely. Faced with the potentially destabilizing effects of the various regional, dynastic and confessional particularisms within the new state, it drove hard for a means of constituting the new nation-state's popular legitimacy, and an ethnic-linguistic conception of Germanness provided the obvious recourse. This, combined with the centralizing logic of the new interventionist state, quickly brought the most vulnerable populations – national minorities in the borderlands, like the Poles – under attack. But beyond this, there was also a powerful National Liberal impetus at work. For the liberal architects of German nationalism the creation of the new state was the beginning rather than the end of unification. Above all (after the liberalization and institutional consolidation of the national economy), they sought to establish what we might call the primacy of the citizen–state relationship in the organization of public life. Apart from the rule of law, the recognition of civil freedoms and the achievement of a representative constitution, this meant eliminating alternative sources of institutional loyalty between the individual citizen and the state, the most important of which was the social and cultural power of the Catholic Church. In these terms the *Kulturkampf* was the necessary accompaniment of territorial unification. Far more than an attack on the Catholic religion *per se* (although liberal anticlericalism of this sort was an important force), it reflected a positive conception of how the new German society was to be ordered. As well as strengthening public control of education (as liberals saw it), it was meant to free the potential for social progress by removing the 'dead hand' of archaic institutions from the restless dynamism of Germany society.

This made German unification a crucial watershed in the German–Polish relationship. By neglecting the liberal content of unification and the liberal momentum of the 1870s, Blanke and Hagen miss the force of this point. Similarly, they both tend to see the *Kulturkampf* as something unleashed primarily by Bismarck, and obscure both the central contribution of National Liberals (like Adalbert Falk, the Minister of Culture in the 1870s) to its inception and implementation and the enormous resonance it possessed for liberals in the provinces. This is important because it explains much of the social and political impetus for the specifically anti-Polish measures as they emerged in the 1880s. Bismarckian ideas of strategic and domestic security (and traditional Junker-cum-bureaucratic prejudices about the weakness of the Polish character) were clearly important to these. But equally significant was the contribution of the National Liberals, who staffed the apparatus of the *Kulturkampf* and provided the most consistent parliamentary supporters for the anti-Polish legislation. It was less that the National Liberals had it in for the Poles directly, than that Polish autonomies were the casualties of some central National Liberal commitments. Curbing the secular power of Catholicism was one of these. But once language was adopted as the badge of nationality and the German language as the functional attribute of citizenship, the way was open for systematic cultural aggrandizement and the rights of Polish and Polish speakers were bound to suffer. Likewise, National Liberals believed in strengthening the independent peasantry in the East, and given the entrenched political power of the East Elbian German landowners, any realistic programme of internal colonization would have to take place at the expense of landowning Poles. In these ways, National Liberals shifted from the defenders of Polish rights to the opponents of Polish nationality.[10]

It is important to remember that a positive conception of nationality rights (the right of self-determination, with protection for national minorities and their culture) is mainly a product of the First World War and the Russian Revolution, although there was a certain amount of movement in this direction before 1914 in the Habsburg Empire.[11] For most of the nineteenth century, liberals amongst the dominant nationalities (for whom the Germans in Central Europe were the pre-eminent example) simply assumed that the smaller peoples of 'lower culture' would eventually assimilate. Usually, this reflected powerful ideologies of progress which assumed the socio-economic and moral superiority of urban metropolitan cultures over parochial peasant ones. Given the chance, it was thought, peasants would willingly exchange their backwardness for the fruits of progress if the oppressive shackles of traditionalism could once be removed. The villains of the piece were the Catholic Church and the landowning aristocracy, the guardians of superstition and the embodiments of frivolity and decadence, who kept the people in moral subjection. If the latter lived in peripheral or remote isolated regions, the problem was all the worse. In principle, therefore, though the clash of different nationalities was the most dramatic form of this process, we are dealing with a more general kind of encounter, between a relatively isolated village world and the exponents of a dynamic metropolitan culture armed with a vision of progress, driving for the cultural unification of the people-nation, and frequently fired with a missionary zeal.[12] Now given this ideological ambience, and the well-known tenacity of the gentry-clerical hegemony in Prussian Poland, it was not easy for German liberals to take up the cause of Polish nationality. They might disclaim hostile intentions against the Polish culture (as did Falk at the height of the Polish *Kulturkampf*), but in the end most of them assumed (with the National Liberal Reichstag group in 1876) that 'bilingualism' was 'a stepping stone towards Germanization' (Hagen, p. 130). Once the power of the Polish church had been curbed, the landed strength of the Polish gentry broken, the Polish peasantry socialized into the virtues of German culture, and the Polish language driven from the public sphere, it was difficult to know what would be left of 'Polishness' other than a quaint customary residue.[13]

In these circumstances it was easy enough for a positively anti-Polish ideology to cohere. Hagen calls this the transition from 'Prussianization' to 'Germanization', meaning 'intensive settlement of Germans in Polish regions accompanied by systematic and forceful efforts, justified in nationalist terms, to undermine the Poles' cultural autonomy, economic strength, and national consciousness' (p. 61). The first stage came under the *Kulturkampf*, with the May Laws of 1873, the administrative substitution of German for Polish in Poznanian secondary and elementary schools, and the 1876 Prussian Language Law making German the sole language of public exchange. The next stage came in 1885 with the expulsion of Polish (and Jewish) non-citizens to Russia and Galicia (reaching some 30,000 by 1887). Originally mooted by Bismarck in 1872, Blanke sees this as 'a long-contemplated, one-shot measure (undertaken in a vaguely nativist rather than specifically anti-Polish atmosphere) rather than the opening gun in a comprehensive anti-Polish campaign' (pp. 21, 48). However, it was quickly followed in 1886 by an elaborate anti-Polish offensive. The centrepiece was the famous Settlement Law which created the Royal Prussian Settlement Commission in Poznania, with a fund of 100 million marks to buy up Polish properties for 'the strengthening of the German element . . . against Polonizing attempts by settling German peasants and workers' (Blanke, p. 66).[14] This was then buttressed by a panoply of additional measures, including everything from new pressure on the Catholic Church (with the German Julius Dinder's appointment to the Archbishopric of Gniezno-Poznan), stricter posting of Polish military conscripts to other parts of Germany, and generous discriminatory subsidies for German schools, to the appointment of German rather than Polish physicians as public vaccinators. As Hagen says, 'a flurry of minor laws and edicts tightened state control over education in the Polish regions, created special German "continuation schools" for Polish youths, to be attended from the time of their departure from elementary school until their induction into the army, and removed Polish language instruction entirely from the elementary and secondary curriculum' (pp. 135 f.). While this offensive was concentrated heavily on Poznan, the measures applied in differing degrees to other areas too (mainly West Prussia, but as Blanke observes, the school measures also applied to Upper Silesia, which was included in a specifically anti-Polish measure for the first time).[15]

After the brief interlude of Leo von Caprivi's Chancellorship between 1890 and 1894, when a significant but piecemeal and ultimately incoherent relaxation of anti-Polish policies took place, there were two further spates of intensified government intervention. The first was in 1897–9, with a major increase in the Settlement Commission's operating capital, the creation of a new slush fund for the direct subsidy of the German cultural infrastructure, a major programme of public works, a new infusion of funds into the schools (this time Polish as well as German), the general harassment of Polish speakers in any public situation (including pressure for the Germanization of Polish names), and a new emphasis on the nationalist responsibilities of Prussian state officials out of hours. The second occurred in 1906–8, with the final Germanization of the schools, the Prussian Expropriation Law of 1908 (allowing for the expropriation of 70,000 hectares of Polish property in Poznan and West Prussia), a further addition to the commission's funding, and the notorious 'muzzle paragraph' of the 1908 Association Law which restricted use of Polish in public assemblies ('the only piece of anti-Polish legislation ever passed by the Reichstag', as Kulczycki reminds us) (p. 215).

But these were more the legislative punctuation marks in an otherwise continuous anti-Polish offensive. The nasty anti-Polish inflection of the *Kulturkampf* and the dramatic departures of 1885–6 certainly established a powerful precedent. But there was still something improvised about these early initiatives. After 1894, by contrast, the anti-Polish activity was more systematically institutionalized, on a continuously rising trajectory. For one thing, the Caprivi interlude radicalized the public atmosphere and produced the first voluntary organizations campaigning on an anti-Polish platform (the Society for the Eastern Marches formed in 1894, preceded by the Pan-German League in 1891). The measures of 1897–9 were the climax of intensive discussions in the Prussian Ministry of State and the bureaucracy, and the Polish question was never far from the centre of government preoccupations. The years between 1897–9 and 1906–8 were also marked by significant legislation, notably the two Settlement Law extensions of 1901 and 1904. Under the tutelage of Johannes von Miquel (Prussian Finance Minister and the dominant voice in the ministry by the later 1890s) and Bernhard von Bülow (Chancellor from 1900 to 1909), the relevant sections of the bureaucracy became permeated with the Germanizing ideology. In the first instance this meant the Settlement Commission itself, together with its increasingly elaborate field apparatus and links to the central ministries in Berlin (Finance, Agriculture, Interior). But it also applied especially to the Culture Ministry (responsible for religion, education, health) under Robert Bosse (1892–9) and Konrad von Studt (1899–1907).[16]

Who was the driving force behind these policies? Traditionally, literature has distinguished Bismarck's essentially conservative interest in order and state security from the more radical motivations of nationalists. As Blanke says, such views 'emphasize the theoretical, ideological distinction between Bismarck and more nationalistic contemporaries, his continuing tendency to think in state rather than ethnic terms, and his lack of concern for ethnic homogeneity' (p. 85).[17] There is something in this. Bismarck's social and ideological formation obviously differed from a right-wing National Liberal like Miquel or a younger generation of radical nationalists like Alfred Hugenberg who set the tone for settlement policies in the field. Blanke makes much of Bismarck's adherence to the traditional Prussian distinction between the Polish peasant (essentially loyal and uninterested in nationalist slogans) and the *Szlachta* (decadent, corrupt, traitorous, the leaders of the nationalist movement, who had forfeited any historic right to independence through mismanaging the pre-Partition state). But these views are, in any case, not so removed from those of the National Liberals, especially if we add in the hostility to the Polish priesthood as the agents of Polonization and the lackeys of the nobility. Liberals had their own reasons for disliking the nobility and the Catholic Church. Moreover, it is hard to escape the feeling that Bismarck's commendation of the sturdy Polish peasant was merely a form of rhetoric. It was certainly without intellectual coherence, for he was also responsible for statements which rivalled the worst Pan-German paranoia. Here he is in the Ministry of State in November 1871: 'the influence of the local clergy hinders the use of the German language, because the Slavs and Romans, in their alliance with Ultramontanism, try to preserve primitiveness and ignorance; all over Europe they are fighting Germanism, which seeks to spread enlightenment'. Or, one month earlier: 'From the Russian border to the Adriatic Sea, we are confronted with a Slavic agitation working hand in hand with the Ultramontanes and reactionaries; we must openly defend our national interests and our language against such hostile activities' (both cited by Hagen, p. 129). Both statements were closer to the rhetoric of the future Pan-Germans than to the vocabulary of Prussian legitimism, and while the peasantry may have been absent from the formal indictment, it was certainly included in the practical remedy.

So Bismarck was right in the forefront of the efforts to 'flay the Poles', as Blanke rightly insists.[18] His own motivation probably did have more to do with classic geopolitical considerations than with the emerging ambitions (and anxieties) of late-nineteenth-century radical nationalism. But I would attach far more importance to the overall climate of nationalist opinion in the 1880s than either Blanke or Hagen. Blanke sees the 1885 expulsions as a meaure which originated mainly with Bismark himself, with the subsequent anti-Polish package growing as a kind of improvised response to the situation this created and as a reaction to the Reichstag censure motion in particular.[19] Hagen tends to set the 1885–6 initiatives mainly in the context of Bismarck's general domestic strategy and his efforts to hold a Conservative/Free Conservative/National Liberal parliamentary coalition together; in these terms the anti-Polish measures are to be seen as part of a general attempt to manipulate nationalism for conservative governing purposes, in the sense of a 'diversionary social imperialism' taken from the work of Hans-Ulrich Wehler.[20]

Such ulterior motives may well have been harboured by Bismarck. But as Blanke allows us briefly to gauge, public opinion had already begun to address the 'decline of the German nationality' in the East independently of Bismarck's move againt the migrants.[21] Of course, Wehler had also argued that Bismarck's manipulation of colonial policy was predicated on the prior emergence of a powerful ideological consensus for colonies in the public sphere, and there are grounds for thinking that Wehler may have underestimated the latter's formative and constructive impact on government thinking.[22] In other words, it is open to question who exactly was leading and who was following. If we consider the general demographic anxieties provoked by rapid industrialization (overall increase, threatening overpopulation, the flight from the land, emigration to non-German settlement abroad, the need to preserve such surplus populations for 'Germandom', and so on) together with the extraordinary upsurge of interest in projects of German colonization (as opposed to the seizing of colonial markets), it is not difficult to see where the impulse for an Eastern

Germanization campaign might come from, and an analysis of public opinion comparable to Bade's study of Friedrich Fabri and the overseas colonization movement would show some interesting results. There is enough evidence in the memoranda of ministers like Gossler and Robert Lucius von Ballhausen (Minister of Agriculture 1879–90) and senior bureaucrats like Christoph von Tiedemann (formerly Bismarck's head of Chancellory and from 1881 *Regierungspräsident* in Bromberg/Bydgoszcz) that such a wider public agitation was beginning to take place.[23] Moreover, the real political impetus for the new Polish policy was National Liberal rather than Conservative. As the excellent work of Nichtweiss and more recently Bade makes clear, Prussian agrarians were decidedly unenthusiastic about the new departures, whether they concerned controls on the cheap agricultural labour of Polish migrants from Russia and Galicia or sinister schemes for the fresh implantation of an independent German peasantry.[24] By contrast the National Liberals (and flexible Free Conservatives like Lucius and Tiedemann) were 'all fire' for the ideas, and quickly set about appropriating Bismarck's legislative proposals for their own ends. As Blanke's evidence makes clear, they were very quick off the mark, successfully smuggling the pro-peasant *Rentengut* concept against Bismarck's inclinations into the final version of the Settlement Law.[25]

Thus both Blanke and Hagen are ultimately too 'Bismarckocentric' in their interpretation of the Germanization measures, although at various points both show awareness of the wider dimension. A more extensive evaluation of the parliamentary discussion, the inner-ministerial deliberations and the activities of the Prussian provincial administration would have built bridges to the analysis of public opinion in this broader sense. Something of the same limitation reappears in Hagen's analysis of the Eastern Marches Society. This is generally very good, building on the previous studies of the organization and introducing some valuable new information about its operations in Poznan.[26] But in stressing the society's character as a propaganda organization and dependence on the government too straightforwardly, Hagen underplays an important element in the overall apparatus of anti-Polish activity, namely the creative nexus between Eastern Marches Society, the insurance, savings and loan, and co-operative organizations in Poznan, Danzig and Königsberg, the Settlement Commission itself, and the central ministerial instances in Berlin. As Guratzsch has shown, between the mid-1890s and 1908 Alfred Hugenberg installed himself at the centre of this organizational network and there are good grounds for regarding him as the real architect of the 1908 legislation.[27] Of course, there are different ways of interpreting this structure of influence, and given Hugenberg's status as a senior civil servant one might be forgiven for seeing his role in the Eastern Marches Society and the *Raiffeisen* movement as a secondary reflection of his official responsibilities. My own view would be that Hugenberg proceeded from a remarkably coherent Pan-German ideology (having been the *spiritus rector* of the league's foundation in 1890–1) and saw himself very much as a Pan-German mole.[28] There was a good opportunity here for some interesting biographical analysis of Hugenberg's Eastern collaborators (Leo Wegener, Ludwig Bernhard, Karl Hayessen, Georg Ganse, Karl Kette, Albert Dietrich, Friedrich Swart and others), who amounted to a younger generation of radical nationalist ideologues born and trained under the empire itself, some of them non-Prussians (and nearly all of them from west of the Elbe). Their dominance of Eastern Marches policy blurred the line between the bureaucratic apparatus of Prussian officialdom and the independent agitation of radical nationalists. The main point is that there was considerably more interpenetration of state and civil society (or the Prussian bureaucracy and the radical nationalist public) in the formation of anti-Polish policy than Hagen seems to allow.[29]

How successful was the anti-Polish offensive? At one level the achievement of the Settlement Commission was impressive: 524,231 hectares of land purchased in Poznan and West Prussia between 1886 and 1918 (some 10 per cent of the total land area); some 734 million marks expended; some 27,744 homesteads created for German farmers, involving a family population of perhaps 150,000, or around 3 per cent of the two provinces' overall population. Taken together with the other kinds of government input (for example, the 25 million marks spent between 1897 and 1914 in cultural subsidies, the public-works programme, or the funding of the schools), this represented an enormous effort. But as Blanke and Hagen both point out, on closer inspection the Commission's balance sheet becomes far less favourable. The availability of Polish estates quickly dried up after the first decade and German lands had to be purchased if the programme was to maintian momentum. Thus 71.5 per cent of the land the commission acquired was previously owned by Germans, while 26.5 per cent of the settlers already lived in Poznan or West Prussia and so added nothing to the existing national balance there. The attempt to break the Polish landowning class must be accounted a failure. Between 1861 and 1886 Poles had lost some 195,000 hectares to Germans or the Prussian state, and in the first decade of the Settlement Commission they lost another 50,000 hectares. But during the years 1896–1914 the trend was dramatically reversed, with a gain of 181,437 hectares in Polish hands. On the one hand, the commission certainly achieved its object of hastening the diminishment of large noble property in the social structure of the Poznanian countryside. Between 1882 and 1907 the percentage of arable land farmed in units of more than 100 hectares fell from 58.5 per cent to 46 per cent. Likewise, the share for peasant farms of 5–100 hectares rose from 29.3 per cent to an impressive 47.3 per cent of the total arable. But on the other hand, it seems clear that these shifts redounded just as much to the advantage of the Polish peasant as the German.[30]

Ultimately the demographic trends were against Germanization. Hagen makes this clear in a chapter called 'Capitalism and the nationality conflict: the Poznanian economy and population, 1890–1914', which is really the analytical fulcrum of his book (pp. 208–24). After the systematic rethinking of 1895–9 German strategy was fairly successful in strengthening the German presence in the villages: in 1900–10 the German population in rural Poznan grew by 11.5 per cent, as opposed to 6.5 per cent for the Poles. However, this simply contributed to correcting the losses of the years 1870–1900 and, at the same time, Germans *lost* ground in the towns: in 1895–1910 the Polish urban population grew by 46 per cent, the Catholic and Protestant Germans by only 29 per cent (reduced to only 23 per cent once the Jewish outflow is included). In crude demographic terms the Germans were fighting a losing battle: 'Between the onset of the *Ostflucht* in the 1870s and the eve of the war, the German-Jewish population grew by only 21%, the Polish population by 40%' (Hagen, p. 218). Paradoxically (given the roots of the Polish nationalist movement in the Poznanian countryside), the German holding operation presupposed the continuation of the primarily rural economy, for if urban industrial development had taken place within the province the surplus Polish population would have been retained and the Polish demographic preponderance would have been completely impossible to contain.

None the less, we should be wary of concluding too easily that German policy was foredoomed to fail. On its own suppositions German policy made sense, given the geopolitical-cum-strategic considerations, the notorious resilience of the Polish nationalist tradition and the long-term spectre of a Polish irredentism, and not least the Prussian state's structural obligation to service the socio-economic basis of the East Elbian aristocracy's regional hegemony. Within these limits, the 'positive Germanizers' as one might call them – National Liberals and Free Conservatives, joined from the 1890s by Pan-Germans and other radical nationalists, collectively the real backbone of the Eastern Marches policy – found adequate space for their own ideal of a sturdy German frontier peasantry. Aside from the colonization programme *per se*, the government orchestrated an elaborate repertoire of subsidies for the German population, through agricultural policies, the manipulation of public employment, public works, the strengthening of the economic infra structure (by regulating the Warta/Warthe River, building port facilities at Poznan, and considerably extending the province's rail network), and the monumental celebration of German culture in the provincial capital (with the opening of the Royal Academy in 1903, the Kaiser Wilhelm Library in 1902, the Kaiser Friedrich Museum in 1904, a new theatre, a new imperial castle, and so on).

The Germanizing strategy was consistent, systematic, quite sophisticated, and not particularly unusual in the context of other 'official nationalisms' of the time.[31] It was presaged in the Polish arena of the *Kulturkampf* in the 1870s, precipitated in the measures of 1885–6, worked during the intensive ministerial discussions of 1895–9 into a fully articulated system, kept well oiled during 1900–6, and ideologically sharpened in a full-scale political confrontation with the Polish nationalist movement in 1906–8. Probably the most significant aspect of this systematization, which as suggested above was already inscribed in the consequences of German unification, was the increasingly *German-national*, as opposed to *Prussian*, terms of reference. As Bosse said in a Landtag speech of 27 February 1896, Prussia was simply 'a German state – not a federal state, which is put together out of individual German, Polish, Danish elements or nationalities; rather we are a German national state' (Blanke, p. 180). This was a decisive repudiation of the older Prussian ideology of citizenship enshrined in the Poznanian Proclamation of 1815. Henceforth the Eastern Marches policy was taken increasingly out of the specifically Prussian sphere and made into an urgent priority of imperial government concern. This was reflected in the Instructions for Officials drawn up by Miquel for the Ministry of State and issued in April 1898, which enjoined Prussian officials in Polish areas to work actively off-duty for the strengthening of 'German national' as well as 'Prussian state consciousness' (Blanke, p. 198). Altogether, and despite the ebbing of radical nationalist activism in Poznan detected by Hagen on the eve of the war (pp. 184 f.), the anti-Polish campaigning achieved a high level of ideological mobilization between the 1890s and 1914. It had fully consolidated the social infrastructure of German cultural dominance in the East, while driving a wedge between the Poles and other oppositional forces in German society. Without foreign assistance there was no reason why the Poles should constitute a serious threat to the Prusso-German state. In effect, the Polish question was rapidly becoming successfully marginalized as something to trouble the mainstream of German party politics.[32]

Not the least of the effects of the anti-Polish drives, though, was the impressive counter-mobilization of the Polish nationalists, and in bringing this essay to a close it remains to say something about the character of the Polish national movement. Each stage of anti-Polish activity elicited powerful affirmations of Polish national identity. In the 1870s the *Kulturkampf* engineered a vital conjunction between the church and the national government, thereby subsuming a threatening inner-Polish conflict between liberals and ultramontanes in the defensive rhetoric of Polish national solidarity; at the same time the Polish peasantry were brought closer within the nationalist orbit (as addressees of nationalist propaganda, at least), as was a larger physical territory, including more isolated areas of Poznan, West Prussia as a whole, the Kashubian areas in the north of that province, and (far more ambiguously) Upper Silesia.[33] The 1885–6 measures stimulated further popular mobilization in a 'deferential' mould, the beginnings of serious economic organizing amongst the Polish peasantry, and the first flickerings of independent Polish politics in the towns (Blanke, pp. 93 ff.). Then after the collapse of the 'loyalist' experiment under Caprivi, the first major fissures in national solidarity opened up, the clerico-gentry notability experienced a sustained challenge from a new urban populist grouping, and the the peasant co-operative movement experienced a powerful upswing of organizational growth (helped, it should be said, by the economic upturn of 1895–6). Finally, after the school strikes of 1906–7 and the fresh legislation of 1908, the clerico-gentry hegemony was decisively upset, and the launching of the National Democratic Association in 1909 signalled a lasting realignment of Western Polish politics (Blanke, pp. 209–33; Hagen, pp. 225–65).

As Kulczycki rightly says: 'By attacking a minority on nationalist grounds, the government actually armed the minority' (p. 220). The distinctive features of the Polish national movement as it responded to this challenge are perhaps well known – a parliamentary representation dominated by the noble/clerical notability, supported by a provincial structure of election committees, with a flourishing Polish-language press, and doubly rooted in a well-developed rural network of economic and cultural 'Organic Work' organizations (the Central Economic Society 1861, the Provincial Union of Peasant Societies 1873, the Union of Co-operative Societies 1871, the Society of Popular Learning/Society of Popular Libraries 1872/1880) – and these are described by Blanke and Hagen in excellent detail. The ideological inheritance of this movement – an historical-cum-political (as opposed to an ethnic) conception of Polish nationality deriving from the old Commonwealth, which rendered the parliamentary leadership open to participation in the institutions of the Prussian state – is also well laid out by the two authors.[34] The interesting question of Prussian Polish history is the internal transformation of this movement between the 1890s and the First World War to the point where (after 1918) a previously unbudgeable clerico-gentry hegemony had been replaced by a regional National Democratic dominance which was equally imposing. One of the great virtues of the works by Blanke and Hagen is their detailed analysis of this political transition.[35]

A number of points can be made about this process. First, 'the political monopoly of the *Szlachta* and the conservatives and their clerical allies' (Hagen, p. 257), solidified by the slogans of National Solidarity and the practical achievements of Organic Work in the 1870s and 1880s, proved extraordinarily resilient. In the first instance, this was based in the specifically gentry institution of the Central Economic Society (CTG) and the informally constituted provincial and local election committees, together with the longstanding organ of gentry opinion, *Dziennik Poznanski* (which originated in 1859 as a predominantly Polish National Liberal paper). But it was also grounded in a popular apparatus of peasant-oriented institutions, from the Popular Libraries and the co-operative network to the gentry-sponsored peasant 'agricultural circles' which by 1913 showed an overall membership of 14,500 in some 350 active circles, or around two-thirds of Poznan's self-sufficient peasant cultivators (Hagen, p. 242).[36] The impressive thing here is the extent to which the Polish landowning class maintained its political and ideological leadership over this extremely well-organized peasantry, which (as we saw) was demographically and economically on the rise between the 1890s and 1914. Yet neither of the independent political formations, Roman Szymanski's populists (who raised their independent standard in Poznan and other towns for the first time in 1892–3) nor the National Democrats (who emerged under the leadership of Roman Dmowski during the later 1890s in the other parts of the Partition), made much of an impression on the Poznanian peasantry's traditional allegiance until shortly before the war. Unlike their compatriots in Galicia or the peasantries of Central and Southern Germany (but not unlike the Catholic peasants of Westphalia or parts of the Rhineland), the peasants of Prussian Poland generated no independent mobilizations before 1914.[37]

Secondly, a key role in this respect was played by the Catholic clergy. As mentioned above, the mobilization of the village clergy behind the national cause was one of the most important consequences of the *Kulturkampf*, and by the 1890s it is clear that priests were a vital category amongst the ranks of political and Organic Work officeholders (Hagen estimates a figure of 28.5 per cent for 1914) (p. 257). As Hagen says: 'In reminding the villagers and town workers of their "holy obligation" to vote according to the electoral authorities' instructions, to join and support the institutions of Organic Work, and to honour the concept of Polish Catholic national solidarity, the clergy clearly served conservative interests to the degree that control of Polish politics rested in the gentry's hands' (p. 242). But the Catholic Church also defined a distinctive ideological position, marked by the formula 'First religion, then nationality', which was a significant narrowing of the pre-1870s tradition of gentry patriotism. Increasingly, it seems, tendencies within the Catholic Church 'concentrated on strengthening the common people's religiosity and national consciousness through organizations and a press', like the Union of Polish Catholic Workers' Societies (ZKTRP) (launched in 1891, with 31,140 members in 271 associations by 1914), its organ of opinion *Robotnik* (The Worker), and the mass circulation weekly *Przewodnik Katolicki* (Catholic Guide) launched in 1895 (with 64,000 subscribers in 1904). Together these two papers 'formed the single largest ideological bloc within the province's Polish press'. It amounted to a 'clerical populism distinct both from gentry conservatism and National Democracy'. As Hagen says (pp. 243 f., also for the preceding):

After 1890 the clergy, apprehensive of their parishioners' susceptibility to socialism, Germanization, and secularization had ceased relying on automatic obedience in the political realm and instead began actively indoctrinating the Polish workers and common people with a popular nationalist Catholicism. The result by 1914 was that the priestly nationalists and their followers had become an important independent force which neither the conservative nor the ND camp could afford to antagonize or ignore.

Thirdly, the main challenge to the gentry before the turn of the century, Szymanski's National People's Party formed in 1893, came from a kind of diffuse socio-political resentment and a growing impatience with the accommodationism of the parliamentary delegation (*Kolo Polskie*) and the clerical establishment, rather than from anything more ideologically coherent. Its emergence reflected a definite strengthening of the Polish urban population under the empire, with the growth of the professions and a limited flourishing of Polish entrepreneurship. As Hagen says, 'Szymanski's populism was the first independent political movement among the nineteenth century Poznanian bourgeoisie. It won support from urban Organic Work activists and educated professionals of bourgeois origins, merchants, artisans and small-scale manufacturers. These were groups whose numbers and prosperity were on the rise after 1870' (p. 149).[38] Ideologically, it was a mishmash of liberal-cum-radical and anti-semitic attitudes which in many ways was classically *mittelständisch*. Blanke provides many excellent quotations to this effect. Thus in Szymanski's mind: 'One cannot count on the nobility any more; Poland exists only in the people and in the middle classes ... The people must protect itself from the downright demoralizing influence of the nobility ... [which] constitutes a genuine danger for the further political development and education of the Polish people'. On another occasion he divided the noble parliamentarians into three classes, 'wastrels', 'crafty card-players', and '*déclassé* place-seekers'. The leading institutions of the Poznanian (and West Prussian) Polish community were dominated by 'untouchable big-shots, representatives of the clergy, of the nobility, or people who belong to their social class'. The election committee should contain 'members of all classes, nobles, burgher, peasant, artisan, workers' (Blanke, pp. 215, 226, 221, 224). However, this general animus against the Polish notability only acquired ideological coherence and organizational muscle with the arrival of the younger nationalist intelligentsia in the later 1890s – first the Young Poland group around Bernard Chrzanowski and

217

Wladyslaw Rabski and the short-lived weekly *Przeglad Poznanski* (1894–
6), and then the National Democrats with their brutally instrumental
subordination of political activity to the ulterior goals of national
consolidation. Their conception of a 'political party based on the
intelligentsia' was something altogether more serious than the vague
caucusing of the Populists, of whom they were generally but patronisingly
supportive. The future clearly lay in combining the political intelligence of
the new nationalists with the generalized mobilization of urban political
resentments achieved by the Populists, a coalescence which actually
occurred between the end of the 1890s and the foundation of the National
Democratic Association in 1909.[39]

How was the conjunction between this new urban nationalism and the
existing Organic Work apparatus in the countryside achieved? In some
ways (this in my fourth point), this is the key to political transition
mentioned above, from the clerico-gentry hegemony of the 1870s and
1880s to the more broadly based and finely articulated radical nationalism
of the final peacetime years (or from a political to an ethnic conception of
Polish nationhood). My own view (although this is stated as such by
neither Blanke nor Hagen) is that it was achieved in the ideological
climacteric of the general school strike. This is obviously where
Kulczycki's exhaustive narrative of the latter comes in useful. As an
analytical survey of the strike – its precursors and origins, the course of
events in 1906–7, the dimensions and distribution of the activity, the
mechanics of individual school actions, the immediate responsibilities of
children and parents, the contributions of the Polish clerical and secular
leaderships, the broader involvement of the Polish political public and, of
course, the reactions of the authorities – his account can hardly be
bettered.[40] But at its centre is an unresolved tension between the general
argument that the strikes were 'spontaneous' (in the sense that they
originated with parents and children, with a primarily religious rather than
a nationalist/political motivation) and the patent involvement of the Polish
national movement once the strikes had begun (through the press,
promotion of protest meetings, distribution of literature, provision of local
leadership, and so on). Kulczycki tends to present this as the normalizing
influence of 'the traditional Polish socioeconomic elite', who channelled
the resistance into established forms of expression.[41]

I would prefer to stress the novelty of the departures in 1906–7. As
Kulczycki points out, the old clerico-gentry establishment was extremely
equivocal in its advocacy of the strike (for example, pp. 119 ff., 173 f.). The
real motor of mobilization was the series of public meetings organized in
Poznan between 1 April and 15 October 1906 (thirty-five in all), and here it
was precisely the National Democrats and clerico-Populists identified by
Hagen who were probably most involved, notably through the co-
ordinating activities of the *Straz* (the Guard) which had been formed in

1905 and through the parochial leadership of priests.[42] The agitation's political climax was the great Poznan rally of 17 December 1906, whose proceedings were dominated by new activists of this kind (and by the shadowy organizing hand of the *Straz*) (Kulczycki, pp. 136 f.). Now, the novel incursion of so many urban activists into the villagers' consciousness (through the *Straz*, older groups like the women's intelligentsia association *Warta* and circles of school students, and the existing organizations of Populists and National Democrats), combined with the effects of the publicity apparatus (press, leaflets, strike bulletins, and so on) and the existential practice of opposition to produce a new kind of popular Polish public sphere. In effect, the experience of simultaneous mass struggle across the entire Prussian Polish region over matters of such quotidian immediacy as schooling and religion precipitated the Polish countryside into a stronger sense of active national belonging, a process which was consummated in the triumphant Reichstag election campaign of January 1907.[43] This provided the necessary impetus for the final unification of the Populists and National Democrats and opened a decisive breach in the walls of popular deference that shored up the gentry's old parliamentary monopoly. In these terms the school strikes marked a key political rupture.

These points are also made by Kulczycki. Thus:

The Polish national movement had *penetrated* the lives of the masses of Prussian Poland to the point of rousing them to put up direct resistance to the Prussian government, something they had never done before. Through the strikes they *participated* in the affairs of Polish society more intensely than they had in the past. The risks they endured and the price they paid indicated that they *identified* their interests with those of Polish society. Parents and children joined the strike for a variety of reasons but they soon embraced the religious and national values that were ostensibly at stake. Following the strike, there was an upsurge of popular support for Polish cultural and social activities. Furthermore, the camaraderie of the struggle enhanced the complementarity of communication habits of the Polish-speaking population. Thus, the school strikes had profound effects on their participants if not on the government against which they were directed. (Kulczycki, p. 218)

This, with its stress on the educational, radicalizing, and unifying effects of the strike (and in its invocation of Karl Deutsch's concepts of social communication), is very well put.[44] Similarly, Kulczycki has a good eye for the shape of the Polish rural community and its 'natural' spokesmen: 'The Polish-speaking peasant often deferred to the judgement of individuals who had a superior social position or a profession that required a degree of instruction like the local organist, miller, or the estate owner and his functionaries: the farm-manager, steward, distiller, and forester' (p. 76).

He is also doubtless right that there was no 'evidence of central direction or coordination by Polish nationalists' in the preparatory stages of the strikes (p. 88). But to postulate an implied dichotomy between a consciously nationalist political leadership and an isolated, primordial and unpolitical peasantry, and to conclude from these judgements that the peasantry *per se* had no developed sense of Polish nationality or of Polish political consciousness before the general strike ('for the vast majority of the population Polish nationalism was more an effect of the school strikes than a cause', p. 219) is going too far. The Polish peasantry had, after all, experienced an extensive and accelerating process of avowedly Polish organization before 1906–7, and on Kulczycki's own evidence showed a fairly sophisticated command of political tactics during the strikes themselves. But despite the excellent local detail, there is little feel in his account for the process of political socialization within the peasantry or for the prior permeation of nationalist ideas in the village culture.

Finally, these books prompt some observations about how the history of 'Poland' should be written. As with any stateless or territorially divided nation, where state organization and cultural formation do not coincide, it is extraordinarily difficult to keep the entire Polish national region clearly in focus during the nineteenth century (quite aside from deciding what the legitimate boundaries of that region should be). In the Polish case this problem is somewhat fudged by the prior existence of the Commonwealth as a pre-Partition Polish state, so that the period between 1795 and 1918 can be represented as a kind of interlude, during which the boundaries of 'historic' Poland are allowed to set the parameters of historical discussion and the continuity of a Polish nation *per se* is simply assumed. But it has become a common insight of the literature on nationalism that territorial state formation and the cultural unification of a people into a shared sense of national belonging are not necessarily the same thing, so that even avowedly national states (or popular nationalist movements) can easily coexist with large subject populations which possessed a very under-developed sense of nationality. In other words, the mere existence of Polish *statehood* before 1795 and the political aspiration thereafter to recreate it should not lead us to think that either the conception or the reality of Polish *nationhood* embodied in the post-1918 state were already in place. The most obvious change in this respect was the increasing tendency of the peoples on the eastern borderlands (Ukrainians, Lithuanians, Belorussians, and Jews) to think of themselves as separate nationalities, divided from the Poles by a combination of language, religion and social place. At the same time, the social-legal confinement of the Polish nation to the *Szlachta* was eroded. Hugh Seton-Watson puts this very well:

Poland until the Partitions was a multi-lingual multi-religious state with a single Polish nation limited to a social class. After the Partitions this changed. The non-Catholic, non-Polonophone populations gradually fell away. Germans, Belorussians and Ukrainians were increasingly drawn towards their kinsmen living in more distant parts of the empires between which Poland was divided, while Lithuanian-speakers (largely on the initiative of compatriots who had emigrated to the United States) began to think of their language-group as a distinct nation . . . Gradually the Polish nation was reduced to a core of Polish-speaking Catholics. At the same time this core expanded as, with the spread of nineteenth century democratic ideas, the class distinctions on membership of the nation melted, and Polish-speaking Catholic – or lapsed Catholic – workers and peasants were drawn into the nation, taking their place beside members of the old szlachta, now largely entrenched in the intellectual professions and other middle strata of society. The process had not gone very far in 1863, when peasants responded rather feebly to the call to insurrection, but was basically completed by the end of the century.[45]

Now, this process of national reconstitution is certainly not peculiar to the Polish case and in fact is a common feature of nineteenth- and twentieth-century national states and nationalist movements.[46] But capturing its full flavour is complicated by the need to integrate the histories of the three parts of the Partition, which bequeathed distinct juridical and political traditions, regional economies and social structures to the post-1918 Polish state. For the nineteenth century most historians dodge this problem by concentrating on a single part of the Partition, usually the Russian or the Austrian, and this tendency is reproduced in the various general histories, where the Prussian lands invariably come off worst.[47] The point I wish to make is that works specifically on Prussian Poland succumb to the same syndrome, by focusing on the core territory of Poznan (and to a lesser extent West Prussia) rather than the areas of Polish habitation as a whole – East Prussia, Upper Silesia, thin scatterings of Pomerania and Brandenburg, and of course Rhineland-Westphalia (and for that matter Berlin). Concentrating (as do Blanke and Hagen) on the two most 'Polish' provinces is perfectly defensible. But for an understanding of the Polish population's 'nationalization', an analysis of the other areas can be just as useful, by exposing some of the unevenness and ambiguities in the process. One way of doing this, as Murphy shows in his careful weighing of the evidence of assimilation and national distinctiveness amongst the Poles in Bottrop, is to look at the national affiliations of the Polish migrants in the industrial West and Berlin.[48] When the 'Ruhr Poles' (whom Wehler estimates at between 350,000 and 450,000 in 1914) are added to the seasonal migrants in Eastern Prussian agriculture from Galicia and Russia (some 400,000 a year by 1914), we have an enormous mobile or transient population whose implications for the social, cultural and political tasks of the Polish nationalist movement in the East are barely touched upon by Blanke, Hagen and Kulczycki.[49] Another way of broadening the analysis would be to compare the apparently successful Polonization of the Catholic Kashubs in West Prussia with the Polish movement's lack of success with the Protestant Masurians in East Prussia.[50] Most interesting of all in this respect would be the heavy industrial region of Oppeln/Opole in Upper Silesia, where the Catholic Centre Party's electoral monopoly was broken from the 1890s by the parallel emergence of the Polish nationalists and the SPD.[51]

Thus the main limitation of the books under review derives from their monographic character, which is also their main source of strength. Kulczycki might have strengthened his evaluation of the school strikes by including more discussion of the Polish nationalist movement as a whole. Blanke and Hagen might have delineated stronger comparative contexts for their analyses by addressing the larger questions of Polish nationality mentioned above, by considering the experience of other subject nationalities of the German Empire (Danes, Sorbs, Alsace-Lorraine), by discussing other national examples (both official nationality and comparable nationalist movements, like the Irish and Ukrainian, or the Hungarian), and by referring to the general literature on nationalism – not as a full component of the books, but as a stimulating comparative dimension to the argument.[52] However, to press these comments too far would be ungenerous. This is a group of excellent monographs, which fill important gaps and make a distinguished contribution to their chosen field. Hagen's, in particular, is extremely well-rounded and enterprising, with a number of additional merits (for example, the deeper historical sweep, the discussion of the Jews and the treatment of Poznanian left liberalism) which I have been unable to include here. Though concerned principally with the specifics of the nationality clash between Germans and Poles, they deliver a number of essential building blocks for the genuinely integrated history of the nineteenth-century Polish national movement which may hopefully someday be written.

CHAPTER 8: NOTES

This essay originally appeared as a review article based on the following books: R. Blanke, *Prussian Poland in the German Empire (1871–1900)*, East European Monographs, No. 86 (Boulder, Colo, 1981 [distributed by Columbia University Press, New York]), pp. xii, 268; W. W. Hagen, *Germans, Poles, and Jews: The Nationality Conflict in the Prussian East, 1772–1914* (Chicago, 1980), pp. x, 406; J. J. Kulczycki, *School Strikes in Prussian Poland, 1901–1907: The Struggle over Bilingual Education*, East European Monographs, No. 82 (Boulder, Colo, 1981 [distributed by Columbia University Press, New York]), pp. xii, 249; R. C. Murphy, *Gastarbeiter im Deutschen Reich. Polen in Bottrop 1891–1933* (Wuppertal, 1982), p. 203.

1 M. Laubert, *Die preussische Polenpolitik von 1772–1914* (Berlin, 1920; 3rd edn, Cracow, 1944), *Eduard Flottwell* (Berlin, 1919), and *Die Verwaltung der Provinz Posen 1815–*

1847 (Berlin, 1923); H. Rothfels, *Bismarck und der Osten* (Leipzig, 1934); Rothfels, *Ostraum, Preussentum und Reichsgedanke* (Leipzig, 1935), and *Bismarck, der Osten und das Reich* (Darmstadt, 1960). See also H. Jablonowski, *Die preussische Polenpolitik von 1815 bis 1914* (Würzburg, 1964).

2 See W. Conze, *Polnische Nation und deutsche Politik im ersten Weltkrieg* (Cologne and Graz, 1958); T. Schieder, *Das Deutsche Reich von 1871 als Nationalstaat* (Cologne and Opladen, 1961). See also the work of their students: H.-U. Wehler, *Sozialdemokratie und Nationalstaat. Nationälitatenfragen in Deustschland 1840–1914* (Göttingen, 1971; originally published in 1962 under a slightly different title); and V. Hentschel, 'Wirtschaftliche Entwicklung, soziale Mobilitat und nationale Bewegung in Oberschlesien 1871–1914' in W. Conze, G. Schram and K. Zernack (eds), *Modernisierung und nationale Gesellschaft im ausgehenden 18. und im 19. Jahrhundert, Referate einer deutsch-polnischen Historikerkonferenz* (West Berlin, 1979), pp. 231–73. It is worth noting that Schieder has sponsored work of some originality on nationalism by drawing on East European scholarship since the early 1970s, whereas Conze has been in the forefront of recent German-Polish exchange. See the following volumes of essays edited by Schieder: *Sozialstruktur und Organisation europäischer Nationalbewegungen* (Munich, 1971); *Staatsgründungen und Nationalitätsprinzip* (Munich, 1974); (with Otto Dann) *Nationale Bewegung und soziale Organisation I: Vergleichende Studien zur nationalen Vereinsbewegungen des 19. Jahrhunderts in Europa* (Munich, 1978). See also Conze's valuable general essay, 'Nationsbildung durch Trennung. Deutsche und Polen im preussischen Osten', in O. Pflanze (ed.), *Innenpoltische Probleme des Bismarck-Reiches* (Munich, 1983), pp. 95–119.

3 H.-U. Wehler, 'Von den "Reichsfeinden" zur "Reichskristallnacht": Polenpolitik im Deutschen Kaiserreich 1871–1918', in *Krisenherde des Kaiserreichs 1871–1918* (Göttingen, 1970), pp. 181–99; 'Deutsche-Polnische Beziehungen im 19. and 20. Jahrhundert', ibid., pp. 201–17; 'Die Polen im Ruhrgebiet bis 1918', ibid., pp. 219–36.

4 See esp.: H.-U.Wehler, *Bismarck und der Imperialismus* (Cologne, 1969), and *Das deutsche Kaiserreich 1871–1918* (Göttingen, 1973).

5 Good introductions to the Fischer Controversy and its reverberations can be found in J. A. Moses, *The Politics of Illusion. The Fischer Controversy in German Historiography* (London, 1975), and G. Iggers, *New Directions in European Historiography* (Middletown, Conn., 1975), pp. 80–122 (reissued in a revised edition, London, 1984). Two of Fischer's students published important monographs on German expansionism in the East during the First World War: I. Geiss, *Der polnische Grenzstreifen 1914–1918* (Lübeck and Hamburg, 1970).

6 See Conze, Schramm and Zernack (eds), *Modernisierung und nationale Gesellschaft*, p. 7.

7 Jackobczyk is the author of many works in Polish. In English see 'The first decade of the Prussian Settlement Commission's activities, 1886–1897', *Polish Review*, vol. 17 (1972), pp. 3–13. He is also joint author of the major study of the German anti-Polish pressure group, the *Deutscher Ostmarkenverein* (also known as the *H-K-T-Verein* or the *Hakatisten* after the initials of the three founders) launched in 1894: A. Galos, F.-H. Gentzen and W. Jacobczyk, *Die Hakatisten* (East Berlin, 1966), the outcome of an East German-Polish collaboration.

8 Of course, like all such statements, this one needs qualification. Works by Wehler, Conze and Geiss have already been mentioned. To them should be added L. Schofer, *The Formation of a Modern Labour Force. Upper Silesia, 1865–1914* (Berkeley, Calif., 1975). In some ways Schofer's valuable book belongs in a category with the ones under review, but its focus is more on the political economy of the regional labour market and only secondarily on the dynamics of the Polish–German nationality conflict. Murphy's study of the Poles in the Ruhr was preceded by C. Klessmann, *Polnische Bergarbeiter im Ruhrgebiet 1870–1945* (Göttingen, 1978).

9 Hagen, p. 60. Here Hagen quotes Otto Karl von Voss, the Minister for South Prussia in 1796, to the effect that 'unity of laws, customs, morals, benefits and burdens, and, if possible, language forges the strongest national bond among large populations' (p. 62). If that is not the modern concept of nationality, it is very close.

10 Note that this was not true of the German left liberals, who divided from the National Liberals first in 1867 and again in 1880–1. See Hagen's discussion of left liberalism in Posen (pp. 288 ff.).

11 See the following: A. J. Mayer, *Wilson vs. Lenin. Political Origins of the New Diplomacy 1917–1918* (Cleveland, Ohio and New York, 1964), pp. 293–393; H. Mommsen, 'Zur Beurteilung der altösterreichischen Nationalitätenfrage', and 'Otto Bauer, Karl Renner und die sozialdemokratische Nationalitätenpolitik in Osterreich 1905–1914', in *Arbeiterbewegung und Nationale Frage. Ausgewählte Aufsätze* (Göttingen, 1979), pp. 127–46, 195–217; H. and C. Seton-Watson, *The Making of A New Europe. R. W. Seton-Watson and the Last Years of Austria-Hungary* (London, 1980); R. Szporluk, *The Political Thought of Thomas G. Masaryk* (New York, 1981), esp. pp. 80–146.

12 For one detailed exploration of this approach: E. Weber, *Peasants into Frenchmen. The Modernization of Rural France 1870–1914* (London, 1977).

13 Liberal ambivalance on the nationality question resembled liberal ambivalence in a related sphere, namely the question of Jewish emancipation. On the one hand, liberals believed in religious toleration and civil equality. On the other hand, they opposed the archaism, superstitiousness and cultural particularism of the Jews' traditional religion. Logically these positions led to the advocacy of Jewish assimilation. But if the Jews shed their attachment to traditional Judaism, what was left of a distinctive Jewish culture? This dilemma has caused much anguish over the past century, particularly with the twentienth-century emergence of a Jewish nationalism linked to the idea of a homeland. For an excellent exploration of both the Jewish and the liberal sides of this discussion, see U. Tal, *Christians and Jews in Germany. Religion, Politics and Ideology in the Second Reich, 1870–1914* (Ithaca, NY and London, 1975), esp. pp. 21–210.

14 The Law's detailed justification included the following statement, whose resemblance to the Frauendienst quotation at the head of this essay is striking: 'The Polish nationality is notoriously seeking, and not without success, to extend itself more and more in certain eastern provinces, while displacing the existing German elements. Such advances, in important regions of the monarchy, by a nationality which, by language and custom, is fundamentally alienated from the life of the Prussian state, demand extensive defence measures in all areas of state administration . . . to prevent the interests of the German population, to prevent the flooding of these regions by Polish elements, and to open the way more and more to German intellect and German culture' (Blanke, p. 67).

15 The fullest account of the 1886 offensive is in Blanke, pp. 55–91. Hagen provides a more cursory treatment, while Kulczycki deals with it as part of his general introduction. See also: J. Mai, *Die preussisch-deutsche Polenpolitik 1885–1887* (East Berlin, 1962); H. Neubach, *Die Ausweisungen von Polen und Juden aus Preussen 1885–6* (Wiesbaden, 1967); K. J. Bade, ' "Kulturkampf " auf dem Arbeitsmarkt: Bismarcks "Polenpolitik" ', in Pflanze (ed.), *Innenpolitische Probleme des Bismarck-Reiches*, pp. 121–42.

16 Bismarck's Minister of Culture had been Gustav von Gossler (1881–91), also a radical Germanizer. This made the brief tenure of Robert von Zedlitz-Trützschler (1891–2) the only break in three decades of continuous pressure on the legitimacy and public practice of Polish national culture.

17 On the whole Hagen also takes this view (e.g., p. 167).

18 The quoted phrase is taken from Bismarck's letter to his sister in 1861: 'Flay the Poles until they despair of life! I have all sympathy for their position, but if we wish to endure, we can do nothing else but extirpate them' (Hagen, p. 125; Blanke, p. 10).

19 Blanke, pp. 39–91. By comparison with his careful dissection of the 1886 measures, Blanke's treatment of the context of the expulsions is somewhat perfunctory.

20 For example, Hagen, pp. 131, 167. For some criticisms of Wehler's ideas in this respect: G. Eley, 'Defining social imperialism: use and abuse of an idea', in *Social History*, vol. 1 (1976), pp. 265–90, and 'Social imperialism in Germany: reformist synthesis or reactionary sleight of hand?', in J. Radkau and I. Geiss (eds), *Imperialismus im 20. Jahrhundert. Gedenkschrift für Georg W. F. Hallgarten* (Munich, 1976), pp. 71–86.

21 Blanke (pp. 41–6) cites two articles in the *Preussische Jahrbücher*, vol. 44 (1879), pp. 32–51 ('Die Kolonisation in unserem Osten und die Herstellung des Erbzinses', by E. von der Brüggen), and *Die Gegenwart*, vol. 27 (1885), pp. 1–3, 19–22 ('Die Rückgang des Deutschtums', by E. von Hartmann). For Hartmann see the useful article by H. Neubach, 'Eduard von Hartmann's Bedeutung für die Entwicklung des deutsch-polnischen Verhältnisses', in *Zeitschrift für Ostforschung*, vol. 13 (1964), pp. 106–59.

22 See esp. K. J. Bade, *Fredrich Fabri und der Imperialismus in der Bismarckzeit* (Freiburg, 1975).

23 See K. J. Bade, ' "Kulturkampf " auf dem Arbeitsmarkt', cit. at n. 15 above. For the wider context of the migrant labour question: J. Nichtweiss, *Die ausländischen Saisonarbeiter in der Landwirtschaft der ostlichen und mittleren Gebeite des Deutschen Reiches. Ein Beitrag zur Geschichte der preussisch-deutschen Politik von 1890–1914* (East Berlin, 1959); B. P. Murdzek, *Emigration in Polish Social-Political Thought, 1870–1914* (New York, 1977).

24 Bade, ' "Kulturkampf " auf dem Arbeitsmarkt', cit. at n. 15 above, pp. 135 ff.; Nichtweiss, *Die ausländischen Saisonarbeiter*, pp. 36–73, and in general.

25 See Blanke, esp. pp. 63 ff. The phrase 'all fire' comes from Lucius's description of Miquel's reaction to the news of the proposal for a settlement law. In this sense I would differ from Hagen, who describes the political constellation behind the Polish policy as 'an openly conservative and antiliberal government reliably supported in the Prussian Landtag by the combined forces of the agrarian conservatives, Free Conservatives, and National Liberals' (p. 131). This was only partially true. The Conservatives were always ambivalent and only came round haltingly to the internal colonization idea on the eve of 1914. The National Liberals were the real partisans in the 1880s and 1890s, particularly through the powerful advocacy of Johannes von Miquel. In this sense the *Ostmarkenverein* and other radical nationalists in the Pan-German and Navy Leagues were the real inheritors of the National Liberal mantle, as the efforts of the new National Liberal leadership around Gustav Stresemann and Ernst Bassermann to strike alliances with them after 1905–6 would tend to confirm. There is some discussion of this in G. Eley, *Reshaping the German Right. Radical Nationalism and Political Change after Bismarck* (New Haven, Conn. and London, 1980), pp. 304–12. In his analysis of the *Ostmarkenverein* in Poznan Hagen does bring out the tensions between agrarian Conservatism and the advocates of a forward anti-Polish policy (see pp. 276 ff.).

26 See R. W. Tims, *Germanizing Prussian Poland* (New York, 1941), and Galos, Gentzen and Jacobczyk, *Hakatisten*. For a summary, see Eley, *Reshaping the German Right*, pp. 58-68.

27 D. Guratzsch, *Macht durch Organisation. Die Grundlegung des Hugenbergschen Presseimperiums* (Düsseldorf, 1974), pp. 26–62. This work is not cited by Hagen.

28 For some discussion of Pan-German politics in this period, see Eley, *Reshaping the German Right*, pp. 242–53.

29 See also G. Voigt, *Otto Hoetzsch 1876–1946. Wissenschaft und Politik im Leben eines deutschen Historikers* (East Berlin, 1978), pp. 28-48; R. Baier, *Der deutsche Osten als soziale Frage. Eine Studie zur preussischen und deutschen Siedlungs- und Polenpolitik in den Ostprovinzen während des Kaiserreichs und det Weimarer Republik* (Cologne and Vienna, 1980), pp. 1–148. Blanke seems to me to underestimate the importance of the *Ostmarkenverein*. See pp. 182 f.

30 The figures are adapted from the summaries in Blanke, pp. 191 f., and Hagen, pp. 208–10.

31 For a stimulating discussion of 'official nationalisms', see B. Anderson, *Imagined Communities. Reflections on the Origin and Spread of Nationalism* (London, 1983), pp. 80–103, a book which should be required reading for all historians of nationalism in one country.

32 This was reflected in the difficulties of the two main opposition parties – the SPD and (more ambivalently) the Centre – in developing a consistent advocacy of Polish nationality rights. It was much easier for the SPD to ignore the Polish question than to develop a principled democratic policy in relation to it, much as the British Labour Party has tended to evade the Irish question for long periods of its existence.

33 See Blanke, pp. 25–33. See also P. Böhning, *Die national-polnische Bewegung in Westpreussen 1815–1871* (Marburg, 1973), and 'Agrarische Organisation und nationale Mobilisierung in Westpreussen', in Conze, Schram and Zernack (eds), *Modernisierung und nationale Gesellschaft*, pp. 161–76. Hagen, pp. 147 f., cites examples of popular resistance to the *Kulturkampf*.

34 This conception of nationality also left the nationalist leadership insensitive to the ethnically defined claims of other peoples inhabiting the lands of the former Commonwealth – Lithuanians, Belorussians, Ukrainians and Jews.

35 Blanke's discussion is contained in two substantial chapters, 'The Populist revolt and the failure of loyalism' (pp. 145–75), and 'The triumph of nationalist enmity' (pp. 209–38), Hagen's in one ' "Each to his own": the Polish national movement, 1890–1914' (pp. 225–

65). Of the two, Hagen's is the more analytical, Blanke's the more narrative account. Kulczycki's account is of a different order, being focused exclusively on the specific issue of resistance to the Prussian school policies rather than on the dynamics of change in the Polish movement as a whole. But in this context his contribution is also extremely valuable. It is worth noting that the Populist agitation amongst the Poles of Poznan and West Prussia can also be interpreted in a larger *German* context. New resentments against the patrician and oligarchic cast of the political process – the informally constituted networks of notables (*Honoratiorenpolitik*) that dominated the localities – were replicated in most parts of Germany during the 1890s. Sometimes they took a popular agrarian form (as in the anti-semitic agitations of Central Germany or the agrarian rebellions in the Centre Party in the south and south-west), sometimes the form of a political critique on the part of urban-bourgeois and petty-bourgeois elements who felt themselves shut out by a traditional notability which was incapable of rising to the challenge of a modern popular politics (as in the emergence of the Pan-Germans and a radical nationalist opposition on the right). Hagen finds the same phenomenon – the claims of 'democracy against the notables' (in the words of the Poznanian Zionist slogan) – amongst the Poznanian Jews (p. 316), but both he and Blanke miss the more general context. See Eley, *Reshaping the German Right*, pp. 19 ff.

36 Blanke's figures are different, citing 373 peasant associations in 1911 with 15,000 members, 'equivalent to 36% of the independent Polish farmers in Poznan' (p. 213).

37 I have tried to address the general comparative question of agrarian politics in 'Anti-semitism, agrarian mobilization, and the crisis in the Conservative Party; radicalism and containment in the foundation of the *Bund der Landwirte*, 1892–1893', in J. C. Fout (ed.), *Politics, Parties and the Authoritarian State: Imperial Germany, 1871–1918* (forthcoming). See also I. Farr, 'Populism in the countryside: the peasant leagues in Bavaria in the 1890s', in R. J. Evans (ed.), *Society and Politics in Wilhelmine Germany* (London, 1978), pp. 136–59; D. G. Blackbourn, *Class, Religion and Local Politics in Wilhelmine Germany. The Centre Party in Wurttemberg before 1914* (New Haven, Conn. and London, 1980); R. G. Moeller, 'Peasants, politics and pressure groups in war and inflation: a study of the Rhineland and Westphalia, 1914–1924' (PhD thesis, University of California, Berk., 1980).

38 The architects of Eastern Marches policy in the 1890s cottoned on to these trends very quickly. Thus in March 1890 Gossler told the Landtag that: 'With the nobility it is all over – that is what the (Polish) papers say – the nobility cannot hold out, the nobility is selling its Polish property . . . Other population groups are presented as the authorized heirs of the formerly powerful nobility. This is a quite conscious struggle of the third and fourth estates – with the nobility it will not last long, then it will be against the clergy'. Around the same time Gossler gave the Ministry of State detailed figures for the growth of the Polish professions in Poznan and West Prussia. See Blanke, pp. 124–5.

39 For details of this merger, see Blanke, pp. 228–9, and Hagen, pp. 231–8. Hagen's whole analysis of the new ideological and political configuration this produced is very fine (pp. 231–65). See also the statement of Chrzanowski in the setting of the 1898 elections, quoted by Blanke, pp. 220 f. For a superb analysis of the ideological transition from 'political romanticism' to 'integral nationalism', see A. Walicki, *Philosophy and Romantic Nationalism. The Case of Poland* (Oxford, 1982), pp. 337–57.

40 Some important individual points emerge: e.g., the ambivalence of Stablewski and the clerical hierarchy; the active role of girls and mothers; the low involvement of Polish teachers; the preference of the populace for formal political process as a means of protesting against the Germanization measures (e.g., through petitions and public meetings, official representations in Berlin by the Catholic Church, and so on) until their patience was exhausted; the relative quiescence of Poznan city; the brutal obduracy of the local and central Prussian authorities, and their tendency to penalize secular rather than clerical strike leaders (and especially parents and children). In general Kulczycki finds (not very surprisingly) that the general strike 'was stronger, that is a larger than average percentage of Polish-speaking pupils joined the strike and persisted in it, where a greater concentration of the Polish-speaking population lived' (p. 116). This was true both of regions and within specific localities. Altogether some 93,000 pupils in more than 1,600 schools throughout Prussian Poland joined the strike in 1906–7.

41 'Where the strike lacked vigour or did not even exist, the locally prominent Polish-

speaking citizens were indifferent or even against the strike (or, as in Silesia, such leaders were scarce). Where it was strong, one can usually detect the hand of the local priest, school board member, national activist, large landowner, or other member of the local socio-economic elite. This, of course, affected the character of the resistance movement. What otherwise might have appeared to be a radical, even revolutionary, movement assumed an air of normality in communities where local leaders endorsed it' (Kulczycki, p. 151).

42 See Kulczycki, p. 80, and esp. pp. 149–50. It was chaired by the former parliamentary loyalist, Jozef Koscielski, and its directorate contained representation from National Democrats and Populists as well the conservative forces. During 1905–7 it seems to have enrolled some 22,000 members and held some 230 meetings. After Prussian complaints Stablewski forbade clerical participation in April 1906. Its fate after 1907 is not clear from the books under review. Blanke (p. 232) and Hagen (p. 234) unjustifiably dismiss its importance, the former very misleadingly.

43 The elections resulted in a great triumph for the Reichstag Polish Circle. Its candidates received 32 per cent more votes than in the last election in 1903 while the number of all voters had increased by only 18.6 per cent. Furthermore, twenty Polish candidates won, forming the largest Polish contingent ever to sit in the Reichstag – in 1903 only sixteen were elected. Most of the Polish gains came in Silesia, primarily because of the end of the Centre's monopoly of clerical support' (Kulczycki, p. 179).

44 See K. Deutsch, *Nationalism and Social Communication* (Cambridge, Mass., 1966).

45 In a review of N. Davies, *God's Playground. A History of Poland*, 2 vols (Oxford, 1982), in *Times Literary Supplement*, 19 March 1982, p. 297. The overall ideological process is brilliantly presented by Walicki, *Philosophy and Romantic Nationalism*.

46 See, for instance, Weber, *Peasants into Frenchmen*, and for some thoughts on the German case, my own 'State formation, nationalism and political culture: some thoughts on the German case', in R. Samuel and G. Stedman Jones (eds), *Culture, Ideology and Politics* (London, 1983), pp. 277–301.

47 This is especially true of R. F. Leslie (ed.), *The History of Poland since 1863* (Cambridge, 1980): though the introductory comments are quite good ('Prussian Poland in the second half of the nineteenth century', pp. 26–35, in a general chapter called 'Triloyalism and the national revival'), Prussian Poland almost completely disappears from the rest of the pre-1914 discussion. Similar criticisms may be made of Davies, *God's Playground*, and rather less so of P. S. Wandycz, *The Lands of Partitioned Poland, 1795–1918* (Seattle, Wash. and London, 1974). The same applies to O. A. Narkiewicz, *The Green Flag. Polish Populist Politics 1867–1970* (London, 1976).

48 See esp. Murphy's concluding chapter (pp. 183–94) and his discussion of 'Nationalism' (pp. 140–164). The strength of his account derives from the meticulous evaluation of the statistical and other evidence for geographical and social mobility, marriage and residential patterns, religion and education, associational life, and out-migration for a single town in the Ruhr, namely Bottrop. Klessmann, *Polnische Bergarbeiter*, is also useful, but is couched at the level of the Ruhr region as a whole. Murphy draws fruitfully on the social historical literature on immigration and ethnicity in the USA.

49 The statistical evidence for Polish migrants in the Ruhr is confused. For a helpful discussion, see Wehler, 'Die Polen im Ruhrgebiet', cit. at n. 3 above, pp. 221–5. For the general phenomenon of Eastern labour migration for the seasonal needs of Eastern agriculture, see Nichtweiss, *Die ausländischen Saisonarbeiter*, and the various essays of Klaus J. Bade, now conveniently summarized in English in 'German emigration to the United States and Continental immigration to Germany in the late nineteenth and early twentieth centuries', *Central European History*, vol. 13 (1980), pp. 348–77. See also (from the Polish as opposed to the German point of view) Murdzek, *Emigration in Polish Social-Political Thought*.

50 We are almost completely ignorant about these two processes. But see the evidence discussed in Conze, 'Nationsbildung durch Trennung', cit. at n. 3 above, pp. 101–5 (Masurians) and 110–11 (Kashubs). See also H. Linde, 'Die soziale Problematik der masurichen Agrargesellschaft und die masurische Einwanderung in das Emscherrevier', *Soziale Welt*, vol. 9 (1958), pp. 233–46; H.-U. Wehler, 'Zur neueren Geschichte der Masuren', *Zeitschrift für Ostforschung*, vol. 11 (1962), pp. 147–72; D. von Oppen, 'Deutsche, Polen und Kaschuben in Westpreussen 1871–1914', *Jahrbuch für die*

Geschichte Mittel- und Ostdeutschlands, vol. 4 (1955), pp. 157 ff.

51   See the parallel essays by W. Dlugoborski, 'Industrialisierung und "nationale Frage" in Oberschlesien mit besonderer Berucksichtigung der Rolle der Migration von Arbeitskräften', and V. Hentschel, 'Wirtschaftliche Entwicklung, soziale Mobilität und nationale Bewegung in Oberschlesien 1871–1914', in Conze, Schramm and Zernack (eds), *Modernisierung und nationale Gesellschaft*, pp. 193–230, 231–73. Schofer, *Formation of a Modern Labour Force*, is relatively silent on the nationality issue.

52   For some leads in the existing literature, see: O. Hauser, 'Polen und Dänen im Deutschen Reich', in T. Schieder and E. Deuerlein (eds), *Reichsgründung 1870/71. Tatsachen, Kontroversen, Interpretationen* (Stuttgart, 1970), pp. 291–318; Hauser, 'Zum Problem der Nationalisierung Preussens', *Historische Zeitschrift*, vol. 202 (1966), pp. 529–41; Hauser, *Preussische Staatsräson und nationaler Gedanke* (Neumünster, 1960); K. D. Sievers, *Die Köllerpolitik und ihr Echo in der deutschen Presse 1897–1901* (Neumünster, 1964); D. P. Silverman, *Reluctant Union. Alsace-Lorraine and Imperial Germany 1871–1918* (University Park, Pa and London, 1972); J.-M. Mayeur, 'Elsass, Lothringen und die Deutsche Frage 1870–1945' in J. Becker and A. Hillgrüber (eds), *Die Deustche Frage im 19. und 20. Jahrhundert* (Munich, 1983), pp. 221–38; J. E. Craig, *Scholarship and Nation-Building: The University of Strasbourg and Alsatian Society, 1870-1939* (Chicago, 1984); H. Zwahr, *Sorbische Volksbewegung* (Bautzen, 1968); G. Stone, *The Smallest Slavonic Nation. The Sorbs of Lusatia* (Cambridge, 1972). Finally, two relevant books for the subject of this essay, which have gone unmentioned in the references above, are: R. Korth, *Die preussische Schulpolitik und die polnischen Schulstreiks* (Würzburg, 1963); H. K. Rosenthal, *German and Pole. National Conflict and Modern Myth* (Gainesville, Fla, 1976).

PART FOUR

The Origins of Nazism

9

The German Right, 1860–1945: How It Changed

This essay was originally presented to a seminar of mainly non-specialists in Cambridge in early 1976. It was consequently an attempt to paint the general picture in brash strokes and broad outlines, at a time when I was trying consciously to step back from the immediacy of my doctoral research. There is consequently a certain raciness to the style and a certain intended incaution to some of the formulations. But when Richard Evans asked me to contribute to a collection of essays by younger British German historians (as we then were), it seemed worth preserving some of the zest of the original, particularly as we hoped the volume might reach something of a student audience. Consequently, it was published (in R. J. Evans [ed.], *Society and Politics in Wilhelmine Germany* [London, 1978], pp. 112–35) very much in the form that it was originally spoken. In fact, the volume of essays seems to have had an impact greater than we had originally anticipated, and during the last five or six years the essays have been widely cited as a kind of programmatic intervention into Wilhelmine historical discussion. This may exaggerate the coherence of the overall volume, but for several of the individual contributions (including my own) it does seem in retrospect to have been the springboard for a relatively distinctive historiographical contribution, certainly in the perceptions of the field as a whole.

That contribution is defined very much by the critique of emergent post-Fischer orthodoxies referred to in my introduction to this collection. In the case of the Evans volume that critique was mounted from a specifically British tradition of social history from the 1960s, stressing locality, people's history, everyday life and 'history from below', and on the whole it is the last of those phrases that has stuck firmest in the minds of the readers. For my own part, I have not been particularly comfortable with that label. It has seemed to me to open the door too easily to a conception of social history which can become too uncritically populist and too affirmative in relation to popular culture and the forms of popular protest. It facilitates a focus on the 'people' in isolation – as workers, peasants, women, and so on – rather than on the class relations – the social relations of exploitation and domination – that structured, constrained and provoked their actions. It can also produce indifference in some of its exponents to political history and events in the state – or 'history from above', as it tended to be called. But as a way of redressing the historiographical balance, the slogan was very attractive and on that basis can well be defended. It is certainly present in my own essay, although mainly I think as a rhetorical figure. Substantively, the essay lays more stress perhaps on the field of relations between dominant and subordinate classes or 'people' and 'power bloc', although those terms themselves were a somewhat later addition to my conceptual vocabulary.

More generally, the essay laid out an agenda for the framework of my book on the German right. This was true of its polemic against simple notions of continuity, of its hostility to manipulative models of political mobilization, of its stress on the

231

petty bourgeoisie, and of its focus on the dynamics of right-wing radicalization. I would now want to amend it in detail and to qualify a number of its stronger generalizations, but it is reprinted here in its original form.

I

Discussion of the past century of German history is still dominated by the events of 1933–45. Knowledge of National Socialism and the desire to explain its victory continue to shape the main trends of German historiography: they help select the subjects of most interest and inform the kind of questions that get asked. This is obviously true of the Weimar Republic, but it affects discussion of the nineteenth century as well. It appears to be equally true of the academic specialist and of the various categories of interested lay people, whether teachers, journalists, students, book-club subscribers, or public-library users. All tend to be attracted by the dramatic quality of the Nazi period, drawn by a mixture of concern and excited morbidity, rather like the crowds at the scene of an unpleasant catastrophe, such as an explosion or an air-crash. This is probably inevitable. If we are honest most historical interests – in a period, a country, a topic – are motivated to some extent by extraneous considerations. The effect is clearest where a national history is dominated by a bout of convulsive change as in the French and Russian Revolutions. On a more modest scale the decline of the Liberal Party, the General Strike, the origins of the welfare state and the Irish troubles are all instances of British history in which an important development has been allowed to structure the preceding history of the respective fields. But to recognize the source of one's interest is easy: it is far more difficult to stop this distorting one's perspectives on it. In the past nationalist historians were notoriously guilty of prejudging complicated processes of historical development, and more recently many radical historians have been finding that the mere celebration of popular struggles is a poor guide to the substance of popular achievement.[1] But the problem is seldom as close to the surface as this. More often it results from a submerged teleological view of the past which reduces historical processes to their known results. In this case a chain of causation can easily be constructed which owes far too much to the vantage-point of the historian.

The recent history of the *Kaiserreich* has fallen into this trap. As suggested above, it is fairly easy to regard 1933 as a terminal point in Germany's historical development and this tendency has been magnified since the early 1960s by the lasting effects of the Fischer Controversy: whereas earlier the older generation had regarded Nazism as an irrational aberration which diverted German history from its true course, their successors have now gone to an opposite extreme by seeing it as the end-product of a continuous authoritarian and manipulative tradition of the

German right since Bismarck; in both cases the history of the *Kaiserreich* is pressed into the service of a larger view of the German past focused on the events of 1933.[2] This has unfortunate implications for our understanding of Nazism, still more of the political movements that preceded it. There is an increasing tendency to interpret the years between the 1860s and 1914 – and the Great Depression in particular – as a crucial founding period which broadly determined the fascist possibilities of the 1920 and 1930s. It is based on a particular analysis of the state and of the ruling coalition which sustained it which is then linked to the problem of Nazism by a rather simple notion of continuity. Underlying this are some important assumptions about the origins and nature of fascism which do justice neither to the phenomenon of Nazism nor to the real character of the Wilhelmine right, still less to the complex processes of change which enabled one to emerge from the other.

My aim in this essay is to subject existing ideas about the long-term origins of National Socialism to some critical scrutiny and in the process to clarify our understanding of the Wilhelmine right. This will involve some consideration of existing interpretations and their weaknesses, together with a brief indication of how the latter might be rectified. I will conclude with some suggestions for an alternative chronology of the right between the early-nineteenth and mid-twentieth centuries.

II

There are two main ways of linking Nazism to an earlier nineteenth-century tradition. The first, which gained currency in the Anglo-American West during and after the Second World War, concentrates on the discovery of intellectual pedigrees, the uncovering of a German tradition of authoritarian thinking through which the appeal of Nazi ideology could be made more readily intelligible.[3] The procedure has normally involved the selection of a number of nineteenth-century intellectuals whose ideas and values are then made to exemplify a set of attributed cultural dispositions; these are then held to be dominant amongst the educated classes and to be proto-Nazi in tendency. Classically this has meant reconstructing the intellectual pursuits of an earlier epoch in the image of Nazi ideology and its familiar terminology. Thus we find Rohan Butler, in *The Roots of National Socialism* published in 1941, arguing that Nazism was merely the political climax of a dominant indigenous tradition. His method is to ransack the German past for any idea with the remotest resemblance to those of the Nazis. He does this for 'the exaltation of the heroic leader', 'the racial myth', anti-semitism, 'the concept of the all-significant totalitarian state', 'the community of the folk', 'the full programme of economic autarky', 'the tradition of militarism', the idea of 'the dynamic originality

233

of German culture in contrast to the superficial civilisation of the West',
'the polemic against reason', 'the supernatural mission of German culture',
'living-space', 'Pan-Germanism', law as folk-law', and finally for the
'abasement of the individual before the state'.[4] All these ideas are described
as in some way distinctively German and all are traced back to the
eighteenth century as aspects of an unbroken linear continuity. The
following quotation is typical of the method: 'The Nazis say that might is
right; Spengler said it; Bernhardi said it; Nietzsche said it; Treitschke had
said as much; so had Haller before him; so had Novalis.'[5]

This is surely a fruitless exercise, the worst kind of traditional intellectual
history, which makes its connections by lifting ideas from their sensible
context. The original impetus was provided by the Second World War,
when the Allies had a pressing interest in finding historical justifications for
their hostilities with Germany. The Cold War then tended to harden this
into a habit of mind, which characterized 'the West' as a sort of historic
zone of freedom and the German past as an equally historic revolt against
it, dating from the romantic-nationalist reaction to the French Revolution.
German exiles, often of Jewish extraction and preoccupied with the
'German Mind', have tended to be the architects of this view, and the most
considerable achievement of the transplanted Central European culture,
the Institute of Social Reseach, whilst avoiding the uncritical identification
of enlightenment with the territorial extent of NATO and substituting the
notion of the 'authoritarian personality' for that of the 'German Mind', has
also mirrored these concerns. So has the work of A. J. P. Taylor, though it
sometimes masquerades as a geopolitical argument about Germany's
strategic position in the centre of Europe. So, too, have the more popular
works best represented by the UNESCO collection of 1955, *The Third
Reich*, and William Shirer's *The Rise and Fall of the Third Reich* – perhaps
the single most influential work of German history since Treitschke.[6] This
is not a totally barren tradition of explanation. In its more sophisticated
versions it has produced important studies of a particular social-cultural
milieu, that of 'the non-political German', the nationalist bourgeois who
preferred a romantic and illiberal anti-modernism – so-called – to the
values of Western liberal democracy.[7] But its basic weaknesses as an
approach to the origins of Nazism and the problem of continuity in
German history cannot be reiterated too strongly: the connections are
made predominantly, even exclusively, in the realms of ideology and
consciousness; the roots of Nazism are seen to lie in a particular frame of
mind.

The second conventional method of placing Hitler in a longer historical
setting is not incompatible with this approach, but has tried to underpin it
with an analysis of the German social formation. This second approach
concentrates on what Bracher has called a continuity of 'authoritarian and
anti-democratic structures in state and society', which obstructed any

liberal evolution towards parliamentary forms before 1918, paralysed the Weimar constitution after 1918, and facilitated the Nazi success in conditions of crisis after 1930.[8] It has been most influential inside Germany itself and has made most headway since the early 1960s when the liberating effects of the Fischer Controversy made historians more receptive to a conceptual framework devised principally by sociologists and political scientists.[9] It focuses on those interests in German society that tried to obstruct the process of democratization and political 'modernization'. Though based primarily in the traditional landowning aristocracy and its allies at the court and in the army and bureaucracy, this reactionary coalition also relied on the leading sections of industry and the majority sentiments of the educated professional bourgeoisie. Together, and beneath the hegemony of pre-industrial authoritarian values, these forces provided the natural basis of government in the unreformed Prusso-German state between the late 1870s and 1918.

As already suggested, this and the other approach to a great extent complement one another. They both diminish the importance of the conventional chronology of political events and they both stress an underlying continuity of authoritarianism which sets Germany apart from the liberal 'West'. One sees this mainly as an intellectual tradition, the other stresses material interests and structures of rule. The first finds Hitler's precursors in the romantic anti-modernists who allegedly inhabited the Pan-German movement and created a cultural disposition towards authoritarianism in the middle class. The second sees them in the coalition of heavy industrialists and big landowners which pulled the strings of government, it is claimed, more or less continuously after 1878–9. In a further sense both approaches share the intellectual patrimony of Talcott Parsons, whose 1942 essay on fascism has left an indelible imprint on subsequent non-Marxist thinking about National Socialism.[10]

I want to argue that both these dominant approaches are deficient and that together they represent an over-simplified view of the continuity problem that has so exercised German historians since the late 1960s. To illustrate this two central ideas may be isolated for critical comment, both of which have entered the conventional wisdom of modern German history. The first is that of 'cultural despair' with its connotations of anti-modernism and romantic opposition to the emerging urban and industrial civilization.[11] A number of weaknesses reduce the value of the social-cultural stereotype associated with this idea. On one count, the real anti-modernists – agrarians, artisans and traditional small businessmen with a grievance against progress – were motivated much less by an intellectual cultural pessimism than by the prospects of *economic* decline. By contrast, the urban middle class with whom the mood of cultural pessimism is normally associated seem readily to have grasped the benefits of the new society with all the buoyancy and self-confidence one could expect in a prosperous and rapidly growing economy. In general they confined their hostility only to certain features of 'modernity', principally those arising from the social and political situation of the new industrial masses and the threats this appeared to contain. Moreover, the idea of cultural despair exaggerates the political impact of a few maverick thinkers (most notably Lagarde, Langbehn and Möller van der Bruck, to name the three chosen by Stern), rests on a selective reading of their work, and ignores the complexity and contradictions of the intellectual climate which gave them meaning. Above all: by concentrating on this social-cultural milieu with its suspicion of conventional politics, it distracts from those organizations in Wilhelmine society which *were* politically more influential and which produced an ideology which was genuinely proto-fascist. In other words, the 'cultural despair' approach tends to focus on the wrong areas of German society.

The second key concept is that of *Sammlungspolitik*. Literally, 'the politics of cohesion' or 'rallying-together', this meant the attempt to unite all anti-socialist forces in a common front against democratic reform, the political expression of a protectionist pact between heavy industry and big agriculture. It has been claimed that this idea supplies the interpretive key to German politics in the entire period between the 1870s and 1933. It denoted a force far stronger than the challenge raised by the reforming left before 1918 and provided the crucial foundations for the right-wing counter-attack against the Weimar Republic.[12] Yet whatever its positive merits, and these have been considerable, the ultimate effect is again reductionist, for this simplifies the development of the right-wing tradition between Bismarck and Hitler and elides the successive problems of readjustment to changed conditions which faced the right in this longer period. Moreover, by stressing the manipulative abilities of the ruling class and the stability of its power-base, it underestimates the extent to which its survival depended on a responsiveness to certain kinds of pressure *from below*.

Consequently this second concept also suffers from failing to focus on a special area of political life which is particularly crucial to this problem, namely that of the forms of petty-bourgeois mobilization. In their respective ways both of the influential approaches outlined above tend to divert our attention from the real foundations of later developments: the *first* by fixing on intellectual currents whose typicality is assumed rather than demonstrated and whose political implications are misinterpreted by referring them forward to Nazism rather than to their own proper and very different contemporary context; the *second* by stressing the manipulative achievement of the 'ruling strata' in equipping themselves with popular support in the new conditions of mass politics, and by neglecting the extent to which this 'modernization' was determined by novel pressures from social groups which had previously been marginal to the political system.

The rest of this essay will consider the problem of petty-bourgeois mobilization by considering areas of the political culture where *masses* of people were set into motion. It is only by this means that we can avoid the tendentious generalizations criticized above, because the attribution of an alleged cultural disposition or state of mind to an entire society surely requires the investigation of a sufficiently large collectivity. Thus Fritz Stern's work has always been vitiated by his narrow biographical perspective: the wider influence of the intellectuals concerned has only ever been illustrated by finding formal traces of their ideas elsewhere; there is rarely any sense of the determinate social context which may have influenced their reception. To rectify this is the first aim of what follows. The second is to question the tendency of recent historians to draw straight lines of continuity between Bismarck and Hitler, and to contest the view that Wilhelmine conservatism and Nazism were just different variations on a single theme of authoritarianism, reflecting the same constellation of industrial-agrarian interests, and distinguished only by the types and levels of political manipulation required by these so-called 'ruling strata' to secure their interests.[13] The gist of the argument is this: that we cannot understand the conditions for the rise of a German fascism without recognizing the existence of a profound metamorphosis in the character of the German right between the 1870s and the 1920s, involving a massive expansion of its social base and a drastic radicalization of its ideology and general political style; and we cannot understand the nature of that radicalization without appraising the novel impact of the petty bourgeoisie on the Wilhelmine political system between the early 1890s and the First World War.

III

By the petty bourgeoisie I mean two groupings of people in a capitalist society: the old or traditional petty bourgeoisie of small-scale producers and owners (artisans, carters, shopkeepers, farmers and other small businessmen) whom in Germany came to be known as the *Mittelstand*; and the newer petty bourgeoisie of salaried employees and white-collar workers (lower-grade civil servants, junior managerial and technical personnel, teachers, clerical workers and certain strata of the professions) known in Germany as the 'new *Mittelstand*'. Though occupying different economic positions these two groupings exhibited enough common characteristics to regard each other – and be so regarded – as members of a larger collectivity. These derived from a process of negative self-definition, for each occupied an intermediate position between the bourgeois and the proletarian which easily induced a profound suspicion of both major classes. The traditional small businessman was strung between self-ownership in the means of production and increasing real dependence on the power of big capital: separated from the working class by the social ideals of small property and independence, yet prevented from joining the ranks of the bourgeoisie proper by poor resources and the rising pressures of technological change and large-scale production. In the same fashion the salaried employee was caught between economic dependence and the self-sealing ideology of white-collar respectability with its status compensations, both resentful of the boss and patronizing of the uncultured worker.

There is room here for only the barest remarks concerning the place of the petty bourgeoisie in the class structure, and as they stand these twin categories are clearly abstractions with limited historical value. There is no doubt, for instance, that in Germany both groupings were in a state of massive flux at the turn of the century as the pace of industrialization imposed new patterns of mobility, recruitment and depletion on to the old petty bourgeoisie, whilst enduring a huge expansion of the new. Moreover, for precisely this reason it is extremely difficult to generalize about the petty bourgeoisie's political affiliations, for at any one time before 1914 it was likely to consist of large numbers who were en route for somewhere else – upwards to join the ranks of the more successful businessmen, downwards into the working class, or sideways between different fractions of itself. There were also serious internal divisions which set old against new, artisans against retailer, small employer against employee, and which seriously inhibited the ideological identity of the petty bourgeoisie as a whole class. This made its political reactions extremely unpredictable and in view of its numerical importance gave it a key role when parties began to compete for mass support.[14] Whilst conceding each of these complexities and acknowledging both the theoretical and empirical difficulties of generalizing about the petty bourgeoisie as a class, particularly in this period, therefore, I want to offer some comments about its impact on the right in the years before 1914 by considering the forms of its political mobilization. I will do this by looking at three different categories of organization.[15]

The first of these categories is that of a rural and small-town protest movement, encompassing the independent and semi-independent peasantry and the so-called *Mittelstand* of shopkeepers, carters, independent craftsmen and petty entrepreneurs. This took the form of defensive sectional organization at a time of rapid industrial and commercial concentration and declining agricultural prices. Small producers and traders started to band together in a series of interest groups of both an occupational and regional character. Artisans, fortified by traditions of guild organization and assisted by some half-hearted protective legislation between 1881 and 1897, found this easier than most: a first national body was launched in 1873, passing into the General League of German Artisans in 1882, and as a result of successive legislation this was paralleled by the

Central Committee of the United Guilds in 1884 and the standing conference of the Chambers of Handicrafts and Trade in 1900.[16] Small tradesmen were less successful. An abortive Association of Traders formed in Berlin in 1878, followed after a decade by the Central Association for Commerce and Trade, which grew from an initiative in Leipzig into a loose umbrella for other regional groups. In both sectors, of course, individual trades retained and expanded their occupational associations, and these were further supplemented by purchasing co-operatives, credit, savings and discount associations, and local defensive unions of artisans and tradesmen.[17] The new national bodies were clearly intended to represent their members' interests at the level of government and their activities registered the first moves towards overt and co-ordinated political commitment. This embraced affiliation with a number of right-wing parties, but not as yet the foundation of an independent *Mittelstand* party as such.[18] The anti-semitic parties which emerged in the 1880s came closest to providing such a new departure,[19] but the proliferating organs of agrarian protest in the 1890s generally succeeded in subsuming *Mittelstand* grievances beneath the rubric of their general protectionist and anti-plutocratic programmes. These included the Agrarian League in 1893 and the Catholic Peasants' Associations, most of which were founded in the 1880s. But they also encompassed a wider variety of political initiatives, ranging from the anti-semitic groups of Central Germany and the regional foundations of the Centre Party in the South to the final exclusion of Adolf Stöcker's Christian-Social Party from the official Conservative Party and the concurrent launching of the National-Social Association in 1896, itself a break-away from the Christian-Socials.[20]

The 1890s must be regarded as the great period of agrarian organization, when the countryside was incorporated into the national political arena and all parties, including the SPD, made systematic efforts to penetrate the rural electorate. This was reflected in the organizational proliferation just mentioned, in the increased participation of rural voters at the polls, and in the greater number of highly contested constituencies in the countryside. In the elections of 1893 and 1898, for instance, the SPD was incomparably more active in rural areas and by 1898 was able to contest all 397 seats but one, though in a number of others it failed to register a single recorded vote.[21] In 1898, moreover, whilst the party experienced serious setbacks in West Prussia, Posen and parts of Pomerania, in the Catholic regions of Prussia and in Bavaria as a whole, it none the less managed an impressive advance in three rural areas: in the seven Mecklenburg seats where almost 10 per cent more votes were polled than in 1893, pushing the Socialist share up to over 40 per cent of the total; in the Province of East Prussia excluding Königsberg, where the party's total vote rose from 12,000 to some 33,000, and in the seats of Rastenburg, Ragnit and Heiligenbeil from between 1 per cent and 5 per cent to between 17 per cent and 23 per cent;[22] and finally in

Hesse, where the party competed fairly successfully with the anti-semites for the votes of small producers. This was a time of tremendous political ferment in the countryside, producing considerable volatility of allegiance in which the simple correlations of rural discontent with unambiguously authoritarian or right-wing politics are not easily made.[23] In some constituencies of Hesse, for instance, the electorate displayed an extraordinary fluidity of allegiance, and anti-semitic, particularist, left liberal, National-Social, Centre and SPD were distinguished by little more than varying shades of anti-Prussian populist radicalism.[24]

The new volatility of the rural electorate and the unprecedented truculence of German conservatism's natural supporters created big problems for the right-wing parties at the very time when they most needed fresh reserves of popular support against the SPD. Paradoxically, the myth of the *Mittelstand* as the strongest pillar in the social order gained in popularity amongst Conservatives just at the point where small producers and owners were starting to repudiate old traditions of deference.[25] This led to new modalities of public life in country areas and helped disintegrate the old informal style of politics in the very places where it seemed most destined to survive. The Conservative Party bore the first brunt of this in the Protestant areas of the rural north-east, for having deflected the rebukes of the Christian-Socials and anti-semites in the 1880s it found itself newly threatened from within in the 1890s by the Trojan horse of the Agrarian League. Then by the 1898 elections the right-wing National Liberal Party found its traditional rural preserves in Hanover, Schleswig-Holstein and the Palatinate under severe attack from the Agrarian League's independent nominees: sitting National Liberals survived the onslaught only by formally committing themselves to the Agrarian League's programme. In the same way the Catholic Centre Party found it hard to keep its peasant supporters without a clear affirmation of protectionist intent: this could be seen in the tensions between the party leaders and the Catholic Peasants' Associations, in the foundation of the Bavarian Peasants' League in 1893 and in the ongoing threat of a Bavarian secession from the national Centre.

In general the 1890s were a period when the groundwork of agrarian organization and agitation proceeded largely outside the effective surveillance of those political parties under whose banner it was officially proclaimed. As yet there was no comparable upsurge of activity by the *Mittelstand* as such. There were faltering attempts at national and regional organization, such as the abortive announcement of a *Mittelstand* Party in Thuringia in 1895, but on the whole artisans and small businessmen had to be content with the Chambers of Handicrafts and Trade established in 1897, their guild organizations and the existing political parties. It was not until later – in 1904 with the short-lived German *Mittelstand* Association and then in 1911 with the more substantial Imperial-German *Mittelstand*

League – that the national organization of the *Mittelstand* took place.[26]

The second category of organization to be mentioned concerns the white-collar fractions of the petty bourgeoisie, the so-called 'new *Mittelstand*' which was so much a product of the growing bureaucratization of economic life after 1890. The comments which follow are necessarily fairly brief, for we know far less about this area than about the traditional petty bourgeoisie, and far less progress has been made in understanding what to all accounts was a highly complex and politically ambiguous phenomenon. By the census of 1907 there were about 2 million 'private' white-collar workers and something like 1½ million employed by the state. One in three of the former were already members of an occupational association. By 1913 the fifty-three white-collar organizations ranged from the combative trade union to the non-combative social association, and politically from the Socialist Central Association of Commercial Assistants with 24,000 members to the right-wing and anti-semitic German-National Commercial Assistants' Association with some 148,000. It has been claimed that distinctively German traditions of status and deference separated white-collar workers 'much more emphatically and unequivocally' from manual workers than elsewhere, and that the German term *Privatbeamter* or *Angesteller* carried a much stronger social charge than the English 'white-collar' or the French *employé salarié*.[27] But even if this was true, which seems unlikely, it would still be a long step to concluding that these strata were somehow easier meat for right-wing predators than in say Britain.

On the contrary, this was in many ways the contested zone of German politics: the 'new *Mittelstand*' was by no means uniformly right-wing in its inclinations. Many of its members joined the liberal Hanse-Union, an anti-agrarian umbrella launched in 1909, for instance, and with its 102,000 members in 1913 the more liberal Association of German Commercial Assistants managed to run its German-National counterpart reasonably close. The Union of Technical-Industrial Officials (23,000 members in 1913) was militantly critical of employers and embraced the strike weapon, whilst even the civil servants' Union of the Salaried embraced progressive demands for heavier taxation of higher incomes, reform of the Prussian three-class franchise and more representative government at all levels. This was perhaps the liberal parties' natural constituency, for as business circles shifted rightwards and the Agrarian League usurped the traditional primacy of the liberals in the northern and central Germany countryside, they were thrown increasingly back on these strata for their votes. But against all this must be set the success of the radical-rightist German-National Commercial Assistants' Association and the attempts to float white-collar equivalents of the company unions between 1911 and 1918. Less obtrusively there was also the apolitical inertia of the older professional organization: the Association for Commercial Clerks of 1858

(127,000 members in 1913), the German Foremen's Association (62,000, founded 1884), and the Association of German Technicians (30,000, also founded 1884). At all events these groupings displayed the typical diversity of the petty bourgeoisie's politico-ideological reactions. The main political division of German society ran through the class rather than to the left of it. By the early years of the Weimar Republic white-collar workers were roughly polarized between the Socialist AfA (General Free Federation of Salaried Employees) with 690,000 members and the right-wing Gedag (Trade Union Federation of German Salaried Employee Organizations) with 463,000.[28]

The third category of organizations I want to consider is rather different, in that it arose not from the defensive needs of occupational or sectional groupings, but from the affirmation of a powerful nationalist commitment of an imperialist, militarist, or cultural kind. These organizations qualify for consideration with the other two categories because by and large they recruited their active membership from precisely the same strata of the old and new petty bourgeoisie. They were the so-call *nationale Verbände*, the nationalist pressure groups, those organizations with the official object of attracting popular backing for the notion of exclusive national priorities, normally from an overtly anti-socialist and anti-liberal perspective. The first was the Colonial Society, formed in 1887 from the coalescence of two earlier organizations. It was followed by the Pan-German League in 1891, the Society for the Eastern Marches in 1894, the Navy League in 1898 and the Defence League in 1912. These were the classic representatives of the milieu. To them must be added cultural organizations with a less aggressive public persona – the Society for Germandom Abroad, the Patriotic Book League, the Christian Book League and the German-Union are all examples – and a range of organizations whose primary responsibility lay elsewhere, but who consciously situated themselves within the same nationalist tradition. The latter included the veterans' associations, the Young Germany Union sponsored by the state in 1911, and the gamut of anti-socialist labour organizations, from the Evangelical Workers' Associations to the company unions and the Imperial League against Social Democracy launched in 1904.

The direct political influence of these groups can easily be over-estimated. Many historians have been misled by their large paper membership and impressive propagandist output into making excessive claims for their political importance. In reality membership tended to mean very little in terms of time, energy and commitment, and supporters were normally required to do little more than read the literature which their subscriptions helped to produce. In this way the *nationale Verbände* probably had a less formative impact on the consciousness of their ordinary members than did the occupational groups or the economic defence leagues. But, on the other hand, they did provide a political

242

platform for a sizeable minority who recoiled from involvement in the conventional political parties and their 'cattle-trading' in the Reichstag, and who sought a practical surrogate in the untainted moral crusading of nationalist education. The Pan-Germans and the naval enthusiasts were bitterly resented by the established party politicans, particularly as they legitimated their agitation from an angry critique of the latter's inadequacy. The nationalist pressure groups were a noisy and disruptive presence in German politics after the turn of the century, and played no small part in radicalizing the general tone of right-wing politics. In this their contribution rivals that of the Agrarian League and its allies.[29]

The point is this: that together these three sets of organizations, most of them founded in a crucial period between the 1880s and the turn of the century, registered a profound seismic shift at the base of German society, which sent heavy tremors of social aspiration upwards to the political surface of the new German nation-state. This was a period of unprecedented social change – of astonishing urban growth, massive migration and pervasive cultural dislocation, in which people were forced either to defend their accustomed way of life or to adapt rapidly and resourcefully to a new environment. We are now very familiar with the efforts of a particular tendency of the German working class – that organized by the SPD – to cope with these problems, and there are many studies of the so-called Social Democratic 'sub-culture' in which the socialist worker was provided, it is claimed, with a self-contained and self-sufficient social and cultural world of trade unions, co-operatives, friendly societies, educational and recreational institutions which included everything from the socialist cycling club to the socialist public house. The great absence in German social history at the present time is any comparable attempt to extend the same degree of imaginative and analytical sympathy to the world of the peasantry, the urban petty bourgeoisie and the *Mittelstand*. Presently, these groups tend to be seen as the voting fodder manipulated at will to the polls by the political managers of the big businessman and the Junker. The point I want to stress, therefore, is that the organizations enumerated above were more often than not the autonomous achievements of social strata who had previously been dormant politically, who were now impelled into action by the desire to protect an older way of life in the case of the *Mittelstand* and peasantry, or to affirm their confidence in the new modernity of the industrial nation-state, in that of the clerical, professional and managerial strata in the town, and finally whose entry into politics was at first deeply resented by the closed establishment which dominated the existing non-socialist parties.

The critical problem of German history between the 1870s and the First World War was thus in many ways that of how the old governing establishment was to absorb this new mobilization. This was the full meaning of terms like 'mass politics' and 'mass society' if they are to have any use at all. They meant not simply the new conditions of universal manhood suffrage and mass literacy, nor just the efforts of manipulative politicians like Bismarck, Bülow or Tirpitz to equip themselves with pliant popular support. They also and even primarily meant that 'the masses have come of age (through elementary education, mass conscription, universal suffrage and the cheap oil-lamp)', and were consequently demanding that their voices be heard.[30] To capture the real changes at work in German society, in other words, the notion of mass politics has to imply not only manipulation from above, but also militant pressure from below.

This is precisely where the currently influential ideas of *Sammlungspolitik*, 'secondary integration', 'caesarism' and 'social imperialism' reveal their limitations. For they all advance the idea of a successful manipulation of popular emotions from above by entrenched elites: this is made into the unifying theme of the entire period between the 1860s and the 1930s, and Nazism becomes merely the most extreme manifestation of an older authoritarian syndrome. But if instead of regarding the pressure groups as the transparent fronts of traditional ruling interests and the ciphers of an unchanging authoritarian tradition, we try to see them as the organic expressions of a powerful and variegated movement of popular protest, with their own distinctive styles of propaganda and agitation, their own aggressive ideologies and their own vigorous corporate identities, and if we try to regard these organizations as the vehicles through which the new techniques of mass agitation were reluctantly and painfully assimilated by establishment politicians, then, it seems to me, we have a more satisfactory means of understanding that radicalization of conservative politics which made possible the rise of a German fascism. If we wish to identify the sources of change in the forms of conservative politics, therefore, it is at the points of friction between the political parties and the pressure groups, the real mass organizations of Wilhelmine Germany, that we must look.[31]

IV

Looking back from the vantage-point of 1933, but bearing in mind the above remarks, therefore, it is possible to regard Nazism as merely the most recent in a succession of right-wing redefinitions, each more advanced than its predecessor in the achievement of a broader social appeal and the appropriation of methods and tactics corresponding more tightly to the needs of the historical moment. It is fatally misleading to use terms like conservatism on the right as conceptual monoliths to be shifted around the century before Hitler at will and with a perfectly autonomous explanatory power of their own. Between the start of the nineteenth century and 1945 the German right underwent some profound changes in its sociological, organizational and ideological complexion, which together constituted an important political metamorphosis. It is possible to see Nazism as one of a series of dissolutions and regroupings at a higher level and on an enlarged basis, through which the German right developed in three sorts of ways: *convulsively*, through a series of protracted crises; *progressively*, by adjusting to changed conditions; and *laterally*, as a result of the convergence of new social and political forces from different directions. Building upon the achievements of recent work, therefore, I want to suggest a broad chronological framework for locating Nazism historically without incurring the distortions of perspective mentioned at the beginning of this essay. Basically, it is possible to distinguish six broad phases in this sense.

The *first* of these spans the two key periods of nineteenth-century legal and constitutional experiment in Germany, that of 1807–12 and that of 1862–79. This was the period of resistance to the new bourgeois civilization, in which the landowning class, whose institutional equivalents were the monarchy, the army and the bureaucracy, attempted to defend its political predominance by warding off demands for unification, constitutional reform and economic rationalization. This general reactionary stance precluded neither the limited progressive contribution of the state bureaucracies nor the detachment of significant sectors of the landowning class and their realignment with the progressive forces, in areas like Hanover, certain parts of eastern and western Prussia and South Germany. Moreover, the territorial fragmentation of Germany as well as its social and economic diversity made for a high degree of uneven development in this respect.[32]

The *second* period extended from 1879 to 1909. This was a phase of significant reorientation away from an entrenched counter-revolutionary stance and of political-ideological consolidation within new positions. It involved a series of compromises with the formerly antagonistic bourgeois coalition, in which conservatives in Bavaria and Prussia came to terms with the newly constituted nation-state, acquiesced in the new constitutional arrangements and recognized the need for political alliance with the new industrial bourgeoisie. There resulted a gradual fusion of social forces into a new hybrid ruling bloc through a progressive realignment of the dominant classes which had been greatly accelerated by the inter-penetration of industrial and agrarian capital in the boom years ending in 1873. The political consummation of this process was the Bismarckian settlement of 1878–9, when the twin compulsions of economic crisis and revolutionary anathema culminated in a new decisive configuration of protectionism and repressive anti-socialism: *Sammlungspolitik*. This naturally entailed a radical transformation of the social base of German conservatism, if we define this to mean the political defence of an existing system of social, economic and political power, as distinct from Conservatism with a capital 'C', which implies a more specific political tradition. But although we may detect the formation of a new dominant bloc at the centre of German society, denoted by its own ideological forms and made sharply visible in the crisis years of 1878–9, the very speed of the realignment – which took a matter of decades rather than centuries as in Britain – produced a high degree of political, that is organizational, fragmentation. In other words, the new socio-economic bloc failed to find its organizational equivalent in a new united party of the right. The old independent parties – Conservative, Free Conservative, National Liberal and Centre – remained as the monuments to important sectional interests and loyalties.

The crucial problem of the German right, for which this organizational fragmentation became a decisive impediment, was the achievement of the necessary political strength to meet the rising threat of the working class. This general problem broke down into three particular ones: the ideological adjustment to conditions of parliamentary democracy and the development of an appropriate scepticism towards proposals for a violent suppression of political debate (that is, through a course of *Staatsstreich* or *coup d'état*, or through some form of a renewed Anti-Socialist Law); the transcendence of sectional divisions within the dominant bloc and an ultimate organizational reconstruction of the right on a unitary basis; and finally, the winning of mass popular support to compete effectively under conditions of parliamentary rule. The last of these three problems proved especially difficult, for the established right-wing parties proved unable to readjust their newly consolidated practice (from the 1860s and 1870s) by paying lip service to the principles of democracy and by mobilizing fresh strata to their banner. This resistance to the demands of new popular forces for recognition – the petty bourgeoisie in town and country, the peasantry, the professional and administrative strata – led to a process of political fermentation beginning in the 1880s and continuing throughout the period, with a phase of accelerating organizing activity in the 1890s. This produced a string of economic interest groups, agitational pressure groups behind nationalist issues like the navy, the colonies, the defence of the German language and culture, and so on, and a number of minor political parties – all standing broadly on the right, but in opposition to the established conservative parties as 'parties of order'. In general the older parties found it difficult to assimilate these new forces or to accommodate them in political alliances – the Catholic Centre Party managed this better than most – and the period was marked by great political tension between old and new groups. The period was characterized by a general failure of the conservative parties to meet the challenge of popular mobilization: their popular base was a diminishing one, and the electoral success of 1907 was largely a temporary diversion from the problem. These were the years of the rise of the petty bourgeoisie, which laid down its own organizations and forged its own distinctive ideologies, whose common characteristic

246

was a militant populist nationalism, and whose point of negative departure was the political exclusiveness of the established party-political oligarchies.[33]

The *third* phase ran from 1909 to 1918, years in which the right engineered a further feat of self-orientation no less far-reaching than the earlier one of 1878–9. It was characterized by a further ideological compromise, this time with the freshly mobilized petty bourgeoisie, and by the decisive acquisition of a genuine popular base. Several factors assisted this development. One was the temporary and partial resolution of the tax question in 1913, which removed a principal bone of contention between industry and agriculture and restored the cohesion of their alliance.[34] Another was the faltering emergence of a new reformist coalition seeking the basis of co-operation with the labour movement, which also helped to drive the conservative forces closer together. A third factor was the deterioration of German capitalism's position in the world market, especially after 1911; and a fourth was the renewed pressure of the working class after the SPD landslide in the 1912 elections. The nationalist panacea supplied the ideological fixative which aided the integration of previously discordant forces. This complex of factors forced a coalescence of the right of great novelty. The protectionist and anti-socialist motifs were still present, but to them were now added a new seriousness in the conciliation of the *Mittelstand* and the expanding white-collar interest. This marked the arrival of the petty bourgeoisie in the magic circle of conservative politics after the angry and divisive altercations of the preceding decades. The circumstances under which the new conservative regrouping was announced to the world symbolized this important development: the so-called Cartel of the Productive Estates was officially proclaimed at the third annual congress of the Imperial-German *Mittelstand* League at Leipzig in August 1913.[35] It was also registered by the growing importance of the Pan-Germans in the counsels of the right.[36] Politically it resulted in calls for a more aggressive foreign policy and a more strident denunciation of parliamentary forms. Its manifestations included an unprecedented willingness to criticize the kaiser, the ideological recourse to the *Volk* as an alternative focus of political legitimacy, a pronounced interest in corporative as opposed to representative institutions of government, and the revival of plans for a *Staatsstreich* or *coup d'état.*

Although clarification of these issues was interrupted by the outbreak of war in 1914, the domestic wrangles concerning the nature of Germany's war aims and the spectre of postwar reconstruction soon gave the changes fresh impetus. Things were clearly tending towards an organizational reconstitution of the right on a unitary footing. Strong evidence was provided by the continuing drift of heavy industry from the National Liberals to the Conservatives.[37] Moreover, by now the latter had been completely reshaped in the image of the Agrarian League and the tone of right-wing politics was set almost entirely by people with strong connections in the respective organizations of the petty bourgeoisie. This was certainly true of the Fatherland Party launched in 1917, the prototype of a future united party of the right. Yet even this was forced to coexist in parallel with the existing parties by maintaining an official restriction of its activities to the field of foreign affairs. It required the trauma of defeat and revolution in the autumn of 1918 before the organizational reconstruction which had been implicit since the 1890s could finally be precipitated.

This initiated a *fourth* major phase of development, in which the German National People's Party emerged from the fusion of five older parties (Conservatives, Free Conservatives, Christian-Socials and the two main anti-semitic remnants) to form the unitary organ of the right.[38] This also marked the definitive victory of populist and pseudo-democratic notions of political activity in conservative ranks, manifest in the very title of the new party. Although the uncertainties of the revolutionary ferment which lasted until the autumn of 1923 gave some scope for fresh contradictions of a moderate-radical nature inside the rightist bloc, the dissenting currents were largely confined to the periphery of the new state, as in the Munich Putsch of 1923,[39] and by the Weimar Republic's period of relative stability between 1924 and 1928 the new party had also consolidated its own legitimacy with some success.

Given the Wilhelmine emphasis of this essay, the *fifth* and *sixth* phases in the chronology of the right require comparatively little description. The former began with the crash of 1929 and the protracted crisis this inaugurated. This first fractured the unity and self-confidence of the dominant conservative organ, the German National People's Party, already under pressure from an independent process of internal factionalism, and then enabled the Nazis to constitute themselves as the largest popular force on the right. The result was a fresh synthesis, on broader social foundations than ever before and on an incomparably more radical basis. The central role of the petty bourgeoisie in the Nazi movement is well attested, though its precise relationship to the state apparatus established after 1933 remains the subject of involved debate. Moreover, the collaboration of big business and the residual aristocracy with the Nazis, despite certain evident uneasiness and the desperation of the July Plot in 1944, extended across the entire life of the Third Reich, though again its precise forms remain to be established. It was not until the defeat of 1945 and the imposition of a new political settlement by the Western Allies that the final and most recent phase began, namely that of adjustment to conditions of parliamentary rule and incipient welfare capitalism.[40]

V

The overall argument of this essay may be briefly recapitulated as follows. It is first premised on the belief that the conditions of petty-bourgeois mobilization are crucial to our understanding of fascism and of National Socialism in particular. There will be exceptions, but on the whole most commentators are agreed on the importance of the petty bourgeoisie in the structure of fascist movements: this is true of the most perceptive contemporary observers like Trotsky, Thalheimer, Gramsci and Bloch, it is also true of subsequent theorists like Parsons and Lipset or Poulantzas, and of recent historical studies like those of Allen, Noakes, or Pridham. If we want to pin down those conditions which *specified* fascism in Germany, which favoured its success there but which were absent in, say, Britain, then there are some grounds for looking closely at the terms under which the petty bourgeoisie was admitted – or compelled its own admittance – to the political system. Secondly, arising from this, I feel that previous historians of the Wilhelmine period have not given this problem sufficient critical attention and have rather smoothed over many of the complexities it presents. Thirdly, I have tried to indicate some of the ways in which these complexities might be dealt with. This is naturally a partial view of Nazism's prehistory, but my aim has been principally to redress the balance by identifying a problem and proposing a framework within which it might be tackled.

The central point deserves one further reiteration. Of course there were manipulative elements at work in the organizations of the petty bourgeoisie, both at their initial foundation and in their subsequent history; of course traditional politicians saw the pressure groups as a vehicle for some much-needed popular support against the Socialists; of course the size and vitality of the autonomous popular movement can easily be exaggerated, whether in the case of the Agrarian League or in that of the *nationale Verbände*; of course the populist complexion of petty-bourgeois ideology must be kept carefully in proper perspective; and of course the petty bourgeois ended up in large numbers in the camp of the Nazis. But we shall not understand the routes which were travelled to that conclusion, nor the nature of the right-wing radicalization which provided some of the necessary preconditions for a German fascism, unless we also appreciate the strength of the popular aspirations and resentments to which the old-style conservative parties were subjected between the 1890s and 1914. In 1900 the Pan-Germans were dismissed as 'beer-bench politicians', the radical peasants of Central Germany were scorned as 'gutter-antisemites', and the extremist agrarian agitators attacked as 'irresponsible meddlers', By 1913 the Agrarian League had reshaped the Conservative Party in its own image, the anti-semites had been successfully assimilated to it, a new national *Mittelstand* organization had given its annual congress for the announcement of a new right-wing front, and the Pan-Germans had become important intermediaries between industrialists and agrarians. Something had clearly happened in the meantime. In 1900 the established politicians saw the petty bourgeoisie as something to be manipulated; by 1913 they had given its organic spokesman grudgingly a voice of their own. The phenomenon I have been trying to highlight is the interaction of manipulative intentions from above with the formulation of demands from below. Because it was only from this *friction* that the forms of proto-fascist ideology and political practice were born.

CHAPTER 9: NOTES

1 For an excellent discussion of these matters see A. S. Kraditor, 'American radical historians on their heritage', *Past and Present*, no. 56 (August 1972), pp. 136–53.

2 The three best discussions of the Fischer Controversy are all in German: A. Sywottek, 'Die Fischer-Kontroverse', in I. Geiss and B.-J. Wendt (eds), *Deutschland in der Weltpolitik des 19. und 20. Jahrhunderts. Fritz Fischer zum 65. Geburtstag* (2nd edn, Düsseldorf, 1974), pp. 19–47; I. Geiss, 'Die Fischer-Kontroverse', in *Studien über Geschichte und Geschichtwissenschaft* (Frankfurt-on-Main, 1972), pp. 108–98; W. Schieder, 'Ergebnisse und Möglichkeiten der Diskussion über den Ersten Weltkrieg', in W. Schieder (ed.), *Erster Weltkrieg, Ursachen, Entstehung und Kriegsziele* (Cologne, 1969), pp. 11–26. But see also J. A. Moses, *The Politics of Illusion. The Fischer Controversy in German Historiography* (London, 1975).

3 For a useful critique of this approach, see G. Barraclough's three articles in *New York Review of Books*, 'Mandarins and Nazis' (19 October 1972), 'The liberals and German history' (2 November 1972), and 'A new view of German history' (16 November 1972).

4 R. D'O. Butler, *The Roots of National Socialism* (London, 1941), pp. 277 f.

5 ibid.

6 For a sample of works following this approach: H. Kohn, *The Mind of Germany* (London, 1966); F. Stern, *The Politics of Cultural Despair* (Berkeley, Calif., 1961); G. L. Mosse, *The Crisis of German Ideology* (London, 1966); A. J. P. Taylor, *The Course of German History* (London, 1945); UNESCO, *The Third Reich* (London, 1955); W. Shirer, *The Rise and Fall of the Third Reich* (New York, 1960). For the work of the Institute of Social Research (the so-called Frankfurt School: Marcuse, Adorno, Horkheimer, Neumann, Kirchheimer, etc.), see M. Jay, *The Dialectical Imagination: A History of the Frankfurt School and the Institute of Social Research 1923–1950* (Boston, Mass. and London, 1973), esp. pp. 113–72.

7 See Stern, *Politics of Cultural Despair*, and the edition of his essays, *The Failure of Illiberalism* (London, 1972). By far the most sensitive discussion of these themes to date is R. Pascal, *From Naturalism to Expressionism. German Literature and Society 1880–1918* (London, 1973), esp. pp. 16–66, 277–314.

8 K. D. Bracher, 'The Nazi takeover', *History of the 20th Century*, vol. 48 (1969), p. 1339.

9 The works of Bracher and Dahrendorf are most familiar to an English-speaking audience, but lesser-known figures in this country have been equally important for West German historians. See, for instance, M. R. Lepsius, 'Parteiensystem und Sozialstruktur: zum Problem der Demokratisierung der deutschen Gesellschaft', in G. A. Ritter (ed.), *Deutsche Parteien vor 1918* (Cologne, 1973), pp. 56–80.

10 T. Parsons, *Essays in Sociological Theory* (Glencoe, Ill., 1964), pp. 104–41. For a useful critique: M. Clemenz, *Gesellschaftliche Ursprünge des Faschismus* (Frankfurt-on-Main, 1972), pp. 96–118.

11 The term has been enshrined for posterity in the title of Fritz Stern's highly influential book.

12 I have discussed the idea of *Sammlungspolitik* in an earlier essay: Eley, '*Sammlungspolitik*, social imperialism and the Navy Law of 1898', *Militärgeschichtliche Mitteilun-*

gen, no. 1 (1974), pp. 29–63. For a summary statement of the conventional usage: H.-U. Wehler, *Das deutsche Kaiserreich 1871–1918* (Göttingen, 1973), pp. 100–5, 48–59.

13 The emphasis on continuity between Bismarck and Hitler implies a definite understanding of Nazism (and of fascism) which has never been properly explicated or theorized as such in the work of the recent Wilhelmine historians. A useful object for future discussion (for which there is no space here) would be to reconstruct that understanding from the often invisible web of theoretical assumptions which holds their argument about continuity together. This may be clarified by the fact that a number of the authors who began work on the Wilhelmine period have now moved on to the Weimar Republic.

14 On the most recent estimate we are probably dealing with upwards of 1.5 million artisans, 0.5 million small traders and 5.0 million small farmers (i.e. those owning less than 20 hectares or 50 acres of land) in 1907. To them must be added some 3.5 million white-collar workers in private and state employment. See J. Kocka, *Klassengesellschaft im Krieg. Deutsche Sozialgeschichte 1914–1918* (Göttingen, 1973), pp. 65 ff., and G. Hohorst, J. Kocka and G. A. Ritter, *Sozialgeschichtliches Arbeitsbuch* (Munich, 1975), pp. 66–77. See also H. Handtke, 'Einige Probleme der inneren Struktur der herrschenden Klasse in Deutschland vom Ende des 19 Jahrhunderts bis zum ersten Weltkrieg', in F. Klein (ed.), *Studien zum deutschen Imperialismus vor 1914* (East Berlin, 1976), pp. 85–114.

15 Again: it is worth stressing that these comments are concerned mainly with right-wing tendencies in the petty bourgeoisie. They do not present an exhaustive survey of its political mobilization and are not meant to suggest that left liberals and Social Democrats made no appeal to these groups of people, for they clearly did. The main point is that during the 1880s and 1890s a political fermentation began which affected the practice of all parties in Germany: in this particular essay I am concerned with the impact of this on just one group of parties, those of the right.

16 For the details of legislation, see the entry under 'Gewerbegesetzgebung' in *Handwörterbuch der Staatswissenschaften*, vol. 4 (3rd edn, Berlin, 1910). See also H. A. Winkler, 'From social protectionism to National Socialism: the German small-business movement in comparative perspective', *Journal of Modern History*, vol. 48 (March 1976), pp. 1–7; Winkler, *Mittelstand, Demokratie und Nationalsozialismus* (Cologne, 1972), pp. 26–64.

17 See R. Gellately, *The Politics of Economic Despair. Shopkeepers and German Politics 1890–1914* (London, 1974), pp. 83–111. In south-west Germany until the turn of the century the 'Trade Associations' organized into an umbrella federation in 1891 performed a common function for artisans, traders and small manufacturers. See Winkler, 'Der rückversicherte Mittelstand: Die Interessenverbände von Handwerk und Kleinhandel im deutschen Kaiserreich', in W. Ruegg and O. Neuloh (eds), *Zur soziologischen Theorie und Analyse des 19. Jahrhunderts* (Göttingen, 1971), p. 166.

18 A *'Mittelstand* Party' was formed abortively in Halle in 1895. See Gellately, *Politics of Economic Despair*, pp. 150 f.

19 The best guide to the confusing universe of the anti-semitic parties is still P. W. Massing, *Rehearsal for Destruction* (New York, 1949), but see also P. Pulzer, *The Rise of Political Antisemitism in Germany and Austria* (London, 1964), and R. S. Levy, *The Downfall of the Antisemitic Political Parties in Imperial Germany* (London, 1975).

20 See the indispensable handbook, D. Fricke *et al.* (eds), *Die bürgerlichen Parteien in Deutschland*, 2 vols (Leipzig, 1968–1970), which contains individual entries on each organization. See also H.-J. Puhle, 'Parlament, Parteien und Interessenverbände 1890–1914', in M. Stürmer (ed.), *Das kaiserliche Deutschland. Politik und Gesellschaft 1870–1918* (Düsseldorf, 1970), pp. 340–77.

21 This was true in twelve constituencies altogether: in six of the ten in Posen, two each in Bromberg and Minden, and one each in Liegnitz and Arnsberg. These were all in Prussia, and all lay in either the Junker or the Centre heartlands.

22 Königsberg itself was already held by the SPD and in both 1893 and 1898 the vote held steady there at around 13,000.

23 The guiding assumption of most work on the agrarian and *Mittelstand* movements before 1914 is that they provided the seed-bed of authoritarianism: they represented the casualties of 'modernization' and stood in direct lineage with the Nazis. There is some

truth in this received wisdom, but as it stands the explanation cuts too many corners. Two points may be briefly made. First: unless we pay meticulous attention to the egalitarian and radical components in the make-up of these protest movements in the Wilhelmine period, we shall not adequately understand the ambiguous strength of the Nazis' populist appeal later on. Second: petty-bourgeois radicalism was perfectly capable of propelling its exponents in either political direction, left or right, and in the Wilhelmine period when masses of traditional small owners were being proletarianized the SPD and liberals benefited as much as the far right. For a sensitive discussion of the *Mittelstand* in its actual Wilhelmine context, see D. Blackbourn, 'The *Mittelstand* in German society and politics 1871–1914', *Social History*, vol. 4 (1977), pp. 409–33.

24 This was particularly marked in Marburg, where in 1898 seven parties fought the election and polled between 995 (SPD) and 2,886 (Anti-Semite) on the first ballot; for the run-off, which the Anti-Semite won against the Conservative (the odd man out amongst the other six radicals!) by 5,417 to 4,937, it is anybody's guess how the spare votes were distributed. In 1903, in a similarly confused fight, the Anti-Semite lost the seat to a National Social, Helmuth von Gerlach, who later became a liberal democrat and pronounced pacifist!

25 See Blackbourn, 'The *Mittelstand* in German society and politics', cit. at n. 23 above, for further discussion of this point.

26 See Gellately, *Politics of Economic Despair*, pp. 148–96.

27 Kocka, *Klassengesellschaft im Krieg*, p. 66.

28 ibid., pp. 65–71; Hohorst, Kocka and Ritter, *Arbeitsbuch*, p. 138.

29 For lack of space these comments may appear unnecessarily elliptical. I have treated the problem of radicalization in more detail in my unpublished thesis, 'The German Navy League in German politics, 1898–1914' (D. Phil., University of Sussex, 1974), chaps 5 and 6.

30 Rassow to Tirpitz, 12 April 1898, in Bundesarchiv-Militärarchiv Freiburg, 2223, 94943. Hermann Rassow, a *Gymnasium* headmaster, was one of the most important naval propagandists of the period.

31 This argument should be considered together with those of two earlier articles: '*Sammlungspolitik*, social imperialism and the Navy Law of 1898', cit. at n. 12 above, and 'Defining social imperialism: use and abuse of an idea', *Social History*, vol. 1 (1976), pp. 265–90.

32 H. Mottek, *Wirtschaftgeschichte Deutschlands. Ein Grundriss. II. Von der Zeit der Französischen Revolution bis zur Zeit der Bismarckschen Reichsgründung* (East Berlin, 1969); W. Conze (ed.), *Staat und Gesellschaft im deutschen Vormärz 1815 bis 1848* (2nd edn, Stuttgart, 1970); L. Krieger, *The German Idea of Freedom* (Boston, Mass., 1957); J. Kocka, 'Preussischer Staat und Modernisierung im Vormärz', in H.-U. Wehler (ed.), *Sozialgeschichte Heute. Festschrift für Hans Rosenberg zum 70. Geburtstag* (Göttingen, 1974), pp. 211–27.

33 This motif is generally neglected in the recent monograph literature. For the best survey of the period, which brings together the findings of the latter, see Wehler, *Das deutsche Kaiserreich*.

34 For an exhaustive analysis of the tax question, see P.-C. Witt, *Die Finanzpolitik des deutschen Reiches von 1903–1913* (Hamburg and Lübeck, 1970).

35 The 'Cartel' was supported by the Central Union of German Industrialists, the Agrarian League and the Imperial-German *Mittelstand* League; there was a looser connection with the Catholic Peasants' Associations, and the various nationalist pressure groups were also represented at the Leipzig Congress, as was the Imperial League against Social Democracy. For the details: D. Stegmann, *Die Erben Bismarcks. Parteien und Verbände in der Spätphase des Wilhelminischen Deutschlands Sammlungspolitik 1897–1918* (Cologne, 1970), pp. 342–408; F. Fischer, *War of Illusions* (London, 1974), pp. 272–90; V. R. Berghahn, *Germany and the Approach of War in 1914* (London, 1973), pp. 145–65.

36 See Stegmann, *Die Erben Bismarcks*, pp. 293–305, 356, 396 f., 449 ff., 480 f., 489 ff.

37 ibid.

38 A. Thimme, *Flucht in den Mythos. Die Deutschnationale Volkspartei und die Niederlage von 1918* (Göttingen, 1969); L. Hertzmann, *DNVP – Right Wing Opposition in the Weimar Republic 1918–1924* (Lincoln, Nebr., 1963); G. A. Ritter, 'Kontinuität und Umformung des deutschen Parteiensystems 1918 bis 1920', in G. A. Ritter (ed.),

Entstehung und Wandel der modernen Gesellschaft (West Berlin, 1970), pp. 342–84.

39 The major exception was the Kapp Putsch in 1920. For the best study of the radical right in this period, see U. Lohalm, *Völkischer Radikalismus* (Hamburg, 1970).

40 The literature on Nazism and fascism is obviously vast. The most useful are probably the following: M. Kitchen, *Fascism* (London, 1976); N. Poulantzas, *Fascism and Dictatorship* (London, 1974); T. Mason, 'The primacy of politics – politics and economics in National Socialist Germany', in S. J. Woolf (ed.), *The Nature of Fascism* (London, 1968), pp. 165–95; Clemenz, *Gesellschaftliche Ursprünge des Faschismus*; E. Hennig, *Thesen zur deutschen Sozial- und Wirtschaftspolitik 1933 bis 1938* (Frankfurt-on-Main, 1973).

10

What Produces Fascism:
Pre-Industrial Traditions or
A Crisis of the Capitalist State?

After all is said and done, and after the dust has settled on the various debates, the origins of fascism remains one of the central preoccupations of German historical writing. If we ever reach a time when discussions of the imperial period can proceed in complete innocence of what comes after, or in disregard for the overall context of the nineteenth and twentieth centuries, the moral-political sensibilities of German historians will have been disastrously blunted. It was this political urgency of historical discussion that attracted myself and many of my contemporaries in Britain and the USA to German history in the first place – the sense that here one's historical research actually *mattered*, and was of something more than academic or antiquarian interest, because we needed to know why and how German society had produced National Socialism and why the forces of democracy and the left had proved ultimately so ineffectual in their resistance. Despite my criticisms of teleology and of the simplifications which vitiate much of the historical work actually produced, this seems to me a compelling and legitimate reason for studying the Wilhelmine and Bismarckian periods (and less compellingly earlier ones too) as well as the Weimar and Nazi periods themselves. My concern has never been to undermine the legitimacy of such a deeper historical perspective itself, but to struggle with the question of how it might best be pursued. The aim of my first book, *Reshaping the German Right*, was to free the imperial period from the more straightforward kinds of 'proto-Nazi' or 'pre-fascist' teleology, but *precisely* that the question of 'origins' could be more effectively posed. Some readers found the concluding passages of that book extremely frustrating from this point of view, but they were left deliberately and provocatively inconclusive in the above sense.

At the same time, it was clear that eventually I would have to return to the problem of fascism as such, both to satisfy my own commitments and to meet the objections of some critics. Readers had a legitimate reason for wondering what I thought on the subject. Throughout the 1970s I had been reading fairly widely in that area, trying to keep abreast of the more important publications on the rise of the Nazis and the collapse of Weimar and poring over the various theoretical debates, and the appearance of a new series of general books towards the end of that decade seemed to provide an appropriate opportunity for organizing my thoughts. The following essay was the result. It was originally published in *Politics and Society*, vol. 12 (1983), pp. 53–82, and is reprinted here unrevised. It seeks to adjudicate what seem to me the two most coherent approaches to the study of fascism, with a view to assembling an agenda for future comparative discussion. It is the very opposite of being the last word, but at present it is the best that I have.

I

The aim of this essay is to explore some of the emerging emphases in current discussions of fascism. In some ways that discussion has entered the doldrums. There was a certain high point in the late 1960s, when the subject was first properly opened up, and when the generalizing ambitions of social scientists and historians briefly converged. Ernst Nolte's *Der Faschismus in seiner Epoche* (Munich, 1963), translated with exceptional speed as *Three Faces of Fascism: Action Française, Italian Fascism, National Socialism* (London, 1965); general surveys by Eugen Weber, Francis L. Carsten and John Weiss; an anthology on the European right edited by Eugen Weber and Hans Rogger; the thematic first issue of a new periodical, the *Journal of Contemporary History*; Barrington Moore Jr's vastly influential *Social Origins of Dictatorship and Democracy* (Boston, Mass., 1966); the *Das Argument* discussions of the German New Left; and three international conferences in Seattle (1966), Reading (1967) and Prague (1969) – all these imparted an excitement and vitality to work on the subject.[1] But in retrospect there is an air of innocence to this activity, whose intense preoccupation with comparison, generalization and theory has tended not to survive the subsequent growth of empirical research. These days people are far more cautious, because the accumulated weight of historical scholarship has seemed to compromise the explanatory potential of the old theorizations.

So what is left once certain old certainties (like totalitarianism or the orthodox Marxist approaches) have been abandoned? The answer, if we consult the most recent publications, is not very much. We know far better which theories do not work (totalitarianism, the 1935 Dimitrov formula, the authoritarian personality, the mass society thesis, monopoly-group theory, and so on) than those which do.[2] There have been certain major interventions – the work of Nicos Poulantzas and the controversy surrounding Renzo De Felice are two that come to mind – but on the whole they have not sparked off much widespread debate.[3] Most writers have tended to settle for a typological approach to the definition of fascism, by using certain essentially descriptive criteria (ideological ones have tended to be the most common) as a practical means of identifying which movements are 'fascist' and which not. Yet this begs the more difficult conceptual issues and leaves the stronger aspects of definition (like the dynamics of fascism's emergence, and its relation to class, economics and political development) to the concrete analysis of particular societies.[4]

Understandably, this is an outcome with which historians can live. In fact, the enormous proliferation of empirical work over the past ten to fifteen years has concentrated overwhelmingly on more immediate problematics, normally with a national-historical definition (for example, on Nazism or Italian Fascism rather than fascism in general). We 'know' far more than ever before, but this remains the knowledge of highly particu-larized investigations. Not surprisingly, a common response has been the philistine cry of despair (or perhaps of triumph). 'Reality' is simply too 'complex'. Radical nominalism easily follows, and there is precious little agreement as to whether fascism even exists as a general phenomenon.[5]

At the same time, there is now a large body of excellent work which lends itself to theoretical appropriation. Some of this is on the less significant fascisms of the North and West of the European continent or on the larger but ambiguous 'native fascisms' of the East, and facilitates a stronger comparative dimension to the discussion. Other contributions are on specific aspects of German and Italian history, including the structure of interest-representation, the sociology of the Nazi movement and the nature of the Nazi electorate in Germany, or the precise dynamics of the post-First World War crisis in Italy. In the longer term this intensive reworking of the empirical circumstances of the fascist victories, on the basis of exceptionally elaborate primary research, often sophisticated methodologies and 'middle-level generalizations', promises to reconstruct our theoretical understanding of fascism. My own object is more modest. For it is clear that the coherence of current research relies on a number of organizing perspectives which derive from the older theoretical literature. These run through the analytical structures of particular works with varying degrees of explicitness and self-conscious utilization. The aim of this essay is to identify some of the perspectives, to explore their strengths and weaknesses, and by drawing on the more recent theoretical discus-sions, perhaps to suggest where future interest might fruitfully be directed.[6]

II

One of the commonest emphases in the literature is a kind of deep historical perspective, which proceeds from the idea of German, and to a lesser extent Italian, peculiarity when compared with the 'West'. In this case the possibility of fascism is linked to specific structures of political backwardness. These are themselves identified with a distinctive version of the developmental process, and are thought to be powerful impediments against a society's ultimate 'modernization'. This 'backwardness syn-drome' is defined within a global conceptual framework of the most general societal comparison. It stresses 'lateness' of industrialization and national unification and their complex interaction, predisposing towards both a particular kind of economic structure and a far more interventionist state. The divergence from 'Western' political development is usually expressed in terms of the absence of a successful 'bourgeois revolution' on the assumed Anglo-French model, an absence which facilitates the dominance after national unification of an agrarian-industrial political bloc with strong authoritarian and anti-democratic traditions. The failure to uproot such 'pre-industrial traditions' is thought to have obstructed the formation of a liberal-democratic polity, and in general this is taken to explain the frailty of the national liberal traditions, and their inability to withstand the strains of a serious crisis. In recent social science this perspective stems from (amongst others) Barrington Moore, Alexander Gerschenkron and the discussions sponsored by the SSRC Committee on Comparative Politics. In contemporary Marxism it has drawn new impetus from discussion of the ideas of Antonio Gramsci. But in both cases the analysis may be traced back to the end of the last century.[7] It exercises a profound influence on how most historians tend to see the problem of fascism, though frequently at a distance, structuring the argument's underlying assumptions rather than being itself an object of discussion.

The argument was put in an extreme, discursive form by Ralf Dahrendorf in *Society and Democracy in Germany* (Garden City, NY, 1967; originally published in Germany, Munich, 1965), which deeply influenced a generation of English-speaking students of German history. It has also functioned strategically in a large body of work dealing with the imperial period of German history (1871–1918), whose authors write very much with 1933 in mind. One of the latter, Jürgen Kocka, has recently reaffirmed Dahrendorf's argument in a particularly explicit way, which highlights the specific backwardness of German political culture.[8] Thus in Kocka's view 'German society was never truly a bourgeois society', because the 'bourgeois virtues like individual responsibility, risk-taking, the rational settlement of differences, tolerance, and the pursuit of individual and collective freedoms' were much 'less developed than in Western Europe and the USA'. Indeed, the chances of 'a liberal-democratic constitutional development' were blocked by a series of authoritarian obstacles. Kocka lists

the great power of the Junkers in industrial Germany and the feudalizing tendencies in the big bourgeoisie; the extraordinary power of the bureaucracy and the army in a state that had never experienced a successful bourgeois revolution and which was unified from above; the social and political alliance of the rising bourgeoisie and the ever-resilient agrarian nobility against the sharply demarcated proletariat; the closely related anti-parliamentarian, anti-democratic, and anti-liberal alignment of large parts of the German ruling strata.

In fact, the 'powerful persistence of pre-industrial, pre-capitalist traditions' pre-empted the legitimacy of the Weimar Republic and favoured the rise of right-wing extremism.

These arguments, which are conveniently summarized in Kocka's essay, are representative for the generation of German historians who entered intellectual maturity during the 1960s, in a fertile and (for the time) liberating intellectual encounter with the liberal social and political science then in its North American heyday. This is particularly true of those historians who have explicitly addressed the question of Nazism's longer-term origins, for whom figures like Karl Dietrich Bracher, Wolfgang Sauer, Ernst Fraenkel, Martin Broszat, M. Rainer Lepsius and Dahrendorf provided early intellectual examples.[9] Here, for instance, is Hans-Jürgen Puhle summarizing the argument in terms which correspond precisely to the ones used by Kocka. Fascism is to be explained by the specific characteristics of a society 'in which the consequences of delayed state-formation and delayed industrialization combined closely together with the effects of the absence of bourgeois revolution and the absence of parliamentarization to form the decisive brakes on political democratization and social emancipation'.[10]

It should be noted that this approach to the analysis of fascism is advanced as an explicit alternative to Marxist approaches, which for this purpose are reduced by these authors polemically and rather simplistically to a set of orthodox variations on themes bequeathed by the Comintern, in a way which ignores the contributions of (amongst others) Poulantzas, the Gramsci reception and Tim Mason.[11] Thus in a laboured polemic against the German new left Heinrich August Winkler gives primary place in his own explanation of Nazism to pre-industrial survivals, which in other (healthier) societies had been swept away. This was the factor which explained 'why certain capitalist societies became fascist and others not'.[12] Or, as Kocka puts it, adapting Max Horkheimer's famous saying: 'Whoever does not want to talk about pre-industrial, pre-capitalist and pre-bourgeois traditions should keep quiet about fascism'.[13]

Kocka specifies this argument in a detailed study of American white-collar workers between 1890 and 1940, which is motivated by an explicit comparison with Germany.[14] He begins with a well-known feature of Nazism, namely its disproportionate success amongst the lower middle class or petty bourgeoisie, and amongst white-collar workers in particular. He then abstracts a 'general social-historical hypothesis' from this – namely, that the lower middle classes develop a '*potential* susceptibility to right-wing radicalization as a consequence of transformation processes which typically appear at advanced stages of capitalist industrialization – and proceeds to test it against the experience of American employees in retailing and industry between the end of the nineteenth century and the Second World War.[15] After careful discussions of social origins, educational background, income differentials, organizational experience and status consciousness, he concludes that American white-collars showed a much lower propensity to see themselves as a distinct class or status group superior and hostile to the working class. This 'blurring of the collar line' helps explain the absence of 'class-specific' political tendencies comparable to those of German employees, because while the latter turned to the Nazis in large numbers, their American counterparts joined with manual workers in support of the New Deal. Thus the comparable socio-economic situations of white-collar workers in the two countries failed to produce identical ideological or political orientations. If this is so, Kocka argues, perhaps the general hypothesis, which seeks to explain the rise of fascism by the 'changes, tensions and contradictions inherent in advanced capitalist societies', needs to be qualified.[16]

Kocka considers a number of explanations for the divergence, juxta-posing German and American particularities in each case. Thus the socialist consciousness and greater independence of the German labour movement, which led to its deliberate isolation in the political system, was not replicated in the USA, and American white-collars had far less reason to construct ideological defences against the left. Secondly, ethnicity frag-mented the potential unity of both workers and petty bourgeoisie far more than religious or ethnic differences did in Germany. Thirdly, the swifter emergence of the interventionist state in Germany tended to emphasize the importance of the collar line and legally cemented the lines of differen-tiation (for example, through the separate insurance legislation for white-collar employees), while, fourthly, the existence of 'a stratified educational system' tended to strengthen the barriers between occupations by lowering the mobility between manual and non-manual jobs. Each of these points is well taken, though the enormous expansion of tertiary employment in Germany after the turn of the century (and hence the broadly based recruitment of the white-collar labour force), is probably understated, as are the conceptual difficulties in mobility studies, which Kocka takes rather uncritically on board.[17]

But Kocka reserves his major explanation for a fifth factor, namely 'the continuing presence or absence of pre-industrial corporatist/bureaucratic traditions at advanced stages of industrialization'.[18] In the USA the absence of feudal traditions has long been seen as a crucial determinant of the country's political culture, permitting the hegemony of democratic citizenship ideals and the containment of class animosity.[19] In Germany, by contrast, the political culture suggests a 'deficit in some essential ingredients of a modern bourgeois or civil society that was closely but inversely related to the strength of Germany's pre-industrial, pre-capitalist, and pre-bourgeois traditions'. In the case of white-collar workers this created much ready support for the fascists.[20]

There is much to agree with in Kocka's account, which is exactly the kind of controlled comparison the field so badly needs. By taking the idea of pre-industrial continuities and arguing it through in a very specific context he enables us to see more clearly its attractions and disadvantages. The very concreteness of the analysis allows the case for the German

Sonderweg – for German exceptionalism – to be made more convincingly probably than ever before. At a general level his conclusions seem unimpeachable. This applies most certainly to his stress on 'the *relative autonomy* of social-structural and socio-cultural developments' within the larger process of capitalist industrialization. As the American material shows, there is nothing in the logic of the latter *per se* to send industrial workers automatically to the left and non-manual ones automatically to the right of the political spectrum (or, one might add, to associate specific ideologies or political attitudes necessarily with any particular social group).

At the same general level, it is hard to quarrel with Kocka's formulation of the pre-industrial argument:

> The uneasy coexistence of social structures that originated in different eras, the tense overlayering of industrial capitalist social conflicts with pre-industrial, pre-capitalist social constellations – the 'contemporaneity of the uncontemporary' – defined Germany's path to an industrial society, but not America's.[21]

But his practical elaboration of this point is not wholly convincing. To single out the primacy of pre-industrial traditions from the larger explanatory repertoire seems arbitrary, not least because some of the major German particularities in Kocka's list – for example, the rise of the SPD, or the constitution of *Angestellten* (employees in the private sector and low-status public employees) as a separate social category by the interventionist state – are formed during industrialization rather than before it.[22] Moreover, though Kocka seems to establish German peculiarity compared with the 'West', what he actually shows with most of his argument is American peculiarity with Europe, certainly with the European continent and in many ways with Britain too.

Ultimately Kocka's view of fascism is confusing. On the one hand, he upholds the relationship between capitalism and fascism ('the susceptibility of the new middle class to right-wing extremism . . . would not have existed without the changes, tensions, and crises that accompanied the creation of an industrial capitalist society'), pointing only to its interaction with older pre-industrial traditions in a complex causal dialectic ('the tension and crises inherent in industrial capitalist systems, on one side, *and* the repercussions of the collision of older traditions with industrialization and modernization, on the other').[23] But, on the other hand, the main logic of his argument definitely gives analytical priority to the pre-industrial part of the equation, making it the real difference between Germany (which went fascist) and other countries (which did not).[24] However, all capitalist societies are forged from pre-capitalist materials, and this is as true of the USA (with its non-feudal configuration of property-owning white democracy) as it is of Germany (with, if we follow Kocka for the sake of argument, its feudal legacy of military and bureaucratic traditions) and elsewhere. In the period of industrialization itself the implied ideal of a 'pure' capitalism without pre-capitalist admixtures (the 'modern bourgeois or civil society' that Germany is supposed not to have been and against which German history is measured) never existed. That being the case the crucial problem becomes that of establishing how certain 'traditions' became selected for survival rather than others – how certain beliefs and practices came to reproduce themselves under radically changed circumstances, and how they became subtly transformed in the very process of renewal. Pre-industrial values had to be rearticulated in the new conditions of an industrial-capitalist economy. It is this process of active reproduction through a succession of new conjunctures between the 1870s and 1930s, surely, that has first claim on our attention.

In other words, Kocka's argument can only be tested on the terrain he deliberately abandoned, namely the immediate context of the Weimar Republic. It is here that white-collar attitudes acquired their specific content and political effectivity, in the vicissitudes of the capitalist economy and the permanent political uncertainty after 1918, for to ensure their disproportionate right-wing orientation (and eventually to harness a fascist potential) required a positive ideological labour, on the part of employers, the state and the right-wing parties. One of the least satisfactory aspects of the pre-industrial argument is a kind of inevitabilism – a long-range socio-cultural determinism of pre-industrial traditions – which implies that German white-collar employees were just never available for left-wing politics until after 1945. This is partly belied by the manifest dividedness of white-collar allegiances until the late 1920s, and once we concede the existence of significant exceptions, as in any historical argument indeed we must (for example, why did the causal chain of pre-industrial status mentalities and right-wing proclivities work for some white-collar groups at different times but not for others?), the pre-industrial argument looks far less compelling. In fact, there is much evidence that in the earlier circumstances of the German Revolution many white-collar workers moved significantly to the reformist left. That the left-wing parties (especially the SPD) failed to respond creatively to these possibilities was less the result of German white-collar workers' ineluctable conservatism (bequeathed by the absence of bourgeois revolution, and so on), than of specific political processes and their outcomes, which were themselves naturally subject to the disposing and constraining influence of social and economic determinations.

Similarly, we can scarcely understand the nature of the 'collar line' unless we also examine the technical division of labour, the social context of the workplace and the position of white-collar workers in the labour process – all of which were experiencing some basic changes in the early twentieth century, in Germany no less than the USA, but which are strangely absent from Kocka's final account. In the end the invocation of pre-industrial ideological continuities confuses these issues, though the argument is handled more constructively in Jürgen Kocka's text than in most others.

III

One point emerges clearly enough from Kocka's account, and that is the limited explanatory potential of a sociological approach to fascism. This should not be misunderstood. I am not voicing hostility to sociology *per se*, either to the use of different kinds of social theory or to the adoption of social-scientific methodology, quantitative or otherwise. Nor am I suggesting that sociological approaches to fascism in particular are completely lacking in value. Quite the contrary, in fact. The careful dissection of the fascist movements' social composition through analysis of the leadership, activists and ordinary membership, and through a long tradition of sophisticated electoral analysis, has been an essential feature of recent research. It has generated an enormous amount of information and many new questions, providing the indispensable foundation for any intelligent reflection.[25]

The problems arise with the larger conclusions. Writers move too easily from an empirical sociology of the fascist movement and its electorate to a general thesis concerning its origins and conditions of success, which is usually linked to conceptions of 'modernization', social change and the impact of economic crisis. Such conceptions combine with the deep historical perspective identified above to suggest that fascism is structurally determined by a particular developmental experience. This is powerfully represented, for instance, in Barrington Moore's celebrated arguments about the relationship of different developmental trajectories ('dictatorship' and 'democracy') to the societal dominance of different types of modernizing coalition (based on specific configurations of landowning and urban-bourgeois elements and their links to popular forces). In German historiography especially, it is strongly implied that fascism follows logically from patterns of partial or uneven 'modernization', which throw unreformed political institutions and 'traditional' social structures into contradiction with the 'modern' economy. In some versions this effectively redefines fascism as a more general problem of political backwardness.

In this sort of thinking the notion of 'traditional' strata, who are unable to adjust to 'modernization' for a mixture of material and psychological reasons, has tended to play a key part. Since the 1920s, for instance, there has been general agreement that fascism originates socially in the grievances of the petty bourgeoisie or lower middle class. In the words of Luigi Salvatorelli in 1923, fascism 'represents the class struggle of the petty bourgeoisie, squeezed between capitalism and the proletariat, as the third party between the two conflicting sides'.[26] This was the commonest contemporary judgement and has been pursued repeatedly by both historians and sociologists, Marxists and non-Marxists alike. Most of the accumulated evidence (and a mountain of continuing research) is assembled in an enormous collection of essays recently edited by Stein Ugelvik Larsen, Bernt Hagtvet and Jan Petter Myklebust, *Who Were the Fascists. Social Roots of European Fascism* (Bergen, 1980), and while the aggregate effect of around 800 pages is hard to assess, it seems to confirm the received assumptions. There have been attempts to suggest that other social groups were ultimately more important in the fascists' makeup, or that class was less important than 'generational revolt'.[27] But on the evidence of *Who Were the Fascists* the fascist movements' social composition seems to have been disproportionately weighted towards the petty bourgeoisie (that is, small-scale owners and producers, together with the new strata of salaried employees, including lower-grade civil servants, junior managerial and technical personnel, teachers, clerical workers and parts of the professions).[28]

At the same time, to call fascism flatly a protest movement of the petty bourgeoisie is clearly an oversimplification. As David Roberts observes in an excellent discussion of 'Petty bourgeois fascism in Italy', the tendency is to 'assume that if we can find social categories enabling us to distinguish fascists from non-fascists, we have the key to explaining the phenomenon', with consequences that are potentially extremely reductionist.[29] As Roberts continues, historians of Italian fascism habitually analyse it 'in terms of socio-economic crisis and the traumas and frustrations which industrial modernization causes the lower middle class', and the same is equally true of writers on Nazism too.[30] As already suggested above, this argument conjoins with another popular thesis concerning the relationship of fascism to 'modernization', where the movement's specificity derives from 'its appeal to certain kinds of people who see themselves as losers in modern technological civilization', who rejected 'the modern industrial world', and took refuge in an ideology of 'utopian anti-modernism'.[31] The problem here is that the correlations between fascist ideology, the support of the petty bourgeoisie and general economic trends are drawn in a way which is too general and mechanical. Though the casualties of capitalist industrialization were certainly prominent amongst the radical right's supporters, this was by no means the whole story.

As David Roberts reminds us, the deficiencies in this standard view 'stem not from the insistence on the petty bourgeois role in fascism, but from the inferences about motivation that are made from this fact of social composition.[32] Summarizing his own argument in *The Syndicalist Trad-*

ition and Italian Fascism (Chapel Hill, NC, 1979), he highlights a quite different ideological tendency in the petty bourgeoisie: so far from 'trying to preserve traditional values and repudiate the modern industrial world', its exponents were firmly committed to a heavily productivist vision of industrial progress, and harboured few 'backward-looking' anxieties about the modern world in the way normally attributed. In fact, they were preoccupied less with the socio-economic problems of declining pre-industrial strata than the long-term political questions of Italy's national integration and cultural self-confidence. Their resentments were aimed less at the bearers of capitalist industrialization than the representatives of a narrowly based parliamentary liberalism (not forgetting, of course, the socialist left, whose growth the latter seemed irresponsibly to permit). In Roberts's view, petty-bourgeois fascism emerged as a critique of 'Italy's restrictive transformist political system' under the radicalizing circumstances of the First World War. As 'political outsiders', its spokesmen presented themselves as a new populist 'vanguard' capable of providing the ideological leadership effectively abdicated (as they saw it) by the old Giolittian establishment. Moreover, their urgency stemmed not just from the shattering experience of the war, but from the ensuing crisis of the *biennio rosso*, with its alarming evidence of Socialist electoral gains, working-class insurgency, and ambiguous *Popolare* radicalism.[33] Under these circumstances, radical nationalism was an intelligible response to the social dynamics of national disintegration. Affirming the virtues of industrial power, productivism and class collaboration, its architects offered a programme of national syndicalism, which 'could mobilize and politicize the masses more effectively and thereby create a more legitimate and popular state'.[34]

In other words, it is worth considering the possibility that fascism was linked as much to the 'rising' as to the 'declining' petty bourgeoisie. Now, on past experience (the celebrated 'gentry controversy' in Tudor–Stuart historiography is a good example) this kind of terminology may create more trouble than it is worth.[35] So let me explain carefully what I mean. Both Germany and Italy were societies experiencing accelerated capitalist transformation, through which entire regions were being visibly converted from predominantly rural into predominantly urban-industrial environments. In both cases the process was extremely uneven (in vital ways functionally so), with equally large regions trapped into social and economic backwardness (the south in Italy, or the East Elbian parts of Prussia and the Catholic periphery of the south, south-west and extreme west of Germany). In Italy the process was the more concentrated and dramatic, producing interesting similarities with Tsarist Russia: for example, the massive spurt of growth from the 1890s to the First World War; the very high levels of geographical, structural and physical concentration of industry, which brought masses of workers together in a small number of centres and created new conurbations with politically volatile populations; the interventionist role of the state, linked to a powerful complex of railway, heavy-industrial, shipbuilding, engineering and hydro-electrical interests, the selective involvement of foreign capital, and a well-knit oligopoly of government, industry and banks; an exclusivist and oligarchic political system; and a dramatic discrepancy between north and south, between a dynamic industrial sector which in all respects was highly advanced and an agricultural one which was equally and terribly backward.

This situation produced complex political effects. Simplifying wildly, we might say that the pace of social change outstripped the adaptive capabilities of the existing political institutions, particularly when the latter were called upon to be responsible to new social forces – agricultural populations concerned for their future in an economy increasingly structured by industrial priorities, urban populations demanding a more rational ordering of their hastily improvised city environment, a potential chaos of private economic interests, the mass organizations of the industrial working class, and the more diffuse aspirations of the new professional, administrative and managerial strata of the bourgeoisie and petty bourgeoisie. It is the last of these groups that interests me here.

For in a situation of widespread political uncertainty – in both Germany and Italy (and, we might add, Austria, Hungary and Spain) an existing political bloc of industrial, agrarian and military-bureaucratic interests entered a protracted period of instability and incipient dissolution in the 1890s from which it never really recovered – large numbers of the educated citizenry experienced a radical scepticism in the appropriateness of the existing political forms, which were largely liberal and parliamentary in type. Acutely conscious of the socio-cultural fissures in their newly unified nations, such people took recourse to a new kind of radical nationalism, which stressed the primacy of national allegiances and priorities (normally with a heavily imperialist or social imperialist inflexion) over everything else. Under circumstances of unprecedented popular mobilization, in which socialists and other 'anti-national' elements achieved an increasingly commanding position for themselves, this lack of confidence in the unifying imagination of the liberal and conservative political establishment acquired an extra political edge. From the turn of the century radical-nationalist voices called for a new drive for national unity, at first as a kind of dissenting patriotic intelligentsia, but more and more from an independent political base, with its own organized expressions and wider social resonance.

In my own work on Germany I have tried to characterize this dissenting radical-nationalist politics as a new kind of right-wing populism.[36] It was to be found above all in the ideology and mass agitational practice of the nationalist pressure groups, for whom the Pan-German League may be considered a vanguard, but which included the Navy League, the Defence League, the anti-Polish movement, and a variety of other organizations. Originating in the regional and local dissolution of the old Bismarckian power bloc (essentially an industrial-agrarian coalition, hegemonically ordered by a right-wing liberal politics), it created a new space for disinterested patriotic activism. Though aimed at the directly 'unpatriotic' activities of the socialists, ultramontanes and national minorities (especially the Poles), this was also motivated by a growing anger at the alleged faint-heartedness of the constitutional government, the old-style conservatives, and above all the liberal parties from whom many of the radical-nationalist activists came by personal background, family, or general milieu.

In other words, radical-nationalists raised a radical right-wing challenge, at first obliquely and then openly, to the established political practices of the dominant classes. If Germany was to enter into its imperialist heritage, they argued, if patriotic unity was ever to be achieved and domestic squabbling overcome, if the work of national unification was to be completed and the nation's internal divisions healed, above all if the challenge of the left was to be met, then a new political offensive to regain the confidence of the people was required. This demand – for a radical propagandist effort to win the right to speak for the 'people in general' – I have called 'populist'.[37] At its height this radical-nationalist agitation produced a generalized crisis of confidence in the existing political system which undermined the latter's hegemonic capability – the ability, that is, to organize a sufficient basis of unity amongst the dominant classes and a sufficient basis of consent amongst the subordinate classes to permit stable government to continue. In Germany this point was reached around 1908–9, and arguably opened the way for a far-reaching reconstitution of the party-political right over the next decade. In Italy the process was more strung out, extending from the intellectual nationalist ferment of the early 1900s to the interventionist drive of 1914–15. Arguably a similar process was unleashed by Spanish Regenerationism after the Spanish-American War.[38]

My suggestion is that we can explain the attractions of radical nationalism (and by extension those of fascism) without recourse to the cultural and economic 'despair' of threatened 'traditional' strata, to concepts of 'anti-modernism', or to the persistence of Kocka's 'pre-industrial traditions'. Those attractions may be grasped partly from the ideology itself, which was self-confident, optimistic and affirming. It contained an aggressive belief in the authenticity of a German/Italian national mission, in the unifying potential of the nationalist panacea, and in the popular resonance of the national idea for the struggle against the left. Radical nationalism was a vision of the future, not of the past. In this sense it harnessed the cultural aspirations of many who were comfortably placed in the emerging bourgeois society, the successful beneficiaries of the new urban-industrial civilization, whose political sensibilities were offended by the seeming incapacitation of the establishment before the left-wing challenge. While I would concur with Roberts that this outlook possessed a definite appeal to a certain type of patriotic intellectual or activist, it is also likely that in times of relative social and political stability the ideology in itself could achieve only a limited popular appeal. But in times of crisis, which brought the domestic unity, foreign mission and territorial integrity of the nation all into question, this might easily change. The dramatic conjuncture of war and revolution between 1914 and 1923 produced exactly a crisis of this kind.

Given the operation of certain recognized social determinations (like the status distinctions between white-collar and manual work, or the deliberate fostering of white-collar consciousness by employers and the state), we should concede a certain effectivity to this specifically political factor when trying to explain the radical right-wing preferences of large sections of the new petty bourgeoisie. There is no space to develop this argument more fully here, and in some ways the knowledge to do so is not yet assembled, given the general paucity of research in the area. Though we are well equipped with data concerning the voting patterns in Weimar elections, for instance, or the relative prominence of different occupations amongst the Nazi Party members, we are still very ignorant about the social histories of the particular professions and categories of white-collar employment. What we *do* know certainly suggests that the avenue of inquiry is worth pursuing. The presence of professionals, managers and administrators amongst Nazi activists is now well attested, and the Nazi state provided plenty of scope for the technocratic imagination – in industrial organization, public works, social administration and the bureaucracy of terror.[39] This sort of evidence moves securely with the direction of the above remarks. At the very least the grievances of the 'traditional' petty bourgeoisie co-existed in the fascist movements with other aspirations of a more 'forward-looking' and 'modernist' kind.

IV

We can take this critique of the 'petty-bourgeois thesis' further. For despite the over-representation of the petty bourgeoisie, fascist parties were always more eclectic in their social recruitment than much of the literature might lead us to suppose. Two observations in particular might be made. On the one hand, peasants proved especially important to a fascist party's ultimate prospects, because the transition from ideological sect to mass movement was achieved as much in the countryside as the towns. This was true of both Italy (1920–1) and Germany (1928–32). Conversely, some of the smaller fascist movements owed their weakness to the country population's relative immunity to their appeals. This applied both to Norway and Sweden, where farmers kept to the established framework of agrarian-labour co-operation, and to Finland, where neither the Lapua movement (1929–32) nor its successor the IKL (Isänmaallinen Kansanliike – Patriotic National Movement) (1932–44) could break the hold of the Agrarian Union and Coalition Party on the smaller farmers.[40] But, on the other hand, it is also clear that many fascist parties acquired significant working-class support. The best example is the Nazi Party itself, with its 26.3 per cent workers in 1930 and 32.5 per cent in 1933. But though higher than the working-class membership of the Italian Fascist Party (15.4 per cent in 1921), this was by no means exceptional. Both Miklós Lackó and György Ránki show that the Hungarian Arrow Cross won much support from workers, in both the more proletarian districts of Budapest and the industrial areas of Nógrád, Veszprém and Komárom-Esztergom.[41]

There is a tendency in the literature to play down the importance of this working-class support in the interests of the 'petty-bourgeois thesis', especially in the German case, where the research is extensive. Certainly, we can admit that the Nazis made most progress amongst specific types of workers. Tim Mason lists 'the volatile youthful proletariat' in the big cities, who went straight from school to the dole, who lacked the socializing education of a trade union membership, and who provided many of the SA's rank-and-file support; the 'uniformed working class' in public employment, especially in the railways, post office and city services; and those in the small-business sector of provincial Germany, 'where the working-class movement had not been able to establish a stable and continuing presence'.[42] It seems clear that the Nazis failed to breach the historic strongholds of the labour movement – the urban industrial settings that contained the 8 million or so wage-earners who voted habitually for the SPD and KPD – and had to be content with those categories of workers the left had failed (or neglected) to organize.

Yet this was surely significant enough. Though not a sufficient basis for contesting the left's core support, it deprived the latter of a necessary larger constituency. As Mason points out, between 1928 and July 1932 the combined popular vote of the SPD and KPD fell from 40.4 per cent to 35.9 per cent, and it was progressively unclear how they were to break through the 'sociological, ideological, religious and, not least, sex barriers' that defined the 'historic' working class in Germany. Mason suggests, in fact, that under the conditions of economic crisis after 1929 these barriers were virtually impassable. By eliminating the chances for either reformist legislation or effective trade union economism, the depression 'robbed the working-class movement of its anticipatory, future-directed role for the working class in general', and 'to the degree that industry and trade shrank, the potential constituency of the workers' parties stagnated'. The effect, Mason concludes, was a disastrous 'narrowing of the political arena of the working class movement'.[43]

This brings us to an interesting problem. In effect, the SPD and KPD were facing under particularly extreme, urgent and dramatic circumstances the classic dilemma of the European left in the general period after the stabilization of 1923–4: how to win popular support for socialism by electoral means, at a time (contrary to earlier predictions) when the industrial proletariat in the classical sense had little chance of becoming a numerical majority of the voting population, and when a reformist practice had ceased to show tangible returns. In the crisis of Weimar, moreover, the cause of socialism had become inextricably linked to the defence of democratic gains. It became imperative for the left to break out of the class-political ghetto for which its entire previous history had prepared it, by building broader political alliances and appealing not only to workers, but to white-collar employees, small owners, pensioners, professional people, students, and so on. Most of all, it was vital to conceive of other than class collectivities, by rallying the people as consumers, as women, as tax-payers, as citizens, and even as Germans – not as some opportunist and eclectic pluralism of discrete campaigns, but as the coherent basis for the broadest possible democratic unity. Yet it was in this democratic project that the politics of the left proved most lamentably deficient, at least until after 1935, when the Popular Front revealed a new strategic perspective. It was less the left's inability to carry the working class itself (though, as Mason points out, in 1930–2 about half the wage-dependent population voted for other parties), than its abdication from this wider popular democratic mobilization that proved most fatal to the republic's survival.[44]

Arguably, it was precisely here that fascism showed its superiority. In the end, the most striking thing about the NSDAP, for instance, was not its disproportionate dependence on a particular social group (the petty bourgeoisie), but its ability (by contrast with the two working-class parties) to broaden its social base in several different directions. The promiscuous adaptability of Nazi propaganda has often been noted, and it was certainly adept at tapping manifold popular resentments, promising all and nothing in the same breath. But this remarkable diversity of social appeal can easily mislead. Though both cynical and opportunist, Nazi eclecticism was also a major constructive achievement. The Nazis rallied a disparate assortment of social and political elements who lacked strong traditions of co-operation or effective solidarity in the political sphere, and often surveyed long histories of hostility and mutual suspicion. From September 1930 to January 1933 the NSDAP was a popular political formation without precedent in the German political system. It not only subsumed the organizational fragmentation of the right. It also united a broadly based coalition of the subordinate classes, centred on the peasantry and petty bourgeoisie, but stretching deep into the wage-earning population.

It did so on the terrain of ideology, by unifying an otherwise disjointed ensemble of discontents within a totalizing populist framework – namely, the radicalized ideological community of the German people-race. The resulting combination was extraordinarily potent – activist, communitarian, anti-plutocratic and popular, but at the same time virulently anti-socialist, anti-semitic, intolerant of diversity and aggressively nationalist. In Germany this right-wing Jacobinism was all the more complex for the absence of a strong existing tradition of popular radical nationalism, though as I have tried to argue above, one had begun to take shape since the start of the century. In Italy, for example, as David Roberts argues, the Fascists had access to the suppressed Mazzinian tradition of unfulfilled radical-nationalist expectations, which they could then recover and transform. In Germany, in the absence of something similar, the recourse to new synthetic solutions (anti-semitism, the race-mission in the East, 'national-socialism') was correspondingly all the more important. There was perhaps something of the same contrast in the difference, say, between the authoritarianism of a Pilsudski in Poland, which could conjure memories of national democracy for its present purposes, and the more radical innovations of the Arrow Cross and Iron Guard in Hungary and Romania. This goes some way to explaining the greater radicalism of Nazi racialism and the apparent irrationalism of the programme's implementation during the Second World War.

This line of argument reinstates the importance of ideology for our understanding of fascism. In particular, it directs us to the contested terrain of popular-democratic aspirations, where the socialist left proved most deficient, the fascist right most telling in their mode of political intervention. Where the left, in both Italy and Germany, kept aggressively to a class-corporate practice of proletarian independence, the fascists erupted into the arena and appropriated the larger popular potential.[45] Of course, putting it like this presupposes an expanded definition of ideology, where it means something more than what happens inside a few literati's heads and is then committed to paper and published for wider consumption. In other words, I mean something more than the well-tried intellectual history so popular with many Germanists during the 1950s and 1960s – that is, not just ideas and attitudes, but also types of behaviour, institutions and social relations, so that ideology becomes materially embodied as well as just thought about (for example, not only the fascist movement's formal aims, but its style of activism, modes of organization and forms of public display). On this basis fascism becomes primarily a specific type of politics, involving radical authoritarianism, militarized activism and the drive for a centralist repressive state, with a radical-nationalist, communalist and frequently racialist creed, and a violent antipathy for both liberal democracy and socialism. Providing these elements are treated not as some revealed unity, but as a set of potentials whose concrete substance may be unevenly and partially realized in 'real' (particular, historical) fascisms, a definition of this kind could be quite serviceable.

V

It is time to draw some of these threads together. My comments have clearly been concerned mainly with the strong German and Italian cases, with occasional reference to fascist movements elsewhere. I have also (mindful of the typology referred to in note 4 at the end of the chapter) confined myself to a particular aspect of the overall problem, namely the 'coming to power' of indigenously generated fascist movements, rather than the less compelling examples of the smaller imitative or client movements, or the dynamics of established fascist regimes. In so doing I suggested that the specificity of the fascist movements resided in a particular capacity for broadly based popular mobilization – a distinctive ideology or style of politics, as the preceding paragraph puts it. Fascism is more extreme in every way. It registered a qualitative departure from previous conservative practice, substituting corporatist notions of social place for older hierarchical ones, and ideas of race community for those of clerical, aristocratic and bureaucratic authority. These and other aspects of fascist ideology are intimately linked to its broadly based popular appeal. Fascism is an aggressively plebeian movement, espousing a crude and violent egalitarianism. Above all, fascism stands for activism and popular mobilization, embracing everything from para-military display, street-fighting and straightforward terror, to more conventional forms of political activity, new propagandist forms and a general invasion of the cultural sphere. It is negatively defined against liberalism, social democracy and communism, or any creed which seems to elevate difference, division and conflict over the essential unity of the race-people as the organizing principle of political life.

At the same time, fascism was not a universal phenomenon, and appeared in strength only in a specific range of societies. In explaining this variation there are two main emphases. One is the deep historical perspective discussed in relation to Jürgen Kocka. At some level of explanation the structural factors stressed by the latter are clearly important and might be summarized as follows: accelerated capitalist transformation, in a dual context of simultaneous national state formation and heightened competition in the imperialist world economy; the coexistence in a highly advanced capitalist economy of large 'traditional' sectors, including a smallholding peasantry and an industrial-trading petty

271

bourgeoisie, 'deeply marked by the contradictions of capitalist development';[46] and, finally the emergence of a precocious socialist movement publicly committed to a revolutionary programme. This complex over-determination (the 'contemporaneity of the uncontemporary', or 'uneven and combined development') characterized both German and Italian history before the First World War, articulated through the interpenetration of national and social problems. Most of the primary analytical traditions share some version of this framework (for example, the political science literature on state formation and the related theories of developmental crises, the particular works of Gershenkron and Barrington Moore, and most of the analogous literature within Marxism).

However, German historians have given this structural argument an additional formulation, which is far more problematic. Evaluating German development (or 'misdevelopment', as they call it) by an external and linear model of 'modernization', which postulates an ultimate complementarity between economic growth and political democratization (which in Germany, for peculiar reasons, was obstructed), such historians stress the dominance in German public life of 'pre-industrial' ideological traditions. The absence of a liberal political culture is thought to have permitted the survival of traditional authoritarian mentalities which enjoyed strong institutional power bases, and which could then be radicalized under the future circumstances of an economic or political crisis. Thus a 'reactionary protest potential' is created.[47] Fascism draws its support either directly from 'traditional social strata', or from newer strata (like white-collar employees) supposedly beholden to 'traditional' ideas. This essentially is Jürgen Kocka's argument.

Though not incompatible with a modified version of the above, the second approach stresses the immediate circumstances under which the fascists came to power. Here we need to mention the impact of the First World War, the nature of the postwar crisis in the European revolutionary conjuncture of 1917–23, the unprecedented gains of the left (both reformist and revolutionary), and the collapse of parliamentary institutions. Together these brought a fundamental crisis in the unity and popular credibility of the dominant classes, which opened the space for radical speculations. Here again, although one was the major defeated party and the other a nominal victor in the First World War, the German and Italian experiences were remarkably similar in these respects. In both cases the radical right defined itself against the double experience of thwarted imperialist ambitions and domestic political retreat, each feeding the other. In both cases the postwar situation was dominated by the public accommodation of labour, whose political and trade union aspirations appeared to be in the ascendant: trade unions acquired a new corporative legitimacy; socialists attained a commanding presence in large areas of local government; the national leaderships of the SPD and PSI occupied the centre of the political stage; and substantial movements to their left (first syndicalist and then communist) added an element of popular insurgency. In both cases, too, liberal or parliamentary methods of political containment were shown to have exhausted their potential, guaranteeing neither the political representation of the dominant classes, nor the mobilization of popular consent. In such circumstances fascism successfully presented itself as a radical populist solution.

In other words, fascism prospered under conditions of general political crisis, in societies which were already dynamically capitalist (or at least, which possessed a dynamic capitalist sector), but where the state proved incapable of dispatching its organizing functions for the maintenance of social cohesion. The political unity of the dominant classes and their major economic fractions could no longer be organized successfully within the existing forms of parliamentary representation and party govenment. Simultaneously the popular legitimacy of the same institutional framework also went into crisis. This way of formulating the problem – as the intersection of twin crises, a crisis of representation and a crisis of hegemony or popular consent – derives from the work of Nicos Poulantzas and its subsequent reworking through the extensive and continuing reception of Antonio Gramsci's ideas into the English language. It has been formulated with exemplary clarity for the case of Nazism by David Abraham, in his *The Collapse of the Weimar Republic. Political Economy and Crisis* (Princeton, NJ, 1981). As he puts it:

> Could no bourgeois political force organize the political unity of the dominant economic fractions out of the diversity and factiousness of their economic interests? Was no political unity possible and no mass political support available within the Republic, despite the single-mindedness of the dominant classes' anti-socialism? Were the maintenance of capitalist economic relations and political democracy so antithetical in *this* conjuncture that abandonment and undermining of the Republic were self-evident necessities for the dominant classes?.[48]

In the context of the Weimar crisis, adjustments within the existing institutional arrangements looked increasingly untenable, and more radical solutions beyond the boundaries of the existing political system consequently became more attractive.

The problem of defining fascism is therefore not exhausted by describing its ideology, even in the expanded sense of the latter intimated above. Fascism was not just a particular style of politics, it was also inscribed in a specific combination of political conditions (themselves the structured, mediate effect of complex socio-economic determinations), namely the kind of dual crisis of the state just referred to. Now, that kind of crisis is normally associated with the Great Depression after 1929, but the postwar crisis of political order between 1917 and 1923 was equally important. The global ideological context of the Bolshevik Revolution and its international political legacy gave enormous impetus to the radicalization of the right, and the more vigorous fascist movements generally arose in societies which experienced serious left-wing insurgencies after 1917–18. As well as Italy and Germany, Hungary, Austria, Finland and Spain are all good examples. Although the recent tendency has been to accept 'that Francoism was *never* really fascism but rather some variant of limited, semi-pluralist authoritarianism', for instance, Paul Preston has argued convincingly that it *was* (at least between the mid-1930s and mid-1950s), and does so partly on the basis of 'the Spanish crisis of 1917–23', which was 'analogous to the Italian crisis of 1917–22'.[49] Moreover, this approach supplies criteria for assessing the seriousness of other crises elsewhere. Thus the formation and fleeting victory of the Popular Front in 1934–7 threatened to create a comparable situation in France, until the break-up of the left government dissipated the gathering concentration of radical right-wing forces.

The operative circumstances were ones which made it possible for the dominant classes to take extreme or exceptional solutions seriously, though never without well-founded hestitation. One such circumstance was obviously the very emergence of the fascists as a credible mass movement, for without the popular materials an 'exta-systemic solution' (in Abraham's phrase) was clearly a non-starter.[50] But, as a generalization, recourse to the fascist option was politically most likely where the left had achieved significant inroads into the administration of state power and the limitation of private capitalist prerogative, or where combinations of entrenched left reformism and concurrent revolutionary activity seemed to obstruct the resolution of economic crisis and the restoration of order. For example, the most persuasive reading of the crisis of Weimar stresses the importance of a kind of social democratic corporatism (embodied in trade union legislation, a Ministry of Labour, compulsory arbitration procedures, unemployement insurance, other welfare legislation, and so on), whose defensive strengths could not be dismantled within the existing constitutional framework of parliamentary decision-making. The structural necessity of fascist remedies (given certain inflexible commitments and requirements among the most powerful fractions of the dominant classes) can then be located in the labour movement's ability to defend the institutional advances of the 1918 Revolution (or more accurately, of the political settlement of 1918–23).[51] When we add the SPD's strong position in provincial and local government, the impressive militancy of the Reichsbanner militia, and the continued vitality of a strategic Marxist-reformist vision amongst the party intelligentsia, the appeal of a radical authoritarian solution becomes all the more intelligible.[52]

This idea of a defensive social democratic corporatism, which within the limits of this essay has to remain theoretically underdeveloped, may well be a fruitful one for the discussion of fascism. It lends a formal unity to the political crisis of Weimar, between the foundering of the Grand Coalition in March 1930 on the issue of insurance legislation, and the precipitation of the Papen-Hitler manœuvre in December 1932–January 1933 by Schleicher's renewed corporatist exploration. *Mutatis mutandis*, the argument also works for the Italian situation in 1918–22, where the presence of a mass socialist party publicly committed to a revolutionary programme (however rhetorically) had effectively thrown the state into paralysis. Here the growing popular strength of the left, its aggressive use of the workers' councils in Milan and Turin, its commanding position in northern local government, and its massive concentrations of regional support, provoked a massive counter-revolutionary backlash, organized through Mussolini's Fascists. In both Germany (1918–33) and Italy (1918–22), and for that matter Spain too (1931–6), we are dealing in effect with limited socialist enclaves (some of them physical, some institutional, some merely attitudinal or ideological) within the existing state, which constituted intolerable obstructions to the kind of stabilization which a powerful coalition within the dominant classes was increasingly pursuing. Arguably a comparable situation threatened to arise in the wake of the Popular Front in France (1934–7), and if the Labour Government had chosen to conduct a stubborn resistance to the demands for conservative stabilization in 1931 instead of capitulating, similar circumstances may have materialized in Britain as well. As Joseph Baglieri says of Italian fascism:

> The movement's functional role against the socialists and the *Popolari* attracted the sympathies and support of all those interests which felt threatened by the post-war mobilization of the lower classes, the incipient process of economic and political democratization, and the breakdown of traditional authority. In the process of crushing the left, the fascists succeeded in offering these interests an alternative sovereignty which successfully stood in for the crumbling Liberal state.[53]

Fascism may be best understood, therefore, as primarily a counter-revolutionary ideological project, constituting a new kind of popular coalition, in the specific circumstances of an interwar crisis. As such it provided the motivational impetus for specific categories of radicalized political actors in the immediate aftermath of the First World War, embittered by national humiliation, enraged by the advance of the left. As working-class insurgency defined the capacities of the existing liberal politics to achieve the necessary stabilization, this radical-nationalist cadre became an important pole of attraction for larger circles of the dominant classes and others who felt threatened by the reigning social turbulence. In Italy, where the socialist movement was generally further to the left than in Germany, and where no equivalent of the SPD functioned as a vital factor of order, this process of right-wing concentration around the redemptive potential of a radical-nationalist anti-socialist terror was far more advanced. But later, in the renewed but differently structured crisis of 1929–34, a recognizable pattern recurred. Elsewhere a similar scenario was scripted, but indifferently played out. Spain and possibly Austria were the closest examples of a similarly enacted fascist solution. Other countries certainly generated their own fascist cadres – in some cases very large (say, France, Finland, Hungary, Romania), in some quite small (say, Britain, Scandinavia). But the severity of the political crisis, and the resilience of established political forms, determined the broader attractions of the fascist ideology.

In the end both perspectives are necessary – the deep historical or long-term structural one *and* the stress on the immediate crisis. But we have to be clear about what exactly each of them may reasonably explain. In particular, the causal primacy of 'pre-industrial traditions' threatens to become both teleological and heavily determinist, locating the origins of fascism somewhere in the middle third of the nineteenth century, when Germany (and Italy) failed to take the 'long hard road to modernity', in Dahrendorf's phrase. Much of this would be perfectly acceptable and in the most rounded of analyses should be complemetary to the other type of approach rather than antithetical. Yet in the works of Jürgen Kocka and other German historians the explanatory claims are far more aggressive than this. The 'pre-industrial traditions' are given a privileged place in the causal repertoire in a way which specifically displaces certain other approaches, those which begin with the interior dynamics of the immediate fascism-producing crisis. What is seen to be the driving contradiction of the latter – the anti-democratic mentalities that left various social groups so receptive to the fascist appeal – is displaced from its own contemporary context on to a much deeper argument about the course of German history and its singularity. This is accompanied by a clearly stated polemical purpose: fascism is to be explained not by its capitalist present, but by the baleful influence of the feudal past. Winkler is quite explicit on this score. The anti-democratic outcome to the world economic crisis in Germany, as opposed to 'the other developed industrial societies', had 'less to do with the course of the crisis itself than with the different pre-industrial histories of these countries. The conditions for the rise of fascism have at least as much to do with feudalism and absolutism as with capitalism.'[54]

This is unncessarily restrictive. Older attempts to take the relationship between fascism and capitalism as the primary causal nexus were indeed inadequate. But that is no excuse for evading the challenge of more recent discussions of fascism or more general theories of the state, forms of domination, and so on. Historical discussions of the relationship between capitalism and fascism are actually proceeding with an unprecedented intensity, as the most cursory glance at current research on the Weimar Republic or the final years of liberal Italy will quickly reveal. But they are doing so in an almost wholly 'empirical' or 'practical' way, without any guiding reference to the larger theoretical issues discussed in this essay. If we are truly to understand the problem, I would argue, it is here – by theorizing fascism in terms of the crisis that produced it – that we shall have to begin.

CHAPTER 10: NOTES

Whatever coherence and value this text may possess owes a great deal to the thoughts and writings of those who have laboured longer and more directly on the subject of fascism than I have myself. My main intellectual debts should be clear from the notes. But my thinking has been shaped over a period of time by the work of three friends and colleagues in particular, who may not always recognize their own ideas after I have finished with them, but who deserve to be handsomely thanked: Jane Caplan, Michael Geyer and Tim Mason.

1 E. Weber, *Varieties of Fascism* (New York, 1964); F. L. Carsten, *The Rise of Fascism* (London, 1967); J. Weiss, *The Fascist Tradition* (New York, 1967); H. Rogger and E. Weber (eds), *The European Right* (London, 1965); special issue entitled 'International fascism, 1920–1945', *Journal of Contemporary History*, vol. 1 (January 1966). The *Journal of Contemporary History* published a second special issue ten years later called 'Theories of fascism', vol. 11 (October 1976). Selections from both issues have been published as G. L. Mosse (ed.), *International Fascism: New Thoughts and New Approaches* (London, 1979). The three international conferences produced the following volumes of proceedings: P. F. Sugar (ed.), *Native Fascism in the Successor States, 1918–1945* (Santa Barbara, Calif., 1971); S. J. Woolf (ed.), *European Fascism* and *The Nature of Fascism* (London, 1968); Institute of History, Czechoslovak Academy of Sciences (ed.), *Fascism and Europe* (Prague, 1970), 2 vols. The first of the two Woolf volumes was recently reissued in a slightly revised form as *Fascism in Europe* (London, 1981).

2 By now there are many critiques of these older approaches. Among the best are: B. Hagtvet, 'The Theory of mass society and the collapse of the Weimar Republic: a re-examination', in S. U. Larsen, B. Hagtvet and J. P. Myklebust (eds), *Who Were the Fascists. Social Roots of European Fascism* (Bergen, 1980), pp. 66–117; M. Clemenz, *Gesellschaftliche Ursprünge des Faschismus* (Frankfurt-on-Main, 1972), pp. 26–57, 96–126, 235–49. In some ways totalitarianism theory in particular has fallen more to the relentless accumulation of monographic research than to frontal critique. For an introduction to that scholarship see: J. Caplan, 'Bureaucracy, politics and the National Socialist state', in P. Stachura (ed.), *The Shaping of the Nazi State* (London, 1978), pp. 234–56; H. Mommsen, 'National Socialism – continuity and change', in W. Lacquer (ed.), *Fascism. A Reader's Guide* (London, 1976), pp. 179–210.

3 N. Poulantzas, *Fascism and Dictatorship* (London, 1974); R. De Felice, *Fascism. An Informal Introduction to its Theory and Practice* (New Brunswick NJ, 1976). Poulantzas's book on fascism has excited little formal discussion by comparison with his other writings, with the major exceptions of an excellent short essay by Jane Caplan and a more abstract piece by Ernesto Laclau. Likewise, De Felice's work has not had a great deal of impact outside the specifically Italian discussion. See: J. Caplan, 'Theories of fascism: Nicos Poulantzas as historian', in *History Workshop*, no. 3 (May 1977), pp. 83–100; E. Laclau, 'Fascism and ideology', in *Politics and Ideology in Marxist Theory* (London, 1977), pp. 81–142; M. Ledeen, 'Renzo De Felice and the controversy over Italian fascism, in *Journal of Contemporary History*, vol. 11 (October 1976), pp. 269–82.

4 For example, see S. Payne's useful general text, *Fascism. Comparison and Definition* (Madison, Wis., 1980), pp. 195 ff., 6 ff., where he proposes a 'descriptive typology' based

on '(a) the fascist negations, (b) common points of ideology and goals, and (c) special common features of style and organization'. The 'negations' involve anti-liberalism, anti-communism and qualified anti-conservatism. The common goals include a new kind of 'national authoritarian state', a 'new kind of regulated, multi-class, integrated national-economic structure', a radical foreign policy, and 'an idealist, voluntarist creed'. The stylistic and organizational features are 'an aesthetic structure of meetings, symbols and political choreography'; militarized forms of mass mobilization; a stress on violence, masculinity and youth; and a 'tendency towards an authoritarian, charismatic, personal style of command'.

This is very similar to the approach of Juan Linz, who has published a number of widely cited and influential essays proposing 'a multi-dimensional typological definition' of fascism. See his 'Some notes toward a comparative study of fascism in sociological historical perspective', in Lacquer (ed.), *Fascism*, pp. 3–121. Personally, though there are many valuable insights to be culled discretely from his work, I find Linz's general argument obscure, inconclusive and confusing in the density of its cultivated empirical complexity. Moreover, the typology described above needs to be extended by a further set of distinctions between the different kinds of fascist movement. One possibility would be the following: (1) indigenously generated movements which successfully came to power (Italian Fascism, Nazism, Francoism); (2) small imitative movements which achieved no particular popularity in their home societies (e.g., the British Union of Fascists, or the various Scandinavian Nazi groups); (3) larger indigenous movements with strong similarities of ideology, sociology and style, but which originated independently of Italian or German sponsorship in a different configuration of social forces, and never took power under peacetime conditions (e.g., Arrow Cross in Hungary, or Iron Guard in Romania); (4) finally, the so-called Quisling regimes installed by the Germans during the war.

5   For a particularly pointless such discussion, see G. Allardyce, 'What fascism is not: thoughts on the deflation of a concept', *American Historical Review*, vol. 84 (April 1979), pp. 367–88.

6   A familiar but none the less important disclaimer should here be entered. By making certain criticisms of existing works, I am *not* trying to discount their value or consign them to the scrap-heap. The point is to open up discussion, nothing more. In certain ways this essay connects with a larger intellectual project, concerned with redrawing the agenda of German historical discussion for the late nineteenth and early twentieth centuries. See D. Blackbourn and G. Eley, *Mythen deutscher Geschichtsschreibung: Die gescheiterte bürgerlich Revolution von 1848* (Frankfurt-on-Main, 1980), and the controversy it has aroused. This book has now appeared in an expanded and revised English edition as *The Peculiarities of German History. Bourgeois Society and Politics in Nineteenth-Century Germany* (Oxford, 1984). This essay originated in a review essay for another journal, and it is only fair to mention the texts that originally provoked it, as they clearly helped formulate the judgements on which the following exposition rests. They include: Lacquer (ed.), *Fascism*; Mosse (ed.), *International Fascism*; Payne, *Fascism*; Larsen, Hagtvet and Mylkebust (eds), *Who Were the Fascists*; H. A. Winkler, *Revolution, Staat, Faschismus. Zur Revision des Historichen Materialismus* (Göttingen, 1978); J. Kocka, *White Collar Workers in America 1890–1940. A Social-Political History in International Perspective* (London, 1980).

7   For discussions of these analytical traditions, see: Blackbourn and Eley, *Mythen deutscher Geschichtsschreibung*, and J. A. Davis (ed.), *Gramsci and Italy's Passive Revolution* (London, 1979). For valuable examples see: A. Gerschenkron, *Economic Backwardness in Historical Perspective* (Cambridge, 1962); B. Moore, *Social Origins of Dictatorship and Democracy* (Boston, Mass., 1966); C. Tilly (ed.), *The Formation of National States in Western Europe* (Princeton, NJ, 1975); R. Grew (ed.), *Crises of Political Development in Europe and the United States* (Princeton, NJ, 1978); and B. Hagtvet and S. Rokkan, 'The conditions of fascist victory', in Larsen, Hagtvet and Myklebust (eds), *Who Were the Fascists*, pp. 131–52, which links the 'violent breakdown of competitive mass politics' to a complex 'geoeconomic-geopolitical model', in which a country's early 'geopolitical position', its 'semi-peripheralization' in the world economy, and its manner of unification supply the vital preconditions for the emergence of fascism.

8   J. Kocka, 'Ursachen des Nationalsozialismus', *Aus Politik und Zeitgeschichte*, 21 June 1980, pp. 9–13.
9   K. D. Bracher, *The German Dictatorship: Origins, Structure and Consequences of National Socialism* (Harmondsworth, Middx, 1973; original German edition 1969); W. Sauer, 'National Socialism: totalitarianism or fascism?, *American Historical Review*, vol. 73 (1967), pp. 404–24, and 'Das Problem des deutschen Nationalstaats', in H.-U. Wehler (ed.), *Moderne deutsche Sozialgeschichte* (Cologne, 1966), pp. 407–36; E. Fraenkel, *The Dual State* (New York, 1941); M. Broszat, *Der Nationalsozialismus: Weltanschauung, Programm und Wirklichkeit* (Stuttgart, 1960); M. R. Lepsius, 'Parteiensystem und Sozialstruktur: Zum Problem der Demokratisierung der deutschen Gesellschaft', in G. A. Ritter (ed.), *Deutsche Parteien vor 1918* (Cologne, 1973), pp. 56–80; R. Dahrendorf, *Society and Democracy in Germany* (London, 1967). By 'German historians' in this context I mean historians in West Germany. It is hard to say exactly how broad this generational experience was, partly because the ideological fronts have changed again since the early 1970s, leaving the most self-conscious exponents of avowedly 'social-scientific' history (e.g. as represented in the controlling group of the journal *Geschichte und Gesellschaft*) feeling relatively isolated within the West German historical profession as a whole. But for a fairly representative example of literature and authors at the height of the earlier liberalizing trend (several of the contributors have since moved quite markedly to the right), see M. Stürmer (ed.), *Das kaiserliche Deutschland. Politik und Gesellschaft 1870–1918* (Düsseldorf, 1970).
10 H.-J. Puhle, *Von der Agrarkrise zum Präfaschismus* (Wiesbaden, 1972), p. 53. The constipated nature of this sentence is an accurate (even benevolent) reflection of the original German.
11 The literature on Gramsci is now enormous. Among the most useful discussions of what he had to say about fascism in particular are the following: A. Davidson, *Antonio Gramsci: Towards an Intellectual Biography* (London, 1977), pp. 185–201; W. L. Adamson, *Hegemony and Revolution. Antonio Gramsci's Political and Cultural Theory* (Berkeley, Calif., 1980), pp. 71–101; C. Buci-Glucksmann, *Gramsci and the State* (London, 1980), pp. 295–324; P. Spriano, *Antonio Gramsci and the Party: The Prison Years* (London, 1979); Davis (ed.), *Gramsci and Italy's Passive Revolution*. For the work of Tim Mason the following are most important: 'The primacy of politics – politics and economics in National Socialist Germany', in Woolf (ed.), *Nature of Fascism*, pp. 165–95; *Sozialpolitik im Dritten Reich* (Cologne, 1977); 'Zur Entstehung des Gesetzes zur Ordnung der nationalen Arbeit vom 20. Januar 1934: Ein Versuch über das Verhältnis "archaischer" und "moderner" Momente in der neuesten deutschen Geschichte', in H. Mommsen, D. Petzina and B. Weisbrod (eds), *Industrielles System und politische Entwicklung in der Weimarer Republik* (Düsseldorf, 1974), pp. 322–51; 'Intention and explanation: a current controversy about the interpretation of National Socialism', in G. Hirschfeld and L. Kettenacker (eds), *Der "Führerstaat": Mythos und Realität* (Stuttgart, 1981), pp. 21–42; 'Open questions on Nazism', in R. Samuel (ed.), *People's History and Socialist Theory* (London, 1981), pp. 205–10.
12 H. A. Winkler, 'Die "neue Linke" und der Faschismus: Zur Kritik neomarxistischer Theorien über den Nationalsozialismus', in *Revolution, Staat, Faschismus*, p. 116, and esp. pp. 74–83. Winkler's essay 'German society, Hitler and the illusion of restoration, 1930–33', in Mosse (ed.), *International Fascism*, pp. 143–60, puts a similar point of view.
13 Kocka, 'Ursachen des Nationalsozialismus' cit. at n. 8 above, p. 11. For exactly similar arguments, see Puhle, *Von der Agrarkrise*, p. 53, and H.-U. Wehler, *Das deutsche Kaiserreich 1871–1918* (Göttingen, 1973), pp. 238 ff., 226.
14 Kocka, *White Collar Workers*. The original German edition appeared as *Angestellte zwischen Faschismus und Demokratie. Zur politischen Sozialgeschichte der Angestellten: USA 1890–1940 im internationalen Vergleich* (Göttingen, 1977). Kocka has by this time accumulated a small mountain of publications on the subject of white-collar workers in one way or another. Among the most important are: *Unternehmungsverwaltung und Angestelltenschaft am Beispiel Siemens 1847–1914. Zum Verhältnis von Kapitalismus und Bürokratie in der deutschen Industrialisierung* (Stuttgart, 1969); 'Vorindustrielle Faktoren in der deutschen Industrialisierung. Industriebürokratie und "neuer Mittel-stand" ', in Stürmer (ed.), *Das kaiserliche Deutschland*, pp. 265–86; *Klassengesellschaft im Krieg. Deutsche Sozialgesch:chte 1914–1918* (Göttingen, 1973), esp. pp. 65–95.

15 Kocka, *White Collar Workers*, p. 5.
16 ibid.
17 Kocka concedes that the inadequacy of the evidence may ultimately vitiate the comparison in this respect. Moreover until Hartmut Kaelble's work the more recent research was mainly on the American side. See Kaelble, 'Sozialer Aufstieg in den USA und Deutschland, 1900–1960. Ein vergleichendes Forschungsbericht', in H.-U. Wehler (ed.), *Sozialgeschichte Heute Festschrift für Hans Rosenberg zum 70. Geburstag* (Göttingen, 1974), pp. 525–42, and *Historical Research on Social Mobility* (New York, 1981).
18 Kocka, *White Collar Workers*, p. 265.
19 For a recapitulation of these debates, see J. Karabel, 'The failure of American socialism reconsidered', *Socialist Register 1979* (London, 1979), p. 204–27.
20 Kocka, *White Collar Workers*, p. 266.
21 ibid., p. 281 f. The phrase 'contemporaneity of the uncontemporary' originates with Ernst Bloch. In some ways it corresponds to Trotsky's 'uneven and combined development' and the Althusserian 'overdetermination'.
22 In other ways the argument seems strained. Thus the suggestion that 'corporatist remnants in German society help explain why working-class status in itself was more important than differences between crafts and occupations' seems both eccentric and obscure, as does the reference to 'the relative insignificance of the line between skilled and unskilled workers in German trade unions and social structure'. See ibid., p. 265.
23 ibid., p. 282 f.
24 This is also true of Winkler, 'Die "neue Linke" und der Faschismus', cit. at n. 12 above, p. 83.
25 Aside from the voluminous contents of Larsen, Hagtvet and Myklebust (eds), *Who Were the Fascists*, there is a useful introduction to such research in R. Mann (ed.), *Die Nationalsozialisten. Analysen faschistischer Bewegungen* (Stuttgart, 1980).
26 Quoted by D. D. Roberts, 'Petty-bourgeois fascism in Italy: form and content', in Larsen, Hagtvet and Myklebust (eds), *Who Were the Fascists*, p. 337.
27 Several authors have suggested that the working class was more important to the social base of the Nazis. See M. Kele, *Nazis and Workers, 1919–1933* (Chapel Hill, NC, 1972); C. J. Fischer, 'The occupational background of the SA's rank and file membership during the depression years, 1929 to mid-1934', in Stachura (ed.), *Shaping of the Nazi State*, pp. 131–59. More recently R. F. Hamilton, *Who Voted for Hitler?* (Princeton, NJ, 1982), has shifted the focus to the 'upper classes' as the decisive factor. The 'generational revolt' argument has been advanced very unconvincingly by P. Merkl, 'Comparing fascist movements', in Larsen, Hagtvet and Myklebust (eds), *Who Were the Fascists*, pp. 752–83.
28 The volume is extraordinarily useful from this point of view, not least because of its genuinely comprehensive coverage of the European continent. P. Schmitter on Portugal, D. Wallef on *Christus Rex* in Belgium, and H. van der Wusten and R. E. Smit on Holland are particularly useful, as are the ten sophisticated essays on Scandinavia.
29 Roberts, 'Petty-bourgeois fascism in Italy', cit. at n. 26 above, p. 337.
30 ibid., p. 338.
31 E. Tannenbaum, *The Fascist Experience: Italian Society and Culture 1922–1945* (New York, 1972), p. 4; H. A. Turner, 'Fascism and modernization', in Turner (ed.), *Reappraisals of Fascism* (New York, 1975), p. 133 f. The view was put in Wolfgang Sauer's seminal article of 1967 and in several of the discussions at the 1967 Reading Conference. See Sauer, 'National Socialism', cit. at n. 9 above; A. F. K. Organski, 'Fascism and modernization', and G. Germani, 'Fascism and class', in Woolf (ed.), *Nature of Fascism*, pp. 19–41, 65–96.
32 Roberts, 'Petty-bourgeois fascism in Italy', cit. at n. 26 above, p. 337. The following quotations come from the same essay.
33 The Partito Popolare Italiano (Popular Party), formed in 1918–19, was Italy's first Catholic party and the political ancestor of Christian Democracy. In the years 1919–22 it became the vehicle for a variegated movement of agrarian radicalism, although the various forces acting to control the latter always ensured that it could never become a peasants' party as such.
34 Roberts, 'Petty-bourgeois fascism in Italy', cit. at n. 26 above, p. 345. This recourse to Mazzini was anything but 'traditional' or 'backward-looking' in the sense normally

intended by such descriptions. As Roberts says: 'In Italy, after all, nationalism was hardly traditional for the society as a whole, and it could still have progressive consequences in such a context. Since these fascists were seeking alternatives to the political patterns that had developed because of the way Italy was unified, it was plausible for them to turn to Mazzini, who represented all the unfulfilled promise of the Risorgimento; his vision of a more popular kind of Italian unity had not been achieved, so it was not merely reactionary nostalgia that led fascists to look to him for ideas and inspiration as they sought solutions to contemporary problems.' For a similar argument in the context of German radical nationalism, see G. Eley, *Reshaping the German Right. Radical Nationalism and Political Change after Bismarck* (New Haven, Conn. and London, 1980), esp. ch. 5, pp. 160–205.

35   There is a useful introduction to the gentry controversy and its historiographical context in R. C. Richardson, *The Debate on the English Revolution* (London, 1977), pp. 90 ff. The problematic nature of trying to establish precise causal correlations between 'rising' or 'declining' social forces and specific ideologies or political movements should be plain. My aim is not to exchange the 'threatened traditional strata' type of explanation for fascism for an equivalent reductionism based on the idea of 'rising new strata' of the white-collar petty bourgeoisie. The point is to think carefully about why exactly radical nationalism (and other aspects of the fascist ideological project) proved so appealing to *different* categories of people. The interesting thing about radical nationalism in Germany was its ability, in a complicated process covering the first two decades of the century, to harness the aspirations of both the old petty bourgeoisie and the new – both the small producers, traders and businessmen in town and country, and the new technocracy of the professional and managerial intelligentsia. If I understand Roberts correctly, his work lends itself to a similar sort of argument in Italy. The problem of fascism then becomes in part the process of unifying, or at least combining on a stable basis, the disparate aspirations of a variegated social base.

36   Eley, *Reshaping the German Right*. The argument is also summarized in Eley, 'Some thoughts on the nationalist pressure groups in Imperial Germany', in P. Kennedy and A. J. Nicholls (eds), *Nationalist and Racialist Movements in Britain and Germany before 1914* (London, 1981), pp. 40–67.

37   My use of the term is not intended to invoke a specific historical experience, like that of Russian or North American Populism in the later nineteenth century. It refers to a broadly based appeal to 'the-people-in-general' against unrepresentative, ineffectual and morally flawed dominant interests. As such, it could become articulated into both a politics of the right and a politics of the left. For the key text in stimulating this specific theoretical usage, see E. Laclau, 'Towards a theory of Populism', in *Politics and Ideology in Marxist Theory*, pp. 143–99. See also S. Hall, 'Notes on deconstructing "the Popular" ', in Samuel (ed.), *People's History and Socialist Theory*, pp. 227–40.

38   For Italy see: A. De Grand, *The Italian Nationalist Association and the Rise of Fascism in Italy* (Lincoln, Nebr. and London, 1978); W. Alff, 'Der Begriff Faschismus', and 'Die Associazione Nazionalista Italiana von 1910', in *Der Begriff Faschismus und andere Aufsätze zur Zeitgeschichte* (Frankfurt-on-Main, 1971), pp. 14–95. For Spain: J. C. Ullmann, *The Tragic Week: Anticlericalism in Spain, 1876–1912* (Cambridge, Mass., 1968).

39   See the following: F. Zipfel, 'Gestapo and the SD: a sociographic profile of the organizers of terror', in Larsen, Hagtvet and Myklebust (eds), *Who Were the Fascists*, pp. 301–11; G. C. Boehnert, 'The jurists in the SS-Führerkorps, 1925–1939' in Hirschfeld and Kettenacker (eds), *Der 'Führerstaat'*, pp. 361–74; Mason, 'Zur Entstehung des Gesetzes zur Ordnung der nationalen Arbeit'; K.-H. Ludwig, *Technik und Ingenieure im Dritten Reich* (Düsseldorf, 1976); A. D. Beyerchen, *Scientists under Hitler: Politics and the Physics Community in the Third Reich* (New Haven, Conn. and London, 1978). See also K.-J. Müller, 'French fascism and modernization', *Journal of Contemporary History*, vol. 11 (October 1976), pp. 75–108.

40   For discussions of agrarian fascism in Italy and Germany, see J. Baglieri, 'Italian Fascism and the crisis of liberal hegemony, 1901–1922', and N. Passchier, 'The electoral geography of the Nazi landslide', in Larsen, Hagtvet and Myklebust (eds), *Who Were the Fascists*, pp. 327 ff., 283 ff. The Scandinavian essays in the same volume are especially useful and show how illuminating the comparison with smaller and more marginal

281

fascisms can be. For Norway: J. P. Myklebust and B. Hagtvet, 'Regional contrasts in the membership base of the *Nasjonal Samling*'; H. Hendriksen, 'Agrarian fascism in eastern and western Norway: a comparison'; S. S. Nilson, 'Who voted for Quisling? For Sweden: B. Hagtvet, 'On the fringe: Swedish fascism 1920–45'. For Finland: R. Alapuro, 'Mass support for fascism in Finland'; R. E. Heinonen, 'From people's movement to minor party: the People's Patriotic Movement (IKL) in Finland 1932–1944'. See Larsen, Hagtvet and Myklebust (eds), *Who Were the Fascists*, pp. 621–50, 651–6, 657–66, 735–8, 678–84, 689 ff.

41 Figures for Germany and Italy are taken from Payne, *Fascism*, p. 60 f. An additional 23.4 per cent could be considered in the Italian case, accounting for agricultural labourers. For Hungary, see M. Lackó, 'The social roots of Hungarian fascism: the Arrow Cross', and G. Ránki, 'The Fascist vote in Budapest in 1939', in Larsen, Hagtvet and Myklebust (eds), *Who Were the Fascists*, pp. 395–400, 401–16.

42 T. Mason, 'National Socialism and the working class, 1925–May 1933', *New German Critique*, no. 11 (Spring 1977), pp. 60–9.

43 ibid., pp. 59, 65.

44 ibid., p. 60.

45 The argument in this and the previous two paragraphs owes much to Laclau, 'Fascism and ideology', cit. at n. 3 above.

46 R. Fraser, 'The Spanish Civil War', in Samuel (ed.), *People's History and Socialist Theory*, p. 197.

47 Kocka, *White Collar Workers*, p. 252.

48 D. Abraham, *The Collapse of the Weimar Republic: Political Economy and Crisis* (Princeton, NJ, 1981), p. 287.

49 P. Preston, 'Spain', in Woolf (ed.), *Fascism in Europe*, p. 332. See also Preston's book, *The Coming of the Spanish Civil War* (London, 1978); R. Carr, *Modern Spain 1875–1980* (Oxford, 1980), pp. 81–97; G. H. Meaker, *The Revolutionary Left in Spain 1914–1923* (Stanford, Calif., 1974).

50 The phrase comes from the title of the penultimate section of Abraham's final chapter, 'Towards the extra-systemic solution', in *Collapse of the Weimar Republic*, pp. 313–18.

51 Here I am abstracting from a number of recent works, which are separated by numerous specific differences and whose authors may not share the particular formulations I have chosen. See, in particular: B. Weisbrod, *Schwerindustrie in der Weimarer Republik: Industrielle Interessenpolitik zwischen Stabilisierung und Krise* (Wuppertal, 1978) and, 'Economic power and political stability reconsidered: heavy industry in Weimar Germany', *Social History*, vol. 4 (May 1979), pp. 241–63; Abraham, *Collapse of the Weimar Republic*; D. Stegmann, 'Kapitalismus und Faschismus 1929–34: Thesen und Materialen', in H. G. Backhaus (ed.), *Gesellschaft: Beiträge zur Marxschen Theorie* (Frankfurt-on-Main, 1976), Vol. 6, pp. 14–75; C. D. Crohn, 'Autoritärer Kapitalismus: Wirtschaftskonzeptionen im Übergang von der Weimarer Republik zum National-sozialismus', in D. Stegmann, B.-J. Wendt and P.-C. Witt (eds), *Industrielle Gesellschaft und politisches System* (Bonn and Bad Godesberg, 1978), pp. 113–29; Charles S. Maier's summing-up at the 1974 Bochum conference on the Weimar Republic, in Mommsen, Petzina and Weisbrod (eds), *Industrielles System und politische Entwicklung*, pp. 950 ff.

52 See W. Luthardt (ed.), *Sozialdemokratische Arbeiterbewegung und Weimarer Republik. Materialien zur gesellschaftlichen Entwicklung 1927–1933* (Frankfurt-on-Main, 1978), 2 vols.

53 Baglieri, 'Italian Fascism and the crisis of liberal hegemony', cit. at n. 40 above, p. 333.

54 Winkler, 'Die "neue Linke" und der Faschismus', cit. at n. 12 above, p. 83.

Index

3534